# Environmental Management

## for Cambridge IGCSE™ and O Level

COURSEBOOK

Gary Skinner, Ken Crafer, Melissa Turner,
Ann Skinner & John Stacey

Second edition

Shaftesbury Road, Cambridge CB2 8EA, United Kingdom

One Liberty Plaza, 20th Floor, New York, NY 10006, USA

477 Williamstown Road, Port Melbourne, VIC 3207, Australia

314–321, 3rd Floor, Plot 3, Splendor Forum, Jasola District Centre, New Delhi – 110025, India

103 Penang Road, #05–06/07, Visioncrest Commercial, Singapore 238467

Cambridge University Press & Assessment is a department of the University of Cambridge.

We share the University's mission to contribute to society through the pursuit of education, learning and research at the highest international levels of excellence.

www.cambridge.org
Information on this title: www.cambridge.org/9781009809009

© Cambridge University Press & Assessment 2025

This publication is in copyright. Subject to statutory exception and to the provisions of relevant collective licensing agreements, no reproduction of any part may take place without the written permission of Cambridge University Press & Assessment.

First published 2017
Second edition 2025
20  19  18  17  16  15  14  13  12  11  10  9  8  7  6  5  4  3  2  1

Printed in Malaysia by Vivar Printing

*A catalogue record for this publication is available from the British Library*

| ISBN | 978-1-009-80900-9 | Student's Book with Digital Access (2 years) |
| ISBN | 978-1-009-80902-3 | Digital Student's Book (2 years) |
| ISBN | 978-1-009-80903-0 | Student's Book eBook |
| ISBN | 978-1-009-80896-5 | Workbook with Digital Access (2 years) |
| ISBN | 978-1-009-80899-6 | Digital Teacher's Resource (2 years) |
| ISBN | 978-1-009-80898-9 | Teacher's Resource Access Card |

Additional resources for this publication at www.cambridge.org/9781009809009

Cambridge University Press & Assessment has no responsibility for the persistence or accuracy of URLs for external or third-party internet websites referred to in this publication and does not guarantee that any content on such websites is, or will remain, accurate or appropriate.

For EU product safety concerns, contact us at Calle de José Abascal, 56, 1°, 28003 Madrid, Spain, or email eugpsr@cambridge.org.

# Our **Cambridge Dedicated Teacher Awards** are an opportunity to show appreciation for the incredible work teachers do every day.

Thank you to everyone who nominated this year; we have been inspired and moved by all of your stories. Well done to all of our nominees for your dedication to learning and for inspiring the next generation of thinkers, leaders and innovators.

## Congratulations to our winners!

**Global Winner**
South East Asia & Pacific
**Sydney Engelbert**
Keningau Vocational College, Malaysia

East Asia
**Pengfei Jiang**
Zhuji Ronghuai Foreign Language School, China

Pakistan
**Saeeda Salim**
SISA – School of International Studies in Sciences & Arts, Pakistan

South Asia
**Meena Mishra**
Dr Sarvepalli Radhakrishnan International School, India

Middle East and North Africa
**Gina Justus**
Our Own English High school- Sharjah- Girls, United Arab Emirates

Sub-Saharan Africa
**Tajudeen Odufeso**
Isara Secondary School, Isara Remo, Nigeria

Europe
**Aynur Bayazit**
Menekşe Ahmet Yalçınkaya Kindergarten, Türkiye

Latin America & the Caribbean
**Ramon Majé Floriano**
Montessori sede San Francisco, Colombia

North America
**Marisa Santos**
Seminole Ridge Community High School, United States

For more information about our dedicated teachers and their stories, go to
dedicatedteacher.cambridge.org

# Endorsement statement

Endorsement indicates that a resource has passed Cambridge International Education's rigorous quality-assurance process and is suitable to support the delivery of their syllabus. However, endorsed resources are not the only suitable materials available to support teaching and learning, and are not essential to achieve the qualification.
For the full list of endorsed resources to support this syllabus, visit www.cambridgeinternational.org/endorsedresources

Any example answers to questions taken from past question papers, practice questions, accompanying marks and mark schemes included in this resource have been written by the authors and are for guidance only. They do not replicate examination papers. In examinations the way marks are awarded may be different. Any references to assessment and/or assessment preparation are the publisher's interpretation of the syllabus requirements. Examiners will not use endorsed resources as a source of material for any assessment set by Cambridge International Education.

While the publishers have made every attempt to ensure that advice on the qualification and its assessment is accurate, the official syllabus, specimen assessment materials and any associated assessment guidance materials produced by the awarding body are the only authoritative source of information and should always be referred to for definitive guidance. Our approach is to provide teachers with access to a wide range of high-quality resources that suit different styles and types of teaching and learning.

For more information about the endorsement process, please visit www.cambridgeinternational.org/endorsed-resources

Cambridge International Education material in this publication is reproduced under licence and remains the intellectual property of Cambridge University Press & Assessment.

Third-party websites and resources referred to in this publication are not endorsed.

# Contents

| | |
|---|---|
| How to use this series | vi |
| How to use this book | vii |
| Introduction | ix |
| 1   Key skills in Environmental Management | 1 |
| 2   Natural resources | 28 |
| 3   Land | 85 |
| 4   Water | 134 |
| 5   The atmosphere and human activities | 196 |
| 6   Ecosystems, biodiversity and fieldwork | 227 |
| 7   Natural hazards | 280 |
| 8   Human population | 316 |
| Glossary | 353 |
| Index | 362 |
| Acknowledgements | 370 |

CAMBRIDGE IGCSE™ AND O LEVEL ENVIRONMENTAL MANAGEMENT: COURSEBOOK

# > How to use this series

We offer a comprehensive, flexible array of resources for the Cambridge IGCSE™ and O Level Environmental Management syllabuses. We provide targeted support and practice for the specific challenges we've heard that learners face: learning a new subject with English as a second language; application of science and data skills; contextualising learning; and more.

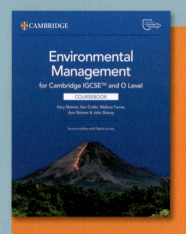

This Coursebook provides coverage of the full Cambridge IGCSE™ and O Level Environmental Management syllabuses. Each chapter explains facts and concepts, and uses relevant real-world examples of environmental management principles to bring the subject to life. Together with a focus on active learning opportunities and assessment for learning, the Coursebook prepares learners for all aspects of their study. At the end of each chapter, examination-style practice questions offer practice opportunities for learners to apply their learning. Answers can be found on Cambridge GO via the activation code found in the front cover.

The skills-focused Workbook has been carefully constructed to help learners develop the skills that they need as they progress through their Cambridge IGCSE™ and O Level Environmental Management courses, providing further practice for key topics in the Coursebook. The Workbook enables independent learning and is ideal for use in class or as homework. Answers can be found on Cambridge GO via the activation code found on the front cover.

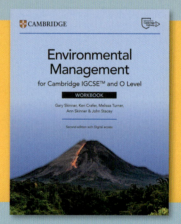

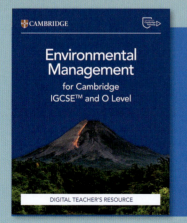

Our Digital Teacher's Resource contains detailed guidance for all topics of the syllabus, including common misconceptions identifying areas where learners might need extra support, as well as an engaging bank of lesson ideas for each syllabus topic. Tests, worksheets and additional case studies with questions are provided, ready to hand out in your lessons. Differentiation is emphasised with advice for identification of different learner needs and suggestions of appropriate interventions to support and stretch learners. Answers for all components are accessible to teachers on the Cambridge GO platform.

# > How to use this book

Throughout this Coursebook, you will notice recurring features that are designed to help your learning. Here is a brief overview of what you will find.

## LEARNING INTENTIONS

These set the scene for each chapter, help you to navigate through the Coursebook and highlight the most important learning points in each chapter.

## BEFORE YOU START

At the beginning of each chapter, there will be a starter activity. These are pair, group or class activities designed to introduce the chapter topic and provide the opportunity for you to show how much you already know about the topic you will be learning.

## REFLECTION

These activities ask you to think about the approach you take to your work and how you might improve this in the future.

## WORKED EXAMPLES

Worked examples show you step by step how to work through a particular process or question, and then provide you with a chance to try it for yourself. You will find this feature helpful for questions that require a mathematical approach to work out the answer.

## KEY WORDS

Key vocabulary for the syllabus is highlighted in the text when it is first introduced. Definitions are given in the margin and can also be found in the Glossary at the back of the book.

## COMMAND WORDS

In the early chapters, command words from the syllabus have been pulled out and will appear in feature boxes. These will remind you of what each command word means and which skills you will need to apply.

## TIPS

These are helpful reminders or notes that will give advice on skills or methodology. You will find them most often near activities or questions, where they will be directly relevant to the task. Different tip types include: Science, Maths, Sustainability, Practical, Problem solving and Critical thinking.

## ENVIRONMENTAL MANAGEMENT IN CONTEXT

This feature presents real-world examples and applications of the content in a chapter, encouraging you to look further into topics. There are discussion questions at the end, which will ask you to think about the benefits and problems of these applications.

### ACTIVITIES

You will find a variety of activities throughout this Coursebook. These provide a good opportunity for you to think about what you have learnt and take part in discussions, or answer questions. Activities will help you to develop different learning styles and provide an opportunity for you to produce your own work either individually, or in pairs or groups.

### FIELDWORK ACTIVITIES

Throughout the book you will find a variety of fieldwork activities. These activities require you to complete a practical task.

### SELF / PEER ASSESSMENT

At the end of some Activities and Practical activities, you will find opportunities to help you assess your own work or the work of your peers, and consider how you can improve the way you learn.

## Questions

Regular sets of questions throughout the book provide you with the chance to check your knowledge and understanding of what you have learnt.

### END-OF-CHAPTER QUESTIONS

These are questions for Chapter 1 to test your knowledge at the end of the chapter. These are not exam-style practice questions but should be used to aid your learning.

### CASE STUDIES

The case studies and the accompanying questions allow you to actively explore specific detailed examples. You are provided with opportunities to produce your own work either as an individual, in pairs or in groups. Note that these are not required learning and are not taken from the syllabus. Our case studies are designed to contextualize your learning only.

### SUMMARY

This feature contains a series of statements that summarise the key learning points you will have covered in the chapter.

### SELF-EVALUATION CHECKLIST

At the end of each chapter, you will find a series of statements outlining the content that you should now understand. You might find it helpful to rate how confident you are for each of these statements when you are revising. You should revisit any topics that you rated 'Needs more work' or 'Almost there'.

### PRACTICE QUESTIONS

At the end of each chapter (except Chapter 1 - see End-of-chapter questions), you will find a set of practice questions that use the command words from the syllabus. To answer some of these, you may need to apply what you have learnt in previous chapters as well as the current chapter you are studying.

### EXTENDED CASE STUDIES

In each chapter, you will find an extended case study that looks at a specific detailed example in a real-world setting. Extended case studies encourage you to think about a particular issue in more depth and will have embedded activities, questions or projects for you to complete. Note that these are not required learning and are not taken from the syllabus. Our case studies are designed to contextualize your learning only.

# > Introduction

*The information in this section is based on the Cambridge International Education syllabus. You should always refer to the appropriate syllabus document for the year of examination to confirm the details and for more information. The syllabus document is available on the website: www.cambridgeinternational.org.*

Welcome to the second edition of our Environmental Management for Cambridge IGCSE™ and O Level Coursebook. This series provides everything that you need to support your course for Cambridge IGCSE™ and O Level Environmental Management (0680/5014), and provides full coverage of the syllabus for examination from 2027.

The chapter order generally follows the same sequences as the topics in the syllabus, with one exception. We have chosen to open the book with a Key Skills chapter to provide you with everything you need to work your way through the rest of the course, enabling you to confidently engage with the more scientific elements of the course from the beginning. You will find that the skills you have learnt in this chapter will be tested throughout the rest of the book – don't hesitate to go back and familiarise yourself with key skills when required.

The various features that you will find in these chapters are explained in the previous two pages. If you have a deep understanding of the facts and concepts that you have learnt, it will help you to answer many of the questions you will meet during your course test. It is not enough just to learn words and diagrams that you can repeat in answer to questions; you need to ensure that you really understand each concept fully. Trying to answer the questions that you find within each chapter, and at the end of each chapter, should help you to do this.

As you work through your course, make sure that you keep reflecting on the work that you did earlier and how it relates to the current topic that you are studying. The reflection boxes throughout the chapters ask you to think about how you learn, to help you make the very best use of your time and abilities as your course progresses. You can also use the self-evaluation checklists at the end of each chapter to decide how well you have understood each topic in the syllabus, and whether or not you need to do more work on each one.

Fieldwork Skills are an important part of your course. You will develop these skills as you perform experiments and other practical work related to the topics you are studying. You will also find lots of activities that take you away from the book to more active forms of learning and application of knowledge. These are good opportunities to engage with your peers and reflect on your learning. We hope you enjoy learning about environmental management. It is an increasingly important and relevant subject that can be challenging but is absolutely vital to understand and appreciate.

Perhaps you will go on to study Cambridge International AS Level Environmental Management or beyond, and become an environmental manager and be involved in a case study such as the ones included in this book!

**Note on maps:** *The boundaries and names shown, the designations used and the presentation of material on any maps contained in this resource do not imply official endorsement or acceptance by Cambridge University Press concerning the legal status of any country, territory, or area or any of its authorities, or of the delimitation of its frontiers or boundaries.*

# Chapter 1
# Key skills in Environmental Management

## LEARNING INTENTIONS

In this chapter you will:

- learn how to plan investigations
- formulate aims and hypotheses
- explore and evaluate sampling techniques
- present data in the form of tables and graphs
- analyse data using statistical techniques
- practise identifying the limitations of methods used and suggesting possible improvements
- present reasoned explanations for phenomena, patterns and relationships
- make reasoned judgements and reach conclusions based on qualitative and quantitative information.

## ENVIRONMENTAL MANAGEMENT IN CONTEXT

### The importance of fieldwork investigation

How do we know about the structure of the Earth's core? While studying **data** from a New Zealand earthquake in 1929, Inge Lehmann, a Danish geophysicist, noticed that waves of energy (seismic waves) were appearing in unexpected locations. This led Lehmann to do further fieldwork, and in 1936 she proposed that the Earth's core is made up of two layers – a solid inner core and a liquid outer core. The two layers are separated by what is now known as the 'Lehmann Discontinuity'. Lehmann's **hypothesis** was confirmed in 1970, when more sensitive seismographs were able to detect seismic waves bouncing off the solid inner core. However, it was through Lehmann's fieldwork investigation that this important scientific discovery was made.

Fieldwork is an important part of studies in environmental management. Most of the knowledge we have today has been developed through the process of **scientific enquiry**. This involves:

- making **observations**
- deciding on an **aim** or guiding question
- formulating a hypothesis
- conducting a scientific experiment
- presenting and analysing data (results)
- testing the hypothesis against the data collected to reach a **conclusion** and an evaluation
- possibly developing a **theory**.

Investigations on the subject of environmental management involve identifying a problem and exploring how it is affecting the environment. You will need to think about:

- planning an investigation
- identifying the limitations of the methods used and suggesting possible improvements
- presenting reasoned explanations for phenomena, patterns and relationships that you have observed in your data
- making reasoned judgements and reaching conclusions based on qualitative and quantitative information.

All these stages involve the use of particular apparatus, skills and techniques, which are explained here and in the following chapters.

### Discussion questions

1. Give an example of some fieldwork you may have conducted in the past. How did it help your understanding of the topic you were investigating?

2. Suggest some suitable hypotheses that you could test in your Environmental Management studies.

### KEY WORDS

**data:** information gathered to investigate a hypothesis

**hypothesis:** a statement on a topic being investigated

**scientific enquiry:** a series of stages, from observation and hypothesis through experimentation to formulating a theory, each of which is designed to answer specific questions

**observation:** the recorded information that results from studying a scientific event

**aim:** the purpose of an investigation

**conclusion:** a statement summarising findings in an investigation

**theory:** an explanation of observations that has been repeatedly tested and confirmed

# 1.1 Planning a fieldwork investigation

Planning an investigation involves formulating an aim and one or more hypotheses. An aim identifies the purpose of your investigation, so you should have a suitable aim in mind when planning. 'To investigate the effects of coal mining waste on soil pH' is an example of an aim. From the aim, the hypothesis or hypotheses arise. A hypothesis is a statement on the topic that you are investigating, and is usually based on prior knowledge or observations. It is a testable prediction that proposes a relationship between two variables. You can find more detail on formulating hypotheses and identifying variables in Chapter 6.

## Apparatus

During your investigations, you will need to be familiar with a range of different tools and apparatus:

- Pitfall trap: Used to collect small animals, such as insects. The trap consists of a container buried in the ground with the top of the container level with the ground surface. The top of the container may be covered, to stop rain entering, with a small gap so insects fall in. The inside of the container is smooth to stop the animals climbing out.
- Pooter: Used to collect small insects and other invertebrates. It is a small jar with two tubes. One tube goes into your mouth so you can apply suction and the other goes over the insect. A mesh over the end of the first tube stops you swallowing the insect.
- Sweep net: Used to collect insects sitting on vegetation. The nets are swept through the grass, trees or shrubs to collect the insects.
- Quadrat: A grid, often (but not always) 1-metre square, which may have wires marking off smaller areas inside, such as 10 × 10 squares. It is used to estimate the abundance of sedentary organisms by counting or estimating percentage cover.
- Transect: A line placed through a habitat, using a tape measure or a piece of string; data is collected on the number and type of organisms at intervals along this line.
- Tray for hand sorting: A sorting tray allows you to sort items based on their physical characteristics.
- Hand lens: A portable magnifier, used to create an enlarged image of small objects.
- 30 cm ruler: A straight measuring device used to measure short distances.
- Metre ruler: A straight measuring device used to measure longer distances.
- pH meter: This measures the hydrogen ion concentration in water-based solutions and determines the acidity or alkalinity. If soil pH is being measured, the probe is pushed into the soil and the reading is displayed on the screen. The probe should be clean and dry before use and kept at a consistent depth.
- Light meter: This measures the amount of light in a particular position. It is held steadily at ground level and pointed in the direction of maximum light intensity, and a reading of the light intensity is displayed on the screen (Figure 1.1).
- Humidity/moisture meter: This measures the concentration of water vapour in the air and is sometimes called a digital hygrometer. Readings should be taken at the same height.

**Figure 1.1:** You may need to use a light meter to check the intensity of light during your investigations.

# Sampling

Once you have decided on the focus of your investigation, you need to think about your **sample**. It is often unnecessary to carry out an investigation on the whole of your target population. It may also be too expensive or time-consuming to do so. For example, it would be impossible to ask everyone in a large town for their views on the effects of air pollution, or to count all the plants in a large field. In these cases, you should plan to work with a sample.

A sample should be representative of the target population. If it is, then a larger sample size will usually give you more reliable results. The target population is the subset of people or organisms to which you can apply the conclusions of the study. For example, if only women are questioned about their views on air pollution, the conclusions can only be applied to women, and they would be the target population.

The sample size is the number of measurements in a sample. Your sample size will also depend on the time and resources available, and the capacity you have for handling the data collected.

You need to think about how you are going to collect the sample – which **sampling technique** are you going to use? Some sampling techniques include:

- pitfall traps
- pooters
- sweep nets
- quadrats (Figure 1.2)
- transects
- aerial photography and drones
- automated sampling.

There is more information about each of these in Topic 6.4.

> ### SKILLS TIP
> During your course, you may need to draw, complete or label diagrams of some of the apparatus described here, so it is a good idea to familiarise yourself with what they look like and how they work.

**Figure 1.2:** This researcher is using quadrats for underwater sampling.

You then need to decide on your **sampling strategy** (Figure 1.3). The main sampling strategies are:

- **Random sampling:** This is when sample points are selected using random numbers to avoid **bias**. Tables of random numbers can be generated by calculators or by smartphone apps. This technique gives every member of the population an equal chance of being selected, but it may also miss out an entire part of the population.
- **Systematic sampling:** This is when sample points are selected using a regular pattern or order, for example, conducting a questionnaire on every tenth person or surveying vegetation cover every 5 metres. This technique gives an even coverage of the population being investigated and is less likely to miss **anomalies** or variations.

1 Key skills in Environmental Management

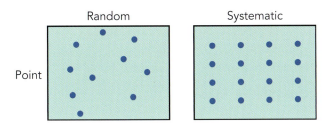

**Figure 1.3:** Random and systematic sampling.

There are examples of each of these sampling strategies in Topic 6.4.

## Questions

1.1 Match the sampling technique to the correct description.

| Sampling technique | Description | |
|---|---|---|
| Pooter | A | A grid, which may have wires marking off smaller areas inside, such as 10 × 10 squares |
| Quadrat | B | A container buried in the ground with the top of the container level with the ground surface. The top of the container is covered. |
| Pitfall trap | C | A small jar with two tubes. One tube goes into your mouth so you can apply suction, and the other goes over an insect. |

1.2 Sample data points are selected using a regular interval or pattern. Which sampling strategy is this a description of?

1.3 Suggest a suitable sampling technique and sampling strategy to use in an investigation into how the size of small rocks changed along a beach profile.

> **KEY WORDS**
>
> **sample:** a group of people or things that is chosen out of a larger number and is asked questions or tested in order to get information about the larger group
>
> **sampling technique:** the method of collecting data in an investigation
>
> **sampling strategy:** the way in which data is collected, either randomly or systematically
>
> **random sampling:** a sampling method in which an area is divided into a grid or given coordinates from a map and the sampling device is placed using random number tables or a random number generator to locate sampling points within this area. For a questionnaire, people may be selected by random selection from a phone book.
>
> **bias:** the action of encouraging one outcome over another
>
> **systematic sampling:** a sampling method in which the sampling device is placed along a line or some other predetermined pattern; the most common pattern is the line of a transect; questionnaires can also be applied systematically. The predetermined pattern maybe every nth metre or every nth person.
>
> **anomaly:** a result or observation that deviates from what is normal or expected; in experimental results, it normally refers to one repeated result that does not fit the pattern of the others

## 1.2 Collecting and recording data

As part of your investigation, you need to decide how to collect and record your data.

## Types of data

There are two types of data: **qualitative** and **quantitative**. Qualitative data is non-numerical and descriptive. Data can be observed but not measured, such as people's opinion on a movie. Quantitative data deals with numbers and can be measured, such as how many people saw a movie or how many people rated it five stars. Quantitative data can be either discrete or continuous:

> **KEY WORDS**
>
> **qualitative data:** data that is non-numerical and descriptive
>
> **quantitative data:** data that deals with numbers and can be measured

- Discrete data is numerical data that has a finite number of possible values and can only take whole numbers, e.g. the number of trees or 1, 2, 3, 4.
- Continuous data is numerical data that has infinite possibilities and can take any value, e.g. temperature, time, speed or 1.5, 1.51, 1.512.

Both qualitative and quantitative data can be either primary or secondary:

- Primary data is collected by you or a group doing the investigation. Examples include practical experiments, surveys or interviews.
- Secondary data has already been collected by people unconnected with the investigation but the data is relevant and useful. Examples include data from social media and the internet, newspapers, books, or past investigations.

Figure 1.4 summarises the types of data.

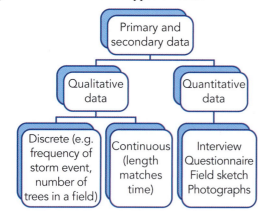

**Figure 1.4:** Types of data.

> **SCIENCE TIP**
>
> To help you remember the difference between quantitative and qualitative data, think:
>
> **Quantit**ative = **Quantit**y
>
> **Qualit**ative = **Qualit**y

> **ACTIVITY 1.1**
>
> Work in pairs. To help you understand the types of data that can be collected, compile two lists based on qualitative data and quantitative data. Decide who is going to write which list. Then, list as many advantages as you can think of for your chosen data type. Afterwards, swap your lists and discuss the results. Now have a go at listing the disadvantages for the data type list you have and discuss your results.

## Surveys and questionnaires

A survey describes a set of questions (a **questionnaire**) and the process of collecting the responses to those questions and analysing the results. Questionnaires can be carried out by approaching people in the street, knocking on people's doors, posting questionnaires, or putting the questions on the internet or on social media (Figure 1.5). When conducting a questionnaire, make sure you consider carefully the day, time and location of data collection, to avoid bias.

**Figure 1.5:** There are also many survey apps available, and companies often gather data by asking customers to complete their own short questionnaires online.

1  Key skills in Environmental Management

Always plan your questions ahead of time, and carry out a **pilot study** to ensure that the people interviewed understand the questions (five respondents would be sufficient) and the answers provide the information you want to analyse. Make sure you explain the aim of the questionnaire and be polite when asking people to complete one. Emphasise that the answers will be anonymous.

A good questionnaire should:

- be carefully worded, so the questions are not ambiguous and people understand them
- be quick to complete, and therefore have a limited number of questions in a logical order
- have **closed questions** at the beginning; you can include **open questions** later in the questionnaire if appropriate (these take longer to record but are useful if more information is required, although the answers might be difficult to record and analyse).

Always thank the respondent once the questionnaire has been completed.

An interview involves talking to a small group of people or an individual. You should have pre-planned questions, and the answers are usually longer than those from a questionnaire.

### KEY WORDS

**questionnaire:** a written list of questions that people are asked so that information can be collected

**pilot study:** a trial run of a questionnaire, which aims to discover any problems with the questions

**closed question:** a question that can be answered with 'yes' or 'no', or by a definite answer

**open question:** a question that requires more than a one-word answer

### ACTIVITY 1.2

Imagine you want to collect some information on how a group of local people feels about living near a copper smelter, as some people have complained that the smelter is making them ill. Copy and complete the following questionnaire to find out about the health of the local population. The first two questions have been written for you. Try to think of five other questions that you could ask.

Introduction: Excuse me, I am doing an investigation on the impact of the copper smelter on the health of local people as part of my Environmental Management studies. Please can I ask you a few questions?

**Q1 Which age range are you?**

Under 21   21–30   31–40   41–50
51–60   over 60

**Q2 How far from the smelter do you live?**

0–500 metres   501–1000 metres
1001–2000 metres   more than 2000 metres

Q3 ..........................................................................

Q4 ..........................................................................

Q5 ..........................................................................

Q6 ..........................................................................

Q7 ..........................................................................

Thank you for your time.

### PEER ASSESSMENT

In pairs, swap questionnaires. Discuss the questions you have each chosen. Were all your questions relevant? Why did you want to ask the questions that you wrote? Decide together how you would ensure that you interview a representative sample of the population. Be prepared to share your ideas with others in your class.

summarises some of the possible hazards and risks posed and safety precautions that should be taken when collecting data.

You should also consider ethics when gathering data, as some investigations involve working with living organisms. Always try to avoid harming the environment. When dealing with people through questionnaires and interviews, keep responses confidential and anonymous.

**Figure 1.6:** Questionnaires are a common way to collect data.

## Risks and safety measures

To collect data safely, you must be aware of potential health and safety issues relating to the equipment you are using (e.g. sulfuric acid or a Bunsen burner) or to the location of the investigation. Table 1.1

**Figure 1.7:** Whether you are conducting an investigation out in the field or in a laboratory, it is important to use protective equipment, such as gloves and goggles.

| Potential hazard | Risk posed | How to manage |
|---|---|---|
| Chemicals | Eye or skin irritation, or possible inhalation | Wear goggles to protect eyes (Figure 1.7), gloves to protect skin and a mask to avoid inhalation |
| Hot equipment | Burns to skin | Wear goggles and use tongs to lift hot equipment |
| Waterborne diseases | Weil's disease contracted through contaminated fresh water | Wash hands thoroughly and ensure open wounds are covered |
| Slippery rocks | Risk of slipping on rocks and causing injury | Wear sturdy, appropriate footwear |
| Wildlife and livestock | Being attacked by aggressive animals | Avoid fields with livestock and keep a safe distance from wildlife |
| Working in an unfamiliar location | Becoming lost | Work in groups, carry mobile phones and tell someone where you will be working |
| Tides | Getting trapped by incoming tide | Check tide timetables before collecting data |
| Weather conditions | Strong sunshine can lead to sunburn or heat stroke; heavy rain can lead to flooding | Check weather forecast; wear a hat to avoid the impact of the sun |

**Table 1.1:** Risks and safety precautions that should be taken when collecting data.

# 1 Key skills in Environmental Management

## Identifying limitations of methods and suggesting possible improvements

The method you choose for collecting data should be achievable and realistic. Even if it is, however, you may still encounter limitations. The quantity and quality of data collected will be determined by available resources, such as time, money, equipment, ICT, transport requirements and the number of people required to collect data from your chosen sample.

The choice of sampling – in terms of type and size – is important, and you should select a suitable sampling method at the planning stage. For example, you might think of using a systematic sampling method for an investigation into vegetation change along a transect, but then realise that some of the sampling sites might be inaccessible.

You should also consider the conditions in which data is collected, such as the weather when conducting a questionnaire. Timing and location of data collection are important too (Figure 1.8). Questionnaires should ideally be done at regular intervals as well as being timed to maximise the number of respondents. Questionnaires may have other limitations – for example, some age groups can be reluctant to answer, and all age groups might not be available if the questionnaire is conducted during working hours.

**Figure 1.8:** Timing and location of data collection, such as questionnaires, can affect results.

Some data-collection methods are subjective – for example, visually estimating sediment shape and size. You may be able to use digital equipment in order to collect more objective information and limit **human error**. If the method involves measuring equipment, make sure that it is **calibrated** before the investigation starts. By repeating the measurements, you can increase the **precision** of your results; or by using another piece of equipment, you may be able to increase their accuracy.

If you use the internet for data collection, you must consider whether the websites you use are biased, or if the information is inaccurate or outdated. Government websites usually provide **reliable** data.

> ### KEY WORDS
>
> **human error:** an erroneous result due to incorrect measurement or misreading a result
>
> **calibrate:** to check and make any necessary adjustments to a piece of equipment to ensure its accuracy
>
> **precision:** how close the measured values of a quantity are to each other
>
> **reliability:** the consistency of a measure – that is, whether the results can be repeated under the same conditions

## Ensuring accuracy

Accuracy is the degree to which the measurement or calculation is close to the true value or a standard. To ensure accuracy in fieldwork investigations, you should always test and, if necessary, calibrate the equipment before starting your investigation (Figure 1.9). This involves adjusting and standardising apparatus – for example, a balance. Apparatus, such as pH meters, also need regular care and maintenance. It is important to keep the use of significant figures that you record consistent and ensure that the number of significant figures is appropriate for the measurement. Nominating one person to be responsible for measurements can ensure accuracy and consistency.

**Figure 1.9:** You will need to calibrate a balance before you begin your investigation.

# Recording data

Data collected in investigations can be recorded in many ways, including by pen and paper, camera, survey apps, voice recorder and spreadsheets. However, drawing up a table is the most common, and often the most useful, way to record the data you are going to collect. Use the following guidelines when creating the table you will use in your investigation:

- If you have two or more columns, the first column should be the **independent variable** (i.e. the **variable** chosen by you); the other columns should contain the **dependent variable(s)** (i.e. the readings taken for each change in the independent variable).
- Columns should be headed with the name of the variable and the appropriate unit.
- Numerical values inserted in the table should just be numbers, without units. They should all be rounded to the same number of decimal places.

See Topic 6.4 for more information about variables.

If appropriate, recording tables may also have:

- a title
- headings for date, day, time and location
- other factors, such as weather
- enough space for all your recordings at each site/sample.

When recording units in your table, it is best to use tally marks.

> **KEY WORDS**
>
> **independent variable:** the variable that is deliberately changed in an experiment
>
> **variable:** a factor in an investigation that changes, can be changed or is controlled
>
> **dependent variable:** the variable that is measured in an experiment

> **WORKED EXAMPLE**
>
> ### Plant coverage
>
> Carry out an investigation for the hypothesis that plant coverage decreases with distance from a footpath.
>
>
>
> **Figure 1.10:** The site chosen to investigate if plant coverage decreases with distance from a footpath.
>
> **Step 1** Decide what apparatus and sampling technique you need for the investigation: a long tape measure for a transect and a quadrat.
>
> **Step 2** Create a transect at right angles to the edge of a footpath. Hold the long tape measure at the edge of the footpath, to measure out 5 metres. Hold it in place at both ends of the transect.
>
> **Step 3** Using systematic sampling as the sampling strategy, at every 1-metre interval along the transect, place a quadrat on the ground. If the plants can be seen as individuals, they should be counted; if not, use percentage cover.
>
> **Step 4** Record the results in a table. The first column should show the distance along the transect line (in metres), the second column should show the percentage coverage for a named species of plant, the third column should show the percentage coverage for a second species of plant and so on (see Table 1.2 as an example).
>
> **Step 5** Draw a conclusion from the data: Plant coverage does decrease with the distance from a footpath.

# 1 Key skills in Environmental Management

## CONTINUED

### Now you try

A student wanted to investigate the impact that grazing goats might have on soil erosion in an area (Figure 1.11). Plants reduce soil erosion by their roots holding soil together. The student decided to carry out a survey of the plants found in three fields. The fields had either no grazing, uncontrolled grazing or controlled grazing. Using a 1 metre by 1 metre quadrat, the student measured the number of plant species eaten by goats and the number of plant species not eaten by goats. Draw a table that the student could use to record the data.

**Figure 1.11:** What impact might grazing goats have on soil erosion?

| Independent variable (units) | Dependent variable 1 (units) | Dependent variable 2 (units) | Dependent variable 3 (units) | Dependent variable 4 (units) | Total % cover |
|---|---|---|---|---|---|
| Distance (metres) | Species 1 (% cover) | Species 2 (% cover) | Species 3 (% cover) | Species 4 (% cover) | |
| 1 | 12 | 25 | 5 | 25 | 67 |
| 2 | 53 | 0 | 3 | 0 | 56 |
| 3 | 23 | 17 | 4 | 11 | 55 |
| 4 | 45 | 3 | 4 | 2 | 54 |
| 5 | 0 | 37 | 3 | 12 | 52 |

**Table 1.2:** Distribution of plant species along a transect line, following a standard layout for tables.

### FIELDWORK TIP

You will find that when processing data, a calculator is a useful tool, so make sure you are familiar with a calculator's basic and more advanced functions.

### MATHS TIP

Make sure you understand and can use the symbols:

= equals

< less than

> greater than

## Compass directions

When recording data, you may find you need to note down the direction in which you are facing or the direction in which a transect runs. To do this, you will need a compass that uses Earth's magnetic field. The needle in a compass is magnetic and so will point to the magnetic North Pole. To use a compass, hold it horizontally so the needle can move freely. Turn the compass so the needle is pointing north (Figure 1.12). The directions on the compass are now the directions from your location. The four main directions are north, east, south and west. Exactly halfway between these directions are north-east, south-east, south-west and north-west. These directions make up the eight-point compass (Figure 1.13).

**Figure 1.12:** A compass being used in a fieldwork investigation.

> **FIELDWORK TIP**
>
> If you have a mobile phone, you can use an app to find a precise direction. The use of left, right, up and down is not appropriate when describing distributions or locations on maps.

**Figure 1.13:** An eight-point compass.

# 1.3 Presenting data

Having collected your data, you next need to decide how to present it. It is important to choose the presentation technique that best suits your data. Whatever way you choose to present your data, always make sure you give it a title, so it is immediately clear what the information shows. In graphs and charts, remember to label the axes and the key if you use one.

Tables of data are simple to design, but it is often easier to see **patterns** and **trends** when data is presented visually – for example, in graphs, charts or diagrams. There are many different types of graph and charts, including **pie charts**, **bar charts**, **histograms**, **line graphs** and **scatter graphs**. Drawings can also be used to record features of specimens that you have examined.

> **KEY WORDS**
>
> **pattern:** something that occurs or repeats in a predictable way
>
> **trend:** a general pattern in data showing an increase, decrease or remaining constant, when smaller changes are ignored
>
> **pie chart:** a chart showing the proportions of different parts making up the total
>
> **bar chart:** a graph showing the data using bars
>
> **histogram:** a graph showing the frequency of a continuous variable
>
> **line graph:** a graph showing the relationship between two quantitative variables
>
> **scatter graph:** a graph with points representing amounts or numbers on it, which may include a line of best fit

## Charts

### Pie charts

Pie charts are circular charts divided into sectors. The sectors show proportions or percentages that relate to the data in each category (Figure 1.14). There should be no more than six and no fewer than two sectors in a pie chart. The data used is often in the form of percentages and can be converted into degrees by multiplying each percentage by 3.6 to give a total of 360°. The sectors are plotted in rank order. The largest sector is plotted first starting at '12 o'clock' or 0° and drawn in a clockwise direction. The second sector is then plotted from where the first one ends.

1   Key skills in Environmental Management

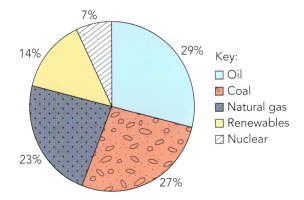

Figure 1.14: A pie chart showing the projected world energy use in 2035.

## Bar charts

Bar charts are useful when one of the variables is not numerical (Figure 1.15). This type of chart is used to show data that fits into categories, such as the total number of plant species at different sites.

A bar chart has two axes, which should be labelled. The bars should be drawn with equal width and with equal spaces between each bar. The bars should not touch.

A divided bar chart can be used to show a set of data that is represented by percentages, and you can use one as an alternative to a pie chart. A single bar representing 100% is subdivided into the different data categories. Bar charts can show two sets of data – for example, climate graphs and population pyramids.

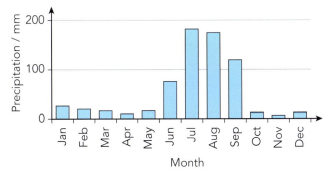

Figure 1.15: A bar chart showing the average precipitation in Agra, India.

## Histograms

A histogram looks like a bar chart without the spaces between the bars, but histograms are used to show frequencies of data in different categories (Figure 1.16) or which change over a period of time. They show a continuous independent variable. On the x-axis, the range of values is divided into intervals – for example, 0–99, 100–199. This is a continuous scale, and the values do not overlap. The y-axis shows the frequency or percentage of the collected data falling into each of the intervals. A vertical bar represents each interval, and the bars are continuous with no gaps between them. The bars should be touching.

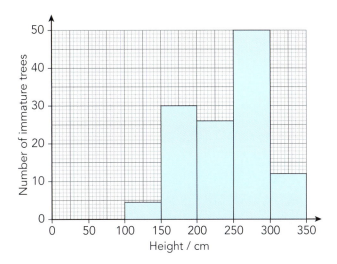

Figure 1.16: A histogram showing the height of immature trees in a plantation.

## Graphs

### Line graphs

A line graph is used when there is a continuous change in the data, often over time. It may show a trend (Figure 1.17). The points should be plotted as crosses or encircled dots, and connected with a clear straight line using a sharp pencil. Make sure that each point is plotted to an accuracy of half of one of the smallest squares on your graph grid.

The axes of a line graph begin at zero. The independent variable goes on the horizontal or x-axis (for example, time), and the dependent variable on the vertical or y-axis. Make sure each axis is labelled with the physical quantity and appropriate unit.

It is important to use a suitable scale, as this will affect the appearance of the line graph. The scales for the axes should cover more than half of the graph grid being used in both directions.

# CAMBRIDGE IGCSE™ AND O LEVEL ENVIRONMENTAL MANAGEMENT: COURSEBOOK

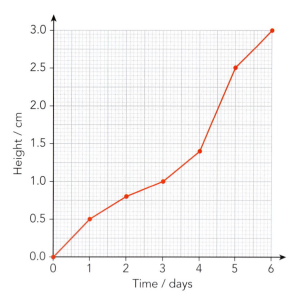

Figure 1.17: A line graph showing the growth of a bean plant over time.

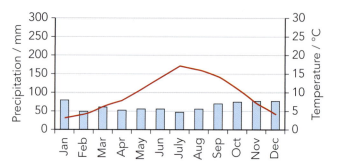

Figure 1.18: A climate graph showing monthly temperature and precipitation in London, UK.

> **FIELDWORK TIP**
>
> When constructing a graph from data collected in a table, remember that you can use the column headings in the table as the axes labels on your graph. Axes labels should include the units for quantities if appropriate.

> **CRITICAL THINKING TIP**
>
> When interpreting a graph, identify an overall trend first and then look for changes in the trend. Trends can be described as going up (increase, rise), going down (decrease, falling, decline), no change (constant, stable) and changing (fluctuating). Also refer to the highest value or peak, and the lowest value. Use data to support your description, if possible.

## Combined graphs

Combined graphs record two related sets of data on the same chart, often in different formats. A climate graph is an example of a combined graph. Temperature is continuous data, so it is presented as a line graph. Rainfall is non-continuous data, so it requires a bar chart. Figure 1.18 is a climate graph for London, UK.

> **ACTIVITY 1.3**
>
> Study Table 1.3, which shows the mean maximum temperature and precipitation recorded in Las Vegas, USA.
>
> Draw a climate graph to represent the data. Use Figure 1.18 to help you.
>
> | Month | Mean maximum temperature / °C | Precipitation / mm |
> |---|---|---|
> | January | 14.1 | 30 |
> | February | 15.7 | 39 |
> | March | 18.7 | 27 |
> | April | 21.9 | 6 |
> | May | 26.9 | 3 |
> | June | 31.9 | 1 |
> | July | 30.6 | 9 |
> | August | 35.6 | 7 |
> | September | 31.3 | 3 |
> | October | 25.5 | 9 |
> | November | 18.0 | 15 |
> | December | 13.5 | 23 |
>
> Table 1.3: Mean maximum temperature and precipitation recorded in Las Vegas, USA.

## Scatter graphs

Scatter graphs are used to see if a relationship exists between two sets of data, and whether that relationship is positive or negative (Figure 1.19). A scatter graph helps you to see if one set of data is likely to change in relation to a second set

1 Key skills in Environmental Management

of data in a systematic way. This change does not necessarily mean that one variable causes the other to change.

Scatter graphs are plotted in a similar way to line graphs, but the points are not joined with a line. The data set that is likely to cause the change is the independent variable, which is plotted on the *x*-axis. The dependent variable is plotted on the *y*-axis. If the scatter graph shows a likely linear relationship, it is then appropriate to plot the **line of best fit** (trend line) by eye, with an equal number of points above and below the line. You should ignore any anomalies in the results when drawing the line of best fit. The line does not have to pass through the origin of the graph, but it should stop at the first or last data point. It should be a single, thin, smooth straight line drawn with a ruler and a sharp pencil.

> **KEY WORD**
>
> **line of best fit:** a line drawn on a graph to show the general trend in the data plotted

> **MATHS TIP**
>
> You should only draw a line of best fit if you have good reason to believe that the intermediate values can be predicted.

### Drawings

A task may ask you to **sketch** something that you have found in your investigation. Sketches should be created with a sharp pencil to give a fine, single line that is unbroken and clear. Leave space around the drawing for labels. Use a ruler to draw each label line and ensure that the end of the label line touches the feature being labelled. Write the labels horizontally. Use a scale bar if appropriate; your drawing should take up at least half the page. Avoid shading and colouring. Figure 1.20 shows a sketch of tectonic plate movement.

> **COMMAND WORD**
>
> **sketch:** make a simple freehand drawing showing the key features, taking care over proportions

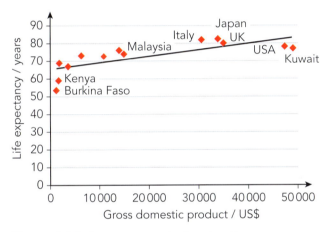

**Figure 1.19:** A scatter graph showing the relationship between life expectancy and GDP for selected countries.

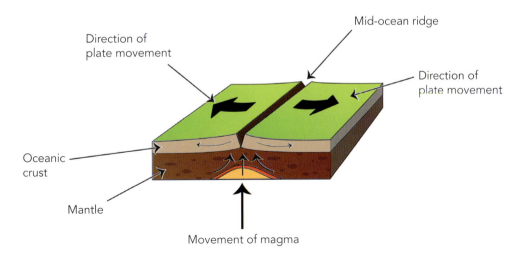

**Figure 1.20:** A sketch showing tectonic plate movement.

15

**Figure 1.21:** Photographs can be used to show changes over time. This photograph shows the impact of flooding.

## Photographs

You can use photographs to show sampling sites. If they are labelled, they can also be used as fieldwork analysis. Photographs are useful because they are an accurate record at the time and can be used next to historical photographs to show changes over time, as can be seen in Figure 1.21. The location of the photograph, time/date taken and direction in which the photographer is facing should be recorded. However, photographs are subjective and biased as the photographer selects what is photographed.

## Questions

**1.4** Match the presentation method that would be best suited to each of the data types described.

| Presentation method | Description |
|---|---|
| Pie chart | Showing the trend of time data |
| Scatter graph | Displaying the proportions of a town's budget spent on various types of flood defence strategies |
| Line graph | Displaying the number of plants collected across 10 sites |
| Bar chart | Displaying the relationship between light intensity and tree height |

**1.5** A student counted the number of Bengal foxes in five different areas over a week. The results are shown in Table 1.4.

| Area | Number of foxes |
|---|---|
| Area 1 | 15 |
| Area 2 | 12 |
| Area 3 | 12 |
| Area 4 | 11 |
| Area 5 | 10 |

**Table 1.4:** Foxes recorded in five areas over the course of a week.

The student has decided to use a pie chart to present the data. What angle should they use for Area 1?

A  15 degrees   B  60 degrees

C  90 degrees   D  180 degrees

**Figure 1.22:** A Bengal fox.

**1.6** A student decided to use a labelled photograph in their data presentation. Suggest one advantage and one disadvantage of using this method.

1  Key skills in Environmental Management

# 1.4 Analysing statistical data

Once you have presented your data in a table, graph or diagram, you need to be able to analyse it by describing and explaining what you can see. For example, can you see any trends or associations and explain them? Simple statistical techniques can also be helpful in analysis. These include working out the **range** (the difference between the largest and smallest values) and the average.

## Working out averages

There are three kinds of average: **mean**, **mode** and **median**:

- The mean is the total of all values divided by the total number of values. It is used when there are no extremes of values, which would distort the mean.
- The mode is the value with the highest frequency.
- The median is the value in the middle after the data has been sorted into ascending order. It is not affected by extreme values.

> **KEY WORDS**
>
> **range:** the calculated difference between the largest and smallest values in a set of data
>
> **mean:** the total of all values divided by the total number of values
>
> **mode:** the value with the highest frequency
>
> **median:** the value in the middle after the data has been sorted into ascending order

## Ratios

Ratios show the comparison in size between two quantities, such as length or area. They are written in the form **a:b or a:b:c**. If a student picked 10 flowers for an investigation, and 6 were white and 4 were red, the ratio between white and red flowers would be 6:4. To simplify a ratio, all parts of the ratio are divided by a common factor, so this can be simplified to 3:2.

Ratios can be written as fractions. Using the example of white and red flowers, there are 3/2 as many white flowers as red flowers. There are 2/3 as many red flowers as white flowers. You can also write this as a fraction of the total: 6/10 flowers are white, which simplifies to 3/5.

To see how simplification works in a more complicated example, imagine a student picks 48 flowers for an investigation; 15 are white and 33 are red. The ratio is 15:33. The common factor is 3, so 15:33 ÷ 3 = 5:11. This is the ratio in its simplest form.

You may want to find the ratio of a part – for example, the ratio of white to red flowers.

2 out of every 10 flowers a student picks are white, so 10 − 2 = 8

8 out of every 10 flowers are red, so for every 2 white flowers there are 8 red flowers.

The ratio is white flowers : red flowers = 2:8, which simplifies to 1:4.

Splitting a total amount into a ratio is an important skill in investigations.

> **WORKED EXAMPLE**
>
> **Ratios**
>
> A student has 99 seeds that need to be divided between three fields: A, B and C in a ratio of 2:3:4. How many seeds should be planted in field A?
>
> **Step 1** Find the total number of parts in the ratio:
>
> 2 + 3 + 4 = 9
>
> **Step 2** Divide the total amount by the total number of parts in the ratio so that you find one part.
>
> 99 ÷ 9 = 11 seeds = 1 part
>
> **Step 3** Multiply the value of one part by the number of parts for field A:
>
> 11 × 2 = 22
>
> **Step 4** Give your answer: 22 seeds should be planted in field A.
>
> **Now you try**
>
> Three fruit pickers, A, B and C, were paid $24 000 in the ratio of 3:4:5 for the number of oranges they picked in a month. How much money does fruit picker A receive?

17

Figure 1.23: Fruit pickers on an orange farm.

Figure 1.25: Examples of how to reduce a ratio to the form 1:n for two forest areas.

Forest A now has a lower ratio of 1:4 compared to 1:6 for forest B, so as a proportion there are more deciduous trees in forest A.

> **SELF-ASSESSMENT**
>
> How confident did you feel working out this ratio? Did you understand all the steps in the worked example or do you feel you need some more practice? Could you work out how much money fruit pickers B and C received?

Finally, you may want to reduce a ratio to the form 1:n or n:1. To do this, divide the whole ratio by the smallest number. In the previous fruit-picking example, the smallest number is 5. Figure 1.24 shows how to form the ratio 1:n. The ratio is now 1:1.6.

$$\div 5 \; \underset{1:1.6}{\overset{5:8}{\circlearrowleft}} \; \div 5$$

Figure 1.24: An example of how to reduce a ratio to the form 1:n.

For example, a student wanted to investigate the number of deciduous trees compared to coniferous trees in two forests and convert the ratio to the form 1:n. The student then wanted to find out which forest had more coniferous trees.

In forest A, there were 30 deciduous trees for every 120 coniferous trees.

In forest B, there were 15 deciduous trees for every 90 coniferous trees.

In forest A, the smallest number in the ratio is 30, and in forest B the smallest number in the ratio is 15. Figure 1.25 shows how the ratios can be converted to the form 1:n.

## Questions

1.7 A student wanted to investigate how temperature varied across an area. Five sites were randomly selected for the temperature readings, and the results are shown in Table 1.5.

   a **Calculate** the mean annual temperature and the mean highest temperature. Write your answers to one decimal place.

   b Calculate the temperature ranges for the mean annual temperature and the lowest temperature.

| Sites | Mean annual temperature / °C | Lowest temperature at each site / °C | Highest temperature at each site / °C |
|---|---|---|---|
| Site 1 | 26.7 | 15.1 | 34.8 |
| Site 2 | 23.4 | 14.5 | 39.5 |
| Site 3 | 28.4 | 12.4 | 32.0 |
| Site 4 | 27.3 | 16.0 | 29.8 |
| Site 5 | 25.4 | 8.9 | 28.2 |
| Mean temperature of all sites | | 13.1 | |

Table 1.5: Results of an investigation into temperature variations across an area.

1.8 In a village of 450 people, the ratio of the numbers of villagers with employment compared to those without employment is 4:5. How many villagers are without employment?

1.9 A student wanted to divide 35 seedlings into a ratio of 2:5. **Calculate** the number of seedlings divided in this ratio.

## 1 Key skills in Environmental Management

**1.10** In 2024, 64% of India's population live in rural areas and 36% in urban areas. Calculate the ratio of the urban population to the rural population.

> **COMMAND WORD**
>
> **calculate:** work out from given facts, figures or information

## Percentages

Percentage means the number of parts per 100, and is shown by the sign %. Being able to work out percentages is a skill that you will use throughout your environmental management studies, and especially when analysing data collected for a fieldwork investigation.

To work out the percentage of an amount, the percentage is converted to a fraction or decimal and then multiplied by the amount.

> **WORKED EXAMPLE**
>
> ### Percentages 1
>
> In 2024, 11% of Nigeria's population of 226 million was estimated to live in the city of Lagos. How many people live in Lagos? Give your answer to one decimal place.
>
> **Step 1** Calculate 11% of 226 million
>
> 11 ÷ 100 × 226 = 24.86
>
> **Step 2** Give your answer: 24.9 million
>
> **Now you try**
>
> A student wanted to investigate fish stocks in a local lake and asked a fisherman how many fish he caught on average in a week. The fisherman said he caught about 60 fish each week, but that 16% of the catch were too small to keep and had to be thrown back into the lake. How many fish were too small to be caught?
>
> **Give** your answer to one decimal place.

> **COMMAND WORD**
>
> **give:** produce an answer from a given source or recall/memory

> **MATHS TIP**
>
> You may be asked to round numbers to a certain number of decimal places. This means the number of digits after the decimal point. Round up if the digit is 5 or more, and round down if it is 4 or less. If the rounding results in a whole number, you should still include the decimal places.
>
> Rounding to 1 decimal place:
>
> 6.423 = 6.4
>
> 6.291 = 6.3
>
> 6.35 = 6.4
>
> 6.95 = 7.0
>
> Rounding to 3 decimal places:
>
> 0.06322 = 0.063
>
> 12.2915 = 12.292

If you want to work out the percentage of two different values, you take the second quantity and divide by first quantity, then multiply by 100.

> **WORKED EXAMPLE**
>
> ### Percentages 2
>
> The total area of Africa is 30.37 million km$^2$. A scientist estimated that in 2024, 10.3 million km$^2$ of land in Africa is at risk of desertification. Calculate the percentage of land that is at risk of desertification in 2024.
>
> **Step 1** Take the second quantity (10.3) and divide by the first quantity (30.37), and multiply by 100:
>
> 10.3 ÷ 30.37 × 100 = 33.91504
>
> **Step 2** Give your answer to two decimal places: 33.92%
>
> **Now you try**
>
> In 2024, global production of oil was 101.5 million barrels per day. Saudi Arabia produced 10 million barrels per day. Calculate the percentage of oil produced per day in Saudi Arabia. Give your answer to two decimal places.

You may want to work out by what percentage your data has increased. To do this, you first need to work out the difference between the two numbers you are comparing:

new number – original number = increased value

Then divide the increased value by the original number and multiply by 100.

To work out percentage decrease, the order swaps:

original number – new number = decreased value

Then divide the decreased value by the original number and multiply by 100.

### WORKED EXAMPLE

#### Percentages 3

In 2014, a region's annual GDP was $90 million. In 2024, the same region's GDP increased to $120 million. Calculate the percentage increase to one decimal place.

**Step 1** Subtract the old number from the new number to find the increased value:

120 – 90 = 30

**Step 2** Divide the increased value by the original number and multiply by 100:

30 ÷ 90 × 100

**Step 3** Give your answer to one decimal place: 33.3% increase.

#### Now you try

The population of Mumbai in India increased from 3 million in 1970 to 22 million in 2024. What is the percentage increase in Mumbai's population? Give your answer as a whole number.

When analysing data, you may have a value and the percentage change but you want to know what the original value was. This is sometimes called a reverse percentage.

### WORKED EXAMPLE

#### Percentages 4

A forest covers 320 km² but has been deforested by 15%. Calculate the original area of forest.

### CONTINUED

**Step 1** Subtract the percentage deforested from 100:

100 – 15 = 85

**Step 2** Work out 1% of the original forest area:

320 ÷ 85 = 3.76

**Step 3** Multiply that answer by 100 to find the original forest area:

3.76 × 100 = 376 km²

#### Now you try

A student counted 120 starfish on a beach. A local person told the student that starfish numbers had decreased by 30% since 2000. Calculate how many starfish were counted in 2000. Write your answer to the nearest whole number.

Figure 1.26: Counting starfish on a beach.

### MATHS TIP

To understand how many significant figures a number has, you can count the digits from the first non-zero number.

So, 1.2 is written to two significant figures. 54,649 is written to five significant figures. 0.001 is written to 1 significant figure, because the zeros are non-significant.

You may be asked to round to 1 or 2 significant figures.

If you need to round to 1 significant figure, look at the second non-zero figure - if it is greater than or equal to 5, round the first figure up. If it is less than 5, round the first figure down.

1 Key skills in Environmental Management

## CONTINUED

When rounding to 2 significant figures, look at the third figure. If this is greater than or equal to 5, then round the second figure up.

For example:

25.8 to two significant figures would round up to 26 because 8 is greater than 5.

3.71 would round down to 3.7 because 1 is less than 5.

0.125 would round down to 0.13 because 5 is equal to 5. 5 is the third significant figure because it is the third number that is not a zero.

If you need to round to 1 significant figure, look at the second figure – if it is greater than or equal to 5, round the first figure up. For example:

26 would be rounded to 30, because 6 is greater than 5, so we round to the nearest multiple of 10, as that is the greatest place value.

25,000 would be rounded to 30,000 because the digit with the highest place value is 2, measured in ten thousands, and 5 rounds upwards.

## ACTIVITY 1.4

Round the following numbers to two significant figures:

1  32,998    4  19,123
2  0.302     5  4,892
3  1.7756

Round the following numbers to one significant figure:

6  22        9  889
7  23,817    10 411,991
8  1.1

Extension: give the person next to you 5–10 more numbers to round to one or two significant figures.

## Scatter graphs and trends

When analysing scatter graphs, if the data points are on or close to the line of best fit, it means there is a strong **correlation** between the variables.

- A positive correlation is shown when an increase in the independent variable occurs at the same time as an increase in the dependent variable.
- A negative correlation occurs when an increase in the independent variable occurs at the same time as a decrease in the dependent variable.
- No correlation is when an increase in the independent variable does not directly affect the dependent variable.

### KEY WORD

**correlation:** a pattern between two variables; this may be due to a causal link between them, but a correlation is not proof of cause

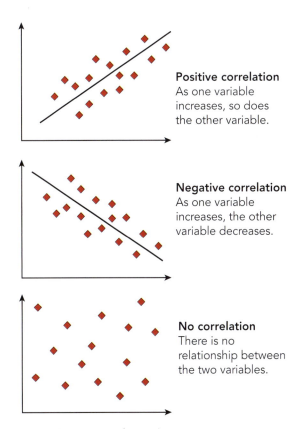

**Positive correlation**
As one variable increases, so does the other variable.

**Negative correlation**
As one variable increases, the other variable decreases.

**No correlation**
There is no relationship between the two variables.

Figure 1.27: Types of correlation.

21

Sometimes a correlation can show a direct link between the two variables. For example, doubling the independent variable results in doubling the dependent variable – they are said to be **directly proportional** (Figure 1.28). Variables are said to be **inversely proportional** when one variable increases and the other decreases.

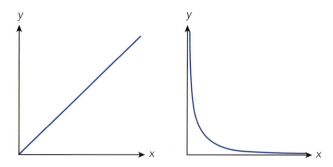

Figure 1.28: Graphs showing variables that are directly proportional (left) and inversely proportional (right).

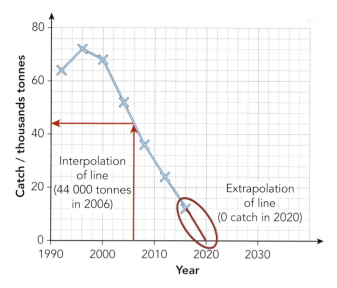

Figure 1.29: A graph to show interpolation and extrapolation.

A student wanted to investigate if more snails appear when it rains. The student stopped counting when 5 mm of rain had fallen, by which time 30 snails had been counted. The student wanted to know how many snails potentially could be counted if 7 mm of rain fell. The graph of these results is shown in Figure 1.30. The extrapolation line shows that at 7 mm of rainfall, potentially 35 snails would be counted. At 1.5 mm of rainfall, around 7 or 8 snails would be counted – this is interpolation.

> **KEY WORDS**
>
> **directly proportional:** a positive correlation when the ratio between the independent and dependent variables is constant – for example, doubling the independent variable also doubles the dependent variable
>
> **inversely proportional:** a negative correlation when the ratio between the independent and dependent variables is constant – for example, doubling the independent variable halves the dependent variable

## Intercepts and gradients

When analysing data on a graph, you may want to calculate the point where the plotted line meets an axis for precise data values that you do not have. This is called the **intercept** and it can be calculated by extending the line from your graph until it reaches an axis. This is called **extrapolation** (Figure 1.29). **Interpolation** is an estimation of values between two known values.

> **KEY WORDS**
>
> **intercept:** the value on an axis where a line meets the axis
>
> **extrapolation:** extending a line on a line graph beyond the range of data collected
>
> **interpolation:** estimation of values between two known values
>
> **gradient:** the rate of change in a variable, calculated by dividing the change in y-value by the change in x-value

1 Key skills in Environmental Management

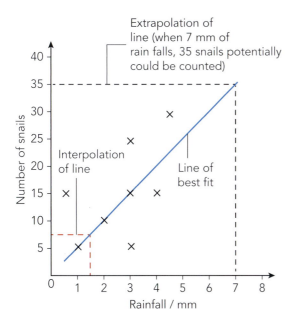

Figure 1.30: A scatter graph showing interpolation and extrapolation.

When analysing graphs, you need to look for any variations in the trend. Does the **gradient** (the rate of change in a variable) change?

> **MATHS TIP**
>
> To calculate the gradient of a straight line on a graph:
>
> - Pick two points on the line that are at least half of the length of the line.
> - Draw a right-angled triangle between the two points.
> - Calculate the gradient using the horizontal and vertical sides of the triangle: $y^1 \div x^1$ (Figure 1.31)

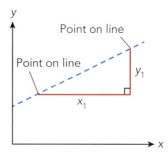

Figure 1.31: Calculating the gradient from a graph.

## FIELDWORK ACTIVITY 1.1

### An investigation into the effect of wood ash on the growth of sweet pea seeds

Figure 1.32: Sweet pea seedlings.

### You will need

- 3 trays filled with the same soil type and quantity
- a measuring ruler
- 30 sweet pea seeds
- 15 g of wood ash
- a measuring cylinder
- a balance for weighing

### Safety

Wear gloves when touching soil to avoid risk of infection.

### Before you start

To make the results of the investigation valid, other variables that might affect the results need to be controlled and kept constant. For this investigation, these could include: type of sweet pea seed, light intensity, temperature, size of the container, ash from the same source, volume of water added to the sweet pea seeds and spacing of sweet pea seeds. You may also want to draw up the results table before you start the investigation.

# CAMBRIDGE IGCSE™ AND O LEVEL ENVIRONMENTAL MANAGEMENT: COURSEBOOK

## CONTINUED

**Method**

- Label the trays A, B and C. Fill them with an equal amount of soil.
- Add 5 g of wood ash to tray B and 10 g of wood ash to tray C. Do not add any wood ash to tray A.
- Plant 10 sweet pea seeds, evenly spaced, in each tray.
- Place the trays in an area that has an equal temperature and amount of light. Give each tray the same volume of water at the same time.
- After day 15, count the number of seedlings that have a minimum of two leaves in each tray every three days until day 30.

**Questions**

1. Why do you think tray A had no wood ash added to the soil?
2. **Plot** a graph to show the results for trays B and C.
3. **Describe** the trend of the graph.
4. Write a suitable conclusion.

## COMMAND WORDS

**plot:** mark point(s) on a graph

**describe:** state the points of a topic / give characteristics and main features

## REFLECTION

How easy did you find this activity? Did you have all the equipment that you needed? Do you think if you had actually carried out this investigation you would be able to describe the method more easily?

## SUMMARY

| |
|---|
| Scientific enquiry involves an aim, hypotheses, designing a method, data collection, data analysis, and a conclusion and evaluation. |
| Suitable apparatus and sampling techniques to collect the data need to be selected. |
| Appropriate sampling strategies must be considered. |
| Data can also be collected by methods such as surveys and questionnaires. |
| Results should be recorded in tables with columns and rows. |
| Risks and safety precautions should always be considered before undertaking a fieldwork investigation. |
| Data should be presented in an appropriate form. This could be charts, graphs, drawings or photographs. |
| Data can be analysed using statistics, from which you need to identify trends. |
| Data collection methods need to be evaluated to identify potential sources of error. |

# 1 Key skills in Environmental Management

## SELF-EVALUATION CHECKLIST

After studying this chapter, complete this table.

| I can: | Needs more work | Almost there | Ready to move on |
|---|---|---|---|
| plan investigations | | | |
| formulate aims and hypotheses | | | |
| describe quantitative and qualitative data | | | |
| understand sampling strategies and techniques | | | |
| understand how to conduct an effective questionnaire and interview | | | |
| describe risks and safety precautions when undertaking data collection | | | |
| present data in the form of tables and graphs | | | |
| analyse data using statistical techniques, such as mean, median and mode | | | |
| understand how to calculate ratios and percentages | | | |
| identify limitations of methods used and suggest possible improvements | | | |
| present reasoned explanations for phenomena, patterns and relationships | | | |
| make reasoned judgements and reach conclusions based on qualitative and quantitative information. | | | |

# END-OF-CHAPTER QUESTIONS

1  Some avocado tree farmers reported that their avocado crops were being eaten by a pest. They wanted to find out how well a pesticide worked against the pest. To investigate, a student marked out two sample areas of the same field as shown in **Figure 1.33**.

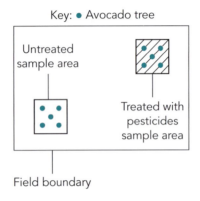

**Figure 1.33:** The two sample areas in the same field.

   a  Give **one** reason as to why the student used two areas in the same field.

   b  State **one** sampling strategy the student could have used to locate the positions of the avocado trees.

   c  All avocado fruit on the trees selected were removed and those infected with the pest were recorded on a table.

   i  Suggest **one** way in which the student could carry out this work safely.

   ii  **Table 1.6** shows the results of the investigation. Calculate the total number of avocados removed in the sample area treated with pesticides.

| Avocado tree | Sample area treated with pesticide | | Sample area untreated with pesticide | |
|---|---|---|---|---|
| | Avocados removed | Avocados infested | Avocados removed | Avocadoes infested |
| 1 | 56 | 10 | 60 | 25 |
| 2 | 48 | 8 | 55 | 22 |
| 3 | 51 | 9 | 45 | 18 |
| 4 | 42 | 5 | 50 | 28 |
| 5 | 33 | 6 | 46 | 19 |
| Total | | 38 | 256 | 112 |

**Table 1.6:** Results of an investigation into how well a pesticide worked against an avocado pest.

## CONTINUED

      **iii** Calculate the percentage of infestation for the treated and untreated sections of the field. Give your answer to the nearest whole number.

      **iv** Determine a suitable conclusion for the investigation.

**2** Table 1.7 shows population data from 2010 to 2025 for Pakistan and the world.

|  | 2010 | 2015 | 2020 | 2025 |
|---|---|---|---|---|
| Pakistan | 194 454 498 | 210 969 298 | 227 196 741 | 249 948 885 |
| World | 6 985 603 105 | 7 426 597 537 | 7 840 952 880 | 8 191 988 453 |

**Table 1.7:** Population data for Pakistan and the world, 2010–25.

    **a** Calculate the percentage of the world's population that lived in Pakistan in 2025. Give your answer to one decimal place.

    **b** Calculate Pakistan's population percentage increase between 2010 and 2025. Give your answer to one decimal place.

    **c** State a suitable graph to present the population data for Pakistan.

**3** A student wanted to record data on traffic. They created the following table to record their data. Suggest **three** reasons why this is not a suitable table.

|  | Number of vehicles at sites 1, 2, 3, 4 and 5 |
|---|---|
| Totals |  |

# Chapter 2
# Natural resources

## LEARNING INTENTIONS

In this chapter you will:

- explore the formation of igneous, sedimentary and metamorphic rocks, and the rock cycle
- investigate the permeability of different types of rock
- explore the different methods of extracting rocks, ores and minerals, and consider why we extract them
- investigate the environmental, economic and social impacts of extracting rock, ore and minerals
- learn how land can be restored and repurposed after rocks, ores and minerals have been extracted, and consider the benefits and limitations of these strategies
- understand what finite resources are and what sustainable management means
- discuss a variety of sustainable strategies for managing rocks, ores and minerals, and consider the benefits and limitations of these strategies
- learn how fossil fuels are formed
- classify energy sources into renewable and non-renewable types
- explore how different energy sources are used to make electricity
- consider the benefits and limitations of different resources
- learn about the different factors affecting energy demand

2 Natural resources

## CONTINUED

- examine how energy sources can be managed efficiently and investigate research into new energy sources
- discover what fracking is, and consider the arguments for and against its use.

## BEFORE YOU START

Look around you. Make a list of all the things you can see from where you are sitting that are made from a material that has been mined or extracted from the ground. (Remember that plastic items are made from oil.) Discuss your lists in pairs. Do you agree that all the items come from materials extracted from the earth?

Now look again at objects in the room around you. In your pairs, choose ten items. For each item, decide whether energy was used in its manufacture, whether energy is needed to operate it, or both. Copy and complete the Venn diagram by putting the items you have chosen in the relevant part.

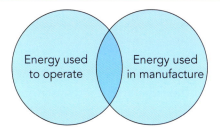

Join up with another pair and discuss your diagrams. Which area has the fewest examples? What other examples from outside the room can you think of that would fit in this area?

## ENVIRONMENTAL MANAGEMENT IN CONTEXT

### Our rocky planet

Not all planets in our solar system are the same. Jupiter and Saturn are gas giants, but Earth is a rocky planet. It is made from rocks and **mineral ores**.

Earth weighs 5 973 600 000 000 000 000 000 000 kg ($5.97 \times 10^{24}$ kg). It has a density of 5.2 g cm$^{-3}$, which makes it the densest planet in the solar system. The reason for this is that Earth's molten core contains a large volume of molten metals, especially iron.

Humans are only able to **exploit** rocks, ores and minerals from Earth's outer layer. There is a large quantity there, but because these resources are not being replaced, they are **non-renewable**, or **finite**. There will come a time when certain rocks, ores and minerals are no longer available, and this will impact the world in many different ways. Coal is the most common example of a natural resource that is running low on Earth. But many other resources are non-renewable, including the materials used to manufacture items that we consider essential, such as mobile phones, computers and batteries.

No one can say for sure when these natural resources will run out. Many previous predictions have proved to be inaccurate, because new **reserves** have been found or because improved technology has made extracting resources more efficient. However, many reserves of resources are in areas such as Antarctica (Figure 2.1), where extracting them could cause significant environmental damage. International agreements are in place to prevent any mineral extraction in Antarctica, but it may prove difficult to maintain this agreement when the world's resources are in short supply.

### KEY WORDS

**mineral:** a naturally occurring inorganic substance; minerals are often solid

**ore:** a rock that contains minerals and metals that can be extracted

**exploit:** to extract and use natural resources for human advantage

**non-renewable (finite):** a natural resource that is being used up faster than it is being replaced so it will eventually run out

**reserves:** stores of a useful resource that can be exploited

29

> CAMBRIDGE IGCSE™ AND O LEVEL ENVIRONMENTAL MANAGEMENT: COURSEBOOK

---

**CONTINUED**

**Figure 2.1:** There are large reserves of resources such as valuable rocks and mineral ores in Antarctica, but an international agreement currently bans their extraction, as there is a risk of major damage to wildlife and the environment.

**Discussion questions**

1. As resources are used up in the future, should the ban on using reserves in Antarctica be removed? Why, or why not?
2. What is more important, the supply of resources for our needs or the conservation of natural **ecosystems**?

> **KEY WORD**
>
> **ecosystem:** all the living things (biotic components) together with all the non-living things (abiotic components) in an area

---

## 2.1 Formation of rocks

There are many different types of rocks, but they are usually organised into three groups based on the way they are formed: igneous, sedimentary and metamorphic.

### Igneous rocks

**Igneous rocks** form when molten rock from Earth's crust and upper mantle cools (Figure 2.2). The molten rock is called **magma** when it is still below the surface. It is known as lava when it reaches Earth's surface.

Magma is found in the mantle. This hot, liquid rock comes under pressure from the rocks above it. When it cools, it turns to solid rock. When magma rises to the surface from volcanoes, it cools and forms lava. Igneous rocks are made from material that was once molten, and they usually contain crystals that form as the molten material cools. Many of these crystals contain valuable minerals that are used in a wide range of industrial processes.

Granite and basalt are examples of igneous rocks (Figures 2.3 and 2.4).

> **KEY WORDS**
>
> **igneous rock:** rock made during volcanic processes
>
> **magma:** molten rock below Earth's surface

2 Natural resources

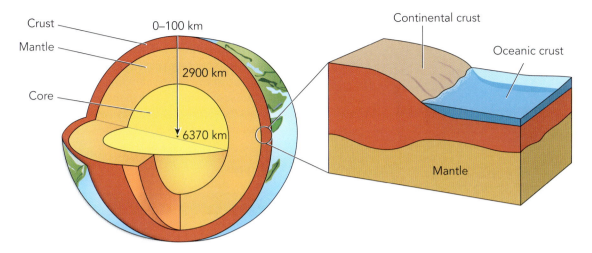

Figure 2.2: The structure of Earth.

Figure 2.3: A piece of granite.

Figure 2.4: A piece of basalt.

Figure 2.5: A piece of limestone.

The sediments include different-sized mineral particles. The smallest particles are clays, followed by silts and then sands. These particles are important in the formation of soils. They are transported by streams and rivers, and then deposited as sediment. Each layer of sediment becomes more compact and harder as it comes under pressure from the newer deposits above it.

Limestone, sandstone and shale are all examples of sedimentary rock (Figures 2.5, 2.6 and 2.7).

## Sedimentary rocks

**Sedimentary rocks** are formed by the **weathering** of existing rocks at Earth's surface, the precipitation of dissolved materials out of solution in water and, in some cases, organic material. Weathering processes release small mineral particles that accumulate to form **sediment**. Over time, layers of sediment build up to form sedimentary rock.

> **KEY WORDS**
>
> **sedimentary rock:** a rock formed from material derived from the weathering of other rocks, or the accumulation of dead plants and animals
>
> **weathering:** the processes that cause rock to be broken down into smaller particles
>
> **sediment:** solid material on Earth's surface that has been moved to a new location through natural processes

31

Figure 2.6: A piece of sandstone.

Figure 2.7: A piece of shale.

## Metamorphic rocks

**Metamorphic rocks** are created from existing rocks when they are exposed to extreme heat and pressure, which causes the structure of the rock to change. These changes can be chemical, physical or both. Sedimentary and igneous rocks can become metamorphic rocks, and a metamorphic rock can become another metamorphic rock. Metamorphic rocks are usually harder than sedimentary rocks.

Marble and slate are examples of metamorphic rocks (Figures 2.8 and 2.9).

Figure 2.8: A piece of marble.

When Earth's crust first formed, all rocks were igneous. These rocks were slowly eroded, releasing small particles that formed sediment. The sediments built up over time to form sedimentary rocks. The rocks that make up Earth's crust are always moving, which creates the heat and pressure needed to form metamorphic rock. All rock types are still being constantly eroded and formed in a process known as the **rock cycle**.

Table 2.1 compares the characteristics of the different rock types.

| Igneous | Sedimentary | Metamorphic |
|---|---|---|
| Made from magma | Made from other rock fragments | Made from existing rock |
| Magma cools to form solid rock | Rock fragments become buried and increased pressure forms a rock | Original rock is changed in form by heat and pressure |
| Mineral crystals sometimes present; the size of the crystals depends on the speed of cooling | Mineral crystals absent | Mineral crystals may be present |
| No fossils present | Fossils may be present | No fossils present |

Table 2.1: Characteristics of the different rock types.

> **KEY WORDS**
>
> **metamorphic rock:** a rock formed from existing rocks by a combination of heat and pressure
>
> **rock cycle:** a representation of the changes between the three rock types and the processes causing them

Figure 2.9: A piece of slate.

2   Natural resources

> **PROBLEM-SOLVING TIP**
>
> Remember – there are only three main rock types. Use what you know about the formation of each one to apply to situations where you need to give information about the properties of specific examples.

## The rock cycle

Figure 2.10 shows the processes by which the three rock types form, and the relationships and interactions between them.

Rocks are always changing. Exposed rock at the Earth's surface may be subjected to weathering caused by:

- biological actions, such as the movement of animals and plant growth
- chemical actions, such as reactions with slightly acidic or alkaline water
- physical actions, such as the action of wind and water, or expansion/contraction by changes in temperature.

Weathering is the breaking down of rocks. When rocks are broken down and moved elsewhere, the process is called **erosion**. The part of the process in which the rocks are moved to a different place is called **transportation**. Being broken down through wind and water are the two most common ways in which rocks are eroded. Local conditions, and the amount or wind and rainfall, dictate which method of erosion is most common in a particular place.

> **KEY WORDS**
>
> **erosion:** the movement of rock and soil fragments to different locations
>
> **transportation:** the process by which rock particles are moved to another location

1. Weathering and erosion break off fragments of surface rock.
2. The eroded rock is transported to another location.
3. The fragments of rock are deposited and build up in layers. As the layers build up, the lower layers are compacted into sedimentary rock.
4. Rock particles bind together in cementation
5. Sedimentary and igneous rocks subjected to heat and pressure underground form metamorphic rocks.
6. At higher temperatures rocks melt to form magma.
7. Magma crystalises as it cools to form igneous rock.

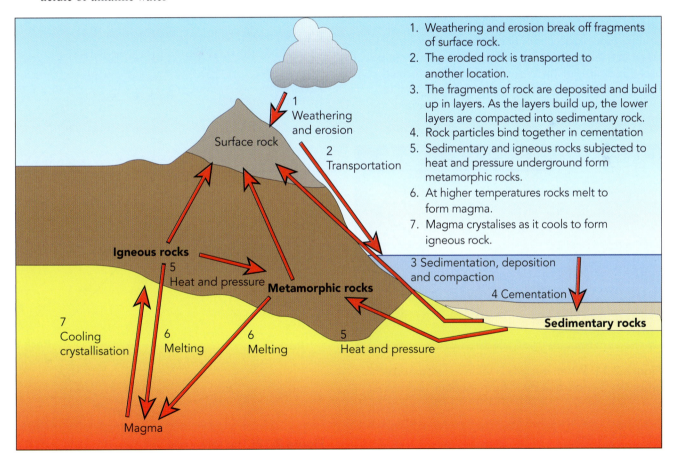

Figure 2.10: The rock cycle and the processes within it.

When the wind drops or the water slows, the rock particles eventually settle, in processes called **deposition** and **sedimentation**. Over time, layers of sediment build up, compressing the layers below in a process called **compaction**.

Finally, the compacted sediment becomes sedimentary rock, through **cementation**. In this process, the pores between the particles in the sediment fill with minerals that have been dissolved in water, which binds them all together like a chemical glue.

These processes all take place extremely slowly. It can take thousands or even millions of years for sedimentary rock to form.

Metamorphic rock also takes a long time to form because it needs intense pressure and heat. The pressure is usually a result of the movement of **tectonic plates**.

In comparison, igneous rocks can form rapidly if the magma cools on the Earth's surface – for example, after a volcanic eruption (Figure 2.11). However, igneous rocks can also take many thousands of years (or longer) if the cooling happens below Earth's crust. The cooling process allows for **crystallisation** to occur. A slower cooling process, deeper in Earth's crust, allows time for larger crystals to form. The size of the crystals can be a useful indicator of the type of rock that has formed. For example, basalt contains closely packed crystals about 1 mm in size, whereas the crystals in granite are often around 5 mm.

**Figure 2.11:** When magma is released from a volcanic eruption, it cools quickly to form igneous rock.

> **KEY WORDS**
>
> **deposition:** the laying down of sediment transported by wind or water
>
> **sedimentation:** the accumulation of sediments, which then form sedimentary rocks
>
> **compaction:** the pressing together of particles over time, reducing the spaces between them
>
> **cementation:** the hardening and joining together of compacted particles
>
> **tectonic plate:** a piece of lithosphere that moves slowly on the asthenosphere; seven major, eight minor and numerous micro plates have been identified
>
> **crystallisation:** the process of crystals forming caused by cooling

## Questions

**2.1** Figure 2.12 shows part of the rock cycle. Name the three types of rock, A, B and C.

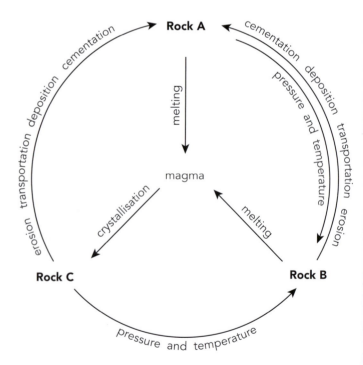

**Figure 2.12:** The rock cycle.

2 Natural resources

**2.2** Name the three types of weathering.

**2.3** Explain why fossils are only found in one of the three rock types.

# Permeable and impermeable rocks

Another way of describing rocks (and soils) is by considering their **permeability** – how easily water is able to pass through pore spaces in them.

**Permeable** rock has interconnected pore spaces that allow water (or other liquids or gases) to pass through it. If a rock has good permeability, water drains away from the surface after heavy rain, for example. Many sedimentary rocks, such as limestone and sandstone (Figure 2.13), are permeable.

**Impermeable** rock does not have as many pore spaces, so water does not drain through as easily. Igneous and metamorphic rocks are usually impermeable, but some sedimentary rocks, such as shale, are also impermeable.

**Figure 2.13:** A magnified image of permeable sandstone. Water can pass through the numerous interconnected pores within the rock.

| KEY WORDS |
|---|
| **permeability:** the ability of water to pass through the pore spaces of rock and soil |
| **permeable:** describing rock and soil that water (or other liquids or gases) can pass through |
| **impermeable:** describing rock and soil that water (or other liquids or gases) cannot pass through |

| COMMAND WORD |
|---|
| **predict:** suggest what may happen based on available information |

| FIELDWORK ACTIVITY 2.1 |
|---|

### Testing the permeability of rocks

**You will need**

- four types of rock (ideally sandstone, limestone, granite and slate)
- four beakers (large enough to fit the samples)
- water

**Safety**

Wash your hands thoroughly before and after the activity.

**Before you start**

**Predict** the permeability of each rock based on its appearance. Compare your predictions with the others in your group.

**Method**

Work in small groups.

- Label the four types of rock A, B, C and D.
- Fill each beaker with water and place a rock sample in each beaker.
- Observe what happens to the rock samples for 5 minutes. Record your findings in a copy of the following table.

35

## CONTINUED

| Rock | Name of rock type | Observations on first placement | Observations after 1 minute | Observations after 3 minutes | Observations after 5 minutes |
|---|---|---|---|---|---|
| A | | | | | |
| B | | | | | |
| C | | | | | |
| D | | | | | |

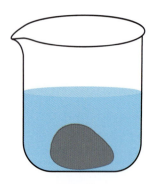

Figure 2.14: Testing the permeability of a piece of rock.

### Questions

1. What did you observe in each of the samples?
2. What does this observation tell you about the permeability of each rock?
3. What do you think would happen if you left the rocks in the beakers for longer?

## REFLECTION

What do you think you learnt from Fieldwork activity 2.1? What process did you follow to reach conclusions? Were there any problems you needed to overcome?

## ACTIVITY 2.1

Create a key that will help someone to accurately identify examples of different types of rock: basalt, granite, limestone, marble, sandstone, shale and slate. Start with a question with a 'yes' or 'no' answer. The answer to that should lead to other 'yes' or 'no' questions, and so on, until eventually the rock can be identified.

The start of a key is shown in Figure 2.15. You can use this starting question or one of your own. Add as many layers and questions to your key as you need.

2 Natural resources

## CONTINUED

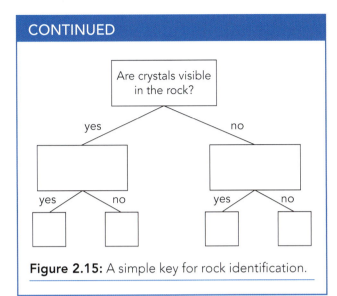

Figure 2.15: A simple key for rock identification.

## PEER ASSESSMENT

In pairs, try to complete each other's keys and give each other feedback. Are there better questions that would help someone identify the rock type more easily or clearly? If possible, try out your partner's key with some different rock samples that your teacher will give you. Does the key lead you to the right answer? You will need to look very closely at each rock sample, using a magnifying glass if possible.

# 2.2 Extraction of rocks, ores and minerals

An ore is a rock that contains minerals and metals. These substances provide many different materials for use in everyday life. Coal and oil are sources of energy and many chemicals used in industry. Metallic ores provide the metals and alloys needed to make products such as computers, mobile phones, cars, wires and batteries. Rocks and the products made from them are also widely used in the construction industry.

## Methods of extracting rocks, ores and minerals

There are three main methods for extracting rocks, ores and minerals from mines:

- Surface extraction is mining on Earth's surface.
- Sub-surface extraction is the removal of material from below the surface.
- Biological extraction is the use of organisms, such as plants or bacteria, to extract material.

### Surface extraction

Open-pit mining (also called opencast or open-cut mining) is used when a valuable deposit is located near the surface. It is often buried below a thick layer of worthless material called the **overburden**, which has to be removed to expose the deposit (Figure 2.16). The overburden is usually stored nearby so it can be used to help restore the area later.

Figure 2.16: In this nickel mine in Indonesia, the topsoil and white limestone overburden have to be removed to reach the deposits of nickel ore below.

Open-pit mines are carefully dug in sections called **benches** (Figure 2.17). The walls of the benches are kept at an angle to reduce the risk of rockfalls. Roads have to be created as the mine gets deeper, to allow the mineral deposit and overburden to be removed. Extracting materials such as sand, gravel and stone, which are widely used as building materials, uses similar surface-mining methods to extract mineral ores.

### KEY WORDS

**overburden:** a layer of rock or soil that has to be removed to reach an ore being mined beneath it

**benches:** layers cut into a mine to allow each level to be excavated

37

Figure 2.17: The sides of this gold mine in Australia mine are cut into benches. The sloped sides reduce the risk of collapse.

Strip mining is another type of surface extraction. It is used to mine horizontal **seams** of an ore. As with open-pit mining, the overburden is removed first. However, because the ore is available in layers or seams, machines are then used to cut these out (Figure 2.18). Strip mining is a common method for mining coal when it occurs near to the surface.

Figure 2.18: A bucket excavator cuts away at a deposit of coal in a strip mine. These machines can remove thousands of tonnes of material every hour.

> **KEY WORDS**
>
> **seam:** a layer of a desired material found in rock
>
> **deep mining:** the process of extracting minerals from deep seabed (depths greater than 200m)
>
> **shaft mining:** a method used to access minerals/ore from the top down

## Sub-surface extraction

Sub-surface mining involves digging tunnels into the ground to reach mineral deposits that are too deep for surface mining. The type of tunnel depends on the geology of the area and the location of the deposits (Figure 2.19). In some cases (often when extracting coal), horizontal tunnels are dug directly into a seam in the side of a hill or mountain.

In **deep mining**, sloping tunnels may be excavated to reach deeper deposits. Mining machinery can then be transported down the tunnels while waste rock and mineral ore are hauled up to the surface in the opposite direction.

The deepest deposits are reached by digging a vertical shaft. Horizontal galleries are then dug into the mineral deposits. **Shaft mining** is more expensive and technically challenging than either horizontal or slope tunnelling, and only large deposits of valuable minerals are mined in this way.

The material is removed from mines by machines. Compared with open-pit mining, any form of shaft mining is more difficult because it needs a supply of fresh air and water drainage. It is also potentially more dangerous, as there is the risk of tunnels collapsing, as well as poisonous gas, explosions and underground fires.

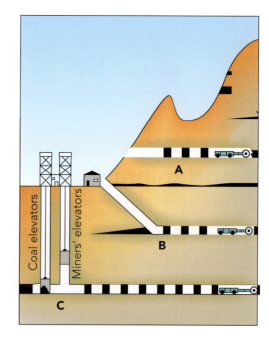

Figure 2.19: Types of sub-surface excavation. **A** Horizontal tunnel. **B** Sloping tunnel. **C** A shaft and horizontal tunnels. The more complex the engineering needed in the mine, the more expensive extraction will be.

## 2 Natural resources

Biological extraction uses living organisms to extract materials from the ground. At the present time, it does not yield the high levels of materials that surface and sub-surface extraction do, but it causes far less environmental damage so it is an increasingly popular method, especially for mining metals.

There are two main techniques for biological extraction:

- **Phytomining:** Some plant species growing in soil that contains a metal can take up that metal through their roots and concentrate it in their cells (Figure 2.20). This is known as **bioaccumulation**. The metal can be extracted by harvesting and burning the plants. This process takes a long time, but it is useful when the concentration of metals is too low to be extracted by other methods.
- **Bioleaching:** Certain bacteria can break down low-grade ores, such as copper ores, to make an acidic solution that contains the **ions** of a metal. This solution can be processed chemically to remove the metal. Again, this is a useful technique where concentrations of the metal are low, and it does not require any special conditions, such as high temperatures. However, it is also a slow process, and the solution produced by the bacteria is acidic, which could impact the environment if it is not managed carefully.

> **KEY WORDS**
>
> **phytomining:** the extraction of materials from the ground using plants
>
> **bioaccumulation:** the build-up of a substance in an organism over time
>
> **bioleaching:** the extraction of materials from the ground using microorganisms, such as bacteria
>
> **ion:** a positively charged particle, usually found as part of a compound

## Factors that affect the decision to extract rocks, ores and minerals

Several competing factors influence whether or not a resource is extracted from an area.

### Exploration

The first challenge is to find the location of suitable deposits. In areas where minerals have not been excavated before, the chances of finding a deposit are low. Even when resources have previously been found in an area, the chances of finding a suitable deposit of metal ores there is only about 1 in 100. For rarer materials, such as gold, the chances may be as low as 1 in 1000. Geologists use information about the rock types in an area to predict how likely it is that a mineral is present. They will then take samples of the rock and test them in a laboratory to see if they contain any useful materials. Further information may be obtained from aerial surveys using aircraft or drones (Figure 2.21).

### Geology

The geology of an area is evaluated when the rock samples are tested. Mining companies want to know what type of rocks are present in the location, and how easily and safely they can be excavated to access the minerals and ores. An analysis of the structure of the rock also helps the company decide on the most suitable method of mining (Figure 2.22).

**Figure 2.20:** Many plants are being tested to evaluate their suitability for absorbing metals by phytomining.

**Figure 2.21:** Drones enable geologists to survey large or inaccessible areas of land for potential ores or minerals far quicker and cheaper than on foot.

**Figure 2.23:** Minerals are often concentrated in layers within the rock, such as this seam of gold.

## Accessibility and terrain

Even if the structure of the rock makes it suitable for extraction, its location might not be favourable. The whole site might be somewhere inaccessible, with no roads into or out of the area, or roads that are not suitable for large mining vehicles (Figure 2.24). The material itself may be deep underground, making it difficult to reach without the use of expensive specialist equipment.

**Figure 2.22:** Information obtained from rock samples can be used to determine the suitability of rock for mining.

Many minerals are not uniformly distributed within the whole rock but are found concentrated in layers, called seams (Figure 2.23). Whether or not these seams are accessible, and the geology of the rock itself, affect the decision whether or not to extract the resource.

**Figure 2.24:** Some areas may have plenty of mineral reserves, but the terrain makes it too challenging to get large machinery into the area to extract them.

## Quantity and quality of deposit

It is expensive to develop a mine. Not only are there the physical costs of extracting the resource from the ground, but there are also linked costs, such as building roads and setting up facilities for workers. Before making such an investment, a mining company needs to be sure that the quantity and quality of the deposit will make this investment worthwhile. For this reason, companies usually carry out additional testing and surveying to learn more about the deposit.

In large mines, such as the marble mine in Figure 2.25, most of the rock can be used. However, this is not always the case. For example, in gold mining, only small amounts of gold are found in the rock, and there are additional stages in the extraction process, including crushing the rock, sieving and washing it, which all have to be factored in.

**Figure 2.25:** Large machinery extracting marble in a mine. The quantity of the resource available influences the decision about whether to start mining the area.

The cost of the extraction process needs to be weighed up against the value of the resource and the potential profits it might yield. Ores are graded on a scale of how much ore is likely to be yielded per tonne of rock. Table 2.2 shows the difference in the mass of gold present in different qualities of ore.

| Grade of ore | Yield of gold in g / tonne of rock |
|---|---|
| Low grade | 0–5.0 |
| Average grade | 5.1–8.0 |
| High grade | 8.1+ |

**Table 2.2:** The yield of gold in different grades of ore.

The cost to transport and process low-grade ore is the same as for high-grade ore. This means that, overall, it will be far less profitable for the mine owners, as the yield of gold will be less from each tonne of rock.

In exceptional circumstances, the ore may be very rich. Some rare examples have provided over 31 g of gold per tonne. Even at this level, the percentage of gold in the ore is only 0.0031%. The mass of ore to be processed at this type of mine is extensive, so it will also result in a very large quantity of waste material.

## Climate and weather

Local climate and weather conditions also need to be taken into consideration. Mining can take place in extreme environments, but climate, weather and landscape can make the process much more complicated (Figure 2.26). Permanently frozen ground (permafrost), such as that in the Arctic tundra, makes excavation difficult. It may also be harder to recruit workers to these environments. As a result, such locations may be more costly both in the equipment needed and in workers' wages, although mining may still go ahead if a company feels there is enough profit in it.

While mining takes place in both extremely hot and cold environments, the costs of operating in these places mean that mining operators usually try less challenging environments first.

**Figure 2.26:** While mining may still be possible in extreme environments, the harsh landscape can affect productivity levels.

## Environmental impact assessment

All forms of extraction have an impact on the local environment. They destroy vegetation, cause the loss of habitats for local wildlife and can cause air pollution. As such, many governments require mining companies to complete an environmental impact assessment before they will grant permission for a mining project to begin. The company must demonstrate that it has considered all the damage its operation is likely to cause. The company must record the likely impact and state what it will do to ensure that negative effects are minimised. It must also outline the processes in place to prevent environmental accidents. Companies may also be asked to show that they have evaluated other sites and that the one they have selected will have the lowest environmental impact.

The cost of meeting the needs of the environmental impact assessment can be high, so companies may feel it is not worth developing a mine at a particular location.

## Cost and profit, supply and demand

**Costs** and **profit** are often the most important factors in determining whether or not deposits of rocks, ores and minerals are exploited. Most independent companies need to ensure they have sufficient income to pay all the costs involved in the extraction process. Indeed, they will aim to make a surplus (profit) that can be used to invest in new equipment or to expand the business.

Prices for different items change over time depending on the number of people who want to buy them. If more buyers are interested in an item, the organisation selling it can charge a higher price. If fewer buyers are interested, prices may be reduced to attract more buyers. This is known as supply and demand.

If prices drop due to a reduction in demand, it may cost a company more to produce an item than they can sell it for. When this occurs, the company may decide not to extract so much. This can cause prices to rise, as demand comes later than supply. There is no way for businesses to know what demand will be or how it might change until it happens, but it is very difficult for mining companies to start or stop production quickly. As a result, the price of raw materials can fluctuate.

Rocks and minerals are non-renewable resources. This means that eventually there will be a shortage of them, which will cause an increase in prices. As a result, deposits that were not originally considered viable may become profitable to exploit (Figure 2.27).

**Figure 2.27:** Many tin mines stopped working when the price of tin dropped lower than the cost of extraction. An increase in global demand for tin might mean some mines in this area restart extraction.

### KEY WORDS

**costs:** the expenses associated with completing an activity, such as the production of a metal ore to sell

**profit:** the surplus made on selling an item once costs have been deducted

### ACTIVITY 2.2

Tin has been used for food storage (tin cans) for many years. However, more recently, demand for tin has increased because it is now used in electrical circuits for computers and similar equipment. Figure 2.28 shows the global price of tin over a period of 34 years.

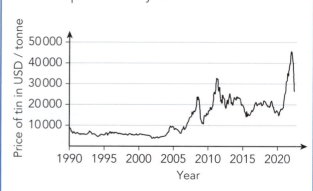

**Figure 2.28:** A graph showing variations in the global price of tin, 1990–2024.

## 2 Natural resources

### CONTINUED

a   Describe the trends shown in the price of tin.

b   Select from the following list the year when the price of tin was highest:

　　1999　　2005　　2011　　2020　　2022

c   **State** the range in the price of tin shown in Figure 2.28.

d   Predict how the price of tin is likely to change in the future. Give reasons for your answer.

### COMMAND WORD

**state:** express in clear terms

### ACTIVITY 2.3

Write five quiz questions about the different factors that companies evaluate when considering whether or not to extract rocks, ores and minerals. Write each question on a separate piece of paper. Make sure the questions are varied and cannot be answered with a simple 'yes' or 'no'. Double check that you know the answers to your own questions.

Get together in groups of four or five and, sitting in a circle, take it in turns to ask one of your questions. Anyone in the group can answer.

### SELF-ASSESSMENT

When you have completed Activity 2.3, note down two topics you feel you understand better as a result of developing your own quiz questions and answering the questions asked by other members of your group. Note down one idea that you still need to spend more time on when revising to understand it better.

# Impacts of extracting rocks, ores and minerals

## Environmental impacts

Environmental impacts from extracting resources from the earth range from large-scale habitat destruction, which reduces biodiversity, to pollution of air, land and water. People living near the site are also affected by noise and visual pollution.

**Ecological impacts**

Even small-scale surface extraction requires that vegetation is cleared. The plants removed have lost a place to grow, and so the animals that depend on the plants for food and shelter are also negatively affected. In deep mining, shafts are dug down to the seams of valuable resources. At the start of the operation, only a small area of land is cleared of vegetation. However, after several years, more habitats are destroyed as the amount of mine waste stored above ground increases, sometimes forming huge heaps (Figure 2.29). These are potentially dangerous, as the waste may shift in heavy rain, for example.

**Figure 2.29:** Deep mining requires the removal of a large amount of waste material to be stored above ground. The longer the mine is in operation, the larger the area affected.

**Noise pollution**

Noise pollution is a problem in large-scale surface mining because the overburden is loosened by explosive charges and then removed by large machines. The noise can change the behaviour of animal species near the mine and cause health problems for people.

43

Deep mining usually produces less noise than surface mining. Mining licences often set limits on the levels of noise and working hours of a mine.

## Water pollution

Water pollution from any type of mine can be a major problem that may continue even after a mine has stopped working. The water that drains through mine waste, or which comes directly from mine shafts, can negatively affect organisms that live in streams and rivers (Figure 2.30). In addition, drinking water supplies can be polluted by drainage from mines, making it unsafe for people to drink.

**Figure 2.30:** Leaching from this copper mine has affected the local water store. While the pollution can be clearly seen here, some pollutants are not easy to see in water samples.

Water pollution is caused by chemical reactions between the water and exposed rocks and mine waste. The water may become acidic and then dissolve toxic metal ions. The combination of acidic water with a high concentration of toxic metal ions kills many aquatic organisms. Some of the metal ions exist only in low concentrations in this water. However, organisms absorb these ions and retain them in their body – a form of bioaccumulation. The concentrations increase further in organisms that are higher up the food chain. This process is called **biomagnification** and can cause the death of top consumers.

## Land pollution and waste management

In the past, mining waste was often put in piles near the point of extraction – in some cases on top of watercourses, which then became polluted with toxic chemicals (Figure 2.31). Sometimes, unstable waste piles collapse, increasing land and water pollution. The affected area may be quite small, but the toxic nature of mine waste means that only a few plants will grow there, even many years after mining has stopped. Today, safe storage and disposal of mine waste is one of the most important aspects of any mining licence application.

**Figure 2.31:** Pollution and land degradation around a copper mine.

Many mining activities release dust particles, which settle on vegetation near the mine (Figure 2.32). The leaves of plants need to absorb light energy to perform **photosynthesis**. If light cannot penetrate the layer of dust, then the rate of photosynthesis – and thus plant growth – is reduced.

Dust from mining activities may also have toxic effects depending on its chemical components and may be dangerous to human health. Mining companies provide safety clothing and breathing masks to protect the health of mine workers. However, many people make a living from 'informal' (illegal) small-scale mining without a licence. Health problems arising from exposure to toxic substances are common among miners working in this way.

> **KEY WORDS**
>
> **biomagnification:** the process in which the concentration of a substance in living things becomes higher at progressively higher levels in a food chain or food web
>
> **photosynthesis:** the process by which plants make (synthesise) glucose using carbon dioxide and water, with sunlight as the source of energy which is captured by chlorophyll in plants

Mining activity is often evident from the damaged landscape. This is visual pollution. Large-scale surface mining will create the most obvious visual pollution. Visual pollution may only be temporary because it is possible to restore the landscape after mining activities have finished.

**Figure 2.32:** Explosives are sometimes used to loosen rock. This causes both noise pollution and dust (air pollution).

## Questions

2.4 State three reasons why illegal mining (mining without a licence) is bad for people and the environment.

2.5 **Discuss** how reduced plant growth can affect an ecosystem.

2.6 Describe how dust from mining impacts living organisms near the mine.

2.7 **Define** the term 'biomagnification'.

> **COMMAND WORDS**
>
> **discuss:** write about issue(s) or topic(s) in depth in a structured way
>
> **define:** give a precise meaning

### Economic impacts

Extracting valuable minerals provides employment for people and taxes for a government. Modern mining is carried out using machines, so only a small number of people will be directly employed to extract minerals. However, if the mineral is refined and processed in the same country, further jobs are created. In many cases, minerals and ores are exported to be used in manufacturing processes in other countries, which creates jobs in the country importing the mineral.

Extraction usually benefits both local and national economies. Jobs are created to extract minerals and to supply transport and mining equipment, as well as during the refining process. If all these activities occur in the same country, it generates significant income for buying goods and services, as well as investing in infrastructure projects (Figure 2.33).

**Figure 2.33:** Extracting resources increases the population of an area, but it may also result in an improvement in facilities and infrastructure, such as roads.

Improvements to transport and services, such as healthcare and education, are almost always required to supply the mining industry and to support the mine workers and their families. Some improvements are paid for by the mining companies as a condition of their mining licence. Taxes (from both companies and individual workers) can provide enough revenue to invest in infrastructure projects that benefit the whole population. Local businesses may also benefit by supplying workers in the area as the local population increases due to the increased industry.

Negative economic effects of extraction include the fact that some local people may lose their livelihoods. For example, farmers may have to give up their land if it is needed to develop the mine.

## Social impacts

The social impacts of mining are often closely linked to its economic impacts. For example, increased employment in an area may result in a higher standard of living. The development of roads and communication networks to supply the mine also benefits the local community.

An increased local population has both advantages and disadvantages. It may bring a greater demand for housing, which can cause a housing shortage that increases house prices in the area. People on lower incomes than mine workers might find housing costs unaffordable. Extraction also needs a large amount of land, so whole communities may need to be relocated.

Table 2.3 summarises the potential social impacts of mining on an area. There may be other impacts specific to the area in which extraction occurs.

| Benefits of extraction | Drawbacks of extraction |
|---|---|
| Improved roads and communication systems (to service the mine) also used by locals | Loss of homes due to land use for mining |
| Improvements to schools and medical facilities (as the population grows to work at the mine) | Relocation will mean communities are not kept together |
| | Local religious/cultural sites could be lost |
| Better community facilities (to meet the needs of a growing population) | A higher population could lead to a shortage of housing in the area |
| Improvements to drinking water supplies / sanitation systems | Loss of cultural identity due to the influx of workers from other areas |

**Table 2.3:** Some of the benefits and drawbacks of mineral extraction.

### ACTIVITY 2.4

Imagine that a company is planning to establish a new mine in your local area. Copy and complete the following table to record the economic and social impacts that the mine would have on local people.

|  | Economic | Social |
|---|---|---|
| Positive impacts | | |
| Negative impacts | | |

When you have completed your table, join up in pairs and share your ideas. Add anything to your table that your partner included that you had not thought of.

### REFLECTION

How did you decide what the positive and negative impacts would be of extraction in your local area? Do you think the impacts could be different for someone in a different location? Why, or why not?

# Strategies for managing damaged landscapes

Management of any mining operation should start with plans for safe waste disposal and end by restoring the land to its original state.

## Land restoration

Methods of land restoration vary between sites, but there some typical processes.

Mines produce a large quantity of waste. Sometimes this can be reshaped to blend in with the surrounding landforms. The deep hole created by the extraction process may also be refilled with some of this material. The overburden is often put back to help with the reshaping of the area (Figure 2.34).

2   Natural resources

Figure 2.34: This huge excavator is replacing the overburden removed from a coal mine in Germany, to help restore the landscape.

Figure 2.35: On the site of old mines, tree roots help to prevent soil erosion and also support a variety of organisms in the area.

Excavation sites need to be returned to as near a natural habitat as possible, so the next stage is to develop a good topsoil to enable plants to regenerate. To start this process, soil from other areas may be imported to cover the surface of the mining site. This creates a good base for plant roots to develop.

Some resources extracted during mining are toxic. Companies monitor water flowing from the site for many years to check for pollution. Contaminated waste can also be treated using a process called bioremediation. This is similar to the methods used for biological extraction. Many organisms can break down toxic substances into other substances that are less hazardous. These organisms can be used to extract toxic materials from an area to make it suitable for growing a wide range of species again. Other microorganisms and plants may be added later to help improve the fertility of the soil once the toxin level has dropped sufficiently to allow them to thrive.

Once soil conditions are right, an area can be replanted with trees. Tree roots stabilise the soil, holding it in place. Trees also support other organisms, providing food and shelter to help establish a new ecosystem (Figure 2.35).

## Repurposing land

Mineral extraction often creates large holes in the landscape. If the rock lining the hole is impermeable, it can be filled with water to form a reservoir. This water could be used for irrigating farmland or processed to provide clean, safe drinking water for humans.

Even though the area may have changed from its original terrain, the restored land could be repurposed into a nature reserve to help increase the biodiversity in the area. The land may also be used for recreation (Figure 2.36), such as sailing on a lake or reservoir, or other outdoor activities.

Sometimes, the holes created by mining are used to contain household waste until they are full. The waste is then covered with soil and planted with trees. This is referred to as landfill.

Figure 2.36: Surface mines can be repurposed into tourist attractions, including adventure activities such as this zip wire.

# The benefits and limitations of land management strategies

Whenever mining takes place, there will be an impact on the environment. The challenge is to address this damage in the most appropriate way. Land restoration

47

allows natural communities to re-establish themselves. However, this can take a long time, and it still requires careful management and monitoring to check for impacts of toxic materials.

The repurposing of mining sites for other uses often provides a quicker solution. However, it does not typically restore the site to its original state. Creating landfill can also cause problems. For example, decomposition in the landfill may generate the greenhouse gas methane, and there is an increased risk of water pollution. However, it does help solve the issue of disposing of large quantities of waste generated by households and industry.

## CASE STUDY

### The Antamina Mine, Peru

Figure 2.37: The Antamina copper mine, Peru. Extraction has meant a significant change to the landscape.

The Antamina mine is a large open-pit mine located high in the Andes Mountains of Peru at an altitude above 4000 metres (Figure 2.37). The estimated reserve is 1.5 billion tonnes of ore. Extraction of copper and zinc ores began in 2001. The mine employs more than 5000 people.

Before mining could begin, more than 100 million tonnes of surface rock had to be removed and placed in waste piles. The ores were then removed and crushed in the processing plant to produce a more concentrated material. The water waste from this process was stored in a compound to prevent water pollution. The concentrated material was then mixed with more water and moved in a 300 km pipeline to the coast. At the coast, this water was removed so that the material could be loaded onto ships.

The mine was expected to stop production in 2022. However, more reserves have been found and increased investment in efficient processing machinery has extended the expected life of the mine to 2029.

### Questions

1. Suggest why the mine was developed in such a remote location.

2. Water pollution is a serious risk at this open-pit mine. Give three reasons why there is a high risk of water pollution.

3. Suggest how the use of pipes for transportation of the material makes the process more sustainable.

4. Explain why it is unlikely that the land will be fully restored to its original condition when this mine stops production.

2 Natural resources

> SELF-ASSESSMENT
>
> You have now studied a lot of concepts relating to the extraction of rocks, ores and minerals. How confident do you feel about the key ideas in this topic? Create a bar chart, like this one, to rate your understanding. Add horizontal bars to show how confident you feel on a scale of 1–10.

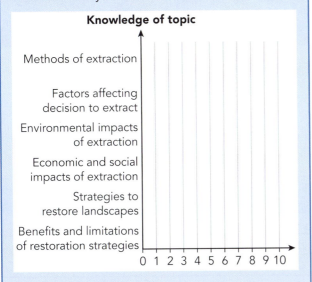

## 2.3 Sustainable management of rocks, ores and minerals

A finite (non-renewable) resource is a natural resource that is being used up at a faster rate than it is being replaced. **Sustainability** means meeting the needs of the present without affecting the ability of future generations to meet their needs. A fully sustainable resource will never run out. Industries such as agriculture and forestry can be sustainable because the resources are biological and can be regrown. However, rock, ores and minerals will not last forever.

> KEY WORD
>
> **sustainability:** the ability to meet the needs of the present without compromising the ability of future generations to meet their own needs

## Sustainable management strategies

Although they are considered to be finite resources, there are several ways of making the exploitation of rocks, ores and minerals more sustainable.

### Reduce and reuse

Reducing and reusing means making better use of products and resources, such as rocks and minerals, so they last longer.

The process of excavating, refining and manufacturing rocks, ores and minerals uses large amounts of energy as well as resources. The amounts of material and resources in manufacturing can be reduced by:

- using building products that contain less material but which are shaped to have the equivalent strength (Figure 2.38)
- processing materials as close as possible to the site where they are excavated, to reduce the fuel used for transportation
- carefully planning which resources are needed and how much of them are required, to limit the amount of waste
- finding new methods of building that reduce the amount of materials required and limit waste, such as computer technologies that can 3D print a house at its final site to reduce the waste materials when items such as bricks are cut to size (Figure 2.39).

**Figure 2.38:** This building brick is as strong as one without the gaps, but it requires less clay to make. Bricks like this are also lighter to transport than traditional bricks.

49

**Figure 2.39:** This house is being 'printed' on site using computer-controlled equipment. Techniques like this use fewer materials than traditional methods and create less waste.

Making new products requires resources, energy and time. One of the simplest ways to reduce the consumption of finite materials is to re-use items that already exist. For example, people could refill glass bottles and jars rather than buying – and therefore creating a demand for new ones – or they could use strong containers or bags instead of single-use ones (Figure 2.40).

**Figure 2.40:** Many single-use containers and bags are plastic, which is made from oil – a finite resource. Plastic items are a major cause of marine pollution. Replacing single-use items with longer-lasting alternatives conserves resources and helps the environment.

## Recycling

Recycling materials makes an important contribution to the sustainable use of rocks, ores and minerals. Many manufactured goods, from cars to cans, can be recycled. Most metals can be recovered and refined back to clean metals to be re-used by industries (Figure 2.41). This takes less energy than processing the ores to make metals. However, there are some issues with recycling.

**Figure 2.41:** Scrap metal in a scrapyard. Recycling metals is far more energy efficient than extracting from metal ores.

Table 2.4 shows the recycling data for several countries in 2022.

| Country | Proportion of all waste that is recycled (%) |
|---|---|
| Australia | 52.9 |
| Brazil | 2.8 |
| China | 24.4 |
| Kenya | 19.9 |
| Mexico | 9.6 |
| Russia | 5.3 |
| South Korea | 67.1 |
| USA | 14.8 |
| Zimbabwe | 21.8 |

**Table 2.4:** Percentage of waste that is recycled in different countries, 2022.

Analysis of this data shows that in 2022, most of the countries listed were recycling less than 50% of their waste, and in all cases there is potential for improvement. It is difficult to find any overall trends in the data, too. For example, there is no clear correlation between the wealth of a county and its success in recycling.

When considering how countries could improve their recycling percentages, it is worth first exploring the reasons why people do not recycle. Some global data is shown in Table 2.5.

> **CRITICAL THINKING TIP**
>
> When analysing data, it is important to understand how accurate the information is before drawing conclusions. Look at the information in Table 2.5. You might ask the following key questions:
>
> - Who collected and compiled this data? Are they impartial? Can they be trusted?
> - Was the data collected in a meaningful way (for example, was there a sufficient sample size that represents the whole population)?
> - Views change over time, so how recently was the data collected?
> - When a category of 'other' is provided, is it a significant proportion of the total? If so, is there another group that should be reported separately within the table?

| Reasons for not recycling | Proportion of people stating this as the main reason (%) |
|---|---|
| Lack of recycling facilities/services | 42 |
| Not knowing how to use facilities correctly | 25 |
| Inconvenience of recycling | 16 |
| Lack of trust in the system | 15 |
| Other | 2 |

Table 2.5: Reasons why people do not recycle.

From the information in Table 2.5, you might consider some of the following ways to encourage more recycling:

- Improve accessibility: Ensure that facilities are available for the main waste types (Figure 2.42). Without these, important resources may be disposed of in landfill sites rather than recovering them for use in new products.
- Make recycling easier: If the process of recycling is too complex, people are less likely to make the effort, particularly if it is easier to dispose of the waste in another way.
- Education: The waste from many households and businesses is made up of many different materials. If people are unsure how to treat different types of waste, they may dispose of it by an easier option. It is important to educate people in the ways that different materials can be recycled.

Figure 2.42: Efficient systems may help increase the rate of recycling. Collection from home and a range of colour-coded bins for different materials increases recycling rates.

## Increasing the efficiency of extraction

Increasing the efficiency of extraction seems an obvious starting point for effective resource use. For example, underground coal mines only remove 55–70% of the coal in a reserve due to the difficulties of extracting the remaining coal safely and cost-effectively. To improve the efficiency of extraction, many mine wastes are now being processed for a second time. This allows valuable materials to be recovered and reduces the risk of pollution from stored mining waste. Techniques such as phytomining may also be useful in obtaining more metals from the waste.

Improvements in the performance of the machines used in mining and processing, as well as using computers in data processing, also increase extraction efficiency. However, surface mining has more potential than underground mining, because it is more difficult to predict geological conditions underground.

## Avoiding resource depletion

The increasing global population puts huge demands on all resources. Without careful monitoring, important minerals and metals may be depleted beyond rescue. Unfortunately, it is not as simple as preventing people from using items made of these key resources. At present, there are no potential replacements available for many resources, and in some cases, the use of these resources may prevent a larger environmental problem. For example, the development of electric cars requires additional quantities of metals such as lithium, which is used in electric car batteries, to be extracted. However, electric vehicles could reduce the reliance on fossil fuels – another finite resource and one that contributes significantly to climate change.

## Use of alternative materials

There is not any one easy answer to the problem of demand for resources. The solution is likely to be a combination of careful use and looking for opportunities to use alternative materials, among other things. Alternative materials may be in greater abundance, therefore reducing the demand for the resource that is in short supply. Switching to other materials may result in a cheaper product or the use of a material that was previously discarded as waste. For example, scientists are working on a scheme to process discarded plastic bottles to use as strengthening for concrete. If successful, this will make stronger concrete (which can be made with less mined materials).

## Legislation and enforcement

While many businesses and individuals are trying to minimise their use – and misuse – of resources, others may continue in their existing practices. Because of this, governments may need to create laws to force a change in behaviour. These include:

- laws requiring businesses to take back products for recycling when their use has ended
- ensuring that all waste disposal is recorded, to monitor types of waste and ensure it is treated correctly
- fines for people who dump waste illegally and do not use approved waste disposal systems
- policing the disposal of waste – for example, businesses may have unannounced spot checks to ensure that they are complying with requirements (Figure 2.43)
- additional taxes for businesses that produce too much waste.

It is important that any new laws are enforced; if people do not comply, they may be fined, lose their business licence or even go to prison.

**Figure 2.43:** Electrical equipment is sometimes referred to as 'e-waste'. Many countries now have laws to ensure that the valuable metal components in these items are recycled.

> **SUSTAINABILITY TIP**
>
> Electrical waste (e-waste) may contain a lot of valuable metals that could be re-used instead of extracting and processing more materials from the ground. Complete an audit at home of all the electrical equipment that you and your family no longer use. Investigate local services that are available to recycle old electrical waste. Were you aware of these local systems to recycle e-waste? What could be done to make local people use them more regularly?

# Benefits and limitations of sustainable management strategies

The benefits and limitations of different sustainable management strategies vary according to the local situation and the type of mineral, ore or rock used. However, there are some general principles, which are outlined in Table 2.6.

2  Natural resources

| Benefits of sustainable management strategies | Limitations of sustainable management strategies |
|---|---|
| It will delay the date of the exhaustion of finite resources. | Recycling of materials may be difficult as products use a lot of different materials. |
| Re-use of minerals or ores means less environmental damage caused by mining/extraction. | Not everyone will recycle, meaning materials are lost. |
| Recycling of materials often uses less energy than refining raw materials/ores. | Sustainable extraction methods may take longer and be more complex to manage. |
| Reducing the volume of material in a product may mean it can be made more cheaply. | Reducing the volume of material used in a product may mean it performs less effectively. |
| Legislation may help restrict the use of rare materials to essential uses / ensure more sustainable approaches are used. | Legislation may not be followed or may be complex to enforce. |
| The need to use alternative materials may be more effective than using traditional methods and materials. | Some alternative materials do not perform as well as the materials they are replacing. Some alternatives may not be recyclable. |
|  | Demand for certain materials may increase, meaning the current supplies need to be supplemented with additional extraction. |

**Table 2.6:** Some benefits and limitations of management strategies.

## Questions

**2.8** Name three 'Rs' relating to sustainable management strategies.

**2.9** Why will it still be necessary to extract more resources, such as metal ores, even if sustainable management strategies are used?

**2.10** Why will the introduction of legislation alone not be sufficient to change people's behaviour regarding the use of finite resources?

## 2.4 Energy resources

Most energy is created by direct **combustion** (burning) to produce heat and light. Combustion requires a suitable fuel source – usually something that contains large amounts of carbon. While items such as wood contain carbon, there are other sources that are far more 'energy dense', producing a greater amount of heat from a unit of fuel. These sources – **natural gas** (methane), coal and **petroleum** (oil) – are known as **fossil fuels** (Figure 2.44).

**Figure 2.44:** Most vehicles rely on fossil fuels as their energy source.

### KEY WORDS

**combustion:** a high-temperature reaction between a fuel and oxygen, commonly referred to as burning

**natural gas:** a naturally occurring flammable gas that contains carbon; the most common example of natural gas is methane

**petroleum:** a liquid mixture of carbon-containing chemicals that is present in some rocks, which is extracted and refined to produce fuels such as petrol and diesel oil

**fossil fuel:** a carbon-based fuel, formed over many millions of years from the decay of living matter

## How fossil fuels are formed

Fossil fuels are produced from the decay of plants and animals. These remains form organic matter that becomes covered in layers of sediment. Over millions of years and buried deep in the ground by further layers, the organic material is subjected to great pressure and heat. The precise conditions, and the type of animal and plant material available, determine whether coal, petroleum or natural gas is produced.

Figure 2.45 shows how coal is formed. The processes for petroleum and natural gas are similar, and are shown in Figure 2.46. In both cases, the dead remains of animals and plants are buried under many layers of sediment, so extracting them involves digging or drilling deep underground. The length of time it takes for fossil fuels to form means that there is only a limited supply.

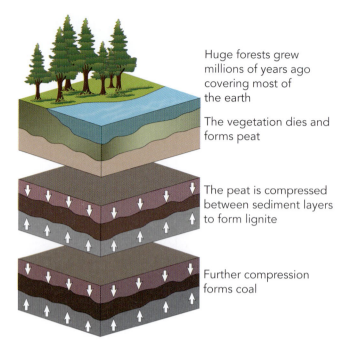

Figure 2.45: The process by which coal is made.

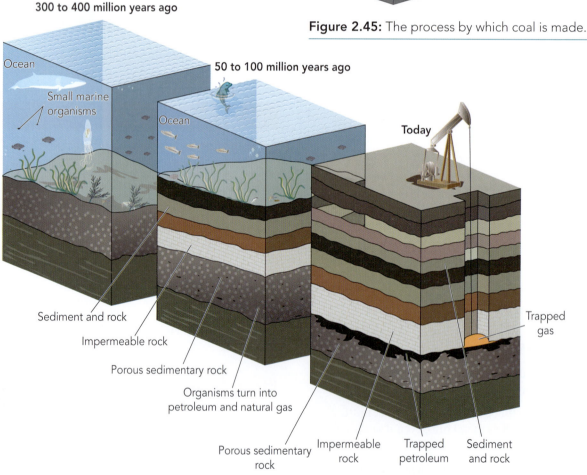

Figure 2.46: Petroleum and natural gas form in a similar way to coal. They are held in a layer of porous rock, which means they can be accessed by drilling.

## Types of energy resources

Energy resources can be classified by whether they are limited resources or available in unlimited supplies:

- Limited resources are often described as being non-renewable (finite). Once they are used, they cannot be replaced.
- **Renewable**, or non-finite, resources of energy are those that can be replenished – they can be used over and over again.

Table 2.7 lists the most common examples of renewable and non-renewable energy types.

| Renewable (non-finite) energy sources | Non-renewable (finite) energy sources |
|---|---|
| Biofuels (**bioethanol**, **biomass**, **biogas**, wood) | Fossil fuels (coal, petroleum, natural gas) |
| Geothermal power | Nuclear power using uranium |
| Hydro-electric power | |
| Tidal power | |
| Wave power | |
| Solar power | |
| Wind power | |

**Table 2.7:** Classification of energy resources.

> **KEY WORDS**
>
> **renewable:** an item or resource that will not be used up or can be replaced; also referred to as a non-finite resource
>
> **bioethanol:** a type of fuel made from plant material that has been fermented to form an alcohol, which can be combusted to provide energy
>
> **biomass:** organic materials from plants and animals that are combusted to produce heat
>
> **biogas:** the gas produced when organic matter decomposes, which is combusted to produce heat; biogas usually has a large proportion of methane

While some of these energy resources are easy to classify, others are more complex. For example, nuclear fuels will last for centuries, and many scientists believe they are a suitable replacement for fossil fuels. However, supplies of the source material (uranium) are finite, so although it will last a long time, it cannot be replaced once it has been used.

Biofuels include the burning of wood, of which there is only a limited amount at any one point in time. However, it is possible to replace felled trees with new ones, so it is classified as renewable.

## Energy resources and the generation of electricity

Most electricity is generated by **electromagnetic induction**. This transforms kinetic energy (energy from movement) into electrical energy using a magnet and loops of a conducting material, such as copper. As the coils are rotated close to the magnet, electricity is generated.

A power source is needed to rotate the coils. This comes from a **turbine** connected to the **generator**. Turbines are designed to provide the rotary motion needed in the generator. This is often achieved by passing a stream of gas or liquid over the turbine blades, causing a shaft to move (Figure 2.47).

Energy resources such as fossil fuels, biofuels, nuclear and geothermal power are usually used to heat water to produce steam. In this simple system, a heat source (in the **burner**) heats up water (in the **boiler**), which is converted to steam. The steam passes over the blades of the turbine, causing them to move. The rotation of the shaft makes the copper coils in the generator move, producing electricity that is transferred by wires to the light bulb.

> **KEY WORDS**
>
> **electromagnetic induction:** a process for generating electricity that uses a magnet and the movement of a metal coil
>
> **turbine:** a machine, often containing fins, that is made to revolve by the use of gas, steam or air
>
> **generator:** a machine that converts mechanical energy (such as movement) into electrical energy
>
> **burner:** a receptacle used to hold fuel as it is burnt
>
> **boiler:** a vessel used to heat water to convert it into steam

Figure 2.48 is a simplified diagram of the production of electricity from a geothermal source. In this case, cold water is pumped under pressure into a layer of hot rocks. The rocks heat the water, and the hot water then returns to the surface under pressure. The hot water heats up a second supply of water using a **heat exchanger**. The steam produced in the second supply moves the turbine, which generates electricity in the generator. Water can then be re-used in the system to continue the process.

> ### KEY WORD
>
> **heat exchanger:** a device used to transfer heat between two fluids at different temperatures

## Wind power

**Wind power** does not rely on the heating of water to produce steam. Figure 2.49 shows a wind turbine. Note the addition of a gearbox to maximise the rotation of the shaft as it enters the generator. The brake will slow down or stop the rotor blade in very windy conditions to prevent the blade being damaged.

> ### KEY WORD
>
> **wind power:** electricity generation using a wind turbine

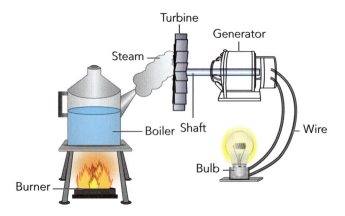

**Figure 2.47:** A simple electricity generation system using a turbine.

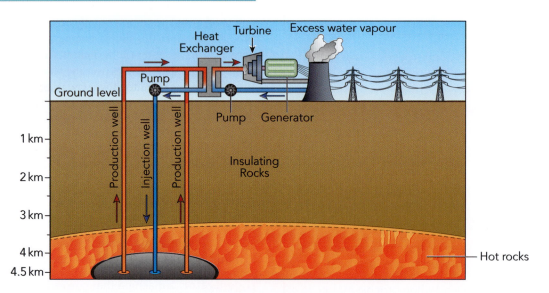

**Figure 2.48:** Production of electricity from a geothermal source.

## 2 Natural resources

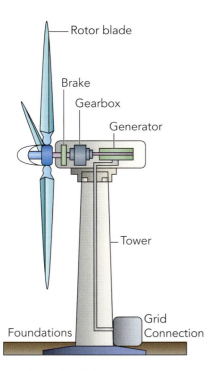

Figure 2.49: A wind turbine.

## Solar power

**Solar power** is the main exception in the way that electricity is produced. Most electricity produced by solar power comes from photovoltaic cells. While the chemistry and construction of photovoltaic cells is quite complex, they all work on the principle that certain materials produce a small electric charge when they are exposed to light. The electricity produced by one cell is small, but a bank of cells organised into solar panels, and a group of panels put together in a large area, can produce a significant amount of electricity (Figure 2.50).

Figure 2.50: Technological advances in the design and manufacture of photovoltaic cells are making them far more efficient. However, many of the metals used within the cells are quite rare and expensive to obtain.

## Questions

**2.11 Compare** the generation systems shown in Figures 2.47, 2.48 and 2.49.

  a  Name the component that is common to all three systems.

  b  Explain the purpose of the components that are not common to all three generation systems in a table like this one. The first row has been done for you.

| Component | Purpose |
|---|---|
| Burner | Location for combustion of fuel to heat water |

**2.12** Rank the three technologies from the simplest to the most difficult to install. Explain the reasons for your choices.

> **COMMAND WORD**
>
> **compare:** identify/comment on similarities and/or differences

## Tidal power

**Tidal power** uses the natural rise and fall in water level in a particular area each day. As the level drops, water is held back by a **tidal barrage** – a small dam that releases water back through a turbine. This creates the electricity using a generator. The amount of power generated depends on the change in tide level throughout the day. Figure 2.51 shows the scale of these constructions.

> **KEY WORDS**
>
> **solar power:** harnessing energy from sunlight
>
> **tidal power:** the use of tides (the natural change in sea levels) to generate electricity
>
> **tidal barrage:** a small dam used to manage water to allow for electricity generation

57

**Figure 2.51:** An example of tidal power generation near St Malo in France. Turbines below the water level rotate as the level changes with the tide.

## Wave power

**Wave power** also uses a turbine and generator to create electricity, but these use the smaller differences in water levels caused by wind action. Power is therefore produced by channelling the energy of waves at sea. Unlike tidal power, wave power is not limited to the regular pattern of the tides. However, electricity generation may stop in calm weather, when there are few or no waves. This type of generation can take place further away from the coast so there is potential to use larger areas.

**Figure 2.52:** The use of new technologies to generate electricity will mean the workers of the future will need different skills to maintain them.

## Hydro-electric power

**Hydro-electric power** also uses a turbine, generator and the flow of water. In most cases, water is stored in a reservoir by a dam (Figure 2.53), although it is also possible to simply use fast-flowing rivers. As water is released through the dam or flows through the river, it causes the turbine to rotate, allowing electricity to be generated from this kinetic energy. One benefit of this system is that provided there is a suitable supply of water, electricity can be generated whenever it is needed.

**Figure 2.53:** The reservoirs created by hydro-electric dams can be a potential store of fresh water, and may be used for leisure or tourism purposes that may create jobs in the area.

### REFLECTION

You have come across a lot of technical and subject-specific words and phrases in this section. Are they all new to you? What strategies have you used to help you remember all these terms? Have they worked? If not, what other methods could you try to help you remember new terminology?

### KEY WORDS

**wave power:** the use of changes in the height of a body of water to generate electricity

**hydro-electric power:** the generation of electricity using flowing water

# Benefits and limitations of energy resources

Deciding which energy resource to use is not always easy, because they all have different impacts, and all have both benefits and limitations. As a result, a range of different strategies may be used to supply the energy needs of a community. Table 2.8 summarises some of the main benefits and limitations of different energy resources. In addition to these general factors, there may also be localised issues that will have an impact.

> **KEY WORD**
>
> **greenhouse gas:** a gas that absorbs radiation and emits the energy as thermal or heat energy, such as carbon dioxide, methane, nitrous oxides and water vapour

| Energy resource | Benefits | Limitations |
|---|---|---|
| Fossil fuels (coal, petroleum, natural gas) | Plentiful supply in some locations. Extraction provides jobs. Existing technology – the fuel is available for most countries to use. | Combustion produces carbon dioxide, which is a **greenhouse gas**. Other toxic gases are produced when combusted, which can affect health. Extraction causes damage to local area. Limited supply – prices rise as the supplies get smaller. |
| Nuclear power (using uranium) | Does not produce carbon dioxide. Small amount of fuel produces large amounts of energy (it is energy dense). Power plants employ lots of people. Fuel is useful for a long time. | Risk of radiation leakage (impact on human health and the environment). Waste products cannot be recycled, as radiation is active for centuries. Limited supply. |
| Biofuels (bioethanol, biomass, biogas, wood) | A renewable resource – bioethanol, biomass and wood are obtained from growing plants; biogas comes from the recycling of waste products. Growing more plants uses carbon dioxide through photosynthesis. | Carbon dioxide and other toxic gases are produced when burnt. A lot of land is needed to grow crops for fuel. Potential removal of natural ecosystems to grow fuel crops. Growing fuel crops may result in food shortages. |
| Geothermal power | Does not produce carbon dioxide. Unlimited supply, as it uses heat from Earth as its power source. | Can be expensive to install. Only certain areas have suitable conditions. |
| Hydro-electric power | Does not produce carbon dioxide. Water can be re-used for other purposes. | Building dams impacts the natural flow of water. Villages and ecosystems may be destroyed when dams and reservoirs are built. |
| Tidal power | Does not produce carbon dioxide. Tidal movements are not dependent on weather conditions. | Limited to specific coastal areas. Impacts on the tourist industry and local fishing areas. |
| Wave power | Does not produce carbon dioxide. A renewable source of power. | Limited to specific areas. Currently not very efficient, so large amounts of resources are needed. Unsuitable for certain weather conditions. |

| Energy resource | Benefits | Limitations |
|---|---|---|
| Solar power | Does not produce carbon dioxide. Sunlight is an unlimited resource. | Only efficient under certain weather conditions. Generation only occurs in daylight hours. Visual impact and potential damage to local ecosystems. Materials used to make solar panels are in short supply. |
| Wind power | Does not produce carbon dioxide. Uses a renewable resource. | Not all locations are suitable. Generation only occurs in certain conditions (at certain wind speeds). Visual impact. Uses a large area. |

Table 2.8: The benefits and limitation of different energy resources.

## Availability of energy resource

Using an abundant local resource has economic advantages. Some countries still have plentiful reserves of fossil fuels, which will keep electricity generation costs lower and so may be favoured over less-polluting methods. Similarly, some countries have easy access to geothermal energy (Figure 2.54) and will choose this over other energy resources that may prove to be more expensive.

## Location of population

If a population lives a long way from the energy resource, the cost of supply increases, as additional pipelines or transport are needed (Figure 2.55). There may also be concerns about the impacts on health for people living near a nuclear power station with the risk of radiation. Some people may need to relocate to allow the exploitation of the energy resource – for example, if an area needs to be flooded to create a reservoir for a hydro-electric dam (Figure 2.56).

Issues may not always be negative, however. The development of a hydro-electric dam may require improvements to infrastructure, such as roads and communication systems. The increase in population needed to operate the site may also mean that improved education and health facilities are built, too.

Figure 2.54: The Blue Lagoon in Iceland is a series of pools heated by geothermal energy from below ground. This in an abundant resource to utilise in this location.

Figure 2.55: Petroleum or natural gas deposits may be located in remote areas. Building a pipeline is one way to transport them to where they are needed, but it is expensive.

2 Natural resources

**Figure 2.56:** The flooding of the River Ter to form the Sau Reservoir in Spain meant the population of a village needed to relocate. Signs of the original buildings are still visible when the water level is low.

## Impact on employment

Exploiting an energy resource impacts people working in local industries, such as farming where agricultural land is no longer available, but it may provide new employment opportunities within the new generation site. The benefits may appear to cancel out the limitations, but this is not necessarily the case if the farmers do not have the skills and qualifications to work at the new site. Pollution to the area caused by the new development may also have a negative impact of other industries, such as fishing.

### CASE STUDY

#### Biofuels: The future of fuels or a misguided technology?

**Figure 2.57:** An aerial view of ploughed land on a sugar cane plantation near Ribeirao Preto, Brazil. The crops from this plantation will not be used for food but for the production of biofuels.

Fuels that are extracted from crop plants are known as biofuels. The three most common types are biogas, bioethanol and wood (the growing and burning of timber to produce heat).

Biogas is the common name for a mixture of gases formed by the decomposition of organic matter in the absence of oxygen (anaerobic decomposition). The main component of biogas, methane, is highly flammable and is therefore suitable as a fuel source. Biogas can be produced from a range of organic wastes, such as animal manure, food waste and household waste.

Bioethanol is a renewable energy resource that is mainly produced by fermenting the sugar found in some crops. Crops that can provide this sugar include maize, wheat, corn, willow, Miscanthus and similar tall grasses, sorghum, and Jerusalem artichoke. These crops are often grown especially for biofuel production. Bioethanol can be used as a substitute for petroleum (gasoline).

Bioethanol is believed to have great potential as a fuel for cars and trucks; it is commonly mixed with petrol or diesel fuels to make these finite resources last longer, but development work is underway to use it as a complete replacement for fossil fuels.

Supporters of bioethanol production state a range of benefits:

- Easy to source: Petroleum is a non-renewable resource, whereas crops can be grown around the world for years to come.
- Reduces greenhouse gases: The burning of fossil fuels causes increased levels of carbon dioxide. While the same is true of bioethanol, the plants grown to provide the fuel use carbon dioxide to produce sugars via the process of photosynthesis.

> **CONTINUED**
>
> - Economic security: Not all countries have a supply of oil, but many can grow suitable crops to produce bioethanol. There is less risk of a lack of energy supply if a country can produce its own fuel.
>
> People who are against the increased use of bioethanol state a range of disadvantages:
>
> - Food shortages: Bioethanol is produced from crops that have high quantities of sugar, which also tend to be food crops. When there are people short of food across the world, it does not seem right to use potential food as fuel rather than for feeding the hungry.
> - Water usage: The crops need a lot of water, which can lead to a shortage of water for humans and their livestock in some areas.
> - Industrial pollution: The amount of carbon dioxide produced by bioethanol may be less than that produced by fossil fuels, but the factories that produce bioethanol do emit pollutants, which can affect local populations.
> - Monoculture: The energy crops used to make bioethanol are grown in the same large fields year after year. This means that nutrients in the soil decrease. Adding fertilisers can cause water pollution and the crop will also need the application of pesticides, which will affect the local ecosystem.
>
> **Questions**
>
> 1. Explain why the production of bioethanol might be more attractive to a country without its own oil supplies than one with large oil reserves.
> 2. Suggest why the growing of biofuels on a worldwide scale is seen to be important, even though there are some clear disadvantages.
> 3. Suggest why a farmer might choose to grow crops for bioethanol production rather than for food production.
> 4. Describe how an increase in demand for biofuels may impact biodiversity.

# Factors affecting the demand for energy

Demand for energy is increasing worldwide, and experts predict that it will continue to do so. Nobody knows exactly how long supplies of non-renewable resources will last, and predictions so far have generally been inaccurate. There are various reasons for this:

- New deposits have been found.
- As prices have increased, some deposits have become economic to exploit.
- New technologies have made extraction more efficient (Figure 2.58).

Despite this, we know that as non-renewable resources become more scarce, prices for them will continue to increase.

There are many factors involved in demand for energy around the world, which are outlined in the following sections.

## Transport

The development of more efficient systems of production means that manufacturers often supply customers all over the world. While this can decrease production costs, it has significantly increased the costs of transportation. Some estimates suggest that there has been a fourfold increase in the number of shipping journeys in the past 20 years (Figure 2.59). Air transport has also increased substantially.

**Figure 2.58:** Oil sands are rich in oils and tars that can be converted into fuels. As technology has improved and prices for fuels have increased, it has become economically worthwhile to extract them.

## 2 Natural resources

**Figure 2.59:** An increase in transporting products internationally means a greater demand for fuel to power the ships.

Ships and planes both need large amounts of fossil fuels to operate. The cost of transporting goods across oceans is high, but the savings in manufacturing still make these forms of transportation attractive to the end customer, even though the energy used in the process is more than if the items were produced locally.

### Personal and national wealth

Domestic demand for energy (and the purchase of manufactured goods) depends on how well off people are within a country. If economic conditions are good, employment is higher so people have more money to spend on luxury items. If economic conditions are poor, households will have less money to spend and will need to make savings. They may limit how much fuel they use and restrict the purchase and use of electrical items, which use energy.

These factors also play a part at a national level. If a country has less income because it is manufacturing less, it will be less able to import foreign goods. A weak economy means:

- less manufacturing (less energy used)
- fewer goods to transport (less energy used)
- an inability to purchase foreign energy supplies.

Sometimes, the impact of reduced manufacturing in one country can affect the global economy. For example, in the mid-2010s, reduced manufacturing in China meant that around the world there was:

- a reduction in demand for steel
- a decrease in the amount of manufactured goods transported by ships

- a decrease in the price of oil (because worldwide demand had decreased as a result of the two factors above).

The global pandemic in the early 2020s meant that for a period of time many factories did not work at full capacity. This had an impact on the amount of energy these factories used and the associated need to transport these goods.

### Climate

Comparing energy use between countries is complicated by typical weather conditions. People living in a temperate climate are likely to experience colder winters than those living in warmer climates. So, the energy demand for heating in colder climates is likely to be far higher (Figure 2.60). In the winter months, people in colder climates also experience fewer hours of daylight, so there is an increased use of electric lighting.

Climate change has resulted in more extremes of weather, including excessive cold and heat. These have resulted in increased energy consumption, particularly from people living in urban areas, who need additional heating or cooling from air-conditioning units.

**Figure 2.60:** People living in colder parts of the world use more energy to heat their homes than those in warmer climates.

### Human population size

Population growth is probably the greatest factor that has affected energy demand. The global population currently stands at more than 8 billion, and there is little sign that this is going to level out. That is a lot of people, consuming a lot of energy and needing a lot of materials to function in their daily lives. Even the production and supply of food and clean water requires significant energy.

## Industry

Energy use per head of population is far lower in traditional farming communities than it is in communities that have become industrialised. Manufacturing requires large quantities of energy in all stages of production. Iron and steel production, for example, has an extremely high energy demand, using fuel to melt iron ore and refine it (Figure 2.61). Additional heat is needed to shape the resulting product.

Developments in manufacturing techniques have resulted in technological advances in the products and have also made these products more affordable. This means that many items are now considered necessities, not luxuries. The increase in demand leads to increasing energy needs for increased production.

## Disruption to and unreliability of supply

People need energy resources to be readily available (Figure 2.62). On a basic level, this may be a need for materials to burn for heating and cooking, but on a larger scale it includes a regular electricity supply to power appliances. While there are still issues with supply in some locations, where supply is reliable it will encourage greater use through the purchase of additional appliances. In this way, demand for electricity increases because of its availability.

**Figure 2.61:** The production of iron and steel requires the use of very high temperatures, needing large quantities of energy.

**Figure 2.62:** Electricity supplies may be disrupted for a number of reasons, including physical damage to the supply system, such as a fallen power line.

## Scarcity of resources

The ability to supply electricity is often linked to the availability of resources that allow it to be generated. This might be because of conflict between countries, which may prevent resources such as natural gas from being imported. Resources may also become scarce due to changes in weather conditions. For example, cloudy weather with little wind affects how much wind and solar energy can be generated. It may also impact wave power, as winds can create larger waves.

# Questions

**2.13** Explain how an increase in the standard of living causes an increase in the demand for electricity.

**2.14** Table 2.9 shows the energy use per person in four different countries in 2021.

| Country | Energy used per person/kWh |
|---|---|
| Central African Republic | 286 |
| Iceland | 165 871 |
| Pakistan | 4 243 |
| USA | 78 754 |

**Table 2.9:** Energy used per person in 2021.

    **a** Calculate the percentage of the energy used by a person from Iceland that is used by an equivalent person from the Central African Republic.

    **b** Suggest reasons for the differences in the energy use between the two countries with higher energy consumption per person and the two with lower energy use.

# 2 Natural resources

**2.15** Iceland relies mainly on geothermal energy as its power source. Describe how this could be used to generate electricity.

**2.16** 'Countries with strong national economies will always use more energy than those with weaker national economies.' How far do you agree with this statement? **Justify** your answer.

**2.17** How could climate change affect the demand for energy?

### COMMAND WORD

**justify:** support a case with evidence/argument

## 2.5 Conservation and management of energy resources

As you have seen, the increased need for energy is due to an increasing population, greater demand from industrialisation and improved living standards. No one knows how long supplies of non-renewable fossil fuels will last, and at the moment not enough energy is being generated from renewable resources to meet the world's needs.

## Strategies for effective energy use

What are the options for resolving this situation? Would governments agree to all countries taking a share of the available energy resources? If so, what happens to countries that are colder and need energy to keep warm and use lights in the winter months? Should industrialised countries cut back on their use of energy while others catch up? It is unlikely that all governments would agree on all of these issues. However, they may be able to reach agreement on the careful management of the resources that are used.

### Reducing consumption

The rapid increase in energy use in the past few years has created the possibility of an **energy gap** – a difference between demand and the available supply.

If this occurs, it will result in **power cuts** and, in the case of fuels such as petroleum, the risk of **fuel rationing**.

### KEY WORDS

**energy gap:** a situation in which demand for energy is greater than the available supply

**power cut:** a period of time when electricity is shut off so people cannot use it

**fuel rationing:** a controlled restriction on the availability of fuel for defined purposes

There are several practical ways of reducing energy consumption. In particular, electrical devices should be turned off when not in use. Many devices have a 'standby' mode that enables them to be accessed rapidly. It has been calculated that the average device uses around 15 watts of power even when it is in this mode. Four or five devices left on standby in a household is the equivalent to leaving an electric light on for the same length of time.

Promoting this strategy has some key benefits. It prevents the need for further investment in infrastructure, and the reductions in energy consumption will not significantly affect people's ability to use equipment. The main limitation is that it is hard to enforce as it will involve changing behaviours, would be hard to monitor and there would be few penalties for failing to do so.

### Insulation

A standard European house (i.e. one in a cooler climate) loses heat through a variety of routes. Figure 2.63 shows the proportions lost.

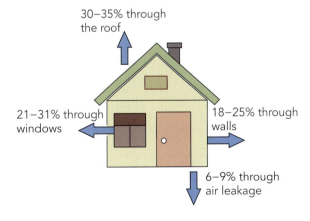

**Figure 2.63:** The percentages of heat lost from an insulated house in a temperate climate.

65

Insulation is one of the most effective methods of reducing this type of heat loss. Using building materials with good insulation properties prevents the loss of heat to the air, in the same way that a blanket keeps a person warm.

In the example shown in Figure 2.63, an insulation layer could be added into the roof space (loft insulation). Most heat is lost through the roof, so investment in this area would have a big impact. Similarly, a lot of heat can be lost through the walls. Some homes are built with a gap between the inside and outside walls. If this cavity is filled with an insulating material, heat will pass through far more slowly than if this space was filled with air. Figure 2.64 shows the construction system for cavity wall insulation. Figure 2.65 shows an alternative system for adding insulation to a wall.

**Figure 2.65:** Installing insulation materials into walls helps retain heat in cooler climates. While expensive, the investment is often quickly paid back in lower heating costs.

In the typical house in Figure 2.63, energy is also lost through the windows. Reducing the size of the windows would limit this, but it would also reduce natural light, so may increase the amount of energy used for artificial light. Instead, energy use can be reduced by double glazing the window. This technique uses two panes of glass with a gap in the middle to act as an insulator. The sealed gap is filled with a clear material, such as an inert gas like argon, or simply air. Further savings could be made using triple glazing (three panes of glass; Figure 2.66), but many people consider this to be too expensive for the amount of energy they are saving.

This strategy has major benefits as, once installed, the impact of insulation is long term. However, it can be costly and sometimes difficult to install into existing homes that were not designed to be as energy efficient. Some historic buildings would be difficult to adapt without changing the character of the structure.

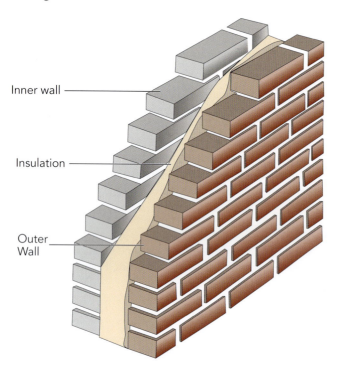

**Figure 2.64:** Cavity wall insulation can be made from a variety of insulating materials.

**Figure 2.66:** A cross-section of a triple-glazed window. The extra layer reduces the heat transfer through the window.

## 2 Natural resources

### FIELDWORK ACTIVITY 2.2

#### How well do materials reduce heat loss?

This simple investigation will help you to evaluate how much heat energy insulation will retain, reducing the amount of energy used.

**You will need**

- three identical glass jars with lids, each lid with a hole for a thermometer or temperature probe
- three temperature probes, for the top of each jar
- boiling water
- a towel or sock
- a piece of paper
- a timer

**Before you start**

Organise a space where all three jars can be placed side by side and the thermometers will be easy to read. Wrap one jar in a towel or place it inside a sock. Wrap another jar with a sheet of paper and secure it.

**Safety**

Take extra care when handling, measuring and pouring boiling water.

**Method**

- Set up the three jars in a row, each with a thermometer (or probe) through the lid (Figure 2.67).
- Label the jars A, B and C.
- Jar A: no covering.
- Jar B: with the covering of paper.
- Jar C: wrapped in the towel or put inside the sock.
- Add the same volume of boiling water to each jar and put the lid on firmly.
- Record the temperature in each jar over 1 hour at 5-minute intervals.
- Present your results in a table and in a line graph.

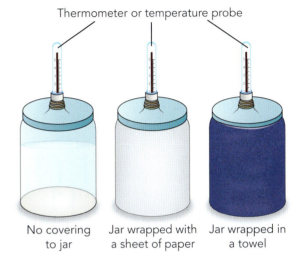

Figure 2.67: How to set up your experiment.

**Questions**

1. What do the temperature changes in jars A and C tell you about the heat loss through glass and through an insulator?
2. Why was jar B included in the experiment?
3. What could be done to make the water stay hotter for longer?
4. Suggest a further experiment that could be done to test the issue of heat loss further.

### CRITICAL THINKING TIP

Review the method for the practical experiment. What aspects of the experiment were kept constant across all three jars? Why is this so important for the accuracy of the experiment?

## Energy-efficient devices

Appliances and machines use energy – either directly as fuel, in the case of vehicles, or indirectly by using electricity to operate. However, a wide variety of new, energy-efficient versions are now available.

Vehicles have become much more efficient in their energy use. Figure 2.68 shows the mean energy efficiency of new cars purchased in the USA between 1975 and 2021. While direct comparisons are difficult due to changes in models, improvements to engine efficiency have clearly allowed cars to travel far further on the same volume of fuel (approximately 6 km per litre in 1975 compared to over 13 km per litre in 2021).

The situation could be improved further with the use of alternative fuels and electric vehicles powered by rechargeable batteries. People could also drive smaller, lighter cars, which would be more energy efficient.

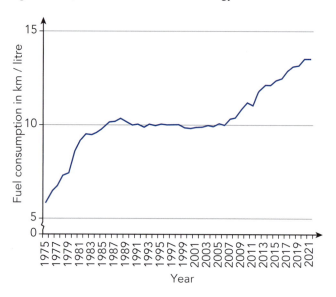

**Figure 2.68:** The increase in the fuel efficiency of new cars in the USA since 1975.

Some countries offer scrappage schemes to remove inefficient machines, including vehicles and electrical appliances. The consumer is paid to trade in their old machine, which is then recycled. The purchase of a new version improves energy efficiency and has a significant impact on air quality. Schemes to make electric vehicles more affordable will reduce the need for fossil fuels, particularly if the electricity is generated from renewable resources (Figure 2.69).

Businesses and individuals will save money, as they are using fewer resources to operate the machines. However, this benefit is only achieved if people can be persuaded to replace existing equipment with more energy-efficient examples. Not everyone can afford new equipment, and scrapping less efficient machines increases the problems of waste management and recycling.

**Figure 2.69:** Schemes to encourage the use of electric cars reduce the consumption of fossil fuels, but investment is needed to make sure there are enough spaces to charge the vehicle batteries.

### SUSTAINABILITY TIP

Once you understand where energy is used inefficiently, you can apply the same principles to an unfamiliar situation. For example:

- Older buildings were not designed to be as energy efficient.
- Old machines could be replaced by newer, more efficient ones.
- People may leave devices unattended.
- A group of people may use multiple items when they could use one between them instead.

However, do not assume that because something is new it uses less energy. Sometimes things are created for convenience or comfort, and they might use more energy than an older device or way of doing things.

2 Natural resources

### ACTIVITY 2.5

Table 2.10 contains information about four types of common light bulb.

| Light bulb type | Compact fluorescent lamp (CFL) | Halogen | Incandescent | Light-emitting diode (LED) |
|---|---|---|---|---|
| Appearance |  | 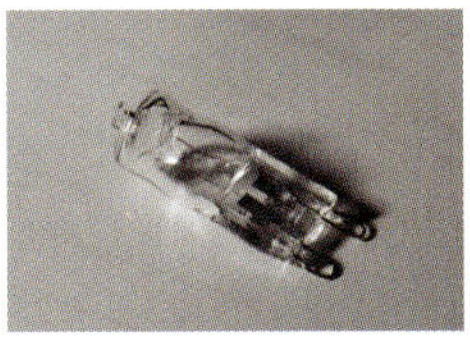 |  |  |
| Energy consumption of a 1600 lumen bulb (W) | 23 | 72 | 100 | 20 |
| Average lifespan (years) | 8 | 2 | 1 | 18 |
| Typical cost to buy<br>* = low<br>***** = high | ** | * | * | ***** |

**Table 2.10:** A comparison of four different electric light bulbs. Source: ResearchGate

a  Present the information about the energy consumption of each type of light bulb in a bar chart.

b  Research the cost of purchasing each type of bulb in your local area. Use the information obtained from your research and Table 2.10 to complete the following tasks:

i  Rank the four light bulbs according to the amount of energy used. Start with the light bulb that consumes the least energy.

ii  Rank the four light bulbs according to their cost to buy and operate over an 18-year period. Start with the cheapest light bulb.

c  Review the use of lighting at your home and school. Make recommendations to improve the energy efficiency of the lighting used.

### MATHS TIP

When drawing a bar chart, remember to:
- use a sensible scale for the data
- use a ruler
- label the axes
- plot the information accurately
- ensure the bars are of equal width
- ensure the bars are not touching.

## Exploiting existing energy

The use of finite resources can be reduced by re-using existing materials to extract the energy from them before they are thrown away. Some countries have introduced schemes to do this but often only on a small scale to test their effectiveness. However, they could be important, especially in places where other ways of disposing of waste are limited.

Anaerobic digestion is the breaking down of organic waste (such as food and vegetation) using bacteria (Figure 2.70). This process takes place in a sealed container and produces biogas, which has a high methane content. Methane is a flammable natural gas that can be used for a variety of heating purposes or for powering vehicles. The composted waste can be used on land to improve the structure of soil and the amount of nutrients it contains.

Household rubbish can be incinerated (burnt) to produce heat, which can be used to generate electricity (Figure 2.71). Many people dislike this process because poisonous gases can be produced during combustion. However, one benefit of it is that the amount of waste from burning (ash) is small and does not take up lots of space when disposed of.

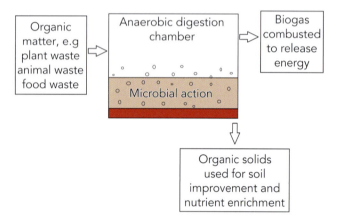

**Figure 2.70:** A simplified anaerobic digestion process.

**Figure 2.71:** A waste incineration facility in the UK. The heat produced is used to produce steam, which powers turbines for electricity production.

Food-processing industries use large quantities of cooking oils in the preparation and manufacture of foods. Once used, these vegetable oils need to be disposed of. Many countries have schemes to collect these oils and recycle them into biofuels that are suitable for running vehicles. In some cases, the biofuels are added to fossils fuels; in others, vehicles may run exclusively using this biofuel.

This strategy ensures that energy resources are used as efficiently as possible, so there is a reduced demand for finite resources and less investment needed in renewable energy solutions. This approach also makes use of materials that may otherwise be wasted. However, it is unlikely that using waste will meet a large proportion of the energy needs in an area. Many solutions also involve the combustion of waste, which may produce additional pollutants as well as the release of carbon dioxide.

## Education on energy conservation

New technologies and innovative designs will only be successful if people understand their benefits. In the same way, people also need to understand the ways in which energy is currently being wasted and what can be done to conserve it.

Figure 2.72 shows the results of research conducted in the UK in 2022. People were asked whether they would be willing to pay more for sustainable products.

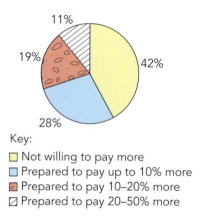

Key:
- Not willing to pay more
- Prepared to pay up to 10% more
- Prepared to pay 10–20% more
- Prepared to pay 20–50% more

**Figure 2.72:** The results of a questionnaire to determine whether people would pay more for sustainable products. This does not match with actual buying patterns. Source: Culturalenterprises.org.uk

While the majority of people questioned said they would be willing to pay more, in varying amounts, 42% said they would not pay extra for a sustainable product. Information on buying trends also suggests that while people say they will pay extra when asked, they do not do so in practice.

2 Natural resources

> **PROBLEM-SOLVING TIP**
>
> You may sometimes come across discrepancies in what data shows and other evidence. For example, the data presented in the pie chart in Figure 2.72 differs from actual sales of sustainable products. You will need to consider why these differences have appeared. It can help to ask yourself questions based on the data and method of collection. Here, you might put yourself in the position of the person completing the questionnaire and ask yourself these questions:
>
> - What factors might influence my answer?
> - What influences my decision most when I choose to buy an item?
> - Why are these not necessarily the same?

This presents a challenge for companies developing new technologies. The educational message must be that despite the initial cost, significant savings can be made in energy bills over the longer term by reducing energy use. This education could be reinforced by including energy-efficiency ratings for new products, so customers can compare products when choosing which to buy (Figure 2.73).

The key to education strategies is to create an increased awareness within the population. Education may help change attitudes to the use of items such as fossil fuels, particularly if there are incentives such as grants to make changes. However, a population will not necessarily decide to change, and it is difficult to enforce change without the use of other strategies such as legislation. It is also a challenge to ensure that the whole population receive the information in a way they can understand.

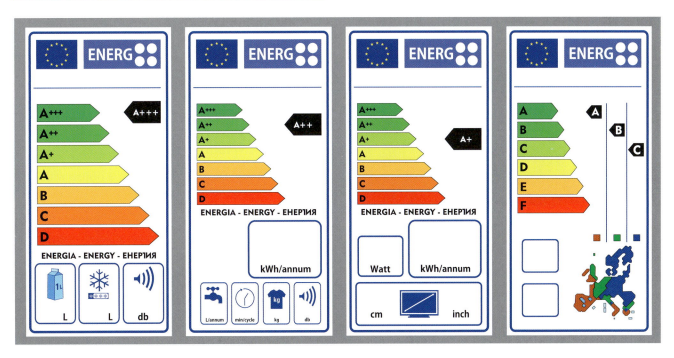

Figure 2.73: Examples of customer information labels for new products. If all products had the same type of information label, people could easily compare the energy efficiency of different models before deciding which one to buy.

## CASE STUDY

### The house that needs no energy input

The challenge for many designers is to develop a house that requires as little energy input to run it as possible. This is particularly difficult in countries where winter temperatures drop below 0 °C.

The Passivhaus Institute in Germany has pioneered the development of building design technology that reduces the energy used to operate a house (Figure 2.74). In a comparable temperate climate, a Passivhaus (or passive house) can reduce the amount of energy used by 90% compared to a 'standard' house in a similar location.

Design features often include:

- high levels of insulation
- airtight construction
- high insulation windows (using special reflective glass and triple glazing)
- use of a heat exchanger to capture excessive heat produced by the occupants
- a ground heat exchanger to capture heat from lower levels in the ground
- solar panels to produce electricity and to heat water pipes.

To date, it has been estimated around 65 000 structures have been built on this principle worldwide, with the majority in Germany and Austria.

### Questions

1. It has been calculated that the energy used by a 'standard' house in a location is 15 dm³ of heating oil per square metre of living space. Calculate the volume of oil that would be used per square metre in a Passivhaus in the same location.

2. The energy savings from this building design are large. Suggest reasons why such a small percentage of houses are built this way, even though so much energy can be saved.

3. Explain why the aim of building a house with no energy input might not be possible.

**Figure 2.74:** The use of different materials and technology can significantly reduce the energy use of a house.

## Transport policies

Transporting products around the world once they have been manufactured, in addition to private transport, uses a significant amount of energy. Governments play a large part in regulating transport and encouraging more efficient use, in the hope of reducing the impact on global oil reserves and improving air quality.

Current government initiatives include:

- regulations regarding fuel efficiency and the quality of exhaust gases from vehicles
- restrictions on where vehicles may travel
- taxes on fuels
- surcharges for travelling to certain places, such as cities, at peak times (Figure 2.75)

## 2 Natural resources

- improving public transport so it is easier and cheaper to use than cars
- improving routes for cyclists and pedestrians so that these are more convenient ways to travel
- encouraging car sharing
- restricting when cars can be used; for example, in São Paulo, Brazil, regulations have been imposed that only allow cars with certain digits on their licence plates to operate on certain days
- providing grants to buy more fuel-efficient vehicles and dispose of older, more polluting vehicles
- providing grants for vehicles that use cleaner technology, such as electric-powered vehicles.

> **CRITICAL THINKING TIP**
>
> Many different transport policies have been implemented all over the world. When giving examples of this kind of policy, make sure that you can explain why the policy is likely to be effective. Imagine yourself in the area where the transport policy has been put in place and think how it would affect you. For example, would it make it easier for you to travel to school? Try to analyse why some strategies will work in some countries or regions, but not in others.

### Battery storage

As you have seen, some renewable energy sources are only efficient under certain conditions, which can mean the energy supply from these resources is inconsistent. For example, solar panels need sunlight, and wind turbines operate best at certain wind speeds. However, the demand for electricity does not follow these peaks and troughs.

Battery storage systems are one way around this problem (Figure 2.76). Excess electricity generation is used to charge batteries, which store the electricity until it is needed. At the moment, technology is only available to set up battery storage systems at a local level. However, there are plans to develop larger storage facilities to supply a greater number of people.

While there are clear benefits to this strategy, there are also limitations. The main one is that reserves of the minerals needed to manufacture the batteries are finite. Some people also object to the installation of battery storage facilities near their homes, as they can cause visual pollution and are perceived as a fire risk if there is a fault in a battery circuit.

**Figure 2.76:** Battery storage systems are being developed to allow the use of electricity at times when demand exceeds supply. These are bulky and use of a lot of valuable resources in the manufacture of the batteries.

**Figure 2.75:** Some cities impose charges for using vehicles at the busiest times and for the most polluting vehicles. In London, UK, the ultra-low emission zone (ULEZ) has resulted in an improvement in air quality but is not popular with everyone.

# Development of new energy resources

Several new technologies and energy resources are currently being developed to help address the energy gap. One of the main new technologies is the use of hydrogen as a fuel. When combusted, hydrogen combines with oxygen to form water, which is not harmful to the atmosphere. Hydrogen for this purpose is produced from either natural gas (**blue hydrogen** fuel) or water (**green hydrogen** fuel).

## Blue hydrogen fuel

Natural gas can be split using a process called steam methane reforming. The results of this split are hydrogen (which forms water when it is combusted) and carbon dioxide, which is captured before it escapes into the atmosphere. In this way, heat is produced from combustion without increasing the amount of carbon dioxide in the atmosphere. This contributes less to climate change and air pollution, but the process still uses natural gas – a non-renewable resource – as its raw material.

## Green hydrogen fuel

Green hydrogen describes a production method where hydrogen gas is produced from water and the energy from other renewable sources (such as solar panels). It uses **electrolysis** to split water molecules into hydrogen and oxygen. The hydrogen is captured and used for combustion, and the oxygen is allowed to escape into the atmosphere. Although splitting the water molecules takes a lot of energy, this comes from a renewable resource and allows the hydrogen to be burnt when needed, such as at night when solar panels are ineffective.

## Ground source heat pumps

A heat exchanger allows heat deep in the soil to be extracted to use in heating homes. The temperatures of this soil are far lower than those available from geothermal energy, so heat from a ground source heat pump cannot heat water sufficiently to produce steam to drive a turbine, for example. As a result, this technology is best suited to the direct heating of buildings in cooler climates, rather than for generating electricity.

> **KEY WORDS**
>
> **blue hydrogen:** hydrogen produced from natural gas
>
> **green hydrogen:** hydrogen produced from the splitting of water molecules
>
> **electrolysis:** the use of electricity to break down molecules into their component elements

## Air source heat pumps

Air source heat pumps (Figure 2.77) use similar technology to ground source heat pumps. An air source heat pump acts much like a refrigerator or air-conditioning unit – but in reverse. The heat exchanger extracts heat from the outside air and transfers it to water to pump the heat generated into a building. As with the ground source heat pump, this type of technology cannot provide enough heat to generate steam to turn a turbine, so it is limited to heating a space or providing warm water in the home rather than electricity generation. Air source heat pumps will often replace the combustion of natural gas to heat homes but will still use some electricity in their operation. This can be provided by sustainable sources.

Figure 2.77: Installing an air source heat pump will reduce the volume of carbon dioxide generated to heat a home.

2  Natural resources

### ACTIVITY 2.6

Complete an audit of your day to identify opportunities to use less energy.
Items might include:

- walking rather than using a car
- making sure lights are turned off when not needed
- using less water (energy is used in its supply and to purify it)
- wasting less food (energy is used in food production and its transportation)
- using natural ventilation rather than air conditioning. When you start your investigations, you will see many more examples.

Use the information from your audit to make an action plan of the top five things you could change to reduce your own energy use. Review your progress after one month to see if you have managed to keep to your action plan.

## 2.6 Fracking

As energy demands continue to increase worldwide, some scientists are concerned that the use of renewable resources cannot be developed at the pace required to meet these needs.

There may be large reserves of fossil fuels in Antarctica, but international agreements are in place to prevent them being exploited due to the significant environmental impact it would have. However, other reserves have been identified that could be accessed using a different – and controversial – technique called **fracking**. This is a way of extracting petroleum or natural gas from shale rock by hydraulic fracturing.

### KEY WORD

**fracking:** the common term for hydraulic fracking – the process of obtaining petroleum or natural gas from shale rock by breaking open the rocks using water, sand and chemicals

## The fracking process

Fracking involves drilling a vertical hole deep underground to reach the fuel-rich rocks (shale rocks). Depending on the location, this may be 2–3 km deep. Water, chemicals and sand are then pumped down into the shale rock layer under pressure. This causes the rocks to fracture (split open), releasing the petroleum and natural gas, which are forced back to the surface and collected. Figure 2.78 shows the process.

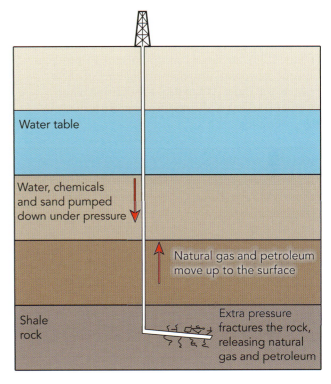

**Figure 2.78:** The fracking process – splitting open shale rocks deep underground.

Regarding the three materials that are pumped into the shale rock layer:

- Sand is used to keep the cracks in the rock open as they occur, allowing the petroleum and natural gas to escape. The sand is sometimes referred to as the **proppant**.

### KEY WORD

**proppant:** a material, such as sand, that is used to keep cracks in shale rocks open to allow natural gas or petroleum extraction

75

- Chemicals are added to stop the blockage of pipes.
- Water is used to act as a carrier for the sand and the chemicals, allowing them to be easily pumped. Water has the benefit of being inexpensive and easily available.

## The fracking controversy

Table 2.11 shows a list of benefits and limitations of fracking. You might notice that the benefits, which tend to be used to support arguments in favour of fracking, are based mainly on economic considerations, while the limitations, used for arguments against fracking (Figure 2.79), are largely environmental. Depending on your viewpoint, the relative weighting of these reasons will differ. Ultimately, the decision about whether fracking is allowed in a country is made by the government.

| Benefits of fracking | Limitations of fracking |
| --- | --- |
| It allows access to more natural gas and petroleum, which are in limited supply. | There is a risk of toxins from fracking entering the water table, affecting water supplies. |
| Using natural gas and petroleum produces less pollution than burning coal, so it is better to extract extra supplies than rely on coal. | The mixture of chemicals used as part of the fracking mixture is toxic and may affect local residents. |
| It reduces the need to import petroleum or natural gas from other countries. | Fracking uses a lot of water, which may reduce availability for other purposes. |
| Shale rock is a long way underground, far below the water table, so poses little risk of water pollution. | Noise pollution: fracking in an area will affect the local community. |
| Petroleum and natural gas have been drilled for many years and this is just another deep method. | Natural areas will be destroyed when new drilling sites are developed. |
| Fracking provides many jobs locally. | Fracturing lower levels of rock may cause earth tremors. |
| The technology is not yet in place to allow the whole world to meet its current lifestyle without fossil fuels. | The longer-term impact of the technology is not known, and any damage done may be irreparable. |

Table 2.11: Benefits and limitations of using fracking to extract petroleum and natural gas.

Figure 2.79: Not everyone is in favour of introducing fracking. The signs at the side of the road are part of a protest against a potential fracking site in the UK.

## Questions

2.18 Governments need to encourage businesses and individuals to become more energy efficient. They can do this in several ways, by legislation (to force a change) or by policies that encourage change. Copy and complete the following table with examples of programmes that have been introduced by governments. One has been filled in for you.

2.19 It has been suggested that in a world with limited energy supplies, governments should reach an agreement to share energy resources equally based on the size of their population. Explain why this might be unfair.

2   Natural resources

2.20 State the main arguments for and against the development of fracking in an area where there has not been petroleum or natural gas extraction previously.

| Forcing change | Encouraging change |
|---|---|
| Restrictions on when cars may be driven |  |
|  |  |
|  |  |
|  |  |

EXTENDED CASE STUDY

### The Island Copper Mine, Vancouver Island, British Colombia, Canada

The Island Copper Mine started production in 1971 (Figure 2.80). It was finally closed in 1995 because there was insufficient ore left to make further extraction economical. It was an open-pit mine and employed 900 people at its peak. During its lifetime, 363 million tonnes of ore were extracted. The ore contained an average of 0.41% copper and 0.017% molybdenum. Extraction involved the removal of a billion tonnes of material in all, at a maximum rate of 170 800 tonnes per day.

The pit produced by the mine was 2400 m long, 1070 m wide and had a depth of 400 m. The waste from the mine, which is called tailings, was disposed of in the sea. Water pollution from the mine was restricted by a 33-m deep, 1219-m long barrier.

The final production figures for the mine were 1 299 978 tonnes of copper, 31 000 tonnes of molybdenum, 31 700 000 g (31.7 tonnes) of gold, 335 994 324 g (336 tonnes) of silver and 27 tonnes of rhenium. These materials were exported to many countries around the world.

**Figure 2.80:** The Island Copper Mine, Vancouver Island, British Columbia, Canada.

During its lifetime, the environmental impact of the mine was carefully managed and monitored. All water run-off from dumps was controlled by a system of water management.

The impacts of the mine can be summarised under four headings:

- Physical: 400 million tonnes of tailings deposited into Rupert Inlet reduced its depth by 40 m. These materials, leading to a reduction in marine biodiversity, regularly smothered the bottom fauna. A small rocky beach was formed where once it was sand, and copper-tainted sediment was found many kilometres away.

- Chemical: Over 25 years of monitoring, no trends were seen in any of the variables measured (pH, oxygen and dissolved heavy metals including copper, manganese and zinc).

- Biological: There was evidence that the water became less clear. The reduction in species diversity on the seabed was the biggest effect. A site near the mine only had 15 species in 1995, whereas a different site sampled away from the mine had 41. Despite early fears, there were no areas found where no life was present.

- Bioaccumulation: There was very little evidence of an increase in the levels of any metals in the tissues of animals. This suggests that neither bioaccumulation nor biomagnification was occurring.

Port Hardy, a small town near the mine, originally had a population of 700 that grew after the opening of the mine to over 5000. The company spent over 2.9 billion US dollars (USD) in the mine's 25 years of life. From early on during the life of the mine, tax was paid at a rate of about USD 3 million per year. The mining company provided 400 houses for its employees, with another 600 being constructed

77

## CONTINUED

by other builders. All the necessary services, including sewerage, roads and water, were paid for and provided by the mining company. The mine's opening also led to the creation of a hospital, a swimming pool, a theatre and some parks.

The plans for the eventual mine closure were in place even when its opening was being prepared in 1969. Nearly 5 million tonnes of overburden were kept and used for land reclamation during the 25 years of the mine and after its closure. The features of the mine covered by the closure plan were the open pit, the waste rock piles, the sea and the buildings.

The open pit was flooded with sea water after closure, creating a 300-m deep lake with an area of 215 hectares. The possibility of using this lake for aquaculture was considered.

A further 200-hectare area was recontoured, and over 600 000 tree seedlings were planted during the life of the mine.

### Questions

1. Explain why the mine was closed in 1995.

2. Calculate the percentage of the total material extracted that was waste. Quote your answer to two decimal places.

3. One of the biggest concerns about the operation of the Island Copper Mine was the possible effect of disposing waste water at sea. Various studies to monitor this started as soon as the mine opened. In one study, a commercially important predator, the Dungeness crab, was checked yearly for the levels of copper and other metals in its tissues over the life of the mine. The data from this study are given in Table 2.12.

| Year | Copper concentration mg / kg wet mass |
|---|---|
| 1971 | 7.0 |
| 1972 | 6.0 |
| 1973 | 5.7 |
| 1974 | 8.1 |
| 1975 | 7.7 |
| 1976 | 9.7 |
| 1977 | 11.8 |
| 1978 | 11.6 |
| 1979 | 9.9 |

| Year | Copper in mg / kg wet mass |
|---|---|
| 1980 | 8.5 |
| 1981 | 8.5 |
| 1982 | 10.0 |
| 1983 | 7.7 |
| 1984 | 9.1 |
| 1985 | 6.5 |
| 1986 | 6.6 |
| 1987 | 6.4 |
| 1988 | 8.1 |
| 1989 | 9.9 |
| 1990 | 10.4 |
| 1991 | 9.0 |
| 1992 | 9.0 |
| 1993 | 10.0 |
| 1994 | 11.0 |
| 1995 | 9.0 |
| 1996 | 10.3 |
| 1997 | 12.3 |
| 1998 | 9.3 |

**Table 2.12:** Copper levels in Dungeness crab caught near the mine.

a  Copy and complete Figure 2.81 using the data in Table 2.12.

b  i  Describe the trend in copper in crab tissue from the opening of the mine until 1977.

   ii  State the year when the concentration of copper in the crabs was the lowest.

   iii  Scientists concluded that the mine did not cause an increase in the concentration of copper in the crabs. State evidence to support this view.

c  Suggest why the Dungeness crab was chosen to monitor copper levels in the tissues of living things in this study.

## CONTINUED

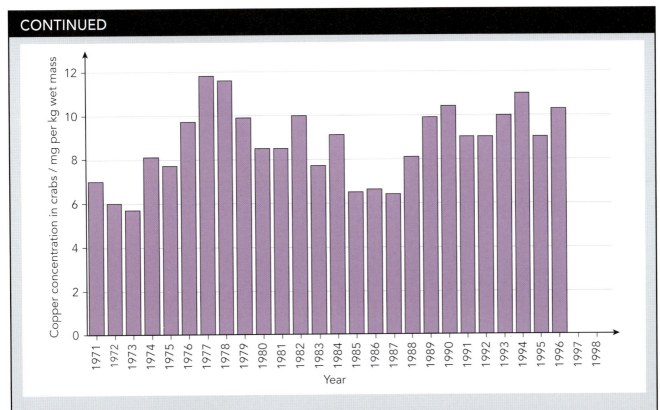

Figure 2.81: Copper levels in crab tissue.

### Project

In small groups, find out more about the Island Copper Mine, using the internet or any other resources available to you. Create a presentation to evaluate how effective the restoration of the area has been since the mine closed in 1995. Ensure that the information you use is provided by reliable sources and provide a balanced opinion so that you can form your own conclusions.

### Further resources

Island Copper Mine, Rupert Inlet

Vancouver Island Copper Mine

Island Copper Mine Location

## SUMMARY

| |
|---|
| Rocks can be classified into three main types depending on how they are formed: igneous, sedimentary and metamorphic. |
| Rocks are continuously forming and being broken down in a process called the rock cycle. |
| Most sedimentary rocks are permeable (water can pass through them easily). |
| Igneous, metamorphic and some sedimentary rocks are impermeable (water cannot pass through them easily). |
| Ores are rocks that contain useful minerals and metals. |
| There are three main methods of mining rocks, ores and minerals: surface extraction, sub-surface extraction and biological extraction. |
| Factors that influence whether or not a particular reserve of a resource is exploited include the geology of the landscape, its accessibility, terrain and climate, the quantity and quality of the deposit, and associated costs and profits. |
| Extraction has environmental, economic and social impacts, including loss of habitat, pollution, and changes to local and national economies and infrastructure. |
| When mining has finished, land can be restored or repurposed in a variety of ways, each of which has benefits and limitations. |
| The use of rocks, ores and minerals needs to be strategically managed in order to conserve the resources and help the environment. |
| Management strategies include recycling, using more efficient extraction processes, laws to manage how much and how resources are used, and finding alternative materials. |
| Petroleum (oil), coal and natural gas are collectively known as 'fossil fuels'. |
| Energy resources can be classified as non-renewable (finite), which includes fossil fuels and nuclear energy, or renewable, such as solar, wind and geothermal power. All have benefits and limitations. |
| Renewable and nuclear resources do not contribute to the overall level of carbon dioxide in the atmosphere. |
| A generator is used to produce electricity but will need a source of energy to power it. |
| Energy demand depends on a range of factors, including the climate, population size and the relative wealth of the population. |
| The use of energy resources can be managed through a variety of strategies, including insulation, education, transport policies and battery storage. |
| New energy resources are being developed, including blue and green hydrogen fuel, ground source heat pumps, and air source heat pumps. |
| Fracking is a technique that may allow for exploitation of additional sources of fossil fuels, but environmental concerns have made it controversial. |

## SELF-EVALUATION CHECKLIST

After studying this chapter, complete this table.

| I can: | Needs more work | Almost there | Ready to move on |
|---|---|---|---|
| describe how igneous, sedimentary and metamorphic rocks are formed | | | |
| describe the processes involved in the rock cycle | | | |
| define 'permeability' and classify rocks as permeable and impermeable | | | |
| explain what an ore is | | | |
| describe a variety of methods for extracting rocks, ores and minerals from the ground | | | |
| explain the environmental, economic and social impacts of extracting rocks, ores and minerals | | | |
| discuss different methods for restoring and repurposing land after extraction, and explain the benefits and limitations of these strategies | | | |
| define 'finite resources' and 'sustainable management' | | | |
| outline some sustainable strategies for managing rocks, ores and minerals, and explain the benefits and limitations of these strategies | | | |
| describe how fossil fuels are formed | | | |
| classify energy sources into renewable and non-renewable types | | | |
| explain how different energy sources are used to make electricity | | | |
| discuss the benefits and limitations of different resources | | | |
| identify the different factors that influence energy demand | | | |
| suggest how energy sources can be managed efficiently | | | |
| outline what research is currently being undertaken into new energy sources | | | |
| state what fracking is and discuss the arguments for and against its use. | | | |

## PRACTICE QUESTIONS

1. **a** Aluminium is produced from a sedimentary rock called bauxite.

   State the name given to any rock that contains a valuable metal. [1]

   **b** The process to extract aluminium from bauxite is shown in the information box below.

   > 5 tonnes of bright red bauxite are made into 2 tonnes of a white powder called alumina (aluminium oxide).
   >
   > The bauxite is usually obtained from open-pit mines. Hot caustic soda solution (an alkaline solution) is added to the crushed rock to get rid of impurities in the alumina.
   >
   > The alumina is then converted into 1 tonne of aluminium in a smelter. To do this, an electric current is passed through the material to heat it and molten aluminium is collected.

   **i** Calculate the mass of solid waste that would be produced from the processing of 25 tonnes of bauxite. [2]

   **ii** Calculate the mass of bauxite that would be needed to produce 25 tonnes of aluminium. [2]

   **c i** Suggest **two** environmental impacts of aluminium production after the bauxite has been mined. [2]

   **ii** Explain how the landscape may be restored after bauxite mining is finished. [3]

2. Figure 2.82 shows a deep coal mine and the area around it.

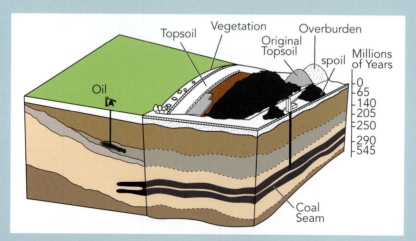

**Figure 2.82:** A deep coal mine and the area around it.

## CONTINUED

    **a** Explain how the coal is extracted from the location shown in **Figure 2.82**. [3]

    **b** State the estimated age of the coal and oil deposits shown in **Figure 2.82**. [2]

    **c** With reference to **Figure 2.82**, and your own knowledge, describe how the spoil heap could be reclaimed. [5]

**3** Figure 2.83 shows how the production of a mineral changed over time.

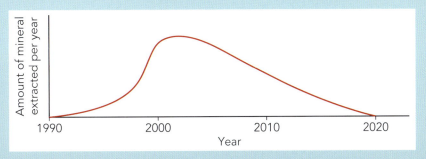

**Figure 2.83:** The production of a mineral over time.

    **a** Choose a word from the list to describe the situation for this mineral in 1990, 2003 and 2020.

        exhaustion      peak production      discovery

        1990……………………………………………

        2003……………………………………………

        2020…………………………………………… [1]

    **b** Explain what might have happened between 2003 and 2020. [3]

    **c** Suggest which techniques could be employed so that the mineral could still be extracted after 2020. [3]

**4** Renewable (non-finite) resources offer opportunities to meet energy needs in a more sustainable way.

    **a**   **i** Name **two** types of biofuel. [2]

        **ii** Identify **two** renewable energy sources that use the power of water. [2]

    **b** Describe how geothermal power is used to generate electricity. [4]

    **c** Obtaining energy from the burning of household waste is one solution to meeting energy needs.

        **i** Give **one** environmental benefit of using waste in this way. [1]

        **ii** Give **one** limitation of using waste in this way. [1]

    **d** Explain the limitations of using solar power to generate electricity. [3]

> **CONTINUED**
>
> **5** Some people argue that while it is a non-renewable resource, a nuclear fuel such as uranium is a suitable replacement for fossil fuels.
>
> State **three** pieces of evidence that might support this view. [3]
>
> **6** Hydrogen is being evaluated as a useful additional resource to supplement existing energy resources.
>
>    **a**  **i**  Define 'green' hydrogen. [1]
>
>        **ii**  Define 'blue' hydrogen. [1]
>
>    **b**  Explain why 'green' hydrogen is thought to be preferable to 'blue' hydrogen. [2]
>
> **7** Different fossil fuels produce different amounts of carbon dioxide and sulfur dioxide when burned.
>
>    **a**  Table 2.13 shows the amount of carbon dioxide produced when you burn each fossil fuel to transfer the same amount of energy.
>
> | Fossil fuel | Units of carbon dioxide produced (based on petroleum = 100) |
> |---|---|
> | Petroleum | 100 |
> | Natural gas | 75 |
> | Coal | 150 |
>
> **Table 2.13:** Relative volumes of carbon dioxide emitted by different fossil fuels.
>
>        **i**  State the most appropriate type of graph or chart to display this data. [1]
>
>        **ii**  Plot a chart or graph to show the units of carbon dioxide produced per fossil fuel. [3]
>
>    **b**  A student observes that the data shows that natural gas appears to be the least environmentally damaging fossil fuel.
>
>       Suggest **three** other factors that should be considered before reaching this conclusion. [3]
>
> **8** Discuss the benefits and limitations of mining for minerals. [6]

# Chapter 3
# Land

### LEARNING INTENTIONS

In this chapter you will:

- discover what soil is made of
- investigate the components of soil that make it good for plant growth
- explore the benefits of loam soils
- learn about the climate and weather conditions needed for optimum growth
- discuss different types of agriculture
- consider various strategies for increasing agricultural yields
- explore the impact of unsustainable agricultural practices
- examine the causes and impacts of soil erosion
- consider strategies for reducing soil erosion.

# CAMBRIDGE IGCSE™ AND O LEVEL ENVIRONMENTAL MANAGEMENT: COURSEBOOK

## BEFORE YOU START

Rank these items in order of importance, with the most important at the top of your list:

nutritious food to eat     reduced deforestation
income for a farming family
low-cost food to eat     choice of food to eat

Compare your list with a partner, then discuss any differences. Try to reach a final order for these factors that you both agree on.

## ENVIRONMENTAL MANAGEMENT IN CONTEXT

### Food for thought

**Agriculture** is not only the largest industry on the planet but also the most important – after all, everyone on Earth needs food to eat. However, agriculture can have serious environmental impacts, so understanding what these are and how they can be managed is very important to the health of the planet.

The challenges are large:

- The human population is increasing by 83 million people per year.
- Approximately 10% of the current human population does not have enough food.
- In the last 40 years, one-third of the land used for growing crops has been lost to erosion and soil exhaustion.
- 80% of all deforestation is for new farmland, which negatively affects biodiversity.
- The use of **fertilisers** and **pesticides** further damages the ecosystems.
- Food production requires large volumes of water, which means that there is less available for drinking.

There are no easy solutions to these problems, but it is clear that changes need to be made. This poses some questions:

- Should 'luxury' foods be banned to ensure that we can grow sufficient basic foods?
- Should everyone be encouraged to eat a vegetarian diet, which has less environmental impact?
- Should technologies such as **genetically modified organisms (GMOs)** be allowed, as they may produce food by using fewer resources?

**Figure 3.1:** Large machines mean more efficient harvesting with fewer workers, but they are expensive to buy, require large fields of the same crop to work efficiently and may damage the soil. Food production needs to be balanced with its environmental impact.

- What impact would these solutions have on people's freedom of choice?

### KEY WORDS

**agriculture:** the cultivation of animals, plants and fungi for food and other products used to sustain human life

**fertiliser:** a natural or artificial material added to the soil to increase its fertility

**pesticide:** a chemical used to control pests, but also, less accurately, used as a collective term to describe pest and disease-killing chemicals

**genetically modified organism (GMO):** an organism whose genetic material has been altered by genetic engineering

## CONTINUED

**Discussion questions**

1 Why is increasing the area used for agriculture not a sustainable option for meeting the demand for more food?

2 Should food production focus on foods that can be grown more efficiently rather than providing a variety of different flavours?

# 3.1 Soils and crop growth

Soil is fundamental to the growth of plants – and ultimately to the success of all living creatures. Soil is a natural resource and needs careful management to keep it in good condition.

## The composition of soil

Soil is a habitat for plants and other organisms. It is made up of four main components:

- mineral particles, which are a combination of rock fragments and other smaller inorganic (non-living) items such as sand, silt and clay
- **organic** content, including living organisms that inhabit the soil (plants, animals, fungi and bacteria) and organic matter from decomposition (Figure 3.2)
- gases, which are held within the spaces (pores) between the particles and organic content of the soil
- water, which is also held within the soil pores (it is this water that enables plants to grow).

The proportion of each of these components varies depending on the type of soil, its mineral particles, the way it has been managed and local climatic conditions.

> **KEY WORD**
>
> **organic:** derived from living organisms

**Figure 3.2:** Living organisms play a part in decomposing the remains of other organisms, releasing nutrients that are then available for plants to use. These processes and the movement of soil animals (such as earthworms) make channels within the soil that allow the gases and water to be held in the soil pores.

# The importance of the composition of soils for crop growth

Most crops require a combination of factors to grow successfully. These include:

- nutrients
- anchorage to hold the roots securely in one place
- a supply of water
- oxygen around the roots to enable the root cells to respire.

The size of the mineral particles also affects the properties of soil, including how well it holds or drains water, its capacity to retain mineral nutrients, and the ease with which crops can grow in it. Particle size also affects how easy the soil is to cultivate.

## Mineral particles

Mineral particles can be classified into three groups, according to size:

- sand
- silt
- clay.

Sand is the largest mineral component of soil. Sand particles are between 0.02 mm and 2.0 mm in size. It is easy to see the individual grains with the naked eye, and sand feels gritty to the touch. The large size and irregular shape of the particles mean that they do not pack together easily, so there are large pores between the grains of sand; this allows water, air and soil organisms to move through sand easily.

Silt particles are smaller than those of sand – between 0.002 mm and 0.02 mm. Silt feels silky or soapy to the touch, and when rubbed between the fingers, the particles slip over each other easily.

Clay particles are the smallest mineral component – less than 0.002 mm in diameter. Their small size means that they pack closely together, making it harder for water to drain through the soil. When damp, clay particles feel sticky and they are easily moulded; when dry, they stick together solidly.

| Particle type | Size of particle | Texture | Characteristics |
|---|---|---|---|
| Sand | 0.02–2.0 mm | Feels gritty | Large pore sizes<br>Drains well<br>Contains large air spaces |
| Silt | 0.002–0.02 mm | Feels silky or soapy | Less friction than sand<br>Particles slippery |
| Clay | <0.002 mm | Sticky when wet | Particles held together tightly<br>Poor air spaces or drainage<br>Forms a hard mass when dried |

**Table 3.1:** A comparison of the three mineral components of soil.

---

### FIELDWORK ACTIVITY 3.1

**Classifying soil**

**You will need**

- a sample of well-sifted soil
- a small trowel or spoon
- a container
- a clear jar
- water

**Safety**

Wash your hands thoroughly before and after the activity.

**Before you start**

Get into groups of six, then join into pairs within your group. Each pair should follow one of the following three methods. Collect a soil sample from just below the surface. Each pair should use soil from the same sample in their investigation. Remove any large roots and stones from the sample before you start.

## CONTINUED

### Method 1: The feel test

- Put a sample of the soil into the container and add a small quantity of water.
- Roll the soil between your hands to make a ball (Figure 3.3).
- Rub the ball of soil between your thumb and fingers to feel its texture:
  - If it feels gritty, it contains a high proportion of sand.
  - If it feels soapy, it contains a high proportion of silt.
  - If it feels sticky, it contains a high proportion of clay.

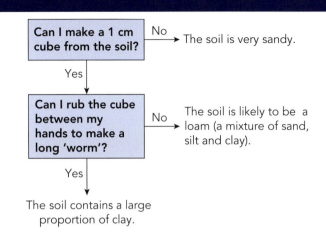

The soil contains a large proportion of clay.

**Figure 3.4:** Flow chart for classifying soil.

**Figure 3.3:** After rolling the soil into a ball, rub it between your thumb and fingers to see how it feels. This will give an indication of the balance of sand, silt and clay.

### Method 2: The moulding test

- Put a sample of the soil into the container.
- Use the water to just moisten the soil – it should not be too wet.
- **Determine** the components of the soil, using the flow chart in Figure 3.4.

> **COMMAND WORD**
>
> **determine:** establish an answer using the information available

### Method 3: The jar test

- Take a sample of the soil and sift it to remove all the stones.
- Add soil into the clear jar until it is approximately one-third full.
- Add water to almost fill the jar.
- Shake the jar vigorously for 2 minutes, then put it down and allow the contents to settle.
- Look at the different soil components (Figure 3.5 shows what the results might look like).

**Figure 3.5:** Components of soil separated out by shaking a sample of soil in a jar of water. The heaviest items fall to the bottom first. Clay particles are so small that they can remain floating in the water for a long time, but they will settle out over a few days.

> CAMBRIDGE IGCSE™ AND O LEVEL ENVIRONMENTAL MANAGEMENT: COURSEBOOK

### CONTINUED

**Questions**

In your groups of six, draw up a table of your results and compare the different tests.

1. Which method do you think gives the best results? Why? Discuss in your groups.
2. Suggest two ways in which this investigation could be improved to ensure that the soil composition of the area is assessed accurately.

### FIELDWORK TIP

When asked to make comparisons, make sure that potential variables are reduced as much as possible. In this activity, the potential variable is the soil sample itself, which is why you were all instructed to use soil from the same sample.

The decision as to which method is most accurate is more challenging. Tests 1 and 2 are based on opinion (qualitative judgements), whereas test 3 could be measured (a quantitative judgement). This means that the results in your group are likely to be closer with test 3 compared to the opinions from tests 1 and 2.

### REFLECTION

How can preliminary work help you to improve your investigation? Think about any difficulties you had with this investigation and note down how you could avoid them in the future.

## Nutrient content

### Soil organic content

The organic content of soil is a combination of living organisms, their waste products and their dead remains. A range of **decomposers** (organisms that break down organic matter) take part in complex interactions that eventually return the nutrients contained within dead matter to a form that plants can use as nutrients (see 'Inorganic ions').

Many different types of organisms are involved in the breakdown of organic matter:

- Earthworms help break down vegetation by digesting it as it passes through their bodies and excreting the remains.
- Fungi feed directly on dead matter and are particularly good at breaking down tough materials, such as woody items (Figure 3.6).
- Bacteria work on organic material at a smaller scale, converting waste products into simple chemicals that can be used by plants.

**Figure 3.6:** Fungi are valuable decomposers, able to break down tough organic matter in soil.

Organic matter also affects the characteristics of the soil. High levels of organic matter have the following positive effects:

- It increases the water-holding capacity of a well-drained soil, absorbing additional water when it is available and releasing it when it is required by plants. This means less **irrigation** is required.

### KEY WORDS

**decomposer:** an organism within an ecosystem that derives its food from the bodies of dead organisms

**irrigation:** the addition of water to a soil

90

- It increases the spaces in the soil. The open, sponge-like structure of organic matter allows air to penetrate, providing gases that are essential for growth processes, including oxygen for respiration.
- It increases the number of decomposer organisms – more organic matter means a more abundant food source. For example, having more worms increases the number of tunnels or burrows in the soil, providing additional drainage and less compaction.
- It prevents the loss of nutrients. Some nutrients are washed away (leached) in excess water. **Humus** – the material left after organic matter has been partially decomposed – can hold onto nutrients until they are needed by plants.

**Inorganic ions**

Plants need carbon dioxide and water in order to produce sugars, which they use mainly as a source of energy. They also require a supply of nitrogen, phosphorus and potassium to construct proteins, and other chemicals to carry out plant processes. These nutrients are typically obtained through the roots of the plant.

In element form, nitrogen and phosphorus are not accessible to a plant, so when scientists talk about the application of nitrogen and phosphorus, they really mean the oxides of these elements, supplied as **compounds**. Potassium, however, is taken up as potassium ions ($K^+$). When dissolved in water, these compounds split, making the ions of the minerals available for uptake by the plant roots (Table 3.2).

| Element name (and symbol) | Supplied as inorganic ion |
|---|---|
| Nitrogen (N) | Nitrate ions ($NO_3^-$) |
| Phosphorus (P) | Phosphate ions ($PO_4^{3-}$) |
| Potassium (K) | Potassium ions ($K^+$) |

**Table 3.2:** The three major nutrients needed by plants.

## Soil pH

The uptake of nutrients by plant roots is affected by the pH of the soil – a measure of its acidity or alkalinity. In absolute terms, the **pH scale** runs from pH 1 (acid) to pH 14 (alkaline). However, soils are only likely to be at the extremes of this scale after major chemical spills or pollution incidents.

The pH of a soil may depend on a number of factors, but in most cases the biggest influence is the type of rock from which the mineral particles are formed or the pH of the water that flows into the area via rivers or lakes. The range of typical pH values found in soil is shown in Figure 3.7.

> **KEY WORDS**
>
> **humus:** dark earth made of organic matter, such as decayed leaves and plants
>
> **compound:** a chemical that combines two or more elements
>
> **pH scale:** a measure of the acidity or alkalinity of a substance, such as soil

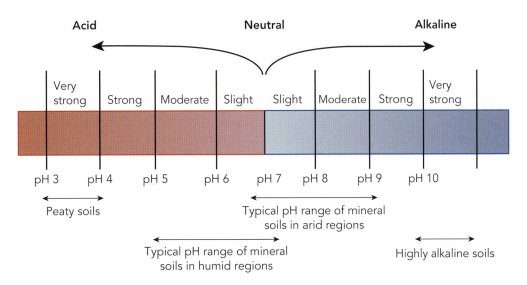

**Figure 3.7:** A scale showing the range of soil pH normally recorded.

| Plant nutrient | Symptoms of deficiency include | Example |
|---|---|---|
| Nitrogen ($NO_3^-$) | Slow growth, yellowing leaves (oldest first) | |
| Phosphorus ($PO_4^{3-}$) | Leaves dull with blue-green colour; leaves fall early | |
| Potassium ($K^+$) | Poor-quality fruits and seeds; leaves with brown edges | |

Table 3.3: Common signs of major nutrient deficiencies in plants.

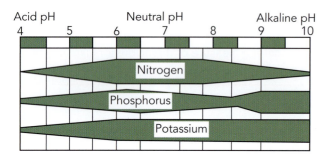

Figure 3.8: The availability of some mineral ions to plants at different soil pH levels.

Some plants do not grow well in certain soils, even when they are supplied with additional fertiliser. For example, sweet potatoes grow better in soil of pH 5.0–5.5 than they do in a more alkaline soil of pH 8. Grown at a pH of 8, sweet potato plants show signs of **nutrient deficiency** (such as yellow leaves), even though the farmer may have provided enough nutrients. The symptoms of mineral nutrient deficiencies vary from plant to plant, but there are some common signs (Table 3.3).

While every plant has its own preferred soil pH, not all nutrients are taken up equally because pH affects their availability. Figure 3.8 shows this effect. At a soil pH of 8.5, there will probably be fewer nitrogen ions and phosphorus ions than there would be at a soil pH of 6 (where the bars in Figure 3.8 are wide). At a pH of 8.5, there is no impact on the availability of potassium ions.

The pH of a soil also has an impact on the well-being of the decomposers that live in it. Different organisms thrive in different conditions, so changing the soil pH can affect the ability of these organisms to break down organic matter effectively.

### KEY WORD

**nutrient deficiency:** the shortage of an important mineral ion essential for healthy growth

## FIELDWORK ACTIVITY 3.2

### Testing soil pH

**You will need**

- a sample of well-sifted soil
- test tubes
- a spatula
- distilled water
- filter paper and funnel
- universal indicator test strips
- pH chart of universal indicator
- gloves

**Safety**

Be aware of sharp stones in the soil sample. Wash your hands after handling soil and test strips, and wear gloves when handling chemicals.

**Before you start**

Select samples of soils from a range of areas in the test location. Choose soil from below the soil surface (in case of surface contamination). Before you start, sift the soil to remove large stones.

**Method**

- Take a small quantity of soil – enough to half fill a test tube using a spatula.
- Top up the test tube with distilled water and shake vigorously for 2 minutes.
- Allow the solution to settle.
- Filter the liquid into another test tube using the funnel and filter paper.
- Test the filtered liquid with the pH test strip.
- Compare the colour on the strip with the colour chart to determine the pH of the solution (and the soil) (Figure 3.9).

**Figure 3.9:** pH test strips are a convenient way of testing the pH of a solution.

**Questions**

1. Was it easy to judge the colour of the solution?
2. Why was distilled water used and not water from another source?
3. Why is it important to select soil from a range of areas and from below the soil surface?

### FIELDWORK TIP

Figure 3.9 shows the pH test in action. The use of gloves not only protects the tester from the risk of toxic materials, but also prevents any substances on their hands affecting the pH of the sample. Using a spatula to fill the test tube also removes another risk of an anomalous (inconsistent) result.

## Pore spaces

Pore spaces are essential for the health of the soil, as they allow water to flow within it and for gases to move between the soil particles. While water tends to adhere (stick) to the mineral components of a soil, large spaces are required to allow excess water to drain away. Figure 3.10 shows the impact of soil particle size on pore spaces.

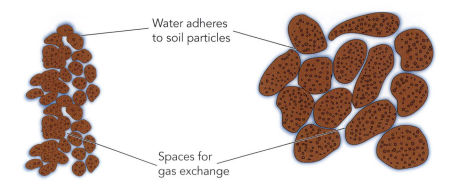

**Figure 3.10:** Soils with large pore sizes tend to be better drained, but they are at greater risk of drought. Soils with smaller pores have a better water-holding capacity, but they are more prone to becoming waterlogged.

Farmers can encourage the best proportion of pore spaces by adding organic matter as needed. This material usually has a larger particle size than the soil, which increases the opportunity for drainage and gas exchange.

## Gas content

All plant cells need oxygen to respire. Without access to this gas, the cells will die. The plant cells in the root of the plant therefore need a supply of oxygen to keep them healthy. Soils with large air pores, such as those with a higher proportion of sand particles, allow for good gas exchange. This provides the oxygen these cells need and removes the excess carbon dioxide produced during the respiration process.

## Water content and drainage

Water is also essential to plant growth. The majority of this is taken up by the plant roots. After heavy rain, the soil may contain large volumes of water, some of which will drain away via the pore spaces in the soil. However, some will be held between the soil particles, and some will also be attracted to the soil particles themselves, meaning that moisture will be available to plants after the water has drained. Soils with a higher proportion of sand tend to drain more easily, as the pores are larger. Soils with a higher proportion of small particles, such as clay, tend to drain less well and have a higher water content.

Humus, derived from organic matter, is also very good at holding water and will retain additional supplies for plants when surplus water has drained away.

## Ease of cultivation

The size of particles, the way they are compacted and the water content also influence how easy a soil is to cultivate. Soils with large particles, such as those with a large proportion of sand, tend to be less dense, so they require less energy to dig/cultivate. They are also easier to drain, so they can be worked sooner after rain. Soils with smaller particles, such as those with a higher clay content, tend to be better at retaining water (so less irrigation is needed). They also retain mineral nutrients better.

Depending on the crop and its particular growing needs, different soil compositions benefit different types of crop.

The addition of bulky organic matter into a soil improves its ease of cultivation, whatever the size of the particles (Figure 3.11). It does this by:

- increasing the water-holding capacity for well-drained soils
- increasing air spaces for poorly drained soils
- improving the general soil structure, making cultivation easier
- increases the number of soil organisms, which will improve soil fertility and structure.

The bulky organic matter may also contain essential nutrients needed by the plant to support its growth.

Figure 3.11: There is no single perfect soil, but farmers can alter a soil by adding organic matter and changing the soil pH. They can also grow plants that prefer the natural conditions of the soil.

## Loam – the ideal soil?

**Loam** soil combines sand, silt and clay, bringing together the benefits of the three main soil mineral particles while minimising many of their limitations:

- Pore spaces: An ideal combination of mineral particles means that pores provide enough space for excess water to drain through, giving the plant roots oxygen from the gases that will take its place.
- Retains moisture: The different-sized particles mean that water is also held via capillary action and by attraction to the mineral particles. As root cells need both oxygen and water, the composition of loam provides the correct growing conditions for longer.
- Inorganic ions and organic content: The best loam soils are very fertile. The combination of the different mineral particles and pore spaces encourages other organisms to flourish; they also need moisture and oxygen. This creates a constant cycle of growth and decomposition that will benefit the plants by providing extra nutrients.
- Drainage: The combination of pore size and a diverse range of soil organisms helps good drainage channels to develop and to remove excess water after heavy rain. This benefits all the organisms in the soil and helps it remain fertile. While plants can withstand waterlogged conditions for a short time, longer periods deprive roots of oxygen, preventing respiration and eventually causing root death.
- Cultivation: Loam soils are less prone to forming a hard surface than clay soils, so are easier to cultivate. Similarly, they will dry out less than more sandy soils, so will need less irrigation.

### KEY WORD

**loam:** a soil that is a mixture of sand, silt and clay, combining the best properties of each

## Questions

3.1 **Identify** the components of the soil that are solids.

3.2 Explain why the proportion of gas in soil varies in different weather conditions.

3.3 Explain how the nutrient content of the soil affects plant growth.

3.4 Explain how the addition of organic matter can improve crop growth.

3.5 Define the term 'nutrient deficiency'.

### COMMAND WORD

**identify:** name/select/recognise

## Weather and seasons

When scientists talk about **weather**, they mean the day-to-day conditions of the atmosphere in a particular location. The weather in different parts of the world can vary a great deal. Further away from the equator, there will tend to be greater differences in mean temperature during summer and winter. In many cases, low temperatures will restrict the growth processes in plants. Similarly, growth may be affected by the availability of rainfall.

### KEY WORD

**weather:** the day-to-day conditions of the atmosphere in a location

Certain parts of the world experience distinct **wet seasons** and **dry seasons**. While not always completely predictable, this pattern can determine when crops are best grown, with the aim of harvesting while there is still enough water for continued growth and when soil is not too waterlogged to allow for seeds to germinate effectively.

> **KEY WORDS**
>
> **wet season:** the time of year when most of the average rainfall occurs
>
> **dry season:** a period of low rainfall

## Weather conditions, photosynthesis and crop growth

All living organisms require certain conditions in order to grow. Unlike animals, plants manufacture their own energy supply through the process of photosynthesis (Figure 3.12). This mainly takes place in the leaves and requires the presence of the green pigment **chlorophyll**. The photosynthesis reaction allows the conversion of carbon dioxide and water into glucose and oxygen using energy from sunlight:

carbon dioxide + water → glucose + oxygen

**Figure 3.12:** In photosynthesis, light energy is captured and turned into chemical energy.

The speed of the photosynthesis reaction depends on:

- the availability of **reactants** (water and carbon dioxide)
- the amount of light energy available
- the temperature
- the availability of chlorophyll
- the size of the plant/leaf area.

Photosynthesis is covered in more detail in Chapter 6.

## Length of the growing season

The growing season is the time available for a plant to grow within the year, and it is dependent upon a combination of the correct temperatures and light levels. Countries further way from the equator tend to experience major differences between summer and winter, and a greater range of temperatures, light intensity and day length. All these factors impact the ability of a plant to photosynthesise. Some seeds, for example, may remain dormant until the correct conditions are provided, to prevent emergence in the incorrect growing season.

Locations where there is less variability will have longer growing seasons. This can be an advantage, as two crops could be grown in the same soil in a year, increasing productivity. Areas with shorter growing seasons may provide a more limited opportunity for growth and perhaps be unsuitable for some crops that take a long time to mature.

## Optimum weather conditions

Some crops are more tolerant of local weather conditions than others, so farmers often use local knowledge of different plant varieties to select the crops that are best suited to the area. For example, the cooler growing conditions of northern Europe are well suited to growing wheat, whereas countries nearer the equator do not experience frosts, making them more suited to growing crops such as bananas, which would be damaged by ice and snow.

It is usually possible to access records of local weather patterns, with detailed measurements of temperature, rainfall, day length and light intensity, all of which will have an impact on the rate of photosynthesis. The farmer can select a suitable crop type and variety to work with the local weather conditions. The farmer can also plan the planting or sowing time for these crops to optimise the weather conditions for both growth and harvesting.

Temperature is a key factor affecting rates of photosynthesis. In higher temperatures, the chemical reactions happen more rapidly, so the plant grows more quickly. At very low temperatures, plants may only

> **KEY WORDS**
>
> **chlorophyll:** the green pigment in plants that traps light energy
>
> **reactant:** a substance used in a chemical reaction

photosynthesise very slowly, meaning poor conditions for crop growing. Very few plants are adapted to cope with freezing conditions (lower than 0 °C), so low temperatures can damage a plant's cells and kill the crop.

Rainfall also affects rates of photosynthesis, as water is a key reactant in the formation of glucose. Water is also essential for a plant to carry out other processes. Plant cells themselves contain a large percentage of water, which is key to maintaining the plant's rigid structure. This is why the leaves on plants that do not have enough water will droop (wilt; Figure 3.13) – and drooping leaves are not arranged in a position to optimise the collection of sunlight.

**Figure 3.13:** Not enough rainfall can result in leaves drying out and wilting.

Too much water may also be a problem for crop growth. Excessive surface run-off due to heavy rain may erode the soil and dislodge plants, particularly in their early stages of growth. If the soil becomes flooded, pores can be filled with water. If this persists, the cells in the plant root will not have access to the oxygen they usually get from the gas in the soil. Without oxygen, the plant is unable to break down glucose to release energy. While other parts of the plant may receive oxygen from the atmosphere, a lack of oxygen in the soil causes the root to die off.

Other weather conditions may also be important factors. Increased wind speeds increase the rate of transpiration from the leaves of the plant, meaning that additional water will need to be taken from the soil to replace it. Increased wind speed may also increase the rate of evaporation at the soil surface, which will reduce the volume of water available to plants.

## Daylight hours

Photosynthesis is more efficient when light intensity is good and days are long. The shorter winter days in many countries north and south of the tropical regions mean that plants here have fewer hours in a day to photosynthesise. While it may not prevent them from growing, they may grow less rapidly than plants that receive longer daylight hours. Some plants also need a minimum day length to produce their crop. Without sufficient day length, these crops may not flower or ripen their seeds.

Table 3.4 compares the requirements of some crops that are grown in different parts of the world. Rice, bananas and maize will all grow within the same temperature ranges, but rice needs far more water, so it can be successfully grown in warm areas with high rainfall or a plentiful water supply. By comparison, wheat prefers cooler temperatures and is the only one of the four crops that could be grown in places that occasionally experience frost and ice.

| Plant | Preferred temperature range (°C) | Minimum temperature (°C) | Water needed to produce 1 kg of crop / dm$^3$ | Soil type |
|---|---|---|---|---|
| Wheat | 22–24 | –15 | 1400 | Well-drained loam |

| Plant | Preferred temperature range (°C) | Minimum temperature (°C) | Water needed to produce 1 kg of crop / dm³ | Soil type |
|---|---|---|---|---|
| Rice | 25–35 | 15 | 2500 | High in clay and silt; good water-holding capacity |
| Banana | 20–30 | 15 | 790 | Well-drained loam |
| Maize | 25–28 | 8 | 1250 | Sandy to loam soil |

Table 3.4: A comparison of the needs of different crops.

## ACTIVITY 3.1

Copy and complete the following table, which shows typical weather conditions. Tick the column relating to the most likely effect these conditions will have on photosynthesis and crop growth.

| Weather conditions | Increases photosynthesis | Remains the same | Decreases photosynthesis |
|---|---|---|---|
| Sunny conditions | | | |
| Heavy rain | | | |
| Drought | | | |
| Cloudy | | | |
| Fog/mist | | | |
| Short daylight hours | | | |
| Snow and ice | | | |
| Weak winds | | | |

> **REFLECTION**
>
> What strategies have you found most useful in remembering information about weather conditions, photosynthesis and crop growth? Share your strategies with a partner.

## 3.2 Food production and crop yield

Agriculture is typically defined as 'the cultivation of animals, plants and fungi for food and other products used to sustain human life'. It is relatively easy to identify the food items, but the 'other products' can include growing timber in a plantation for house-building or fuel, growing plants to produce medicines, breeding fish for fish oils, or growing roses to produce table decorations in restaurants.

## Types of agriculture

The types of agriculture used in different parts of the world depend on a number of factors, including:

- climate
- technology
- culture
- economics.

With such a range of different farming products, grown in different ways, it is useful to group types of agriculture together using various classifications.

### Subsistence farming and commercial farming

**Subsistence farming** is the cultivation and production of food to meet the needs of the farmer growing it and their family. There is very little surplus food; if there is any surplus, it is often exchanged (bartered) for other things that the family needs and perhaps a small amount of cash. Subsistence farmers aim to grow almost everything they need.

**Commercial farming** is the cultivation of products with the main focus of selling them for cash (Figure 3.14). Commercial farmers aim to grow crops to obtain money to buy the things they need. While some of the food may be used by the farmer (and their family), this is only a very small proportion compared with the amount that is sold.

**Figure 3.14:** Commercial farms often use technology and large machines to increase yields and reduce the costs of production.

> **ACTIVITY 3.2**
>
> In pairs, research an example of a subsistence farm and a commercial farm, using the internet or any other resources available. Suggest reasons why each type of farming takes place in that location.
>
> Using your research, create an information poster that compares and contrasts the two types of farming. Use images to support your observations.
>
> Display your posters around the classroom, then walk around this 'exhibition' to see what other pairs have included in their posters.

> **KEY WORDS**
>
> **subsistence farming:** agricultural production focused on supplying the family with food
>
> **commercial farming:** agricultural production focused on selling the produce for a profit

## Arable farming and pastoral farming

Another way of describing farming is by the type of product.

**Arable farming** is the production of plants for consumption by humans. Examples include growing rice, maize, wheat and soybeans. The scale of production (the size and number of fields) can vary greatly, and there are examples of subsistence arable farmers and commercial arable farmers.

**Pastoral farming** is the production of animals or animal-related products. This may also be known as livestock farming or grazing (Figure 3.15). Plants such as grass or grain may be grown on the farm but they will be used to feed the animals. Pastoral farms can produce meat or other animal by-products, such as milk, wool or eggs.

A third type of farming exists: farms that grow crops for food as well as rear livestock. This is commonly referred to as **mixed farming**.

**Figure 3.15:** Sheep are raised on livestock or pastoral farms.

## Intensive farming

Farm production can also be described by evaluating the relative yield compared with the size of space used and the types of plants that are cultivated.

**Intensive farming** is where large amounts are produced from smaller areas of land (Figure 3.16). This style of production tends to have high inputs in terms of labour, fertilisers or machinery.

Intensive farming is often very efficient, so why is it not used more widely? Various factors influence this. While yields are high, so are the costs involved, which can be a barrier for many farmers. Similarly, some people prefer to avoid intensive farming on ethical or environmental grounds. It can negatively affect local ecosystems and, in the case of livestock, there are welfare issues associated with keeping animals in small, confined spaces (Figure 3.17).

**Figure 3.16:** In intensive farming, plants such as lettuces are grown close together to prevent wasted space. The crop is designed to be sold, as there would be too much for a family to consume.

**Figure 3.17:** Chickens kept for intensive egg production. While this is very space efficient, some people dislike this type of production as animals are kept in unnatural conditions.

> **KEY WORDS**
>
> **arable farming:** the production of crops from land
>
> **pastoral farming:** farming that focuses on breeding and rearing livestock
>
> **mixed farming:** farming that practises both rearing livestock and growing crops
>
> **intensive farming:** farming that aims to maximise the yield from an area by using a large amount of resources

## Monoculture

**Monoculture** is a method of farming where only one crop is grown in a field at a time. Many farmers using this technique will often grow this one crop across all their land. This has the benefit of developing advanced skills and knowledge about that crop, which may help to maximise yield. Monoculture often leads to the development of larger fields, which enables larger machinery to cultivate the crop more efficiently, as it will all be ready for harvest at one time. The risk with this approach is that the entire crop would be susceptible to a pest or disease. Monoculture is not confined purely to food crops – for example, commercial forests may be planted with only one type of tree to make harvesting and management easier.

The types of farming discussed previously can be combined. For example, you might have an intensive, commercial, arable farm, which may include the use of monoculture, or a subsistence, pastoral farm.

> **KEY WORD**
>
> **monoculture:** the practice of growing only one crop or keeping only one type of animal on an area of farmland

# Increasing food production and crop yields

The world's population is predicted to increase to 9.7 billion people by 2050, having reached 8 billion in 2022. This is an increase of 21%. The associated need for an increase in food production, when additional land is not always easily available, will mean that there will be an increased focus on different techniques to increase the efficiency of current production systems.

## Mixed cropping, intercropping and crop rotation

### Mixed cropping

In many parts of the world, monoculture – the planting of just one crop in an area – is less common than mixed cropping, which involves growing more than one type of plant. This has several benefits. It means that the resources in the soil, such as nutrients, are used more efficiently. If the plants grow at different heights, for example, they can use the same space without too much competition. If one plant has a deeper root system, it can be grown in the same area as a plant with a shallower root system. A smaller, sturdier plant can act as a support for a taller, more unstable crop.

### Intercropping

**Intercropping** is when rows of different crops are grown in between established rows of a main crop (Figure 3.18). Typically of shorter duration than other types of mixed cropping, intercropping is intended to maximise the use of space and other resources in a field. It is often used in new plantations when the main tree crop will take a while to mature. Other plants can be grown at ground level and provide a profit for the farmer while the main plantation matures.

**Figure 3.18:** An example of intercropping – here, pineapples are being grown in the gaps between young rubber trees to maximise the space and prevent soil erosion.

> **KEY WORD**
>
> **intercropping:** the technique of growing other crops between the rows of a main crop, maximising the use of nutrients and water

## Crop rotation

**Crop rotation** means growing different types of plants in different plots each year. Related groups of plants are grown together during a season. Then, at the start of the next season, they are moved to a fresh plot of land that has just been used for a different plant group. There is a planned sequence to the rotation.

Growing the same type of plant in the same plot year after year often results in a decrease in yield over time. It can also cause:

- a build-up of diseases in the soil that affect plant growth
- an increase in the pests that attack the plants
- a depletion in soil nutrients, because the same crop uses the same ratio of nutrients each year.

Moving a crop to a different piece of land each year means that:

- diseases in the soil affecting that plant are left behind and have nothing to infect
- pests need to find the new site and so their numbers are reduced
- the soil in the new plot is more likely to have the nutrients the crop needs.

Some plants, known as **legumes**, contain nitrogen-fixing bacteria in their root nodules, which take nitrogen from the air and convert it into a form that the plant can use. This not only benefits the legume while it is growing but also adds to the nitrates of the soil for any crop that follows.

Figure 3.19 shows an example of a simple crop rotation and how each crop benefits another. In this example, a large plot of land has been divided into four smaller areas, each to contain a particular type of plant:

- Legumes: plants in the pea and bean family, which are able to fix nitrogen from the air using bacteria in nodules on their roots.
- Leafy crops: a range of vegetables grown for their leaves, which require a lot of nitrogen fertiliser (left in the soil by the legume roots). These plants are grown in a plot the season after legumes.
- Root crops: plants that have deep root systems, which help to break up the soil. A lot of soil cultivation is needed to harvest the roots. Legumes like well-cultivated soils and so benefit from being grown in a plot the season after root crops.
- Fallow: the land is left to rest, so no crops are grown.

While the original planned rotation consisted of four plots, depending on the amount of land available, it is

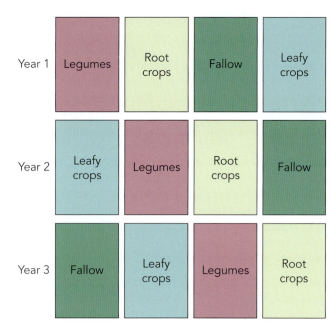

**Figure 3.19:** An example of a four-part crop rotation.

possible to use a three-plot system, without the fallow plot (when the ground is given a chance to replenish its resources naturally).

The process varies depending on the local seasons and crops grown, and crop rotation has been adapted to different situations. For example, some mixed farms include grazing in their rotation rather than the fallow plot, and the animals naturally fertilise the plot as they feed.

The use of crop rotation helps reduce the numbers of pests and diseases, and requires less fertiliser (if legumes are included). However, it is less useful if one of the crops to be grown has little commercial value (in the case of commercial production) or little nutritional value (in the case of subsistence farming), as this would impact the effectiveness of the land being cultivated. Another advantage to this system is that crops can be ready to harvest at different times, which means that the farmer needs less labour and less machinery overall.

### KEY WORDS

**crop rotation:** the practice of planting different crops on the same plot of land year after year to improve soil health, make efficient use of nutrients, and reduce pests and diseases

**legumes:** plants that contain nitrogen-fixing bacteria in their roots to produce a source of nitrates

## Improved methods of irrigation

Farming accounts for almost 70% of the water used in the world today, so it is important that the agriculture industry uses water efficiently and responsibly.

## Drip (trickle) systems

Drip systems – sometimes called 'trickle systems' – use a series of flat polythene hoses laid onto the surface of the soil between the rows of crops. When additional irrigation is needed, water is transported to these hoses through pipes and released slowly at the soil surface via tiny holes in the hoses. Some systems have microtubes (emitters), which allow water to drip directly onto the plant. An example layout is shown in Figure 3.20. Table 3.5 compares the advantages and disadvantages of this system.

## Rainwater harvesting

Many farmers look for opportunities to store water while it is abundant for use later when it is in short supply. Rainwater can be collected from field **run-off** or from the roofs of buildings. This is known as **rainwater harvesting**. Rainwater is transferred by pipes or drains to a water storage facility, such as a water tank or reservoir. However, large expanses of open water are at risk of evaporation in high temperatures, and they are also a potential breeding ground for the *Anopheles* mosquito, which spreads malaria. Underground or covered sources are more expensive to develop but suffer from less water loss.

| Advantages | Disadvantages |
|---|---|
| Water is placed directly at the base of the plant | Expensive to install and complex to maintain |
| The system can be automated and controlled via computers | Small particles such as grit can block tubes |
| Water is used very efficiently | Inflexible: cannot easily be moved |

**Table 3.5:** Advantages and disadvantages of drip irrigation systems.

> **KEY WORDS**
>
> **run-off:** the process by which water runs over the ground into rivers
>
> **rainwater harvesting:** the collection of rainwater – for example, from the roofs of buildings – and storage in a tank or reservoir for later use

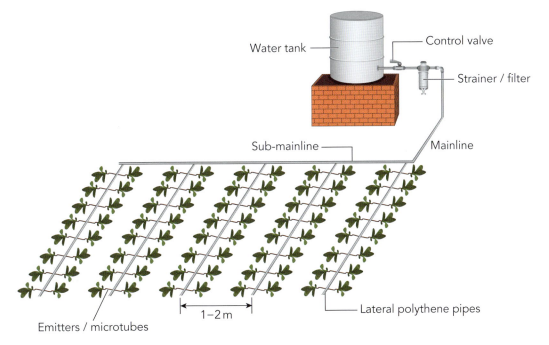

**Figure 3.20:** An example of a drip irrigation system. Plants are watered directly through either microtubes (emitters) or a porous hose.

> **CAMBRIDGE IGCSE™ AND O LEVEL ENVIRONMENTAL MANAGEMENT: COURSEBOOK**

> **SUSTAINABILITY TIP**
>
> In most parts of the world, water is a valuable resource. In some countries, it is in short supply and/or it is costly to purchase potable (drinkable) water. If you grow any crops at home, look at the way they are irrigated:
>
> - Are there ways of using water more effectively?
> - Could the savings in water use be easily measured?

when there is more water in the soil (so it is heavier), which extends the cultivating season.

**Figure 3.22:** Monitoring of the conditions in a crop of sunflowers allows water to be applied automatically when the computer identifies it is needed for optimal growth.

**Figure 3.21:** Digging a new well will provide additional water supplies for irrigation, but it is also needed for other purposes.

As well as basic cultivation tasks, attachments can be added to a tractor to allow efficient application of fertilisers or pesticides. Tractors also have the capacity to transport large loads, which is useful at harvest time.

Large machines work best in large fields, because time is lost when they need to change direction. This has led to the removal of natural vegetation, such as trees and hedges, so that the big machines can operate smoothly, which can affect biodiversity in an area.

## Automated watering systems

Technology means that crops can be monitored 24 hours a day, to identify their optimum growing conditions, whether they are growing in a greenhouse or in a field. Recording devices placed in the field will monitor soil moisture, temperature and light levels (Figure 3.22). A computer can identify when additional irrigation is needed, and this can be applied without the farmer's input. Such technology can be a considerable investment, but it means there is less risk of providing too little or too much water to the crop, and it saves the farmer time.

**Figure 3.23:** One tractor can do the same work in a day as many people.

## Genetically modified organisms

Farmers have always tried to develop new varieties of crop plants. Traditionally, this was done by selecting the best examples of plants or livestock and using these to produce the next generation. However, it was often many generations before any significant changes could be seen.

Genetic modification gets faster results. Technology has enabled scientists to map the genetic material (DNA) of different plant and animal species, which has given

## Mechanisation

In the past, growing many types of crop was labour intensive, and the available workforce limited the amount of land that could be cultivated. Since the introduction of machines such as tractors, larger areas can be cultivated more easily by one person (Figure 3.23). Machine power makes work like ploughing much easier them a greater understanding of how short sections of DNA called **genes** relate to the characteristics of a living organism. Scientists can insert a piece of DNA from one organism into the genetic code of another to create a genetically modified organism (GMO).

There are many different reasons for genetically modifying plant species:

- Disease and pest resistance – genes can be cut from a resistant plant and added to a crop plant.
- Nutritional value – plants can be developed that are more nourishing.
- Allow the growth of plants in inhospitable areas.
- Higher yields.
- Herbicide resistance, which would allow farmers to spray the whole crop and its weeds but only affect the weeds.
- Less use of pesticides, if the GMO plant is pest resistant.
- Grow crops with longer storage lives, leading to less food wastage.

Concerns about the development of GMOs include:

- the unknown impact of the new characteristics on human health
- the products are not natural
- the genes might get into wild plants if they interbreed with GMOs
- issues for other insects caused by insect-resistant varieties.

## Controlled environments

One of the largest variables affecting crop yield is the growing environment – for livestock as well as crops. Over very large areas, it can be difficult or expensive to try to control the environment. Over smaller areas, it is possible to invest more money in controlling the environment, resulting in a product that can be sold for a high price and so make a profit.

### Greenhouses

**Greenhouse** is a collective term for structures that support the controlled growth of plants. Many greenhouses use transparent plastic sheets made from, for example, a polycarbonate, which is stronger than glass and often sold as a double-walled material, providing good insulation against colder external air temperatures, reducing the cost of the internal heating (Figure 3.24).

**Figure 3.24:** Built with an aluminium frame, the sides of this modern greenhouse are constructed of glass and the roof of double-walled polycarbonate (which is stronger and a better insulator than glass). The mixture of glass and polycarbonate mean this cannot be described as a 'glasshouse'.

The term 'greenhouse' also includes structures such as polythene tunnels (polytunnels), where plastic film is stretched over large metal hoops (Figure 3.25). These are cheaper to install than more robust greenhouses, but they are not as effective in controlling the environment and do not last as long.

**Figure 3.25:** A polythene tunnel (polytunnel) is a relatively cheap structure that is commonly used for growing food crops.

### KEY WORDS

**gene:** a sequence of DNA that is responsible for a characteristic of a living organism

**greenhouse:** a building made of glass or similar transparent material that is used to manage the environment for plant growth

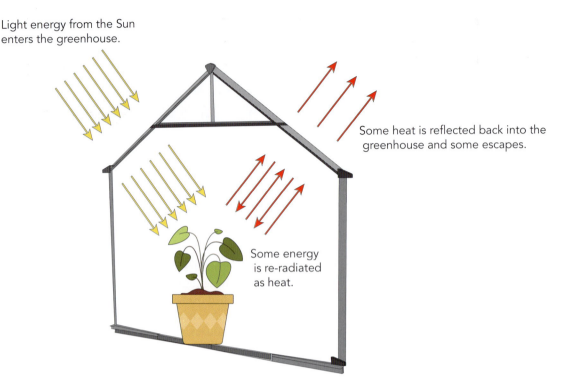

Figure 3.26: How a greenhouse works: light energy is re-radiated as heat, and some of that heat is reflected back into the greenhouse, enhancing plant growth.

All greenhouse structures work in the same way. Sunlight passes through the glass (or other transparent material). Moving through this material causes the wavelength of the energy to change, converting a proportion of the energy into heat. Once inside the greenhouse, the heat is trapped, so the inside temperature becomes warmer than outside (Figure 3.26). Glass is more effective than plastic in converting the sun's light energy into heat.

Greenhouses allow growers to manage many different environmental conditions, which are summarised in Table 3.6.

### Hydroponics

Soil is very variable so farmers may need to make modifications to turn it into an ideal growing environment. At a large scale, this is not cost-effective, but it can be worthwhile within a greenhouse. Scientists have developed a range of different composts and growing media that can remove the need for soil completely. The plants are grown in a material that is the same for each crop and which provides an ideal structure. This successful technique has been taken even further: growing plants using just water and dissolved nutrients. This is called **hydroponics**.

One of the most common hydroponic techniques is to float plants on polystyrene rafts on a reservoir of moving water (Figure 3.27). Water flows through the roots of the plants and is recycled. Sensors measure the amount of key nutrients in the water and add more as they are needed. Air is bubbled into the nutrient solution to ensure the plant roots have enough oxygen to respire.

---

**KEY WORD**

**hydroponics:** growing plants without soil, with the nutrients the plant needs dissolved in water

## 3 Land

| Growth factor | How it might be increased | How it might be decreased |
|---|---|---|
| Temperature | Operate greenhouse heating system | Open roof ventilators |
| Light level | Use supplementary lighting | Use shading material in the roof |
| Humidity | Use misting units to add moisture to the air | Open roof ventilators or use extractor fans |
| Day length | Use supplementary lighting at the end of the day | Use shading material in the roof and curtains at the side |
| Water | Use a sprinkler or irrigation system | Install drainage material underneath the pots or beds |

**Table 3.6:** How greenhouses help to manage growing factors.

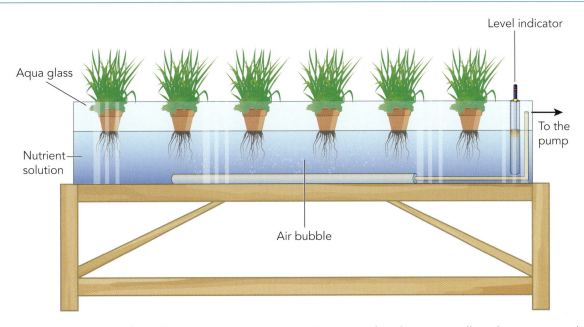

**Figure 3.27:** An example of a hydroponic growing system. Sensors within the system allow the process to be automated once it is set up.

Table 3.7 outlines some of the advantages and disadvantages of hydroponics.

| Advantages | Disadvantages |
|---|---|
| No need for soil. | Expensive to set up. |
| Can be used anywhere (there are even experiments being carried out in space). | Only suitable for small production areas. |
| It is an intensive system that can provide high yields. | Requires a lot of technical knowledge. |
| Easy to harvest. | Any diseases present will rapidly spread through the water supply to all plants. |
| Plants get exactly the nutrients they need in the irrigation water. | Plants can die quickly if conditions are not maintained at optimum levels. |
| Water is recycled, so it is used efficiently. | |
| There are no weeds, pests or diseases in the 'soil'. | |
| No pollutants are released into the environment. | |

**Table 3.7:** The advantages and disadvantages of hydroponics.

**Aeroponics**

In aeroponics, rather than the plant roots coming into direct contact with water, they are sprayed with a fine mist of water, which contains the mineral nutrients the plant requires for optimum growth. This gives the roots water and sufficient oxygen to allow for effective respiration in the root cells. There are some limitations to aeroponics, however. It is a more difficult and expensive system to install, and care must be taken to ensure that the nozzles spraying the fine mist do not become blocked, as this would prevent the plant from receiving sufficient water.

## Questions

3.6 State two ways in which the use of large machines can increase the yield from an area of land.

3.7 State two reasons why some people are concerned about using genetic modification to develop new varieties of crops or livestock.

3.8 Explain how the rate of photosynthesis may be increased within a greenhouse.

3.9 State two benefits and two limitations of using a hydroponic system to grow crops.

3.10 Describe why each of the following components is needed in a hydroponic growing system to enable effective plant growth:
- nutrients
- consistent water supply
- aeration of roots.

## Managing grazing

Too much grazing of an area weakens vegetation and can lead to its death if it is not given a chance to recover (Figure 3.28). The situation becomes worse in extreme weather conditions, such as periods of drought or excessive rain. Animals' hooves also compact the soil and trample plants.

To prevent these problems, farmers can allow specific areas of land time to regrow, effectively rotating the land that the animals have access to. Damage to the soil and the natural vegetation can also be limited by reducing the number of animals kept in an area.

**Figure 3.28:** A comparison of grazed and ungrazed land in Australia. The grazed area on the right does not contain any small plants or shrubs. When the rains return in the wet season, there is an increased risk of soil erosion where plants are not present to hold the soil.

## Urban farming

Any available land can potentially be used to grow crops or keep livestock, including in towns and cities. For centuries, families have grown additional crops or kept livestock to supplement other food sources. More recently, the idea of producing crops in urban areas has been adapted to use new techniques such as hydroponics or protected structures, which provide all the plants' requirements (Figure 3.29). Urban farming allows food to be cultivated in places where supplies may be limited due to transportation difficulties, for example.

**Figure 3.29:** This facility is growing crops in an underground space below a city using artificial light and hydroponics.

# 3 Land

## Agroforestry

Agroforestry is a specific type of mixed cropping in which crops are grown among trees (Figure 3.30). The foliage of the trees will often help protect the crops underneath from extreme weather. Planting of crops below the trees helps to maximise the space available but also will provide additional vegetation coverage to help reduce the risk of soil erosion when heavy rains occur.

**Figure 3.31:** Animal manure is an example of an organic fertiliser. Its bulky nature means that it is also useful for improving the properties of the soil.

**Figure 3.30:** Agroforestry allows for more than one crop to be grown in an area at the same time. Here, beans are being grown at the base of bananas. The bananas provide the beans with shade. The beans (a legume) provide the bananas with additional nitrates.

Manure and compost are quite bulky because they contain a large amount of organic matter, which means they are also good soil improvers, increasing the water-holding capacity of sandy soils and the number of air spaces in compacted, clay soils (see 'Ease of cultivation').

Bulky organic matter is also used as a **mulch** to be applied around crops. Applying the organic material as a thick layer reduces evaporation from the soil underneath and also helps supress weeds from growing to compete with the crop. Over time, soil organisms will incorporate this organic mulch into the soil, improving the soil structure too.

## Inorganic and organic fertilisers

Fertilisers contain minerals such as nitrogen, potassium and phosphorus, which are essential for healthy plant growth. When used correctly, fertilisers increase crop yield because they add to the nutrients already present in the soil. The wide range of fertilisers available is often classified into two groups: organic and inorganic.

### Inorganic (NPK) fertilisers

Inorganic fertilisers are made in factories (Figure 3.32). Different plants need different ratios of nutrients for optimal growth, so manufacturers use different mixes of ingredients to make the fertilisers better suited for particular crops.

### Organic fertilisers

Organic fertilisers are substances derived from natural (typically living) sources. This is usually animal manures (Figure 3.31), but it also includes composted plant materials (crop residue). Other examples of organic fertilisers are bone meal (ground-up animal bones), hoof and horn (these parts of the animal ground up), or dried blood. If a farmer has a mixed farm, they may have a plentiful supply of manure to use on their crops.

> **KEY WORD**
>
> **mulch:** a thick layer of organic matter applied around plants that feeds, retains water and reduces weed growth

**Figure 3.32:** Inorganic fertilisers are manufactured in a factory. This allows them to be more consistent in their content and reliability.

Table 3.8 outlines some of the advantages and disadvantages of organic and inorganic fertilisers.

| Fertiliser type | Advantages | Disadvantages |
|---|---|---|
| Organic | Uses natural resources<br><br>Bulky types also supply organic matter to improve the soil | Can be unpleasant to handle<br><br>Bulky types are harder to transport<br><br>May be variable in composition |
| Inorganic | Can be manufactured to meet a particular crop's need<br><br>Can be easier to store | Cost of manufacture<br><br>Transportation costs |

**Table 3.8:** The advantages and disadvantages of different types of fertiliser.

The three major nutrients – nitrogen, phosphorus and potassium (NPK) – are needed in relatively large quantities. A shortage of any one of these nutrients means plants will not grow at the optimum rate. A significant shortage can result in a deficiency disease. Fertilisers provide the nutrients that help the plants build protein and also the final quality of the plants harvested.

Inorganic fertilisers are often cleaner and less unpleasant to handle than composts and manures. They are also less bulky, so they can be stored and transported more easily. Many intensive commercial farms use inorganic fertilisers because they are also more uniform in nutrients from batch to batch, easy to obtain and easier to apply to crops using machinery.

### ACTIVITY 3.3

In small groups, do some research to find two examples of organic fertilisers and two examples of inorganic fertilisers. For each fertiliser, note down:

- the proportion of each inorganic ion it supplies
- the crops it is best suited for
- how much it costs
- the rate at which it should be applied on a field.

Calculate the cost to apply to a field at the recommended rate.

In your groups, discuss how you would decide on which fertiliser would be the best choice for a named crop.

## Chemical control of pests

The growth of a crop plant can also be reduced by attacks from other organisms that can feed on it, weaken it and sometimes kill it. These organisms – insects, weeds and fungi – are collectively known as **pests**, and the chemicals used to control them (**insecticides**, **herbicides** and **fungicides**) are called pesticides.

**Weed control**

A weed is a plant that is growing in an inappropriate place, where it may cause problems. For example, 'jungle rice' (a grassy plant that is common throughout Asia) competes with cultivated rice because the two plants thrive in similar conditions (Figure 3.33). Jungle rice uses space and nutrients that the food crop needs.

In a system of crop rotation, weeds may also take the form of the previous year's food crop growing among the next crop. For example, if some potato tubers are missed during harvesting, they can survive in the soil, grow and shade the next crop (such as peas or beans), reducing that crop's yield.

Weeds need to be controlled because they:

- compete with crops for water, light and nutrients
- reduce the quality of a seed or grain crop (the weed's seeds affect the purity of the crop for sale)

### KEY WORDS

**pest:** an animal that attacks or feeds on a plant

**insecticide:** a chemical that kills insects

**herbicide:** a chemical used to control weeds

**fungicide:** a chemical used to control fungal diseases

# 3 Land

**Figure 3.33:** 'Jungle rice' (left) is a common weed among rice crops. It grows in a similar way so is difficult to remove from a field of rice (right).

- might be poisonous, either to livestock or to humans
- make cultivation difficult, tangling up tools and clogging up machines
- can block drainage systems with excessive growth
- can be a source of pests and diseases that also attack the crop
- can look untidy, which might have an impact in tourism areas.

Weed-killing chemicals (herbicides) can clear uncultivated areas of all previous vegetation before sowing or planting a crop, or to selectively kill weeds growing among a crop. Most herbicides are applied in a liquid form via a sprayer that splits the liquid into very fine droplets. These form a thin covering on the weeds, allowing the chemical to act. In windy conditions, droplets are likely to spread over a wide distance, meaning that farmers have to apply herbicides carefully so they do not damage the crop or other vegetation, impacting the local ecosystem (Figure 3.34). An alternative method is to use herbicide granules, which are heavy enough to fall to the ground when applied and do not stick to the leaves of most plants. The herbicide starts to act as the granules dissolve in the water within the soil.

Before using herbicides, a farmer needs to take the weather conditions into account. Wind affects the spray pattern, which can affect other plants. Heavy rain soon after application will wash the herbicide off the leaves of the weeds or cause the chemicals within granules to leach into the surrounding area. In extreme sunlight, droplets of herbicide can act like a lens and scorch foliage. In addition, some herbicides work more efficiently on plants that are actively growing, so in temperate climates these can only be applied during the growing season.

**Figure 3.34:** Herbicide sprays are effective at killing weeds, but they must be applied carefully in order not to harm the environment or the operator. Larger areas can be treated using sprayers mounted on tractors.

### Fungus control

A crop **disease** may be caused by fungi, bacteria or viruses (**pathogens**). Of these three groups, fungal diseases are most common in crops. Like herbicides, fungicides are usually applied as sprays to the leaves of a crop.

> **KEY WORDS**
>
> **disease:** a pathogen (fungus, bacterium or virus) that attacks a plant
>
> **pathogen:** a collective name to describe disease-causing organisms (bacteria, fungi and viruses)

111

Again, there is an environmental risk if fungicides are applied incorrectly because they will affect other organisms in the area. Many chemical control compounds can also be poisonous to humans, so farmers may need to wear personal protective equipment (PPE) while using them. If chemical residues remain in the crops, they can pose safety concerns if the concentrations get too high.

**Insect control**

The most common pests of plants are insects. A chemical used to control insects is called an insecticide. All parts of the plant may be vulnerable to insect attack – roots, stem, leaves, flowers, fruit and seeds – meaning that farmers need to closely monitor their plants. Rapid action is needed when insects are detected as many types breed very quickly, meaning that the problem can soon spread to the whole crop.

Insects may reduce the yield of a crop. Damage to leaves or roots may reduce the rate at which the plant can photosynthesise, meaning the crop is reduced, but damage may also reduce the quality of the crop or the ability of the crop to be stored (such as grain).

As with weeds and diseases, chemical controls are widely used, but there is a risk of non-target species also being affected.

## Biological control of pests

Chemical control of pests results in substantial increases in yield for farmers, so they are very popular. However, many people are concerned about the effect that pesticides have on the environment and ecosystems. For example, fewer insects means there is less food for their predators (small birds and reptiles). This in turn means there is less food for top consumers, such as birds of prey. In addition, the chemicals from pesticides do not break down in animals' bodies, so when they are eaten by predators, the chemicals can accumulate until they reach toxic amounts. For this reason, people are looking for natural, biological ways to control pests.

One option is to find natural predators of the pest that can be bred in large enough quantities. When introduced to a crop, they feed on the pest and therefore control the infestation. Common examples include:

- control of caterpillars (which eat the leaves of a crop) by a bacterium
- use of parasitic wasps to control insects that feed on the sap of plants
- use of chickens to eat insects that attack the roots of plants.

There are also examples of controlling weeds (such as using caterpillars that prefer only one type of plant; Figure 3.35) and fungi (by using other fungi, which specifically feed on the identified species).

Table 3.9 summarises some of the advantages and disadvantages of biological methods of controlling pests.

**Figure 3.35:** The caterpillar of the cinnabar moth is a natural predator of ragwort. Ragwort is poisonous to livestock. Farmers can use these caterpillars instead of herbicides to control this weed.

| Advantages | Disadvantages |
|---|---|
| No chemical residues are left in the crop. | The effect of the control is not as immediate as with chemical controls. |
| No impact of sprays on the surrounding ecosystem. | Climatic conditions might mean the pest breeds faster than the predator, so the problem is not controlled. |
| Once introduced, the population of the control agent should increase and breed, so there is no need for reapplication. | The predator might not stay on the crop and move elsewhere, instead of feeding on the intended pest. |
| When the pest has been controlled, the lack of food will mean the predator will naturally reduce in numbers. | The predator might escape into the local countryside and impact the natural ecosystem and food web. |
| There is no need to wear protective clothing when applying the predator. | |

**Table 3.9:** The advantages and disadvantages of biological methods of pest control.

# Questions

Research in North America has examined the impact of weeds on wheat – a very important crop for farmers in both the USA and Canada. These countries are major world producers and supply many other countries. Table 3.10 shows the results of this research.

|  | Mean yield loss / % | Potential loss of production / million kg | Potential loss in value / US$ million |
|---|---|---|---|
| **Winter wheat** | | | |
| USA | 25.4 | 10 511 | 2 193.7 |
| Canada | 2.9 | 93 | 19.6 |
| Total | 23.5 | 10 500 | 2 191.4 |
| **Spring wheat** | | | |
| USA | 33.2 | 4 843 | 1 135.3 |
| Canada | 8.0 | 1 566 | 367.2 |
| Total | 19.5 | 6 673 | 1 392.7 |

**Table 3.10:** A calculation of losses due to weeds in potential yields of winter and spring wheat.

3.11 Which country and type of wheat has the greatest percentage loss in potential yield?

3.12 Suggest why is the potential loss of wheat crops in Canada less than in the USA

3.13 A student says: 'Controlling weeds will mean that wheat will achieve its maximum yield.' Do you agree with this statement? Give reasons for your answer.

3.14 A farmer plans to control the weeds in the wheat crop shown in Figure 3.36 using a chemical herbicide. Explain why this would be the best method for this crop.

> **PROBLEM-SOLVING TIP**
>
> To accurately draw conclusions, it is important to check how valid the data is to the situation you are assessing. Ask yourself:
>
> - Who has published the research? Are they independent or are they funded by a group with a specific interest?
> - How was the information collected? Was the sample of a suitable size? Was the sample representative?
> - When was the research completed? Some situations change over time and the information may not be valid now.
> - Where was the location of the study? Observations in one part of the world may not be valid in other places due to difference in climate and biodiversity.
>
> In the example above, the data in the table may be relevant to wheat harvests in the USA and Canada, but may not be applicable if you are making a decision about rice harvests in Vietnam.

**Figure 3.36:** North American wheat is an important part of the global food supply.

## PEER ASSESSMENT

Assess how well you have understood all the different strategies to increase food production and crop yield. Write five quiz questions to ask the group on the subject. Make sure the questions are varied and cannot be answered with a simple 'yes' or 'no'. Make sure you know the correct answers. Have a quiz within your group where everyone must answer each other's questions.

# The impacts of unsustainable agricultural practices

Agriculture uses more land and water, and employs more people, than any other industry in the world. So, the sector has a significant responsibility towards our planet and its people. Mismanagement of farming systems can have a serious impact on Earth.

## Overproduction of food

Allowing farmers to choose which crops to grow can result in too much of a particular crop. When demand outstrips supply, farmers can charge more for their crops, but if a product is widely available and there is more of it than people want to buy, some of it may be wasted. If a farmer does not make a profit in a particular year, they may start to grow a crop that others have made a profit from that year, resulting in oversupply of that crop and undersupply of different crops the following year. As a result, waste is generated in several ways:

- Waste from overproduction: Too much of a crop might mean that some will not be sold (Figure 3.37).
- Waste of storage space: It may take longer to sell a crop, so buildings are needed to store the spare harvest. Some crops need special conditions so they do not spoil.
- Waste of transportation: To sell all the crop, a farmer may need to travel longer distances, using more fuel, etc.
- Waste of quality produce: If a crop starts to decrease in quality because it has not been sold quickly enough, it will be worth less money.
- Waste of labour: The farmer may have to employ staff to help grow and care for the crop, which is not an efficient use of time and labour if too much crop is produced.

**Figure 3.37:** Overproduction of a crop may mean it is not cost-effective to harvest as the price in the market is too low to cover the costs. As a result, food is wasted.

## Food shortages

Many subsistence farmers choose to grow the type of plants that will feed their families most effectively (either directly from the plant harvest or by feeding livestock). However, commercial farmers may make different decisions about which plants to grow, and the most profitable crops may not be the best choice for feeding the wider community.

Crops grown purely for sale and not for use by the farmer themselves are referred to as **cash crops**. Examples include cotton, coffee, soybeans and palm oil. Often, these are grown where the land is most fertile, and some crops, such as cotton, need large volumes of water. As a result, the opportunity to grow food to meet the needs of the local population is lost. A similar situation is taking place with the increase in demand for biofuels to replace the finite resources of fossil fuels. The production of crops to convert into fuel may be more profitable for the farmer than growing food crops.

### KEY WORD

**cash crop:** a crop that is produced with the primary aim of making money rather than feeding the farmer and their family

## Mismanagement of irrigation

As more and more countries face water shortages, the agriculture industry is coming under increasing pressure to use water wisely and to recycle it wherever possible. Without rain or additional irrigation, crop growth slows and crops may even die. A shortage of water in the soil also makes it more prone to wind erosion.

At the other end of the scale, too much irrigation also has negative effects. Large amounts of water run-off will carry away some soil particles, causing soil erosion. When wet, air pockets are lost, and the surface of the soil can become hard and compact (soil capping), which makes it more difficult for plants to grow through the soil. If the water content is too high, the soil can become too heavy to cultivate and machines may get stuck (Figure 3.38). Waterlogged soils also prevent plant roots getting enough oxygen to respire, and plant cells start to die. Nutrients dissolve in the water in soil, and as water drains away nutrients are taken with it.

The salt content of soil can increase with too much water (salinisation). Estimates suggest that 20% of irrigated land has become saline in the last 20 years. Salts dissolve into the water within the soil but are normally at their highest concentrations deeper down. When soil becomes waterlogged, the salts are able to move within it. When water eventually evaporates from the soil, the salts are left behind. If the salt levels become too high, plants will have difficulty taking up water (by osmosis), and water supplies may also become unsuitable for drinking.

Figure 3.38: If heavy machines are used when soils are too wet, they will damage the structure of the soil and may also get stuck.

### ACTIVITY 3.4

a  Too much water might be as much of a problem for plants as too little water. Working in small groups, copy and complete the following table to describe how the amount of water can affect certain growth factors.

You will need to complete some additional independent research to complete this task fully.

|  | Too little irrigation | Too much irrigation |
|---|---|---|
| Nutrient availability |  |  |
| Root growth |  |  |

Join up with another group and compare your conclusions. Did you include the same factors in each column? Add any information to your table that you feel is relevant based on your comparisons.

b  In your original groups, prepare for a debate on the motion: 'Agricultural crops should be given priority use of water, as it is needed to produce food'. Research your ideas and make sure you can justify your decisions in case of opposing viewpoints. Keep a record of the sources of information that you used to support your argument, and be prepared to demonstrate that these sources are accurate and unbiased.

## Overuse of pesticides

Regular use of one particular pesticide chemical can cause **resistance** in a pest population, whether insects or weeds. This means that the toxic chemical no longer kills all the target individuals. Figure 3.39 shows how resistance develops with insecticides. It takes a number of generations before an insect becomes fully resistant, but many insects have short life cycles, which means a number of generations can occur in just a few weeks.

### KEY WORD

**resistance:** the ability of a living organism to survive when exposed to a toxic chemical (such as a pesticide or herbicide)

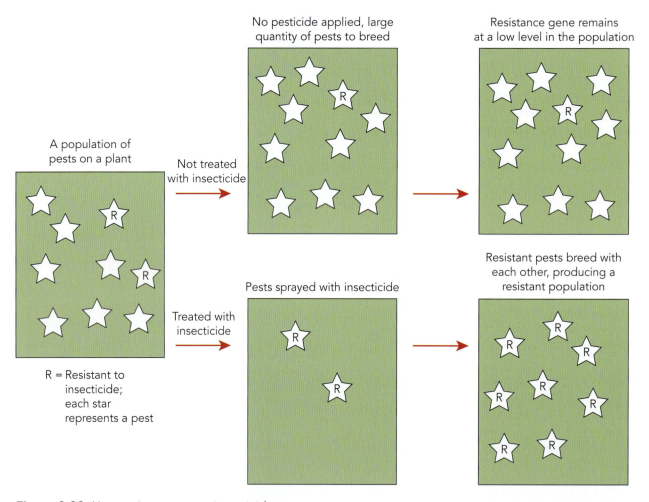

Figure 3.39: How resistance to an insecticide occurs.

Once an insect is no longer being controlled effectively by an insecticide, farmers tend to apply an increased dose to improve the effect. This may work in the short term, but it can cause a build-up of resistance even more rapidly. The best practice is to use a range of different pesticides.

Sometimes, the population of the pest increases to a higher level than it was to begin with, in a phenomenon known as **pest resurgence**. The insecticide may have been successful in killing the pest insect, but it may also have impacted the insect's natural predators, either by being toxic to them too or by removing their food source. The loss of the predator eventually allows the pest insect to resurge.

Insecticides can also kill beneficial insects such as bees, which affects the pollination of plants. A change in the availability of insects can impact the wider food web, because many animals feed on insects.

> **KEY WORD**
>
> **pest resurgence:** a situation where a population of a pest increases to a higher level after an initial reduction caused by the use of a pesticide

## Overuse of fertilisers

All soils have a maximum mineral nutrient level. Continuing to use fertilisers above this level can cause negative effects.

Heavy rain can dissolve the mineral nutrients and carry them away as it runs off the land or soaks through the soil (leaching). Excess water containing dissolved fertilisers drains into rivers and lakes. This **nutrient enrichment** upsets the natural balance of nutrients there. Too many nitrate and phosphate ions can cause **eutrophication** (see Chapter 4).

**Figure 3.40:** The leaching of nitrate or phosphate ions causes nutrient enrichment of watercourses, causing algal blooms to occur. This prevents light from reaching organisms living in the water.

Nutrient enrichment can also affect the growth of plants in the soil directly. Too much fertiliser can cause excessively lush growth, where the plant grows too rapidly and is unable to support itself. Lush growth is more susceptible to pest and disease attack. An imbalance of nutrients (such as a high nitrogen-to-potassium ratio) can cause a plant to produce lots of foliage and be less likely to flower, which is not the desired effect if the crop is the fruit.

> **KEY WORDS**
>
> **nutrient enrichment:** an increase in the level of nutrients in a habitat or ecosystem
>
> **eutrophication:** a sequence of events starting with enrichment of water by mineral nutrients or organic matter that leads to a reduction in oxygen levels in the water and the death of fish and other animals

## Questions

**3.15** A farmer has been using an insecticide to control an insect pest for many years. They have identified that the insecticide is no longer effective.

    **a** Explain why the insects are no longer being controlled by the insecticide.

    **b** Suggest two ways the farmer could prevent a similar problem from happening again.

**3.16** Scientists monitor the impact of fertiliser application on farms on the local water supply.

    **a** Explain how fertilisers applied on a farm can leach into water supplies.

    **b** Describe how nutrient enrichment affects plants growing in that soil.

### Exhaustion of nutrients in soils

In contrast to the application of too many nutrients in fertilisers, many forms of agriculture result in a lack of nutrients in the soil. If plants are grown repeatedly in a soil with no nutrient replenishment, the plants will take up all the available inorganic ions needed for healthy growth processes. Future crops will lack these essential nutrients, causing a reduction in yield.

A lack of organic fertiliser also means a reduction in the organic content of the soil. This causes a gradual decline in the organic content, impacting the soil structure and its ability to hold water, which affects the success of future crops.

### Removal of natural vegetation

Many crops do not naturally occur in the areas where they are grown. Others are the result of such extensive breeding processes that they no longer share the characteristics of their parent plants. Such crops do not support the wide range of organisms that would be found in natural vegetation.

The demand for food to supply the increasing world population often results in more land being converted to farm production. Loss of natural habitats means there is less habitat available for many species and in some cases may cause extinction (see Chapter 6).

Natural vegetation may also be lost in other ways, where farming methods do not include effective soil management techniques. **Overcultivation** can result in the exhaustion of a soil; nutrients are not replenished and the continued working of the soil damages its structure, reducing pore spaces. The overworking of the soil also removes any remaining natural vegetation.

**Overgrazing** is the term used to describe the damage caused by the actions of too much livestock in an area. The hooves of the animals compact the soil, making it less suitable for plant growth. Intense grazing activity means that any natural vegetation is consumed.

## Monoculture and intensification

While monoculture increases the efficiency of farming in an area, it does have some limitations. Most notably, the focus on a single crop often means the removal of other plants or animals, as they reduce efficiency and may potentially be a source of pests or diseases for the intended production (Figure 3.41). This type of production also tends to be intensive, so other organisms that could be competitors may be removed. For example, naturally occurring (wild) flowers could be considered weeds, as they will compete for light, water and nutrients. Removing this competitor species impacts the biodiversity of the area.

**Figure 3.41:** Lavender plants grown for medicinal purposes grown intensively as a monoculture. Note the lack of other plants in the field.

## Soil erosion

Unsustainable agricultural practices often result in impacts to the soil and the organisms living within it. While the effects are varied, they often result in conditions that increase the risk of soil erosion – the loss of the most productive soil layer, the topsoil (Figure 3.42). Without this, it is difficult to grow plants effectively, which impacts not only yield but also the provision of plants for livestock to graze on.

**Figure 3.42:** Unsustainable agricultural practices are a cause of soil erosion. Whatever the precise reason, the impact is always the same – a loss of productive soil in an area.

### ACTIVITY 3.5

Consider the local production of food at a site in your region.

- How many of the strategies to increase food production listed in this chapter can be seen?
- Are there any other strategies that may be used?
- Are there any signs that the production is having impacts on the natural environment?

Note down three ways local production could be made more sustainable. Get together in small groups and discuss your ideas.

### KEY WORDS

**overcultivation:** the excessive use of farmland, causing yield to decline due to soil exhaustion or land degradation

**overgrazing:** repeated grazing, causing damage to or death of plants

# 3.3 Soil erosion

Soil erosion is a naturally occurring process that affects all types of land and plays an important role in shaping the landscape. Soil erosion usually occurs slowly, except in the case of natural disasters. However, human activity can result in broad, rapid changes to the landscape.

Figure 3.43 shows the different layers within the soil.

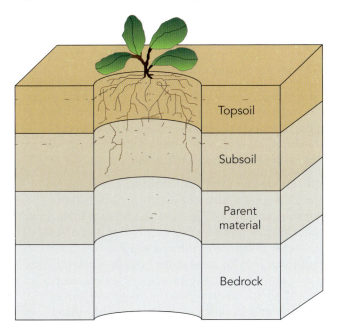

**Figure 3.43:** The horizons (layers) of soil. Most plant roots are found in the topsoil.

# Causes of soil erosion

The topsoil, located just below dead leaves and plants, is the most fertile layer of soil. The structure of topsoil allows the most root growth, because it holds water but also supports air spaces. Topsoil is often a dark layer because it contains organic matter and potentially a large quantity of nutrients. Loss of this layer can significantly affect the fertility of the soil.

## Unsustainable agricultural practices

Soils that are cultivated regularly start to lose structure: ploughing or digging breaks up large clumps into smaller ones. In the short term, this is good for even sowing and the development of seedlings, but the mechanical breakdown of soil means that the smaller particles are easier to move and more vulnerable to erosion. These are not the only causes, however – many of the unsustainable agricultural practices listed previously have an impact on soil erosion.

## Deforestation

Deforestation to meet the demand for wood, and for land to graze livestock and grow crops, has had a catastrophic effect. The roots of existing plants help bind the soil together. Once these are removed, the soil structure is not strong enough to withstand intense rainfall. Flash flooding and other rainwater run-off picks up topsoil and moves it away from its original location. Tree roots are useful in slowing down the speed of flowing torrents of water and providing places for any soil that is carried along to get trapped and deposited. When vegetation is removed, there may be nothing left to prevent run-off and soil erosion (Figure 3.44). Areas of rainforest that are cleared for cultivation often suffer severe erosion because the original vegetation was the only factor binding the soil together. Growers may need to relocate because the erosion means that crops can no longer grow in the affected areas.

**Figure 3.44:** The removal of vegetation means soil is no longer held in place by plant roots. Here, the rain has formed gullies, making the area unsuitable for farming.

## Farming on steep slopes

Soil is formed from the parent rock, so it is not surprising that the rock cycle affects the location and depth of topsoil. Within the rock cycle, materials are transported by wind and rain from exposed areas and deposited as sediment in low-lying areas, such as valleys. This is a risk on all steep slopes, but plant roots help prevent the loss of all these soils. Many farming practices remove these plants, leaving soil more vulnerable to movement.

## Bare soil

Grazing livestock can reduce vegetation to nearly ground level. Constant hard grazing weakens the plants because they do not have sufficient foliage to photosynthesise. So, they will gradually die out. Lack of vegetation cover means that there are no longer plant roots to hold the soil together and so it becomes vulnerable to erosion. Large numbers of animals within an area will also trample down the plants, damaging them in the process (Figure 3.45). Animal hooves compact the ground, which reduces the number of air spaces in the soil, reducing root growth and further weakening the plants.

**Figure 3.45:** A combination of low rainfall and too many livestock has resulted in a lack of vegetation. This ground is at risk of soil erosion.

## Wind and water erosion

Without vegetation, soil is more exposed to winds. Winds cause the water content of soil to be lost through evaporation. The soil becomes lighter and particles no longer stick together. Further winds cause these to separate, with lighter particles blown to new locations.

Water is also a significant factor in soil erosion:

- Heavy rain, with large droplets, dislodges soil particles, which are then loose enough to be eroded in other ways.
- Excess water that cannot be absorbed by the soil will transport it away from the area. Water infiltration may also be reduced if the soil surface has been capped (by large water droplets), or compacted by feet or machines.
- Gullies and streams contain a large volume of water moving at speed. This erodes soil, forming deeper and deeper crevices. Gullies are initially formed as rainwater run-off flows across the land. Where there is a natural slope in the soil, rainwater moves faster, creating a stronger scouring effect.

## The impacts of soil erosion

Soil erosion can have an impact far beyond the area where it takes place. Some of the most significant effects of soil erosion are explored in the following sections.

### Silting of rivers

Flowing water eventually enters rivers and lakes. As it slows down, the soil being carried along starts to settle, silting up these watercourses. The silt can reduce the volume of water that the river or lake can hold, so there may be flooding after heavy rainfall.

Silt deposits can form small lagoons, providing new breeding opportunities for insects, such as malaria-carrying mosquitoes. Silt can also affect the quality and availability of water for drinking. Water that is high in silt may affect the health and viability of aquatic organisms, burying them at the bottom of the silt layer. It may also prevent light from reaching the leaves of aquatic plants, which affects the oxygen content of the water and its ability to provide a healthy living environment (Figure 3.46).

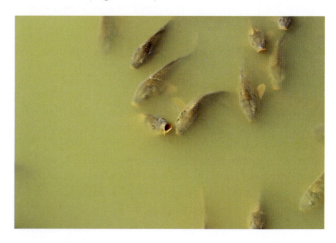

**Figure 3.46:** Soil erosion may impact fish in rivers, as it can reduce their ability to extract oxygen via their gills.

## Desertification and reduction in crop yield

Most plants require nutrient-rich, deep topsoil for healthy growth. With the productive layer of topsoil gone, plants cannot grow well – subsoil does not have enough nutrients, air spaces or water flow to support the same level of growth. The structure of the subsoil does not allow plant roots to penetrate easily. This results in a reduction in crop yield. If the soil cannot support growth, desertification starts to take hold. With few plants surviving, not enough organic matter re-enters the soil to improve its fertility, so the problem worsens. Desertification makes it harder to grow crops because of the unfertile soil, but it also means that there are fewer plants for livestock to feed on. As productivity drops, people may be forced to move away.

## Mass movement

When rain falls on a natural slope, gravity pulls it down the hillside. As it does so, the volume of water increases and so does its speed. Both these factors dislodge soil, which is then carried along in the surface run-off. When the speed of the water decreases (typically in a valley or at the mouth of a river), soil particles are deposited.

If there are no natural barriers, the hillside is left without any useable topsoil, crops are washed away and areas where the soil has been deposited are covered in thick, silty mud. In some cases, whole villages can be submerged by mudslides, causing loss of life and property. When washed further down into rivers or lakes, the silt can cause transport issues as well as damage to the ecosystem.

In addition to loose topsoil being carried by run-off to cause mudslides, some water may penetrate deeper into the soil, loosening the whole or much of that soil layer. This moves all together to cause a landslide. In more extreme cases, rockslides may occur too. Whatever the type of material moved, the impact is similar – damage to anything further down the slope and the loss of vegetation in the area where the slip has occurred.

## Loss of habitats and biodiversity

Topsoil is an important habitat for many organisms and a key part of the ecosystem. When soil is eroded, these creatures lose their habitat. Animals supported by local vegetation have fewer sources of shelter and food. Eventually, the whole ecosystem may be affected, which brings additional problems, such as an increase in pest organisms if their predators are forced away from the area. The changes to the habitat may also impact biodiversity – the variety of animal and plant life that the habitat is able to support.

## Effects on people: malnutrition, famine and displacement

With a drop in productivity from the land, people may not be able to grow or raise enough food to eat. They may be at risk of **malnutrition**, and an area may start to suffer from **famine**.

Local people – sometimes whole communities – are forced to relocate to new areas in order to find soil that will support agriculture. They may take their livestock with them, as they are valuable possessions. Large numbers of people moving in this way can cause problems for the wider region, with potential conflict between the displaced farmers and the original farming communities. Even if a displaced group is able to find land to cultivate, there will be a significant delay before any planted crops will yield any food. Foraging for food and fuel can have a negative impact on the natural vegetation in the new area.

The need for food and a clean water supply becomes a priority when populations are displaced, and foreign aid agencies focus on providing basic food and medical needs in order to prevent people dying and avoid a crisis developing (Figure 3.47).

**Figure 3.47:** Sometimes the location of temporary encampments for populations and the need for agreement between different countries results in a delay in getting the right aid to those who need it.

### KEY WORDS

**malnutrition:** not having enough of the correct nutrients to eat, causing ill health

**famine:** a lack of access to food, often over a large area

## CASE STUDY

### Wind erosion – an American tale

One of the best-known examples of the effects of erosion caused by the wind occurred across the prairies of the USA and Canada in the 1930s. Farmers had converted grassland into arable cropland, cultivating large areas using tractor-drawn ploughs. The area experienced extreme drought and the soil, no longer held together by the deep-rooted grasses, was blown around in the wind in huge dust clouds (Figure 3.48). These dust clouds, known as 'black blizzards', were so dense that they choked humans and livestock. They also impacted cities and shipping in the ocean over 3000 km away.

The effects were so severe that whole farms became unsuitable for use. Topsoil that was originally up to 2 metres deep – some of the most fertile in the country – had been lost. It is estimated that over 400 000 km² of land was affected, displacing approximately 500 000 people who lost all their farmland and their livelihood. Other estimates suggest that over 75% of the topsoil was lost from the area.

The impact of this environmental disaster spread far beyond these farms, causing severe damage to the economies of the two countries. In the USA, the government purchased 45 000 km² of land from farmers to prevent it from being used for arable production and to allow it to return to grassland.

**Figure 3.48:** Soil drifting over a farm in the 1930s as a result of severe erosion.

### Questions

1. Suggest reasons why this area may have experienced extreme soil erosion.
2. Suggest two reasons why farmers were allowed to work in this way.
3. State two major impacts of this extreme soil erosion.
4. Suggest how the purchase of land by the US government would have helped to address the problem.

## Strategies to reduce soil erosion

Keeping soil healthy and avoiding erosion are essential for the production of good crops and the health of the local ecosystem. There are several ways in which farmers work to reduce soil erosion.

### Terracing

**Terracing** is a common technique that prevents the erosion of soil by rainwater on steep slopes. As identified previously, mudslides, landslides and rockslides are major risks linked to steep slopes.

Figure 3.49 shows how terracing changes the shape of a hillside to reduce the risk of soil and rock movement.

Remodelling a hillside into a series of terraces (or steps) means that when heavy rain does occur, it is less likely to run down a slope. The water sits within each of the terraced areas for longer, rather than quickly running off, and most of it will soak into the soil. Some crops benefit from standing water – for example, terracing is often used for the cultivation of rice, where the plants are grown in pools of water (Figure 3.50).

> **KEY WORD**
>
> **terracing:** the artificial development of flat areas (for growing crops) in a sloping terrain

3   Land

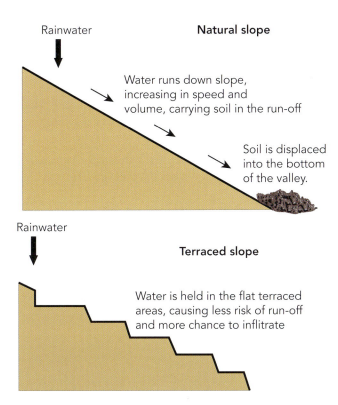

Figure 3.49: The impact on terracing on soil erosion. Flat areas tend to have a reduced water flow, decreasing the risk of topsoil being carried by run-off.

troughs run along the contours of the land, rather than up and down it. Each plough furrow holds back water and stops torrents running down the slope, thus preventing the formation of larger gullies and surface run-off. This technique, known as **contour ploughing**, is suitable in a number of situations and can be used on all gradients of slope (Figure 3.51). The furrows help to prevent soil erosion after land has been left with vegetation for a while until new seeds can germinate.

Figure 3.51: A large farm in Brazil, where the soil is ploughed along the contours of the land, helping to reduce soil erosion by water running down the slopes.

## Bunds

Often linked to terracing, **bunds** are artificial banks at the edges of growing spaces, designed to hold back water. This technique is especially useful for crops that need to be submerged or that require very moist soils, such as rice. Figure 3.52 shows how water is retained. The lack of water flow also means any soil that has been eroded from higher up the slope will be deposited in that terrace, increasing the quantity of soil available to the crop and potentially increasing its fertility.

Figure 3.50: Terracing in a rice field in Vietnam. Water is prevented from running down the hill quickly, which reduces soil erosion and helps the crop grow.

## Contour ploughing

Similar to terracing, when an area of land is ploughed, there are benefits to making sure that the ridges and

### KEY WORDS

**contour ploughing:** a technique where the furrows caused by ploughing follow the contours of the land

**bund:** an embankment constructed around the edge of an area to reduce the loss of a liquid (such as water)

123

# CAMBRIDGE IGCSE™ AND O LEVEL ENVIRONMENTAL MANAGEMENT: COURSEBOOK

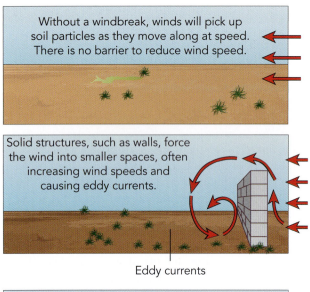

**Figure 3.52:** Bunds (banks of soil) are useful for holding back water and preventing soil erosion from run-off. The bund also helps to protect the soil from wind erosion, depending on its height and the direction of the prevailing wind.

**Figure 3.53:** Natural wind breaks are more effective than solid structures because they reduce the speed of the wind as it flows through the foliage.

## Wind breaks

**Wind breaks** are a useful tool for reducing wind erosion. While many different materials can be used, natural vegetation is one of the best. Many artificial wind breaks aim to reproduce the same effect as natural wind breaks. Figure 3.53 shows how wind speed is reduced. Natural wind breaks can also have other benefits:

- They can provide additional habitats for beneficial insects (or other animals) that help control crop pests.
- The roots of the wind break will help to hold back soil if the area is prone to erosion by run-off.

**Figure 3.54:** A farm in New Zealand using wind breaks to protect crops from wind damage.

> **KEY WORD**
>
> **wind break:** a permeable barrier, made of either living vegetation or artificial material, used to reduce the impact of the wind in an area

## Questions

**3.17** A farmer wishes to cultivate a steeply sloping field. Suggest two techniques they could use to prevent excessive soil erosion.

**3.18** State two benefits and two limitations of planting a wind break at the edge of a field.

**3.19** Suggest one other (non-natural) way that a wind break could be made.

# CASE STUDY

## Flower power

The Netherlands has a long agricultural history. Its temperate climate and fertile soils are ideal for growing a wide range of crops and pasture.

The Netherlands' location within Europe has made it a strong trading nation for hundreds of years. Good transport links have helped the country to develop the largest wholesale flower markets in the world, importing flowers from across the globe and selling them on to customers across Europe and beyond. In addition to trading in cut flowers from across the world, the fertile land within the Netherlands is used for growing flower bulbs, especially tulips. This is done on a large scale and, to increase the productive space, low-lying lands have been drained and large embankments (dams) built to hold back the water. The soil is peaty (contains a high level of organic matter) and is managed using drainage systems to take away extra water, which is then pumped outside the dams. Draining the low-lying land has allowed the growers to produce large fields on reclaimed ground without the need to remove natural vegetation. This process has also meant that the fields can be given straight edges, so using the large cultivation machines is very efficient.

Figure 3.55 shows an area of flower bulb production. The production of bulbs is mechanised: tractors do most of the work, with special attachments for planting and harvesting the bulbs, and additional equipment for applying fertiliser and pesticides. Large areas of land can be cultivated, and the crops are cared for by a small number of workers, so costs are lower and more competitive than in other countries.

Tulip bulbs are planted very close together to maximise the use of the land. This means that a lot of nutrients are needed from the soil, so the growers use large quantities of chemical (inorganic) fertilisers. The bulbs are a high-value crop, so the growers also work hard to prevent the spread of any pests or diseases and typically control these problems with chemical sprays.

**Figure 3.55:** An area used for cultivation of flower bulbs.

Tulip growers can get two 'harvests' from the same crop. Bulbs are lifted from the crop in late summer and sold around the world. In addition, the tulip flowers are picked and sold through the Netherlands' wholesale cut-flower markets, again being transported around the world. The flowers are cut in the spring, which is useful for the flower growers because there is employment for workers over a longer season.

### Questions

1. **a** Describe the type of agriculture used by the flower growers in the Netherlands.

   **b** Wind erosion is a major problem. Suggest three reasons why this might be the case.

2. Describe the risks to the ecosystem if pesticides are applied by tractor.

3. This land is some of the most fertile in the Netherlands, yet the farmers are growing flowers rather than food. Discuss arguments for and against allowing farmers to choose their own crops to grow.

Figure 3.56: The use of clover also helps by adding a source of nitrogen ions to the soil to benefit future crops.

## Maintaining vegetation cover

As you have seen, cultivated soil is most vulnerable to erosion when there is little to hold it together. Cultivation removes many of the natural safeguards from soil erosion: the soil is broken up into smaller, more uniform pieces and any plant growth on the surface is removed. This is usually done at a time in the year when the soil is relatively lightweight, because if it was heavy with water, it would be too difficult to cultivate.

It is relatively easy to reduce this risk by maintaining a cover of vegetation on land for as long as possible. This might mean planting an additional 'cover' crop to help maintain the health of the soil. Some farmers will sow a legume, such as clover, immediately after a crop has been harvested (Figure 3.56). While this does not produce a product that can be sold, the clover helps to prevent erosion and (as a legume) means there will be more nitrogen in the soil for the next major crop. Later, the clover can be ploughed into the soil immediately prior to sowing.

The 'no dig' method uses the same principle. Existing vegetation is left right up until a new crop is ready to be sown, but then rather than cultivate the soil, the farmer applies a herbicide to kill off existing weeds (Figure 3.57). The ground has not been disturbed and the roots of the original vegetation still bind the soil together until the new crop has started to establish itself. However, there are still risks with this method: herbicide residues can build up in the soil and affect the crop, and if control of the cover vegetation is ineffective it will compete with the new crop as a weed.

3 Land

Figure 3.57: Herbicides can be used to kill off unwanted vegetation without the need for digging.

## Adding organic matter

Soil is more at risk if it is left uncovered, if it has been broken down into small particles and if it is lightweight, and so has a low water content. This last issue can be addressed by adding more organic matter, such as animal manure or composted plant material, to the soil.

Additional organic matter has a number of positive effects. It provides additional air gaps in heavy soils, increases the number of organisms in the soil (because they are feeding on the organic matter), adds nutrients and improves the general soil structure to prevent soil erosion (Figure 3.58). Organic matter holds extra water, preventing the soil from drying out and being blown away. Having larger, more irregularly sized particles, it forms a base for other soil particles to bind to. An increase in organic matter, as well as increasing the general fertility of the soil and therefore more vegetation on the soil surface, allows plants to develop stronger and more widespread roots, which help hold the soil together even when the tops of the plants are removed during cultivation.

Figure 3.58: Adding organic matter improves the soil structure, adds nutrients and improves the water-holding capacity of a soil too.

### ACTIVITY 3.6

In pairs, research the methods used in your local area to manage the impact of soil erosion. Use the internet or any other resources available to you. Use the following questions to guide your research:

- Why are these methods used, rather than some of the other options you have read about in this section?
- Is the management of soil erosion perceived to be a priority for local farmers?
- How is the local perception of soil erosion shaped by experience?
- If you were presenting a case for better soil management practices, what type of information would you collate?
- What would be the best way of helping farmers to change practices that they have been following for generations?

Prepare a short report summarising your findings.

### REFLECTION

Did Activity 3.6 help you to understand the practical purpose and application of different techniques? Do you have a clear idea of how soil erosion occurs and how it can be prevented? If not, what other learning strategies could you use to help you remember this topic?

### PEER ASSESSMENT

Swap your final report with another pair. Read your classmates' report and assess it. Did they identify similar methods to you and similar reasons for their use in your local area? Write a short paragraph of feedback, identifying two things that they did well and one area in which their report or research could be improved.

Read the feedback you get on your own report and discuss it in your pairs. Use it to decide how you could improve the next time you approach this type of task.

## EXTENDED CASE STUDY

### Controlling pests naturally – a flawed decision

During the 19th century, sugar cane plants were introduced into Australia as the country became populated by Europeans. Records show that there were plantations in the Brisbane area as early as 1862. Plantations were densely planted and tended to be grown as monocultures (only one crop was grown in an area); today, the plantations are highly mechanised.

As the numbers of sugar cane plantations grew, so did the incidence of pests. Two native beetle species caused major problems: the adults ate the leaves of the crop and their larvae ate the roots. These beetles proved difficult to control because the adults have a tough skin that repels pesticides and the larvae are buried in the soil so are not easy to spray. When pesticides were used, not only were they not very effective on the pests but they also killed many other insects and upset the natural ecosystem. Australian scientists looked at other areas of the world and read reports of increased yields in plantations in Hawaii, the natural location of cane toads. Cane toads are relatively large and eat a wide range of different insects (Figure 3.59).

A small number of cane toads were imported into Australia in the 1930s, bred successfully and released into the local plantations. Unfortunately, it was then discovered that the cane toad was not particularly effective at controlling the beetles on the Australian sugar cane but preferred to eat other insects and animals in the area. It has been estimated that there are now over 200 million cane toads in Australia. They have bred rapidly because:

- they outcompete native animals for food
- they outcompete native animals for habitat space

Figure 3.59: Cane toads were introduced into Australia, where they had a huge environmental impact.

- they have no natural predators in Australia
- if attacked, they produce a toxic liquid on their skin
- they are mobile and the population area increases by approximately 50 km per year.

Cane toads reduce the number of natural organisms within an area. The local population of the Argos monitor, a large lizard, can be reduced by as much as 90% once the cane toad arrives in its community. The lizards eat the toads but die from the toxin on the skin, and the death of the lizards and increase in toads affects the whole food web. Figure 3.60 shows the spread of the cane toad population and what scientists believe to be the potential range of the toad.

Scientists are now looking for ways to control the spread of the cane toad. One suggestion is to infect the cane toad population with a viral disease that will spread among them when the adults mate. The population is too widely spread and numerous to simply collect or trap.

# 3 Land

**CONTINUED**

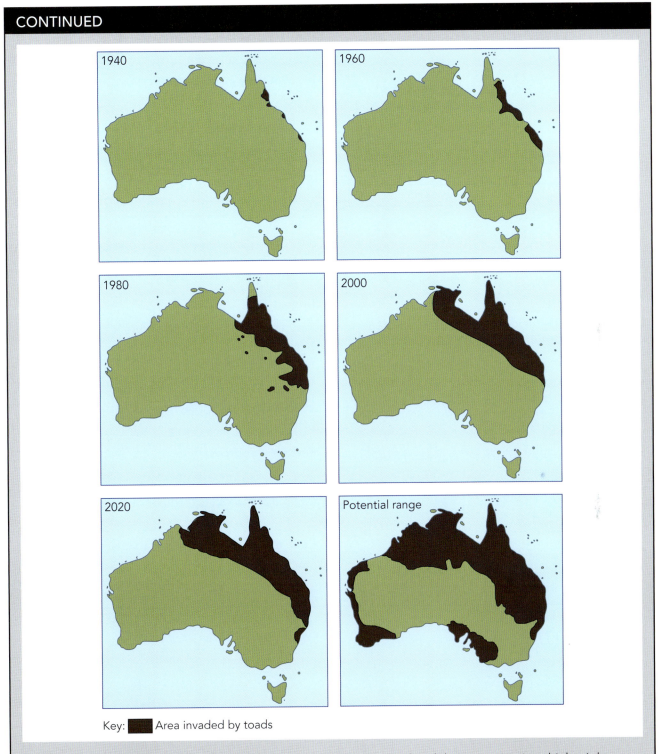

Key: Area invaded by toads

**Figure 3.60:** Maps of Australia showing the spread of the cane toad and the area scientists think might be at risk from invasion.

## CONTINUED

### Questions

1. Copy Table 3.11 and then circle the words that best describe the type of agriculture used to farm sugar cane plantations (choose one from each pair).

| subsistence farming | commercial farming |
|---|---|
| pastoral | arable |
| intensive | extensive |

Table 3.11: Sugar cane plantations.

2. Suggest how the introduction of sugar cane plantations increased the numbers of the native beetles.

3. a  Describe the current location of the cane toad population in Australia.

   b  Using Figure 3.60, estimate the percentage of the total country that could potentially have a suitable habitat for the cane toad population. Circle the correct answer: 85% 75% 45% 25%.

   c  Suggest why scientists have not included all of Australia in the potential range for the toad.

4. Suggest reasons why the spread of the toad has been so rapid.

5. Outline the checks the scientists should have made before releasing the first toads in Australia in the 1930s.

6. Biological control is widely regarded as preferable to the use of chemical pesticides, yet this introduction has been an environmental disaster for Australia. Give an argument to support the use of other biological controls in the future.

7. Suggest some benefits and limitations of the current plan to infect the cane toads with a virus that will kill them.

8. The sugar cane plantations still have problems with the beetles that eat the leaves and roots. Cane toads have not provided a solution. Suggest another method that could be used to control the beetles.

### Project

Research another example where a biological control method has been unsuccessful and one where it has been successful. Use the internet and any other resources available to you. Put together a short presentation to give to your class or a group of your classmates. Use maps and graphics to show your findings.

### Further resources

*Good Bugs Gone Bad*, National Wildlife Federation

*Biological control*, College of Agriculture and Life Sciences

*Cane toad*, Department of Primary Industries and Regional Development

3 Land

## SUMMARY

| |
|---|
| The key components of soil are mineral particles, organic content, water and gases. |
| Soils also contain mineral ions, whose uptake by plants is dependent on the soil pH. |
| Loam soils contain an ideal combination of soil components for plant growth. |
| Weather conditions impact plant growth and photosynthesis. This will affect the choice of suitable plants to grow in a location. |
| Agricultural practice can be defined by the types of products it creates, the level of inputs needed to do so and the main purpose of the production. |
| An increase in food production and crop yield can be achieved by a range of strategies, including specific production systems, additional of irrigation and fertilisers, the use of improved varieties, and the management of pests. |
| Unsustainable agricultural practices include overproduction of food, the choice of crops grown and the methods used to achieve this production. |
| Removal of natural vegetation and the use of monoculture and intensive methods reduces biodiversity and risks an increase in soil erosion. |
| Soil erosion is caused by wind and water erosion. |
| Soil erosion is a greater risk where land is sloping and agricultural practices leave the soil bare. |
| Soil erosion causes the movement of soil and rocks, resulting in the silting of rivers and desertification. |
| Soil erosion causes losses in habitat and biodiversity and reduces plant growth. |
| Reduction in plant growth can mean a reduction in crop yield, resulting in malnutrition, famine and the displacement of people. |
| Strategies to reduce soil erosion include reducing the impact of sloping land, using wind breaks and maintaining vegetation cover. |

## SELF-EVALUATION CHECKLIST

After studying this chapter, complete this table.

| I can: | Needs more work | Almost there | Ready to move on |
|---|---|---|---|
| identify the different components of soil, including sand, silt and clay | | | |
| describe how the different components of soil make it good for plant growth | | | |
| explain the benefits of loam soils in crop growth | | | |
| describe how climate and weather conditions affect crop growth, including wet and dry seasons | | | |

## CONTINUED

| I can: | Needs more work | Almost there | Ready to move on |
|---|---|---|---|
| discuss different types of agriculture | | | |
| define sustainable food production and describe various strategies for increasing agricultural yields | | | |
| explain the impact of unsustainable agricultural practices on both people and the environment | | | |
| describe the causes of soil erosion and determine the impact they have | | | |
| discuss a variety of strategies for reducing soil erosion. | | | |

## PRACTICE QUESTIONS

1. State the **four** components of soil. [4]

2. A farmer adds some fertiliser to their land.

   a State what this will do to the soil fertility. [1]

   b A test of the farmer's soil shows it has low organic content, explain why organic content is important in supporting plant growth. [2]

   c Give **three** ways that a farmer might know their plants are short of mineral nutrients. [3]

3. a **Figure 3.61** shows terms relating to types of agriculture and their descriptions.

   Draw one line from each term to its correct description. [3]

| Term | Description |
|---|---|
| subsistence farming | farming that aims to maximise the yield from an area by using a large amount of resources |
| pastoral farming | farming that is focused on selling the produce for a profit |
| monoculture | farming that focuses on breeding and rearing livestock |
| intensive farming | farming that is focused on supplying the family with food |
| | farming in which only one crop is grown or one type of animal is raised |

Figure 3.61: Terms relating to types of agriculture.

## CONTINUED

    b  Suggest **three** ways that changes to farming practices have helped to feed a growing world population. [3]

    c  State **two** ways that crop rotation can help increase the yield of a crop. [2]

4  Human activity is increasing the rate and extent of soil erosion.

    a  Explain how leaving bare soil increases the risk of soil erosion. [2]

    b  i  Define topsoil. [1]

        ii  With reference to topsoil, describe the impact that soil erosion may have on habitats and biodiversity. [3]

    c  Strategies to reduce soil erosion include terracing, bunds and wind breaks.

        **State one** way that each strategy reduces the risk of soil erosion.

        i    terracing  ……………………… [1]

        ii   bunds       ……………………… [1]

        iii  wind breaks ……………………… [1]

5  Intercropping is identified as a useful way of helping to prevent soil erosion.

    **Suggest three** other benefits of intercropping. [3]

6  With agriculture accounting for around 70% of all water use globally, it is essential that farming practices are optimised to use water in the most efficient and sustainable way.

    a  Suggest **three** ways that farmers can improve the efficiency of their water use. [3]

    b  Describe how a drip irrigation system works. [3]

# Chapter 4
# Water

**LEARNING INTENTIONS**

In this chapter you will:

- explore how the water cycle works
- consider how people obtain safe fresh water and what they use it for
- learn the names of the main oceans
- discover what potable water is and how water is treated to make it safe, and learn about the availability of safe drinking water across the world
- examine the process, benefits and limitations of desalination
- explore the use, benefits and limitations of multipurpose dams
- investigate the causes of water pollution, and its effects on people and the environment
- discuss methods for improving water quality
- explore how malaria and cholera spread, how they can be controlled, and the benefits and drawbacks of strategies to control water-related diseases
- investigate the impact of overfishing and overharvesting of marine species
- discover what marine aquaculture is and the effects it has on the marine environment
- evaluate the ways in which the harvesting of marine species can be managed successfully
- explore the causes and impacts of oil pollution on the marine environment, and strategies to minimise its impact
- learn about different types of plastic, including biodegradable, non-biodegradable and microplastics
- consider the impacts of plastic pollution and evaluate strategies for managing it.

# 4 Water

## BEFORE YOU START

Water can exist in several states. Think about what these are and how water can change from one state to another, then discuss with a partner the importance of this property of water.

Do you know the names of the world's major oceans? Your teacher will give you a blank map of the world. On your copy, label as many oceans as you can, then pair up and compare your maps. Can you name them all between you?

The oceans are at risk from exploitation and pollution. In your pairs, discuss and make notes on what you know about the uses of different types of plastic and the problems that plastic pollution can cause in the oceans. What solutions can you suggest for these problems?

After your discussion, join up with another pair and compare notes. Then, work together to create a poster designed to educate people on the problems of plastic pollution and how they can be addressed.

## ENVIRONMENTAL MANAGEMENT IN CONTEXT

### The bountiful oceans

Only 29% of Earth's surface is actually land, leaving the oceans covering 71%. The vast majority of this area, however, remains relatively unknown. Only about 10% of the ocean is over **continental shelves**, where the water is relatively shallow. The remaining 90% of the ocean is over an **abyss**. Not only are these deep regions almost impossible to access, but they are also very unproductive. Over 50% of the biological productivity of the oceans occurs in the 10% that is over the continental shelves, and 95% of all commercially caught fish are found here, too.

Fish are by far the most important resource that humans obtain from the oceans. This term can include true fish, or finfish, but also shellfish and other animals that live in the sea and can be eaten (Figure 4.1). World fisheries yield about 90 million tonnes / year and **aquaculture** (the cultivation of organisms under controlled, semi-natural conditions) yields 88 million tonnes / year.

The main fisheries are located on the continental shelves. This is because the water is shallow there, so light can penetrate and there is more oxygen than further down. In addition, nutrients from the land are abundant on the shelf. All these features make the continental shelf a good place for the growth of plants and therefore the fish that depend on them. So, despite its vast size, the ocean's depth and low productivity mean it is a relatively minor source of food for humans. However, most of the food harvested from the ocean is animal-based and so is rich in proteins, fats and oils, which makes it nutritious and much needed by those living at subsistence level.

**Figure 4.1:** Freshly caught fish at a fishmonger's shop.

### KEY WORDS

**continental shelf:** an area at the bottom of the ocean near the coast of a continent, where the sea is not very deep

**abyss:** a very deep hole in the ocean, which seems to have no bottom

**aquaculture:** the raising of water animals, such as fish, for food or the growing of plants in water for food

## CONTINUED

The ocean has appeared so vast to humans in the past that it was long assumed that we can have no effect on either it or its ecosystems. However, it is now becoming clear that fish stocks are declining because of **overfishing** and pollution by such things as oil and plastics (Figure 4.2). This is becoming a huge problem, even in the open ocean. For example, more than 250 000 tonnes of waste plastic are currently circulating in five huge ocean regions known as **gyres**. It is estimated that an ambitious plan to clean this plastic up will take nearly 50 years, but it will achieve nothing if we carry on dumping plastic. In addition, with the world's population now in excess of 8 billion, many commodities could become harder to obtain. The most essential of these is probably safe drinking water, and only a very small proportion of the water on Earth is safe to drink. However, it is possible to derive safe drinking water from sea water by desalination.

The message is clear: the ocean is a very important part of life on Earth. It still has much to offer us, but our use of it needs to be better managed in the future than it has been in the past.

### Discussion questions

1. What do you think is the most important use that humans make of the oceans?
2. What problems do you think arise from plastics and oil ending up in the oceans?

**Figure 4.2:** Plastic bottles and polystyrene are major sources of ocean pollution.

### KEY WORDS

**overfishing:** when the number of fish caught is greater than the rate at which the fish reproduce, leading to a fall in fish numbers in an area

**gyre:** a circular pattern of ocean currents

## 4.1 Water sources and supply

Although more than 71% of Earth's surface is covered by water, only 3% of this water is fresh (non-salty) and potentially usable by humans. This is about 42 million km³ of fresh water. However, much of this water is locked up in the polar ice caps or glaciers. In fact, less than 1% of Earth's fresh water is readily available for people to use (Figure 4.3).

This amounts to 420 000 km³, which is about 60 million litres of water for every person on Earth. On average, one person uses about 1.5 million litres a year, directly (for drinking and washing) and indirectly (in the manufacture of products that a person uses).

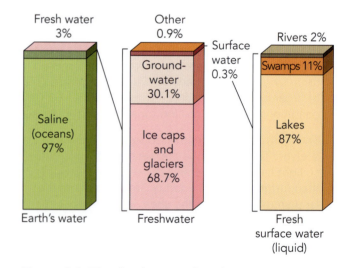

**Figure 4.3:** The distribution of Earth's water.

## WORKED EXAMPLE

### The world's water

Only 3% of the world's total water is fresh (non-salty) and potentially usable by humans. Calculate the total amount of water on Earth if there are 42 million km$^3$ of fresh water.

3% is equal to 42 million km$^3$

1% is equal to one-third of 42 million km$^3$

So, 1% is 42 ÷ 3 million km$^3$

= 14 million km$^3$

Then, 100% is 14 × 100 million km$^3$

= 1400 million km$^3$

### Now you try

a   Only 1% of the fresh water on Earth is readily available, which is about 60 million litres per person. Assume there are 8 billion (8000 million) people on Earth. How many litres of readily available fresh water are there?

b   On average, one person uses 1.5 million litres of water a year. Calculate this as a percentage of the water readily available per person (60 million litres).

## MATHS TIP

You can think of percentage calculations in terms of the equation:

percentage = part ÷ total × 100

The important point is to recognise the correct total out of which you are being asked to find a percentage.

It might seem that there is plenty of water for everyone, but half of the available fresh water is found in just six countries: Brazil, Russia, Canada, Indonesia, China and Colombia. In addition, much of it is not suitable for drinking. So, there are many challenges to providing people with enough clean, safe drinking water.

## The water cycle

The 1 386 000 000 km$^3$ of water on Earth is a fixed amount that neither increases nor decreases. However, water exists in different forms and is found in many places. At one time, a particular water molecule may be within ice in a glacier, but at another time it may be in a raindrop. Or it may be in the ocean or in a fast-flowing river in the far north.

**Figure 4.4:** Glaciers are slow-moving rivers of ice. They may melt, turning to liquid water that runs into the sea.

Changes to the water's state will often lead to a change in where it is. For example, the ice in a glacier may melt and become liquid water; it may then enter a river that flows into a lake (Figure 4.4). With the warmth of the sun on the lake, water may **evaporate** and become vapour. This vapour can then rise into the sky, **condense** and form clouds. Under certain circumstances, the water in these clouds will fall as rain or snow, called **precipitation**. It may then enter the soil and be taken up by the roots of plant, to be transported up the plant in the transpiration stream. This movement is driven by the loss of water from the plant in the process of

## KEY WORDS

**evaporation:** the process in which liquid water turns into vapour – the opposite of condensation

**condensation:** the process in which water vapour turns in to liquid water – the opposite of evaporation

**precipitation:** the process in which liquid water (as rain) or ice particles (as snow or hail) fall to Earth due to gravity

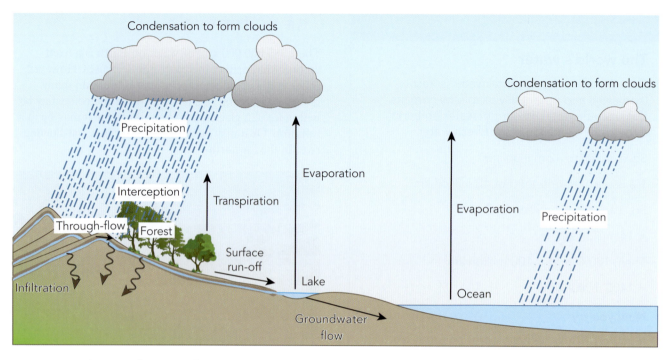

Figure 4.5: The main features of the water cycle.

transpiration. Other possibilities are that the water will flow along the ground in a process called **surface run-off**, be trapped by the leaves of plants (a process called **interception**), or enter the ground by **infiltration** and then become part of **groundwater flow** (if it flows through rocks) or **through-flow** (if it flows through soil).

All these changes in the state of water and its place on the Earth are summarised in the water cycle (Figure 4.5).

> **KEY WORDS**
>
> **surface run-off:** the process in which water runs over the ground into rivers
>
> **interception:** the process in which precipitation is stopped from reaching the ground surface by the presence of trees and other plants
>
> **infiltration:** the process in which water seeps into the ground
>
> **groundwater flow:** the process in which infiltrated water flows through rocks
>
> **through-flow:** the process in which infiltrated water flows through the soil

In summary, the water cycle consists of:

Water stores: salt water oceans and freshwater ice sheets, glaciers, ground water, atmosphere, lakes and rivers.

Water is then transported between stores by: precipitation, interception, surface run-off, infiltration, through-flow, ground water flow, transpiration, evaporation and condensation.

# Sources of fresh water for human use

## Why humans need water

There are a variety of sources of freshwater available such as; rain and snow in the atmosphere, surface water consisting of rivers, lakes and reservoirs, ground water in aquifers and wells, and desalination from the oceans.

Humans need water for domestic, industrial and agricultural purposes. However, the required quantities vary around the world. In general, high-income countries (HICs) use the most and low-income countries (LICs) use the least. But LICs use most of their water in agriculture, whereas HICs use most for industry. In the home, water for drinking and cooking only accounts for about 3% of domestic use (Figure 4.6).

4 Water

For example, in middle-income countries (MICs), about 50% of domestic water is used for washing and flushing the toilet, and a further 20% is used for washing clothes.

**Figure 4.6:** Water for domestic use needs to be especially safe; only around 74% of people worldwide have access to safely managed drinking water.

In LICs, much less domestic water is used for these purposes, although the proportions vary.

Water is also used in a wide range of industrial processes, such as for cooling in the production of electricity. Water is often described as the 'universal solvent' because many different substances will dissolve in it. This makes it very useful in industry.

By far the greatest use of water in agriculture is for irrigation (Figure 4.7). Plants need water to transport minerals and food, to keep their cells rigid, and to combine with carbon dioxide to make food in photosynthesis (see Chapter 3). This means that a reliable supply of water is needed for reliable crop growth. In addition, domestic animals require water to drink.

**Figure 4.7:** The most widespread use of water in agriculture is for irrigation.

## Water from the atmosphere and surface water

Water that is evaporated from Earth is stored in the atmosphere in clouds. When precipitation occurs, it falls as rain and snow, and enters systems such as rivers, lakes and **reservoirs** (Figure 4.8). This is called **surface water**.

**Figure 4.8:** Lakes are a source of surface water.

Rivers, reservoirs and sometimes lakes are major sources of water for human use. Water can be taken from a river by simply dipping a bucket into it, and this is still the only way to get water in many parts of the world. At the other extreme, some countries have huge national projects to provide people with a store of water. These often involve building a reservoir, which may be created behind a dam (Figure 4.9) or by the side of the river (a bankside reservoir).

Water that is fit for domestic uses such as drinking, washing and cooking is called **potable** water. Usually, river water is not safe to drink, but it can be treated to make it potable. **Service reservoirs** are another type of water storage system in which treated – and therefore potable – water is stored for use. **Water towers** and underground **cisterns** are examples of service reservoirs.

> ### KEY WORDS
> 
> **reservoir:** an artificial lake where water can be stored
> 
> **surface water:** water in lakes, rivers, reservoirs and swamps
> 
> **potable:** safe to drink
> 
> **service reservoir:** a reservoir in which potable water is stored

139

Figure 4.9: Dams provide a wall to store water behind in a reservoir.

be dug by hand or bored into rock with machinery. If the water in the aquifer is not under pressure, it has to be raised to the top of the well. This can be done by simply lowering a bucket on a rope, by using a hand-operated pump (a common method in LICs) or by using a motor-driven pump (more typical in MICs and HICs). If the water is stored under pressure, the aquifer is referred to as an **artesian aquifer**. Water from

## Water from the ground

There is a lot more **groundwater** than there is surface water. Vast quantities of water are stored in the spaces of porous rock, such as limestone or sandstone (see Chapter 2). Stores like this are referred to as **aquifers** (Figure 4.10), which is where about 30% of all global freshwater supplies are held. Aquifers fulfil a significant proportion of human water needs.

The most common way in which water is obtained from aquifers is to sink **wells** into them. A well can

> **KEY WORDS**
>
> **water tower:** a type of reservoir where potable water is stored for immediate use
>
> **cistern:** a vessel in which water, usually potable, is stored, forming a type of covered reservoir
>
> **groundwater:** water in the soil and in rocks under the surface of the ground
>
> **aquifer:** water that is stored in porous rocks under the ground
>
> **well:** a hole bored or dug into rock to reach the stored water
>
> **artesian aquifer:** an aquifer in which the water is under pressure

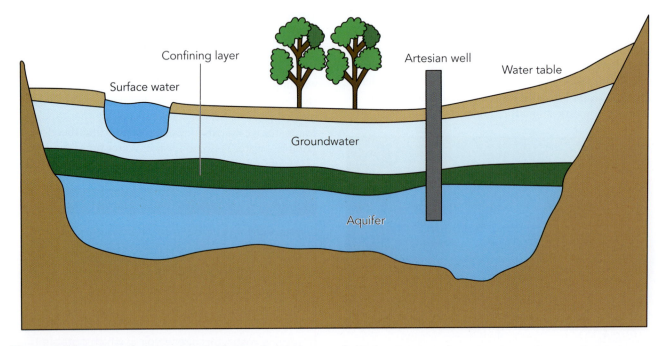

Figure 4.10: An aquifer, showing the layer of rock that confines the water and an artesian well.

a well sunk into an artesian aquifer (an artesian well) will rise to the surface on its own.

## Water from the oceans

There are five major oceans on Earth (Figure 4.11):

- Atlantic
- Pacific
- Indian
- Southern
- Arctic

In some parts of the world, surface water and groundwater sources do not provide enough, so people use water from the oceans. In order to make it safe for people to use, the salt has to be removed through a process called **desalination**.

> **ACTIVITY 4.1**
>
> Look at Figure 4.11. Find the five major oceans and write down a description of their positions. For example, the Atlantic Ocean is surrounded by North America to its west and north, with Europe and Africa to the east. South America lies south of the Atlantic Ocean, where it joins the Southern Ocean.

> **KEY WORD**
>
> **desalination:** the process of removing salt from water

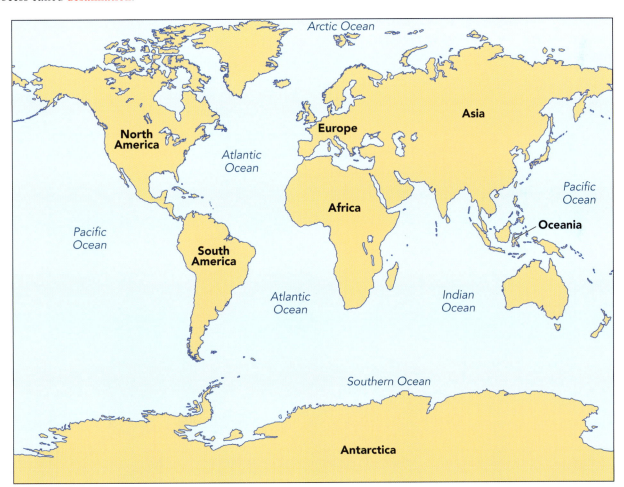

Figure 4.11: The location of Earth's five major oceans.

> **CAMBRIDGE IGCSE™ AND O LEVEL ENVIRONMENTAL MANAGEMENT: COURSEBOOK**

> **REFLECTION**
>
> Do you feel that drawing diagrams helps with your learning? Is there another way that suits your learning style, such as making up a poem incorporating the information needed? Discuss this with members of your class to see if there are any other learning methods that might be useful to you.

## Questions

4.1 Copy and complete the following paragraph about the water cycle:

Liquid water is found on the surface of the Earth in ............, ............ and ............ It is also found inside plants. Water turns from a liquid to a gas, water vapour, in a process called ............ The water vapour then ............ to form clouds. Liquid water falls from clouds to the Earth in the process of ............ Some of the water is prevented from reaching the ground by plants in the process of ............ Water that reaches the ground may enter it in a process called ............ The rest enters rivers by ............

4.2 Explain why nearly 70% of the water on Earth is very difficult for humans to use.

4.3 Using Figure 4.3, calculate the percentage of Earth's water that is in lakes. Show your working.

4.4 Suggest and explain which of groundwater, surface water, or ice caps and glaciers is likely to be the main source of fresh water for humans.

## Water treatment

To make water potable (safe to drink), it is needs to go through four stages (Figure 4.12):

- Screening: this removes large objects such as plastic and coarse grit.
- Sedimentation: substances called coagulants are added, which make dirt particles and dissolved chemicals in the water stick together and then sink to the bottom.

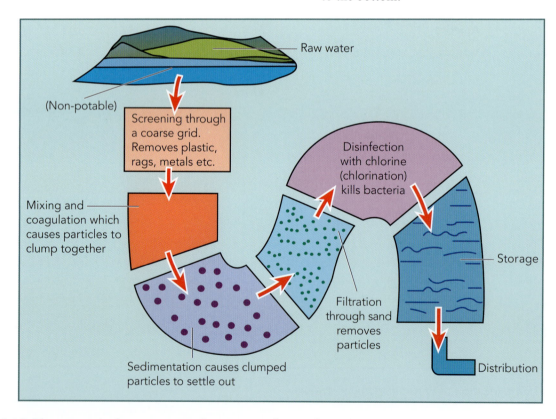

**Figure 4.12:** The stages in the treatment of water to make it safe to drink.

- Filtration: the water is filtered through sand to remove substances that have not already been removed by sedimentation.
- Chlorination: finally, chlorine is added to the water to disinfect it and kill off any disease-causing organisms (pathogens) that remain.

# The availability of safe drinking water around the world

A sufficient supply of potable water depends not only on there being enough rainfall, but also on a country's capacity for building and maintaining pipes and water-storage facilities. Sewage needs to be separated from the drinking water, and drinking water needs to be treated before it can be delivered for safe use.

### ACTIVITY 4.2

In groups of three or four, carry out some research into the current availability of safe drinking water around the world. You might find the Joint Monitoring Programme (JMP), run by the World Health Organization (WHO) and UNICEF, useful. You can either focus on one particular country or take a global perspective. You could also research what programmes are being developed to bring safe drinking water to people around the world.

Produce a presentation (for example, a poster, slide show or leaflet) to deliver to your class explaining the present state of affairs and the consequences of a lack of safe drinking water. Make sure you include the sources of your facts.

### PEER ASSESSMENT

After each group has presented its findings, score the presentations on the following aspects:

- The quality of the facts that they have presented. How many were included? How detailed were they? Did the group use reliable sources for their data?
- The variety of facts presented.
- How much understanding you now have of the issue.

### CONTINUED

For each aspect, award marks as follows:

5 = Superb

4 = Very good

3 = Good

2 = Lacking some information

1 = Needs improvement

As a class, give each group some constructive feedback so they can work to improve next time they do a similar activity.

### REFLECTION

Did this activity help you to understand the supply of safe drinking water around the world? Do you think you learn information better if you discover it for yourself? Does having to present your findings help you to consolidate your understanding?

## Water scarcity

One important factor when considering a country's water wealth is the amount of rain it receives. Using this measure, Brazil and Russia, for example, are two of the most water-wealthy nations, and the United Arab Emirates and Kuwait are two of the most water poor. However, there are other factors to consider, such as the number of people who need water. Water scarcity occurs when the amount of available fresh water does not meet demand (Figure 4.13). It is defined by the United Nations (UN) as an area that has less than 1000 metres$^3$ of fresh water available per person. Less than 500 metres$^3$ of water per person is defined as **absolute water scarcity**.

### KEY WORD

**absolute water scarcity:** defined by the United Nations (UN) as an area that has less than 500 metres$^3$ of water per person

**Figure 4.13:** Many rural communities in countries like Myanmar do not have easy access to drinking water. Here, a woman carries fresh water from a lake.

China has one of the largest populations in the world – more than 1.4 billion in 2023. The total water availability in China is about 2800 km$^3$, which gives approximately 2075 metres$^3$ of water per person. This does not fall into the category of being water scarce; however, these figures suggest that China does experience **water stress**. In 2023, earth.org reported that 17 countries suffered extremely high baseline water stress in 2020, 12 of which are in the Middle East and North Africa (Figure 4.14). The six most water-stressed countries in the world are Bahrain, Cyprus, Kuwait, Lebanon, Oman and Qatar. This is mostly driven by low supply and high demand.

Just as access to safe drinking water varies from country to country, it also varies within countries. In China, roughly half the population lives in the northern part of the country, where only one-fifth of its freshwater supplies are located. As a result, many northern provinces suffer from absolute water scarcity.

A lack of water may be due to low rainfall and/or high levels of evaporation. This is referred to as **physical water scarcity**. However, a country or region may suffer from **economic water scarcity**. A country may have a lot of water but cannot afford to extract it, purify it and make it available for the population.

> **KEY WORDS**
>
> **water stress:** a measure of the amount of fresh water used in an area compared to the quantity of renewable freshwater resources
>
> **physical water scarcity:** a situation in which there is simply not enough water for human needs
>
> **economic water scarcity:** a situation in which there is enough water available, but there is not enough money to extract and/or treat enough of it for human needs

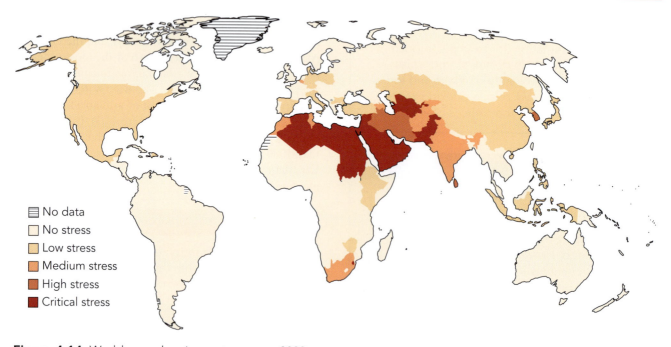

**Figure 4.14:** World map showing water stress, 2020.

## Urban and rural regions

There is often a contrast between rural and urban areas. In many cities and towns, more people have access to both clean, treated water and better sanitation than in rural areas in the same country (figure 4.15). The main reasons for this difference are as follows:

- There is greater wealth in cities, along with more wealthy people.
- Large numbers of people can act together to pressure authorities into providing safe drinking water.
- It is cheaper to install piped water when many people live close together than it is in a scattered rural community.

However, this is not always the case. Overcrowded cities face huge challenges in maintaining good sanitation. People who do not have basic sanitation services, such as private toilets, have to defecate outside – in street gutters, behind bushes or into open bodies of water – which risks contaminating sources of drinking water. Food that is irrigated using untreated water can cause illnesses.

Worldwide, many women and girls suffer the burden of collecting water, especially in rural areas. In 2023, WHO reported that in 7 out of 10 households without water supplies, it was women who had to fetch the water, which could take them up to six hours a day, significantly impacting their education.

**Figure 4.15:** In some places, fresh water is delivered to businesses in huge tanks. Here, a truck is delivering treated water to a restaurant in Cuba.

## Global inequalities in water and sewage treatment

Even if water is available, it may not be safe to drink (Figure 4.16). There are many ways of ensuring that water is potable, but all of them involve two main features:

- Sanitation systems ensure that dirty water does not mix with water intended for human use (sewage needs to be removed and treated; it must not mix with water intended for domestic use).
- Water-treatment processes ensure that the water supplied to people is safe to drink.

**Figure 4.16:** A bottle of water intended for drinking, taken from a river rather than a treated water source in Ethiopia.

Worldwide, sanitation and clean water are not available to everyone. In 2000, the UN said that its aim was to reduce the number of people by half that did not have regular access to safe drinking water and basic sanitation by 2015. It reached that goal five years earlier than anticipated, in 2010. However, despite this progress, 2 billion people are still using below-standard sanitation facilities, and 653 million have no sanitation facilities at all (Figure 4.17). The UN has set a new target to ensure the availability and sustainable management of water and sanitation for everyone in the world by 2030. There has been positive progress, with access to safely managed drinking water globally increasing from 69% in 2015 to 73% in 2022. However, progress is slow, and demand for water is rising so fast that water scarcity is predicted to increase.

**Figure 4.17:** This slum in Mumbai, India, is home to around one million people, living in poor sanitary conditions.

# Desalination

Drinking salt water can cause health problems and, eventually, death, so the water must go through desalination to remove the salt. Two processes can be used to make saltwater safe to drink: **distillation** and **reverse osmosis**.

## Distillation

In the process of distillation, water is heated until it boils and then released as vapour (steam), leaving the salt behind. The vapour is cooled and condensed as liquid water, which is then pure and potable. Figure 4.18 shows the process of distillation. Desalination plants using this method are mainly found in energy-rich countries, such as those in the Middle East.

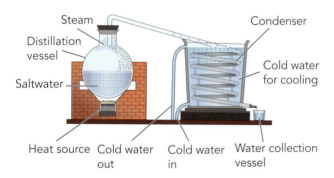

**Figure 4.18:** Desalination by distillation.

Desalination by distillation is about 10–30% efficient. The process leaves highly concentrated salt water (brine) in the flask, which needs to be disposed of and can be a source of pollution. The process of distillation also requires a lot of energy, which can be expensive, so only wealthier countries can afford it. Much of the energy used in desalination comes from fossil fuels, which leads to a large amount of atmospheric pollution. However, the alternative of transporting fresh water from more remote sources also requires energy. So, the desalination process may be no more costly than other methods of providing fresh water unless there are alternative local sources.

## Reverse osmosis

In reverse osmosis, saltwater is pumped at high pressure through very fine membranes (Figure 4.19). The membranes allow the water molecules to pass through, but not the salt molecules.

Desalination by reverse osmosis is about 30–50% efficient, and most new desalination plants use this technique.

As with distillation, brine is a **byproduct** of reverse osmosis. This contains several pollutants, including chlorine and chemicals used in the desalination process. In both desalination processes, the brine is often pumped back into the oceans, causing **ocean acidification** among other effects. It may also be at higher temperatures than sea water, which is harmful to marine life. Reverse osmosis also requires energy but less than distillation.

> ### KEY WORDS
>
> **distillation:** the purification of a liquid by boiling a solution so that the liquid evaporates and can be collected when it condenses at a lower temperature
>
> **reverse osmosis:** the purification of water by pumping it at high pressure through fine membranes
>
> **byproduct:** something that is produced as a result of making something else
>
> **ocean acidification:** a decrease in the pH of an ocean caused by the uptake of carbon dioxide

4 Water

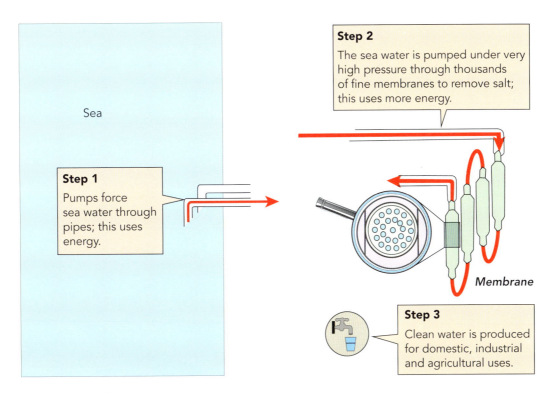

Figure 4.19: Desalination by reverse osmosis.

## Multipurpose dam projects

Dams are constructed with a number of aims in mind:

- Flood control: the amount of water released out of the dam can be controlled, so after heavy rainfall, the flow of water from the dam can be increased to prevent flooding behind it (Figure 4.20).

- Hydro-electric power: the water from the reservoir can be released and allowed to flow through a turbine, producing electricity (Figure 4.21). The amount of electricity produced will depend on the height of the reservoir above the watercourse and the speed with which the water flows through the turbine.

Figure 4.20: This dam is releasing water to prevent flooding after heavy rainfall.

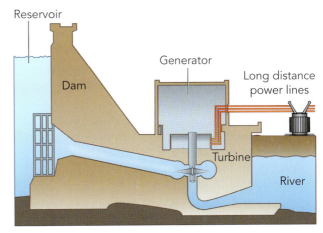

Figure 4.21: The structure of a dam.

147

- Irrigation: water from the reservoir can be used by farmers to water their land, which is particularly valuable during times of drought. Some dams have canals through which water is directed to irrigate farmland.
- Water storage and supply: by building a dam across a river, water is slowed down. The water level behind the dam rises and creates a reservoir for storing the water.
- Transport: once a river has been dammed, it can provide a more suitable navigable watercourse – for example, it can maintain a minimum water level all year round, which is needed by ships and can provide access by boat to otherwise inaccessible areas.
- Recreation: the reservoir can be used for various activities, such as swimming, fishing and other water sports. An increase in wildlife can attract birdwatchers.
- Tourism: the reservoir creates a visually pleasing environment that attracts tourists, who may also come to take part in the increased recreation activities.
- Fish farming: fish farms can be set up in the reservoir.

Dams can be useful in all the ways described previously. However, there are also some drawbacks to constructing dams:

- Cost: dams can be very expensive to plan and build.
- Relocating people: people who live in the area where the dam is being built may need to be relocated. When deciding whether or not to build a dam, the number of people involved needs to be considered as well as the cost of relocating them.
- Loss of land: developers also need to consider how much land will be lost to flooding when building the dam and what its value is.
- Disruption to ecosystems: when a dam is constructed, it can prevent fish from swimming upriver beyond the site of the dam. This can disrupt the breeding and life cycles of the fish and other aquatic organisms.
- Changes to water supplies: a dam reduces the flow of water, so supplies for people living downstream of the dam will be affected.
- Reduction in soil quality: soil downstream of the dam may no longer be enriched by the natural flooding of the original river course (Figure 4.22).
- Siltation: over time, sediment sinks to the bottom of the reservoir and reduces its storage capacity.
- Structure deterioration: the dam's structure, which is under a lot of pressure, may deteriorate and eventually fail.

Despite these arguments, dams may still be a superior energy-generating alternative to the burning of fossil fuels, because they produce electricity without greenhouse gases and pollutants.

Figure 4.22: Built in 1971, the Aswan High Dam in Egypt harnesses the waters of the Nile for hydro-electric power and irrigation. Since then, the fertility of the Nile delta has declined due to a lack of silt that used to be deposited by the Nile's natural annual flooding patterns.

## Questions

4.5 Look at the lists of the uses/benefits and limitations of dam projects described previously. Copy and complete the following table by adding each benefit or limitation in the right place.

|  | Benefits | Limitations |
| --- | --- | --- |
| Environmental |  |  |
| Economic |  |  |
| Social |  |  |

4.6 Explain the ways in which a multipurpose dam project might be considered unsustainable.

## CASE STUDY

### A multipurpose dam on the Ramganga River at Kalagarh, India

In 1961, the construction of a large multipurpose dam was started at Kalagarh across the Ramganga River, which is a tributary of the Ganges in India. It was completed in 1974 (Figure 4.23). The dam:

- is 127.5 metres high
- generates 451 million units of power annually from three 66 MW power houses
- has a reservoir area of 80 km$^2$
- stores 2447.6 metres$^3$ of water
- has a catchment area made up of 57% forests, 8% grassland and 30% agricultural lands.

**Figure 4.23:** A satellite image of the Ramganga Dam, Kalagarh, India.

In its construction:

- no crop lands were submerged, and there was no flooding of railways or roads
- there was no need to relocate any people
- 42 km$^2$ of forest and 25 km$^2$ of plantations were submerged
- the owners of the forests were paid compensation, and plantations in an adjoining area were afforested
- an area of 0.075 km$^2$ was landscaped, and tourist facilities were installed.

The dam is in a highly seismic area, and so a seismological observatory with the latest equipment was installed.

Since construction:

- flooding of a large area around the dam can now be controlled
- wildlife has increased and many species of migratory birds have been attracted to the reservoir
- the reservoir's water quality is suitable for aquatic life and for use in irrigation
- hundreds of square kilometres of land in the Ramganga floodplains are now being used successfully for agriculture
- little treatment is needed to make the water safe to drink
- Delhi receives 5.67 metres$^3$ of water per second through concrete pipes.

Over 10 000 jobs were created by the building of the dam, and 3000 officials and workers are employed in the maintenance of the dam project. The transport infrastructure has also been improved: Kalagarh is now well connected with important cities such as Delhi.

In a report in 2014, some local farmers claimed that the dam was affecting their crops and their fish catches. They said that the dam gates were opened and closed to suit the water level in the dam. Their land therefore received a variable amount of water, ranging from extreme flooding to near drought. This pattern meant they were losing crops.

In addition, the annual floods of the Ramganga River used to bring in fine silt and replenish the fertility of the soil, but now the dam has altered the sediment characteristics by bringing in coarse sand instead.

Fish have become isolated above the dam and only get released to the lower river below the dam when the dam gates are opened. This disruption to their breeding cycles has led to a decrease in fish size, number and diversity.

> CAMBRIDGE IGCSE™ AND O LEVEL ENVIRONMENTAL MANAGEMENT: COURSEBOOK

## CONTINUED

### Questions

1. Suggest reasons why the dam took 13 years to be completed.
2. Explain why:
   a. a seismological observatory was built
   b. authorities are monitoring sedimentation behind the dam.
3. To what extent do you agree that the dam is beneficial to:
   a. local people
   b. India?

   Explain your answers.

### CRITICAL THINKING TIP

In the case study on dams, you were asked to think about the benefits of the dam to local people and to the country as a whole. You were provided with a substantial amount of data to use for this. However, it is important to be aware of any bias there might be in data like this. For example, the groups who want to build the dam for commercial reasons will present figures that suit their needs. Would local people provide different reflections of the impact of the dam's construction on their way of life? Can you put a numerical value on the loss of a person's land? Financial compensation may not be sufficient to offset the disruption.

### ACTIVITY 4.3

Imagine that someone has proposed to build a new dam in your local area. Split into two groups:

- One group should brainstorm arguments against the dam being built.
- The other group should come up with arguments in favour of it being built.

Each group should elect two members to present the arguments to the other group. After the presentations, open the floor to questions from each side.

At the end, everyone in the class should cast their vote either for or against the proposal. Who presented the most persuasive arguments?

### REFLECTION

How did you find the experience of debating this topic? Was it challenging? Fun? Interesting?

Although you were presenting for one side of the argument, could you also see the other side?

Did you have an opinion on this issue before you carried out the activity? If so, did you find it difficult to appreciate the reasons given for the opposite opinion? Did the debate persuade you to change your opinion?

# 4.2 Water pollution

The more that water is used, the greater the chances that it will become polluted and so unusable.

## Sources of water pollution

### Domestic waste and sewage

Domestic wastewater is generated by many activities, with much of it due to 'washing', whether that is clothes, utensils or skin. This is non-sewage wastewater, often referred to as 'greywater'. Wastewater often contains chemicals, such as phosphates, from detergents, and these can cause eutrophication. It may also contain fats and oils along with other dissolved solids. These can provide nutrients for microorganisms, which increases the demand for oxygen and ultimately reduces the amount of oxygen in rivers and lakes. Pharmaceutical, health and beauty products can also find their way into greywater, as can several heavy metals, such as lead and mercury.

4 Water

Figure 4.24: In some areas, sewage pipes eventually run out into bodies of water, such as rivers, which may be sources of fresh water that people use for drinking and other purposes.

**Sewage** wastewater includes urine and faecal material. This is carried away from houses and other buildings in both cities and small villages via drains called sewers. It is then either dumped as it is or converted into a form that is less harmful (Figure 4.24). The two main issues with sewage are that it contains pathogens and organic material. Sewage treatment has to tackle these two elements.

## Plastic waste

Plastic waste in fresh water comes from a range of sources, from people discarding plastic objects such as drinks bottles into watercourses, to the disposal of domestic items such as contact lenses and sanitary products in the sewerage system. Microplastics can be particularly harmful. Plastics in all their forms can cause problems if aquatic creatures get tangled up them or if the creatures ingest them.

## Industrial processes

Industry uses a wide range of chemicals, such as caustic materials (those that may corrode or burn organic tissue) and heavy metals, which can be harmful to both humans and the environment. Because of water's excellent solvent properties, many of these chemicals end up in water bodies. Waste from industry is often discharged into rivers and lakes. Gases from industrial chimneys enter the atmosphere, where they dissolve in water and form acid rain (see Chapter 5). The bodies of living things are at least 75% water, and so these water-soluble pollutants can easily enter organisms and cause problems.

## Agricultural practices

Modern agriculture makes use of many chemicals, such as pesticides, herbicides and fertilisers. All of these are water-soluble and can cause pollution in water bodies. Nutrients such as nitrate and phosphate can enter water from farming practices, such as the use of fertilisers, as well as from industry and domestic outputs. In addition, organic matter can enter water directly as sewage, as well as from other sources (Figure 4.25).

> **KEY WORD**
>
> **sewage:** waste matter that is carried away in sewers or drains from domestic (or industrial) buildings

151

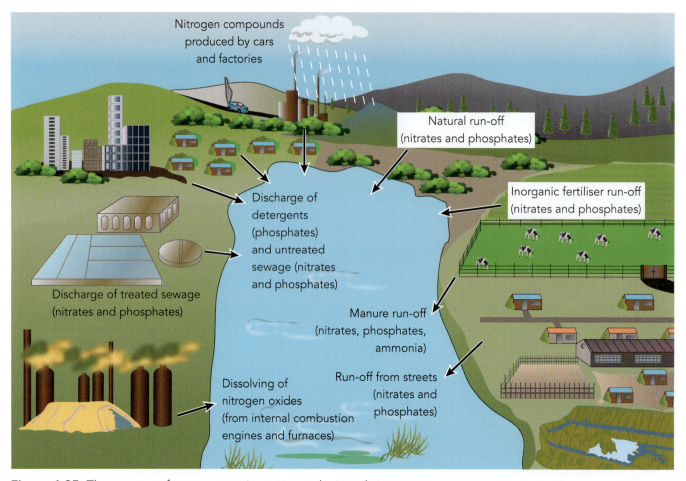

Figure 4.25: The sources of excess organic matter and minerals in water.

Any increase in nutrients in a river or lake will cause a rapid growth of **algae**. This is called an **algal bloom** (Figure 4.26). The death and decomposition of these algae cause a drop in oxygen levels in the water.

> ### KEY WORDS
>
> **algae:** plant-like, photosynthetic organisms that lack true stems, roots and leaves
>
> **algal bloom:** the rapid growth of algae in water, caused particularly by a surge of nutrients

Figure 4.26: An algal bloom on Lake Champlain, Vermont, USA.

4 Water

## Impacts of water pollution

Some of the impacts of water pollution on people and the environment are explored next.

### Infectious diseases

Having plenty of water does not necessarily mean that there is plenty of safe water to drink. For example, poor sanitation can lead to infected water (Figure 4.27), which is linked to the transmission of waterborne diseases such as cholera and typhoid, as well as dysentery, intestinal worm infections and polio.

Cholera is a disease caused by a bacterium, and symptoms can show themselves as soon as a few hours after being infected, up to five days. It is characterised by vomiting and diarrhoea, which can lead to dehydration and death. The main treatment is to rehydrate the person. A vaccination against cholera also now exists. Despite this, case numbers remain high: in 2022, they were 472 697 cases, with 2349 deaths, although these figures may not be completely reliable.

**Figure 4.27:** This sign on a beach alerts swimmers to contaminated water due to raw sewage being diverted into the canal behind the beach, after heavy rains. High levels of bacteria were detected.

### Industrial and agricultural processes: biomagnification and bioaccumulation

Many industrial processes use and produce a variety of toxic substances. Some of these may enter bodies of water and cause immediate harm and even death to the organisms living there. Even if a substance only enters the water in small amounts, it can increase in concentration as it passes up a food chain, by a process called biomagnification. The best-known examples of biomagnification are with heavy metals and some pesticides.

Many industrial processes involve the use of heavy metals, such as lead, mercury and cadmium. These metals are toxic and can be stored in the bodies of plants and animals, including humans, and by such bioaccumulation they may build up to high levels, which can cause illness.

Pesticides are designed to kill living things but not humans. However, because human physiology has much in common with other living organisms, pesticides can also have negative effects on humans. Insecticides will kill both the target species (the pest) and non-target species, which can include the natural enemies of the pests. Pesticides are generally water-soluble, so water pollution by these chemicals is a major concern. These chemicals will enter water-based food chains and result in bioaccumulation and biomagnification.

### The effects of acid rain

When fossil fuels, such as coal and oil, are burnt, the gases sulfur dioxide ($SO_2$) and oxides of nitrogen ($NO_x$) are produced. They enter the atmosphere and can be blown long distances. These gases react with water in the atmosphere to form acids. Then, when it rains, these acids fall to the ground as **acid rain** (Figure 4.28).

The pH of water is a measure of how acid or alkaline it is. A pH of less than 7 is acid, 7 is neutral and above 7 is alkaline. The pH range is from very acidic (0) to very alkaline (14). Rain usually has a pH of between 5 and 6, so is always slightly acidic. Acid rain has a pH lower than this – values as low as 2 have been recorded, which is about the same as battery acid.

When water in a river or lake is acidified, organisms struggle to survive. Fish lay fewer eggs, and young fish may be malformed. Acid rain can also lead to **leaching**

> **KEY WORDS**
>
> **acid rain:** rain that has been made more acidic by the presence of sulfur dioxide and oxides of nitrogen
>
> **leaching:** the movement of a soluble chemical or mineral away from soil, usually caused by the action of rainwater

153

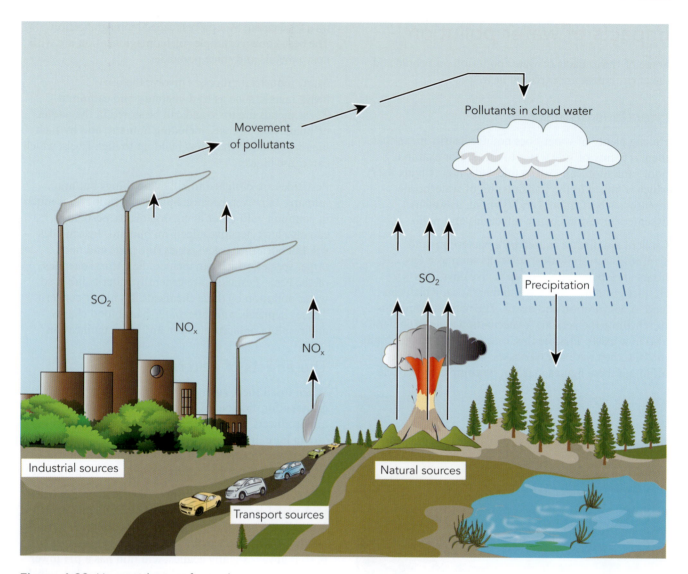

Figure 4.28: How acid rain is formed.

of heavy metals, such as aluminium, lead and mercury, from the soil into the water. This leads to further harmful effects. Aluminium, for example, clogs fish gills and can cause suffocation. Another effect is that essential minerals, such as calcium and potassium, are washed out of the lake or river. This reduces algal growth, leaving less food for fish and other animals. The direct and indirect effects of acid rain and run-off of heavy metals from surrounding soils affect the whole ecosystem.

## Eutrophication

When water bodies receive nutrients from leaching through soil or from fertilisers blowing into them, there is nutrient enrichment, which results in increased plant growth, especially of algae. When these plants die and decompose, it uses up oxygen, lowering the levels of oxygen in the water. The same thing occurs when organic matter enters water through sewage and is broken down by bacteria. Most living things rely on oxygen, so other organisms in the water may die. This process is called eutrophication (Figure 4.29).

4 Water

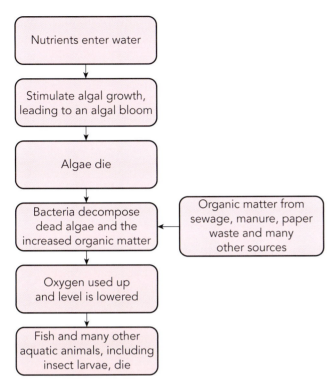

Figure 4.29: A flowchart showing how eutrophication occurs.

### PROBLEM-SOLVING TIP

When discussing the water and carbon cycles, it is useful to use scientific terms, such as 'eutrophication', but it can be challenging to learn them. Eutrophication is a word that is used to summarise a particular series of steps, or a process. Other words and phrases that do a similar thing are: photosynthesis; respiration; water, carbon and rock cycles; and malaria life cycle. Try to find techniques that will help you remember these, such as creating a memorable sentence using the first letter of each process in the sequence or drawing a colour-coded flowchart as a visual aid.

### FIELDWORK ACTIVITY 4.1

#### The effect of mineral concentration on plant growth

It is easy to look at the effects of increasing mineral concentration on the growth of plants by using a floating pond weed, such as duckweed. You need to set up a range of solutions containing increasing amounts of minerals and then follow the growth of the plants.

#### You will need

- pond weed, such as duckweed
- houseplant food
- Petri dishes or glass bowls
- beakers
- forceps or a brush to handle the duckweed

#### Before you start

Plants can make organic matter by using carbon dioxide and water. However, they need various minerals as well to grow. If grown in water solutions containing different mineral concentrations under controlled conditions, the effect of these minerals on growth can be observed.

#### Method

- Make a range of solutions, each with a different concentration of houseplant food – from diluted to strong. You could use 100%, 75%, 50% and 25% of plant food.
- Pour each of your solutions into a Petri dish or glass bowl.
- Place the same number of duckweed plants onto the surface of each solution and count them (Figure 4.30).
- Place the dish with plants in a well-lit place.
- Count the number of plants at regular intervals over the next few days.

155

> ### CONTINUED

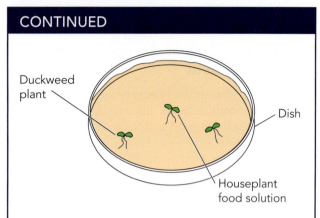

Figure 4.30: Duckweed plants in a Petri dish.

#### Questions

1. Plot graphs to show your data, including graphs of the number of plants plotted against time (in days) for each concentration of solution, and a graph of the number of plants at the end of the experiment plotted against the concentration of the solution.

2. Calculate the doubling time of the number of duckweed plants at each concentration of solution.

3. Write a conclusion about the effect of the strength of houseplant food solution on the duckweed growth.

4. Suggest what the implication of this effect of solution concentration might be for a pond.

## Strategies for improving water quality

### Improved sanitation

An improved sanitation facility is defined as one that separates human excreta from contact with humans. This can be achieved using a variety of toilet types:

- A flush toilet uses a holding tank for flushing water and a water seal that prevents smells. A pour flush toilet has a water seal but uses water poured by hand for flushing. In both cases, the waste needs to be removed in one of two ways:
  - by connection to a system of sewer pipes, called sewerage, that collects human faeces, urine and waste water, which is then removed from the house
  - by connection to a septic system, which consists of an underground, sealed settling tank.
- A pit latrine with a platform is a dry pit fully covered by a platform that is fitted with a seat over a hole, or just has a hole, in the platform. The platform covers the pit without exposing the contents, other than through the hole. Sometimes, these latrines are ventilated to take away smells.
- A composting toilet is a dry toilet into which vegetable waste, straw, grass, sawdust and ash are added to the human waste to produce compost (Figure 4.31).

Figure 4.31: Pouring sawdust into a composting toilet.

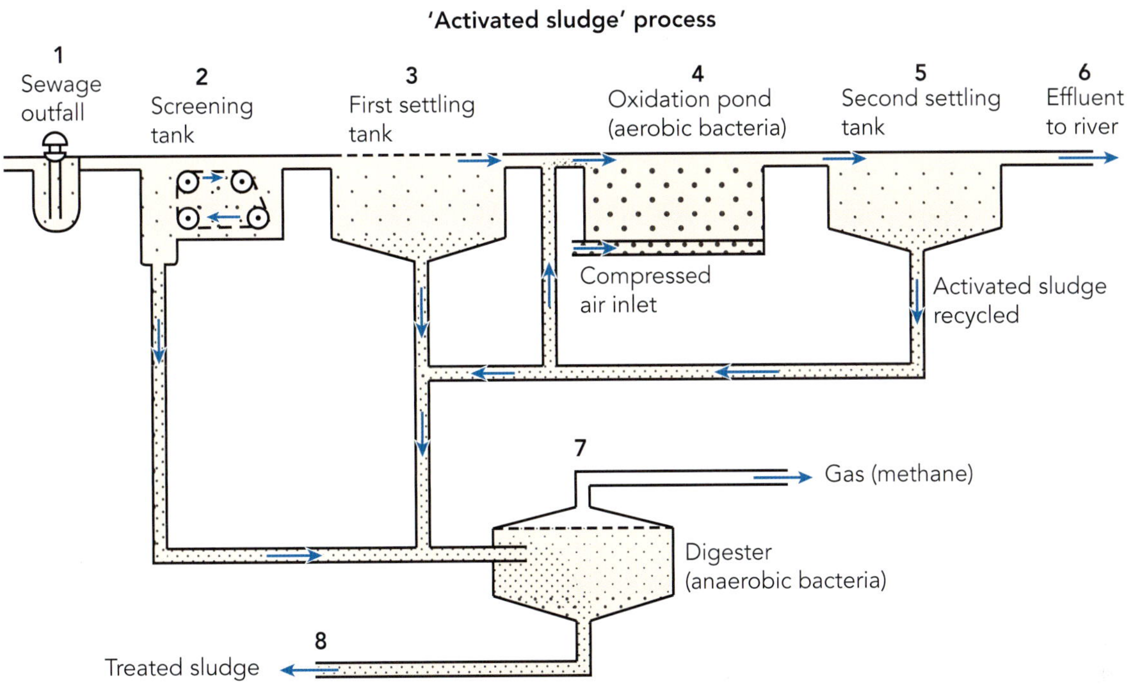

4 Water

'Activated sludge' process

1 Sewage outfall
2 Screening tank
3 First settling tank
4 Oxidation pond (aerobic bacteria)
5 Second settling tank
6 Effluent to river
7 Digester (anaerobic bacteria) — Gas (methane)
8 Treated sludge

Compressed air inlet

Activated sludge recycled

**Figure 4.32:** The stages in a sewage treatment plant.

## Sewage treatment

The main aim of sewage treatment is to reduce the biological oxygen demand (BOD) of the sewage – the amount of oxygen it would use up if released directly into a river or lake. The main stages of a sewage treatment works (shown in Figure 4.32) are described as follows:

1 Sewage outfall: waste water from homes, and sometimes industry, is taken to a sewage treatment works in sewers.
2 Screening tank: large objects are removed from the waste water using a coarse grid.
3 Primary treatment, first settling tank: the solid organic matter, mainly human waste, is allowed to settle to the bottom of the tank. This settled material is called sludge, which is treated in the sludge digester (see step 7). The cleaned water overflows the sides of the tank and is taken to the next stage.
4 Secondary treatment, oxidation: the water is pumped into a tank, where oxygen is bubbled through it. This encourages the growth of bacteria and other microbes, which break down dissolved organic matter (which causes the BOD).
5 Secondary treatment, second settling tank: the water enters the second settling tank, where the bacteria settle to the bottom, forming more sludge. This cleaner water overflows the sides of the tank as **effluent**.
6 The effluent is discharged into the environment, usually a river.
7 Sludge digester: here, oxygen-free conditions are created that encourage the growth of bacteria, which break down the sludge, releasing methane, which can be burnt.
8 The treated sludge can be dried in sludge lagoons (Figure 4.33) and used as organic fertiliser on farmland.

In some sewage works, tertiary treatment is also carried out. This may involve further filtering of the effluent or its chlorination. This produces even cleaner effluent, which may be needed to protect the habitat into which it is released.

> **KEY WORD**
>
> **effluent:** a discharge of liquid waste

157

**Figure 4.33:** Checking a supply pipe of a sludge drying lagoon in a sewage treatment plant.

## Pollution control and legislation

We can reduce the amount of gases that contribute to acid rain by substituting fossil fuels used to produce energy. To reduce $SO_2$ emissions, low-sulfur varieties of fossil fuel should be used. $NO_x$ emissions can be reduced by burning with a cooler flame or adjusting the air-to-fuel ratio. Clean Air Acts have been passed to encourage power plants and others to employ some or all of these methods so that they stay within permitted emission levels.

Governments around the world have been tackling pollution through legislation. Industries in participating countries are required to monitor the pollution they cause and keep it within set levels. Such legislation puts pressure on the polluters to find ways to reduce the pollutants. There can be fines for exceeding set limits. Companies may be prosecuted and, in extreme cases, forced to close down. They might need government agreement on strategic plans to reduce pollutions levels. Incentives can also be used to encourage companies to take part, such as grants or tax relief for those that achieve a reduction in pollution.

> ### ACTIVITY 4.4
>
> Work in small groups to research the bi-national Great Lakes Water Quality Agreement (GLWQA), which was devised in 1972 and celebrated 50 years in 2022. Work together to create a report on the programme. Include the following information:
>
> - where the programme took place
> - what problem triggered the initiative in the first place
> - what updates to the agreement have been made since 1972 and why
> - what successes the programme has had, including animals that have returned to the area.
>
> Try to include some data and statistics in your report.

> ### PEER ASSESSMENT
>
> Swap reports with another group. Read through the other group's report and compare it with your own. Did they find facts and statistics that you have not included? Give the other group feedback by commenting on two things that you liked about their report or that they did well, and suggesting one way in which you think the report could be improved.

## Questions

4.7  Explain why it would not be a good idea to use water from ponds or small lakes in preference to water harvested from a roof.

4.8  What is the main reason for the removal of solid organic material in sewage treatment?

4.9  Explain the difference between water treatment and sewage treatment.

4.10 Distinguish between the terms 'bioaccumulation' and 'biomagnification'.

## 4.3 Water-related diseases

**Water-related diseases** include waterborne diseases such as cholera, which are caused by pathogens, but also water-bred diseases such as malaria, where mosquitos use water for breeding.

### Malaria

Malaria is caused by a microscopic organism called *Plasmodium*, which is carried by and multiplies inside the female *Anopheles* mosquito (Figure 4.34). The mosquito is therefore not the cause of the disease but is a **vector** for the disease-causing organism.

Malaria is water-related because the *Anopheles* mosquito requires water to breed. It lays its eggs in still water, where the larvae develop. Mosquitoes pass the *Plasmodium* – and so malaria – into the human bloodstream when they bite. A non-infected mosquito can acquire the *Plasmodium* parasite when it feeds on the blood of an infected human. The relationship between mosquitoes, *Plasmodium* and human beings is best understood with a life-cycle diagram (Figure 4.36).

The symptoms of malaria are flu-like and include fever and chills at first, but the disease can be fatal. In 2022, there were an estimated 249 million cases of malaria, most of them in sub-Saharan Africa, with about 608 000 deaths in 85 countries.

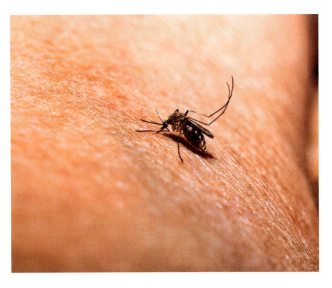

**Figure 4.34:** A female *Anopheles* mosquito biting a human.

### KEY WORDS

**water-related disease:** a disease that uses water in some way in order to spread, such as malaria (mosquitos use water to breed)

**vector:** an organism that carries a disease-producing organism, such as the mosquito which carries the malarial parasite

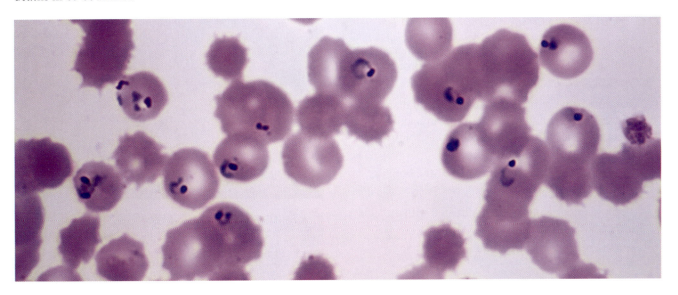

**Figure 4.35:** Malarial parasite (magnification × 400)

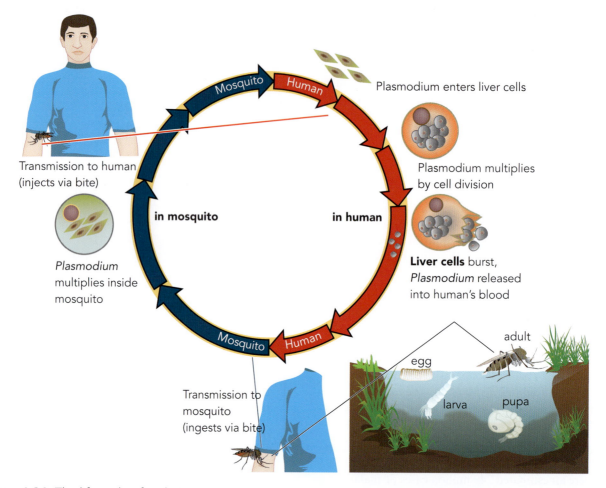

Figure 4.36: The life cycle of malaria.

## Strategies to control malaria

Prevention and control of malaria are best achieved by avoiding mosquito bites. Individuals can protect themselves by:

- avoiding being outside between dusk and dawn in countries where malaria mosquitoes are active – the species of the *Anopheles* mosquito that transmits malaria only flies at night
- wearing clothing that covers most of the body
- using insect repellent
- sleeping under a mosquito net treated with an insecticide (Figure 4.37)
- spraying the inside of accommodation with insecticide
- taking antimalarial drugs
- being vaccinated against the disease.

Figure 4.37: Sleeping under a mosquito net can help to prevent catching the disease in areas where malaria transmission is a risk.

For governments, strategies for malaria control are focused on controlling the vector. This can be achieved by:

- spraying insecticide inside buildings, including houses
- draining wetland areas to remove mosquito-breeding sites
- biological control – such as introducing fish, which eat the larvae and pupae of the mosquito, into ponds and other bodies of water
- pouring oil onto the surface of the water where mosquitoes breed, which stops the larvae from breathing and stops the adults from laying eggs
- sterilising male mosquitos.

### SCIENCE TIP

Be careful not to confuse malaria with bacterial diseases, such as cholera and typhoid. Bacteria breed in the water. Malaria is caused by a **parasite**, which breeds in an insect, and the insect breeds in water. This difference affects how the disease is contracted and how the disease-producing organism is eradicated.

### KEY WORD

**parasite:** an organism that lives in or on another organism; it gains nutrition from that organism but gives the host organism no benefits

## Strategies to control cholera

Earlier, you saw how cholera is spread through contaminated water. One crucial element in preventing transmission of this disease is to ensure that sewage and drinking water do not come into contact with each other. Therefore, good sanitation is crucial, with sewage being removed directly to a treatment works, and water being boiled or treated/chlorinated before it is delivered to people to drink.

Attention to good hygiene is also important, as is the thorough cooking of food. Contaminated water should not be used to wash food, and hands should be washed after contact with any faecal material. Use of efficient latrines is essential.

If there is any doubt about whether water is safe to drink, simply boiling it can eliminate most harmful organisms. Vaccinations are also now available to help prevent cholera.

## Benefits and limitations of strategies to control water-related diseases

Removing the malarial parasite from the population would eradicate malaria completely. Controlling the mosquito's breeding would result in there being fewer mosquitos to bite uninfected people; however, this would only achieve a reduction in infections. Techniques that actually destroy the parasite are better in the long term. However, these are expensive, whereas controlling the breeding of mosquitoes is relatively cheap and can be put into action by the people themselves, simply by such actions as removing any stagnant water or using oil on the surface of pools.

Improvements in diagnosis, treatment and prevention have led to a decline in both cases of and deaths from malaria. However, it is unlikely that these methods will result in its elimination. In 2022, there were 249 million cases reported, with 608 000 deaths. The mosquito vector is developing a resistance to insecticides, and the parasite is also becoming resistant to available drugs. More attention needs to be given to people who are infected by the disease but have no symptoms. It is clear that new methods for controlling malaria are needed.

When it comes to infectious diseases, people can take responsibility themselves for simple actions like hand washing and boiling water. However, treatment of water for drinking and the safe, efficient removal of sewage are more expensive and require government action. Total removal of infectious diseases can be achieved, but the maintenance of this is an ongoing issue. Any lapse in sanitation would quickly lead to the reintroduction of disease.

## Questions

**4.11** Drugs, vector eradication, improved sanitation, clean water supply and chlorination are all ways of dealing with water-related diseases. State which one of these would be most suitable for controlling malaria and which for cholera. Explain your answers.

**4.12** The use of nets to sleep under and biological control are both methods to help reduce the incidence of malaria. What are the reasons for each method? Discuss when each one would be most appropriate.

## 4.4 Marine aquaculture

### The impact of exploiting marine species

Every year, more than 90 million tonnes of fish are harvested. The number of fish that can be caught each year depends on several factors, but most importantly on the amount of fish stocks available. This will vary due to the number of mature fish capable of producing the new generation of young fish. However, fish species also need suitable environmental conditions and an adequate supply of their own food source. There is a delicate balance between these factors.

### Overfishing and overharvesting of marine species

The global fish catch grew almost every year from 1950 until the late 1980s. Since then, there have been fluctuations but no trend of growth (Figure 4.38). After a peak of 96 million tonnes in 2018, there were slight declines of 4.5% in 2019 and a further 2.1% in 2020.

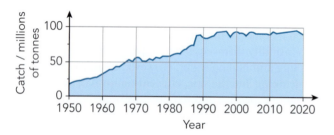

**Figure 4.38:** The change in total marine fish catches between 1950 and 2020.

This lack of growth may be partly explained by overfishing and **overharvesting**. At least 75% of the world's marine fisheries are threatened. The number of fish caught is partly based on how many are available, so sustainable fishing means monitoring how many fish are left in order to still be able to provide for the next generation of fishers and their customers.

The yield from world fisheries has only remained relatively constant because it has been possible to switch to new species. A look at some of the major food providers of the past provides strong evidence of overfishing. One of the best examples is the fate of the North Atlantic herring. In the 1950s, an estimated 3000 million herring per year were taken to ports in the UK. The stock of fish at that time is estimated to have been about 2 million tonnes. Fishing based on how many fish are available led to an increase in the size and power of the fishing boats. By the early 1970s, hardly any herring were left, with stocks of less than 100 000 tonnes.

Another example is that of the Peruvian anchovy fishery. At its peak, this single fishery yielded more than 12 million tonnes of fish. However, the fishery suffered an enormous collapse in the early 1970s. Figure 4.39 shows fluctuations in yields from the Peruvian anchovy fishery between 1950 and 2022.

Part of the reason for this collapse was overfishing, which meant that the fish were being caught before they could breed. But sometimes managing marine species is limited by natural events, which can affect the size of fish stocks.

The most important fisheries in the world are located where the system of currents stirs up decaying material from the seabed, which is rich in mineral nutrients. This is called **upwelling** (Figure 4.40). Because it affects **phytoplankton** growth, this area supports very large fish populations, mainly of the small herring-like fish anchoveta.

> **KEY WORDS**
>
> **overharvesting:** exploiting a natural resource until its supply is diminished to the extent that it is no longer sustainable
>
> **upwelling:** areas where minerals at the ocean floor are brought to the surface by currents
>
> **phytoplankton:** small organisms in the sea that can make their own food and upon which almost all other sea creatures depend for their food (via food chains)

4 Water

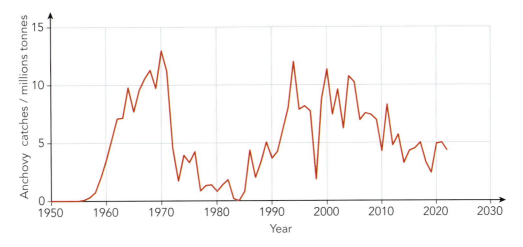

**Figure 4.39:** Yields of the Peruvian anchovy fishery, 1950–2022.

## WORKED EXAMPLE

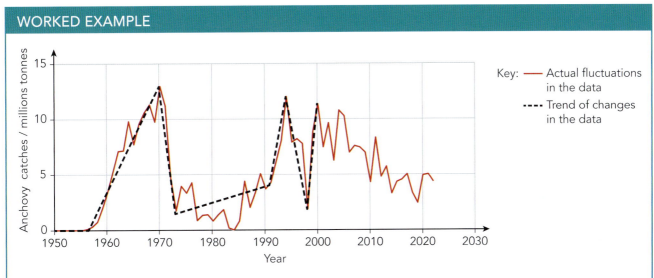

**Figure 4.40:** Sketch the main changes on a copy of the graph.

### Fishing trends

Look at Figure 4.39. Describe the trends in fish catch from 1955 until 2000.

**Step 1** Ignoring the minor fluctuations, consider the main changes and years when there was predictable change.

**Step 2** Sketch your thoughts on a copy of the graph (Figure 4.39).

**Step 3** Note down the key points: "There is a steep rise from around 1957 until 1970. It then falls until 1974. After that, there is quite a lot of fluctuation at a low level, with a minimum in 1984. From 1990, there is a steep rise, a steep fall from 1995 and then a recovery in 2000." This is more than enough detail for a description of a trend.

> CONTINUED
>
> **Now you try**
>
> Figure 4.41 shows a survey of the fish caught in a fishery over a 24-year period. Look at the graph and the key, and describe the trends in the size of fish caught between 1996 and 2020.
>
>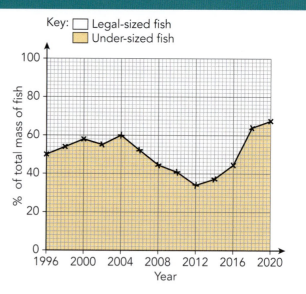
>
> **Figure 4.41:** The fish caught, shown as legal-sized and under-sized fish, as a percentage of the total catch, over a 24-year period from 1996 to 2020.

> **SCIENCE TIP**
>
> When describing a trend or trends, make generalised descriptions. Words such as 'increase', 'decrease', 'constant', 'plateau' and 'fluctuate' are likely to be most useful.
> Use a dictionary to remind yourself what these words mean.

> **KEY WORDS**
>
> **target species:** the species that is the subject of a fishing effort
>
> **bycatch:** animals caught by fishers that are not the intended target of the fishing effort

## Effect on target and bycatch species

The symptoms of severe overfishing are a reduced catch of the **target species**. However, these are not the only casualty. Wherever fish are caught commercially, the wrong species, the wrong sex or individuals that are too small are also caught. These non-target individuals are referred to as **bycatch**. For example, worldwide it is estimated that for every shrimp caught, nearly six other fish are also caught (Figure 4.42). In the tuna-fishing industry, dolphins often become entangled in the tuna nets. The public has become so concerned about this form of bycatch that tinned tuna often carries the label 'dolphin-friendly'.

**Figure 4.42:** Trawl net bycatch from a shrimp fishery in the Sea of Cortez, Mexico.

The most obvious cause of overfishing is the increasing demand for fish as food. However, technology and improved fishing methods have also played a major part. Much bigger boats, which can work a long way from a port for many weeks, are now used. In addition, it is now possible to find fish easily using sonar and detailed weather data. However, one of the most important developments has been the creation of huge nets, which scoop up everything in an area, including unwanted fish and other species. Almost half of everything caught in nets like these is regularly discarded as bycatch.

Another impact of the exploitation of fish is that they get progressively smaller. For example, between the 1930s and the 2000s, the average cod became 12 cm shorter and weighed nearly 2 kg less (Figure 4.43).

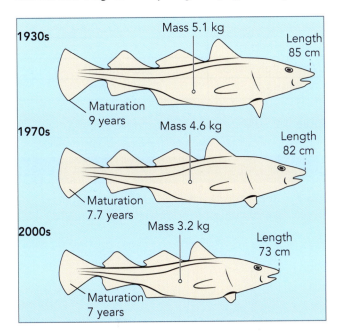

**Figure 4.43:** The decline in size of cod caught.

## Effect on food chains

Overharvesting of any particular species can have an effect on other organisms in the food chain or food web. For example, herring are preyed on by cod. When herring are overfished, cod populations suffer as well. Tuna are both predators and prey – they eat smaller fish and invertebrates, and are preyed on by sharks and whales. If any break occurs in any one chain, the whole food web can be disrupted.

**Figure 4.44:** A type of seaweed called kelp is being harvested on a marine aquaculture ranch in China.

## What is marine aquaculture?

Marine aquaculture is the practice of farming marine species in captivity, including fish, crustaceans (mainly lobster, shrimp and prawns) and seaweeds (Figure 4.44). Although aquaculture has been carried out for hundreds of years, it is becoming increasingly common as populations of wild marine species decline. For example, warm-water aquaculture of cobia is widespread, with around 53 000 tonnes being produced in 2018–2020.

## Impacts of marine aquaculture

Marine aquaculture has both positive and negative impacts. These are summarised in Table 4.1.

| Positive impacts | Negative impacts |
| --- | --- |
| It reduces the exploitation of natural fisheries by providing more food outside of fisheries. | Organisms might escape and disrupt the natural ecosystem. |
| It increases the food supply for people by adding extra stocks of fish and other seafood. | Farmed fish are much more susceptible to diseases and parasites than wild fish, so disease might spread through the caged organisms to natural populations. |

| Positive impacts | Negative impacts |
|---|---|
| It boosts local economies by providing employment to local people. | Local food webs may be disrupted. |
| It can be regarded as a renewable resource. | Pollution caused by waste materials may lead to nutrient enrichment, which can affect the marine ecosystem. |
| It is less dangerous to harvest stocks from a marine aquaculture environment than out in the open ocean. | Energy is needed to maintain aquaculture, such as for regulating the temperature and circulation of water. |
|  | Farmed organisms require feeding, and this has to be sourced. |

**Table 4.1:** Some of the positive and negative impacts of aquaculture.

## Questions

**4.13** Suggest some advantages of marine aquaculture compared with harvesting wild fish populations. Use the following headings:

   a  the environment
   b  fishers
   c  consumers.

**4.14** Table 4.2 shows the status of world fisheries. Suggest what percentage of world fisheries could be described as unsustainable, and explain your answer.

| Fishery type | Tonnes caught per year (world total = 90 000 000 tonnes) |
|---|---|
| Recovering | 2 000 000 |
| Depleted | 5 250 000 |
| Underfished | 7 750 000 |
| Moderately fished | 20 000 000 |
| Overfished | 55 000 000 |

**Table 4.2:** The status of the world fisheries.

### WORKED EXAMPLE

**Pie chart data**

Draw a pie chart to show the data in Table 4.2.

**Step 1** Work out the proportion of the number of degrees in a circle (360°) that each fishery type represents.

For recovering fishery, it is 2 000 000 ÷ 90 000 000 = 0.022.

Then 0.022 × 360 = 8°.

So, the recovering fishery's share of the 360° pie is 8°.

**Step 2** When you have worked them all out, draw a circle, mark the centre and draw a (vertical) radius straight up to the top of the circle.

**Step 3** Measure and draw in the highest angle first of 220° clockwise from the vertical. See figure 4.45.

**Step 4** Repeat for each of the fishery types in descending order of size, as shown.

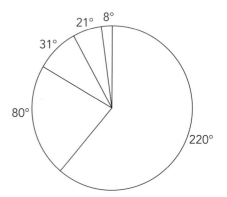

**Figure 4.45:** The pie chart with all sectors marked out to the correct degrees.

4 Water

> **CONTINUED**
>
> **Step 5** Colour and label the pie chart and/or add a key.
>
>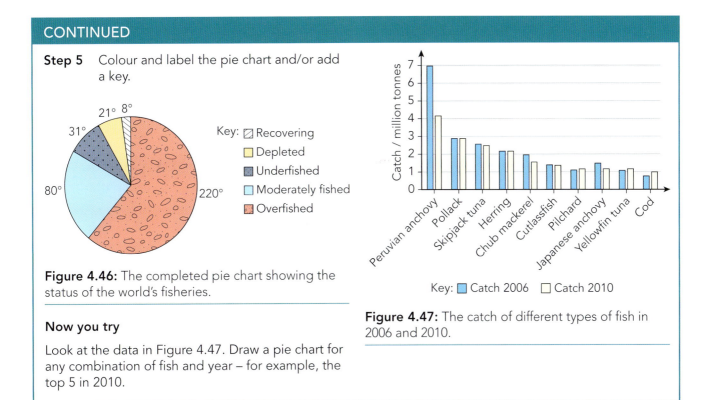
>
> **Figure 4.46:** The completed pie chart showing the status of the world's fisheries.
>
> **Figure 4.47:** The catch of different types of fish in 2006 and 2010.
>
> **Now you try**
>
> Look at the data in Figure 4.47. Draw a pie chart for any combination of fish and year – for example, the top 5 in 2010.

## Strategies for managing the harvesting of marine species

Every country with a coastline has a zone of 200 nautical miles around it that the UN Convention on the Law of the Sea (UNCLOS) has designated an **economic exclusion zone**. Inside this zone, countries must manage the harvesting of marine species in a sustainable way.

### Nets and boats

The use of huge nets to fish efficiently is causing many problems. These types of nets include:

- trawl nets, including bottom trawl nets, which catch all kinds of unwanted species and damage the seabed
- drift nets, which drift with the current and are not anchored; these are often used in coastal waters
- dredge nets are dragged along the seabed, mainly to catch shellfish and other types of fish living in the mud, so they dig in with teeth or water jets.

Figure 4.48 shows these and some other types of fishing nets.

The bigger the net, the larger the catch. Certain net types, such as drift nets, are now banned from use in particular areas because they will catch anything in their path. In 1992, the UN banned drift nets longer than 2.5 km.

A more important consideration, however, is the net's mesh size. If the mesh is too small, the net will catch juvenile fish, which reduces the number of fish available to grow to maturity and reproduce.

The General Fisheries Commission for the Mediterranean (GFCM) adopted an agreement stating that a minimum 40 mm square-mesh **cod end** (the closed end of the net) or a diamond-mesh size of at least 50 mm should be used for all trawling activities exploiting bottom-living fish and shellfish. A diamond-shaped

> **KEY WORDS**
>
> **economic exclusion zone:** the zone around a country's coastline that is under the control of that country
>
> **cod end:** the closed end of a fishing net

167

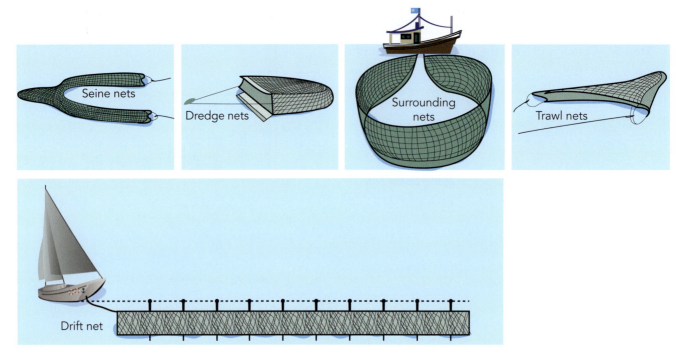

Figure 4.48: Some of the many types of nets used to catch fish.

mesh catches fish more easily, and for this reason a square mesh panel is often included in an otherwise diamond net (Figure 4.49).

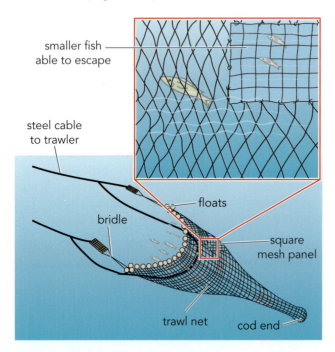

Figure 4.49: A square mesh panel in an otherwise diamond mesh net allows the escape of smaller fish.

A similar factor is the size of the boat, which affects the quantity of fish that can be processed and stored on board. Also, the bigger the boat, the bigger the net it can drag along. Some countries have now introduced limits on the size of boats that are allowed to harvest fish and other marine species.

## Sustainable fishing methods

When nets are not a viable option, more targeted methods can be used, such as the pole and line method. This involves using handheld or mechanically operated poles, with baited hooks attached. It is a much more sustainable method of fishing, as it is highly selective, with very little or no bycatch.

## Quotas

Imposing **quotas** is one of the most important ways to manage fisheries. Legislators – usually governments but sometimes multinational organisations (such as the EU) – set limits on how many and what type of fish

> **KEY WORD**
>
> **quota:** the legal limit on the amount of fish that can be caught

may be caught. Scientists use a wealth of information from networks across the world to help the legislators set sensible limits. If they get it right, enough fish should be left to reproduce and replenish the fishery for the following season. Studies show that a fishery managed with a quota system is half as likely to fail as one that is unmanaged.

## FIELDWORK ACTIVITY 4.2

### Estimating fish population sizes

**You will need**
- a large quantity of beans
- a bag
- a marker pen

**Before you start**

In order for quotas to work, a sensible figure must be set. The size of the quota depends on the population of the target fish species. The size of the yellowfin tuna population in an area of the Indian Ocean was estimated using a method called mark – release – recapture. Fish were captured and marked with a microchip, then released back into the sea. A month later, fish were captured in the same area again. On the first occasion, 127 fish were caught and marked. On the second occasion, 174 fish were caught and 12 of these had a microchip. The formula for calculating the population from these results is:

Population =

$$\frac{\text{number of fish caught on first capture} \times \text{number of fish caught on second capture}}{\text{number of marked fish caught on second capture}}$$

So, in this case it is: $127 \times 174 \div 12 = 1842$

This method assumes that the proportion of marked fish in the whole population is the same as the proportion of marked fish in the second capture. So, in this case, 12 is to 174 as 127 is to x, where x is the actual population.

You can simulate the mark – release – recapture method using some beans and a marker pen. This will allow you to practise your maths skills and think about real-life situations faced by fisheries scientists.

**Method**
- Put four handfuls of beans into a bag, without counting them.
- Take a handful of beans back out: this is your first capture.
- Count these beans and record the number (A).
- Mark these beans with a marker pen.
- Put these marked beans back into the bag, then shake the bag.
- Take a handful of beans from the bag without looking: this is your second capture.
- Count the total number of beans you took (regardless of whether they have a marker pen dot or not) and record your answer (B).
- Count the number of those beans that are marked and record this number (C).
- Return all the beans to the bag.
- Use the figures in the equation given previously for yellowfin tuna, to calculate the size of the bean population in the bag. Population = $A \times B \div C$
- Count the total number of beans in the bag and compare this figure with your calculation.

the total number of beans calculated from the mark-capture exercise =

the total number of beans from actually counting them =

**Questions**

1. You were asked to take a handful of beans from the bag **without looking** at your second capture. This reflects free movement of the organisms throughout the area. If this was not the case and some moved less than others (for example, older ones moved around less than younger ones), what effect would this have on the population estimate?

2. If the method of marking the organism caused it to be harmed so that it was less likely to be recaptured in the second sample, what would be the result on the estimate of the population?

## Closed seasons, protected areas and limited numbers of fishing days

Governments and other legislative bodies can also pass laws to limit the number of fishing days, or close fisheries down for part of the year – usually during the breeding season. As with quotas and closed seasons, some fisheries are protected by preventing fishing in certain areas, often where the target species is known to breed.

## International agreements and conservation laws

Some fisheries are protected by conservation laws. For example, the Magnuson–Stevens Fishery Conservation and Management Act is the main law governing marine fisheries in the USA. It was first passed in 1976 and has undergone numerous amendments. Its aims include controlling the country's territorial waters, conserving fishery resources and enforcing international fishing agreements. It also aims to develop underused fisheries and protect fish habitats.

Inside the economic exclusion zone, it is the right and responsibility of a country to manage its fisheries. However, to regulate fisheries in international waters, international agreements are needed. This led to the UN Convention on the Law of the Sea (UNCLOS). A good example of where such agreement is needed is the Mediterranean. In this narrow body of water, a 200-nautical-mile exclusion zone has no meaning. The countries bordering the sea operate 12-nautical-mile zones and beyond that, they have to reach agreements on how to manage fish stocks.

These agreements are monitored, with varying levels of success, by different countries. A model system is the one operated by the African country of Namibia. Here, larger vessels in its waters have on-board observers, air patrols detect and deter unlicenced vessels, and all landings are monitored at the country's two fishing ports. In addition, all vessels in the exclusion zone must keep daily logs of their catches.

## The limitations of strategies to harvest marine species

There are many benefits to be gained from implementing control over harvesting marine organisms. However, there are drawbacks too.

Any law or agreement is only as good as the level of enforcement that goes with it. Because the oceans are so vast, it is difficult to monitor fishery laws and agreements. Monitoring organisations based in ports have more success.

Because fishing is important for both income and food for many people, there is a huge incentive for illegal activities. Quotas can easily be avoided by simply not declaring how many fish are being caught. Overstretched authorities may not be able to check every boat, and fishers may be willing to risk under-declaring the size of their catch on the chance that they will not be checked. It is not difficult to use a net with an illegally small mesh size, and where patrols are inadequate, fishers frequently trespass in areas where they are not supposed to fish.

**Figure 4.50:** Trawler net full of Whiting fish.

4 Water

CASE STUDY

### The Newfoundland cod fishery

Off the coast of western Canada is an area called the Grand Banks. Its location and some features are shown in Figure 4.51. For more than 500 years, this area was known for having huge numbers of fish, especially cod. Indigenous peoples and early settlers were able to feed themselves and make a living from this fishery. The stock never seemed to be affected and, after the Second World War, commercial fisheries were attracted to the area.

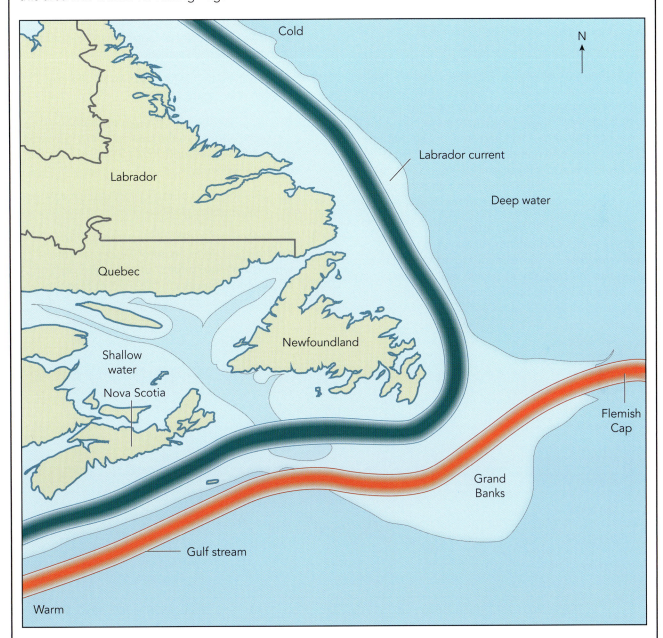

Figure 4.51: The Newfoundland cod fishery.

## CONTINUED

Catches declined very quickly, and the fishery collapsed completely in 1992 (Figure 4.52). A ban on fishing was hardly necessary, but the Canadian government did bring in a ban and paid pensions to many of the 40 000 people whose livelihood had disappeared. Despite this ban and the huge hardship that followed, the fishery is still very poor compared with its former status.

Until 1950, the fishery was not under threat because the technology simply did not exist to catch the fish in unsustainable numbers. After this date, however, more and bigger ships started to trawl the area with huge nets. These took many more cod, a huge amount of bycatch, including smaller fish that are food for cod, and damaged the seabed bed where young cod feed. This pattern continued into the 1980s, but signs of the imminent collapse should have been seen much earlier, in the 1970s.

Today, more than 30 years after the ban was implemented, cod catches remain very low. However, there is some encouraging news that suggests the stocks have grown well in a small part of the region called Smith Sound. Some researchers think that these healthy fish are about to recolonise the whole area. Time will tell.

### Questions

1. The case study states that the Canadian government placed a ban on cod fishing. This could have had to do with where, when and how much can be caught. Explain these different types of restrictions.

2. a Describe the pattern shown by the cod catch in Figure 4.52.

   b Calculate the percentage fall in the catch of cod between the peak around 1967 and the trough around 1976. Show and explain your working.

   c Give the date of the lowest catch between 1900 and the peak catch.

3. Devise a short explanatory paragraph to be read by people as an introduction and then a questionnaire to find out about the opinions of Newfoundlanders in the light of recent news about cod in Smith Sound.

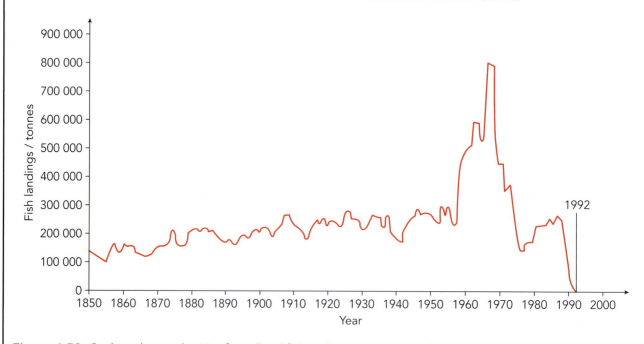

Figure 4.52: Cod catches at the Newfoundland fishery between 1850 and 2000.

## 4.5 Marine pollution

There are two main forms of pollution significantly affecting the world's oceans: oil and plastics.

### Oil pollution

Oil is a toxic material, and oil spills can cause great damage. Crude oil (the unprocessed form of oil, extracted straight from the ground) is thick, dark and sticky. It is also flammable.

#### Causes of oil pollution

The main causes of marine oil spills are:

- offshore oil extraction, due to leakage from oil rigs
- onshore extraction leading to run-off into the ocean
- oil pipelines that move oil to storage, which may have leaks
- shipping and transporting the oil, which carries the risk of collision or damage to the oil tankers (Figure 4.53)
- the cleaning of tanks on oil tankers, which takes place at sea
- oil from oil refineries.

Table 4.3 lists of some of the largest oil spills ever recorded and their causes.

**Figure 4.53:** The oil tanker *Exxon Valdez* being towed for repairs after it ran aground in 1989, causing a disastrous oil spill.

| Oil spill | Location | Cause of spill | Approximate amount of crude oil spilt / thousand tonnes |
|---|---|---|---|
| Kuwait oil fires | Kuwait | War | 136 000 |
| Kuwait oil lakes 1991 | Kuwait | War | 5 000 |
| The Lakeview Gusher 1910 | USA | Onshore oil extraction | 1 200 |
| *Deepwater Horizon* 2010 | USA coast/Gulf of Mexico | Offshore oil extraction | 575 |
| *Ixtoc 1* 1979 | Mexico/Gulf of Mexico | Offshore oil extraction | 475 |
| *Atlantic Express 1* 1979 | Trinidad and Tobago | Oil tanker collision | 287 |
| *Fergana Valley* 1992 | Uzbekistan | Onshore oil extraction | 285 |
| *ABT Summer* 1991 | Angola | Oil tanker | 260 |
| *Amoco Cadiz* 1978 | France | Oil tanker crash | 223 |

**Table 4.3:** Location of large oil spills and their causes.

> ACTIVITY 4.5
>
> Work in small groups to research and plot on a world map the areas where most oil is produced. Then mark the countries that import the most oil. Draw lines to highlight the main shipping routes between these countries. On your map, also indicate dangerous ocean areas, with things such as rough seas and icebergs. Display your finished maps as a gallery in the classroom.

## Impacts of pollution on marine and coastal ecosystems

However, this does not tell the whole story, because the amount of oil spilt does not necessarily indicate the level of environmental impact. The oil tanker Amoco Cadiz released a far smaller volume of oil than many of the other spills shown in Table 4.3, but it had a far greater impact because of the spread of the oil and the difficulty in cleaning it up. Oil spills at sea generally have a far greater impact than those on the land. Environmental damage also occurs around the world as a result of small spills, the washing and cleaning of boats, and through seepage from the seabed.

Whatever the cause, the impact can be significant. The damage to or removal of any marine organism will have an impact on the food web for the area, potentially resulting in either food shortages for animals that use the initially affected organism as a food source, or a population explosion of organisms if their predator has been removed. Oil spills can cause the extinction of a species within a locality; if that species is already critically endangered, the loss of one more local population may mean the loss of the entire species.

Some of the known effects of an oil spill on particular organisms and habitats are listed in Table 4.4.

| Organism/habitat | Description | | Impact of oil |
|---|---|---|---|
| **Phytoplankton** | Microscopic organisms living in the sea water with the ability to photosynthesise. They provide food for many larger organisms. | | Oil floats on the surface of the water and prevents light from entering. This prevents the phytoplankton from photosynthesising, so they die. |
| **Seaweeds** | Large plants living mainly in costal habitats, although some live at sea (*Sargassum* weed). | | *Sargassum* tends to sink. Coastal seaweeds are smothered and thus unable to photosynthesise, which affects the organisms that depend on seaweed for food and shelter. |
| **Crustaceans** | Crabs, lobsters and shrimps are the main crustaceans found in the sea. They all have a hard exoskeleton. The number of legs varies, but most are decapods with ten in five pairs. | | Smothered and affected by the toxic chemicals in the oil. They do have the ability to move away. |
| **Fish** | Different species are present throughout the oceans. Some feed on phytoplankton and some prey on other fish. They are food for mammals and birds. | | Shortage of food due to the reduction in phytoplankton. Oil floating on the water surface prevents gas exchange. Fish become short of oxygen and die. Fish are also affected by the oil through direct contact, as it affects their gills. |

| Organism/habitat | Description | Impact of oil |
|---|---|---|
| Birds | Mobile over large distances, feeding on fish, often diving into the water to catch them. Others wade at the coastal edge, feeding on fish and shellfish. | Shortage of food as fish and other creatures die. May consume oil when eating fish (which can be toxic). When hunting for food, feathers become coated in oil, affecting their buoyancy and ability to fly. |
| Marine mammals | Marine-based mammals such as dolphins and whales will often travel great distances, chasing prey. | Food sources are depleted by the impact of the oil. The mammals may also swallow oil while feeding, which will be toxic to them. A coating of oil will affect their skin, etc. |
| Coral reefs | A complex ecosystem and the habitat for a wide community of organisms. | An oil slick will prevent sunlight from reaching plants and phytoplankton, preventing photosynthesis from occurring. Lack of oxygen will cause other species to die. The impact on the balance of the whole reef might cause complete devastation. Areas of reef may become covered in oil. |
| Beaches | A distinct ecosystem supporting a range of land-based and aquatic organisms. | Oil is often washed in by tides, coating rocks. Organisms living in shallow water and rock pools may be killed by the toxic effects of the oil. Animal food sources will be affected. |

Table 4.4: The effects of an oil spill on different organisms and habitats.

# Questions

4.15 Referring to Table 4.4, explain why the amount of oil spilt does not have a direct correlation with the amount of environmental damage that results.

4.16 Why does preventing light from reaching the surface of the sea have such a big effect on the marine ecosystem?

4.17 Describe one way of preventing an oil spill and one way of mitigating (making less severe) its impact.

## Preventing oil spills

As long as oil is being used and transported, there will continue to be oil-pollution incidents. However, countries are cooperating to develop strategies to reduce the number of marine oil spills and avoid the spillage of other substances that may affect the environment.

**MARPOL**

The International Maritime Organization, a UN group that supervises the safety and security of shipping, obtained agreement for the MARPOL (Marine Pollution) treaty. MARPOL is the International Convention for the Prevention of Pollution from Ships. It sets out a number of regulations covering pollution by oil, sewage, rubbish and toxic liquids, among other things. The agreement was first signed in 1973, updated in 1978 and came into force in 1983. Prior to MARPOL, it was common for ships to dispose of waste or clean their storage tanks in the middle of an ocean, with unknown environmental effects.

Under the MARPOL regulations, rules have been introduced to cover the process of transferring crude oil from one vessel to another while at sea – a common cause of smaller oil spills. All tankers must be certified to show they have appropriate systems in place and records to show that they are being used. Failure to comply with these regulations can result in a large fine or the ship not being given permission to leave port until suitable systems are in place.

### Tanker design

Experts have also focused on the design of ships themselves. The most likely reason for a significant oil spill from a tanker is some form of damage to the hull, so two design features have been added to modern tankers:

- An increase in the number of compartments in the hull of the ship; if there is damage in one section, the contents of the whole hull are not lost.
- The introduction of **double-hulled** tankers. A double-hulled ship is one that has been built with two hulls, so that if there is damage to the outer layer (or plate), the contents are still held securely by the inner plate (Figures 4.54 and 4.55). The cost of building double-hulled tankers is significantly more than the cost of a single-hulled ship, but the risks of oil spillage are far less.

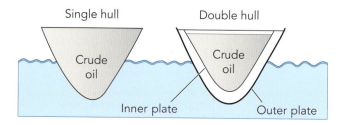

**Figure 4.54:** A cross-section through single-hulled and double-hulled tankers. The inclusion of another layer (plate) provides protection for the cargo if the outer plate is punctured.

### KEY WORD

**double-hulled:** a ship design that uses a second layer, allowing the cargo to remain safe if the external layer is damaged

**Figure 4.55:** The *Eagle Austin*, a double-hulled oil tanker, arrives at the Port of Corpus Christi, Texas, USA, hauling crude oil from the UK.

| Hazard | Severity | Likelihood | Risk rating | Controls proposed | Notes |
|---|---|---|---|---|---|
| Oil spill | 5 | 2 | M | (depends on situation) | |

**Table 4.5a:** Risk assessment for an oil spill.

| Severity rating | | Likelihood rating | |
|---|---|---|---|
| 1 | No discernible consequences for the environment | 1 | It could happen, but it probably never will |
| 2 | Restricted to a very local area | 2 | Only likely to occur in very abnormal circumstances |
| 3 | Moderately widespread consequences should be expected | 3 | Likely to occur at some stage in the operations |
| 4 | Widespread consequences for the environment | 4 | Will almost certainly occur at some point |
| 5 | Very long-term environmental damage | 5 | Expected to occur on a regular basis |

**Table 4.5b:** Severity and likelihood ratings for risks.

## Risk assessments

A risk assessment involves four main stages:

- Hazard identification: What could possibly go wrong? What are the hazards involved in what we are going to do?
- Likelihood analyses: How likely is it that any of these things will go wrong?
- Consequence analysis: What would be the problems caused by any of these things going wrong?
- Measures to be taken: What can we do about the hazards to reduce their likelihood and impact?

Because of the complex chemical nature of crude oil, each of these processes is a major undertaking.

Tables 4.6a, 4.6b and 4.6c show aspects of a typical risk assessment form for an oil spill.

| | | Severity | | | | |
|---|---|---|---|---|---|---|
| | | 1 | 2 | 3 | 4 | 5 |
| Likelihood | 1 | L | L | L | L | L |
| | 2 | L | L | L | M | M |
| | 3 | L | L | M | M | M |
| | 4 | L | M | M | H | H |
| | 5 | L | M | M | H | H |

**Table 4.5c:** Risk rating matrix, allowing risks to be judged as low, medium or high.

## Regular maintenance

Regular or preventive maintenance is designed to ensure that equipment used to handle and transport oil is in working order. This is one way of helping to prevent oil spills and leaks. For example, the failure of the blowout preventer caused the 2010 *Deepwater Horizon* spill (Figure 4.56). A blowout preventer is a specialised valve used to seal and control an oil well, to prevent the uncontrolled emission of oil from the well – a so-called blowout. In the aftermath of this disaster, new rules were introduced about the maintenance of blowout preventers.

**Figure 4.56:** The mobile offshore drilling unit sits directly above the damaged *Deepwater Horizon* blowout preventer, while crews attempt to try and plug the wellhead.

## Minimising the impact of oil spills

Even with good planning and design, oil can still be spilt. The main focus in such a situation is to reduce the impact of the spillage. The technique used will depend very much on local weather conditions, the proximity to land and the calmness of the sea. There are various common strategies, such as:

- Improved navigation systems for ships: some oil spills have been the consequence of accidents, and improved navigation systems are key to avoiding these.
- Floating booms: a boom is a floating barrier that can be used to surround the oil slick and prevent it from spreading to other areas. This process works well when the spill only covers a relatively small area and the sea is calm. It can also be used as a barrier to protect environmentally sensitive areas (such as a river estuary) while a spill is dealt with. Booms do not work very well when the sea is rough and stormy, which are conditions that are sometimes the cause of damage to a ship (Figure 4.57).

**Figure 4.57:** Floating booms close off Newport Harbor, California, USA, to prevent oil from entering the waterway.

- Detergent sprays: these help to break down the oil slick into smaller droplets and disperse it. The smaller droplets of oil will float away and degrade over time. Detergents are most effective on smaller spills, but recent research has suggested they can cause more environmental damage than the crude oil itself. Coral reefs appear to have a low tolerance to detergents.

- Skimmers: these clean the water without changing the chemical or physical properties of the oil. Using a material that oil easily attaches to, the skimmer drags oil off the seawater surface, which is then mechanically scraped off into a container. This system is often used once an oil slick has been contained within a boom. It is a very useful technique, but skimmers will not work effectively in rough or stormy sea conditions (Figure 4.58).

**Figure 4.58:** Oil gathers on a skimmer in the environmentally sensitive Talbert Marsh wetlands, California, USA, after an oil spill from an offshore oil platform in 2021.

- Sorbents: these are materials used to absorb oil. Peat, vermiculate and clay are three common natural sorbents, and there are synthetics too. They tend to be used with smaller spills or in the final stages of major clean-up operations (Figure 4.59).

**Figure 4.59:** A worker checking oil-sorbent booms in Prince William Sound, Gulf of Alaska.

- Controlled burning: oil is highly inflammable and can be removed quite easily by burning. This technique was used after *Deepwater Horizon*, with over 400 controlled burns, removing about 250 000 barrels of oil from the sea (Figure 4.60).

**Figure 4.60:** A controlled burn of oil from the *Deepwater Horizon* spill.

### FIELDWORK ACTIVITY 4.3

#### Oil pollution simulation

**You will need**

- a large shallow tray filled with water
- food colouring that is water-soluble
- food colouring that is oil-soluble (if available)
- vegetable oil
- pipette
- a stick
- feathers
- a small spoon
- string
- detergent.

**Safety**

Make sure you do not ingest any of the liquids used in this investigation.

**Before you start**

In this investigation, you are going to simulate some of the methods used to minimise the impacts of an oil spill. Before you start, re-read the previous list of common strategies.

**Method**

- Place a drop of vegetable oil (cooking oil) onto the water surface.
- Make the 'oil slick' more visible by adding a water-soluble dye.
- Dip a stick into the water and describe what you see.
- Dip a feather into the mixture and describe what you see.
- Try to remove the oil with a small spoon (this represents skimming). How successful is this method?
- Carefully place a piece of string onto the surface of the water so that it floats and then pull it in one direction (this represents a boom). How successful is this method?
- Add some detergent to the tray (this represents detergent spraying). How successful is this method?

**Questions**

1. Draw up a table to compare the three methods of oil removal or dispersal, and say which is which.
2. How could you simulate sorbents and controlled burning?

## CASE STUDY

### *Exxon Valdez*: An environmental disaster

**Figure 4.61:** A spill of crude oil causes significant environmental damage and is costly to put right.

Alaska is a unique area for wildlife, with harsh weather conditions. As a result, the local ecosystem is fragile, and animals are well adapted to the local weather conditions and food sources.

On 24 March 1989, the *Exxon Valdez* oil tanker left the port of Valdez in Alaska fully loaded with oil. An inexperienced junior officer in charge of the ship steered the tanker wide to avoid ice in the shipping lane and collided with the nearby Bligh reef. The tanker was of single-hull construction, and the jagged rocks of the reef created a large hole in its side, allowing around 36 000 tonnes of oil to escape into the sea. The local area, the bay of Prince William Sound, was soon covered in oil. The slick spread far and wide: oil was reported to have reached beaches over 1000 km away from the incident (Figure 4.62).

The accident had a major impact on local wildlife: large numbers of killer whales (orca), eagles, otters, seals and thousands of sea birds were killed in the first few weeks. Many of these organisms had either come into direct contact with the oil or ingested it while hunting for food. The toxic effect of the oil caused slow, painful deaths. The crude oil also impacted the local stocks of herring and salmon, both of which are important for the local fishing industry.

Even though people were on the scene rapidly, the oil had already spread across the sea's surface. Detergents were used to try to break up the slick, but there was insufficient wave action for this to work efficiently. A second attempt to apply detergent (this time by aircraft) missed the target area. So, an alternative method was tried: to cause an explosion in the oil slick to get the oil to burn. The trial explosion did cause the oil to burn but also led to health problems for local villagers, so no more attempts were made.

The remoteness of the site meant there was a delay in getting equipment such as booms and skimmers to the site. While some areas of the slick were successfully held back by the booms, the skimmers could not cope with the quantity of oil clinging to seaweed and soon clogged up. It has been calculated that only around 10% of the ship's cargo was recovered because so much oil was swept into remote rocky coves that were difficult to reach.

More than 25 years later, it is still possible to find oil on local beaches – a potential toxin to all wildlife. Items such as shellfish, which filter feed from the local water, are polluted with oil and unfit for humans to eat, although birds and otters still do. The impact on local wildlife is immense: researchers looked at 32 animal types and habitats, finding that only 13 had fully recovered. They concluded that the ecosystem will never be entirely restored. Since this disaster, changes have been made to try to prevent such an accident from happening again.

### Questions

1. Outline the causes of the accident.
2. Explain why so many large mammals have been affected by the oil spill.
3. Other than the environmental damage, how have locals been impacted by the oil spill?
4. Changes have been made as a result of the *Exxon Valdez* incident. Suggest three recommendations you would make to prevent a similar accident from occurring.
5. Environmentalists argue that extraction of oil so close to the Arctic Circle should be banned because the area is so environmentally sensitive. Give an opposite argument in support of oil extraction.

**CONTINUED**

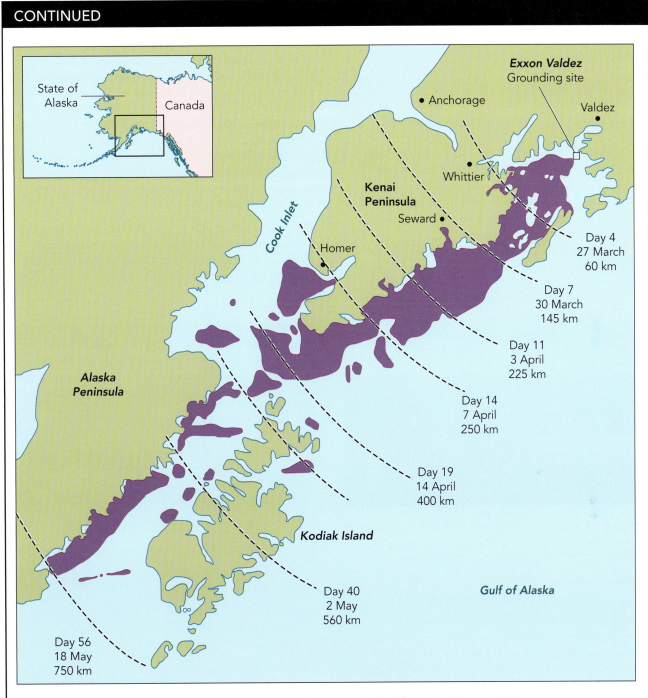

Figure 4.62: A map of the affected area, showing the spread of oil from the *Exxon Valdez*.

# Plastic pollution

Besides oil, the other big contributor to marine pollution is plastics.

> **CRITICAL THINKING TIP**
>
> When discussing and analysing information around the topic of pollution, always be clear and specific about which pollutant you are referring to. Do not just use the word 'pollution', as the problem takes many forms. The type of pollution you are talking about will inform your approach to formulating an opinion and evaluating solutions.

## Conventional plastics

Conventional plastics are made from fossil fuels. They are notable for their durability, but this feature also lies at the heart of the problems associated with them. Conventional plastics can take thousands of years to break down, so they are referred to as non-biodegradable (Figure 4.63).

**Figure 4.63:** Conventional plastics have to be disposed of in landfill, which takes up space and is unsightly.

## Bioplastics

One solution to reduce the reliance on fossil fuels is to make bioplastic – that is, plastic from renewable, biological materials, such as vegetable oils and starches. As well as avoiding using fossil fuels, some of these materials are also biodegradable, but not all. Bioplastics are now being used in many products, including packaging and bottles.

## Biodegradable and non-biodegradable bioplastics

'Biodegradable' means that a plastic can be completely broken down by bacteria and fungi in water or soil. The products of this breakdown are biomass, water and gases (carbon dioxide and methane). This should ideally happen within a few weeks or months at most. Some bioplastics take longer than this and are referred to as 'durable' rather than biodegradable.

Bioplastics are popularly believed to all be biodegradable. However, a bioplastic is considered non-biodegradable if it cannot be broken down easily by microorganisms. Some 50% of bioplastics fall into this category and so are considered as non-biodegradable and are considered to pose the same risk as conventional plastics. The reason for this is due to several factors including the fact that the conditions for decomposition are not usually present in recycling facilities and that the processing of the plastic changes the biological material in such a way to make it more difficult to biodegrade.

Different types of plastic require different environmental conditions, such as oxygen, light and temperature (abiotic), and the bacteria and fungi involved (biotic) – all these affect the rate at which the plastic breaks down.

## Microplastics

When larger, non-biodegradable plastics break down, they usually do so into smaller pieces of plastic, less than 5 mm in length. This is known as microplastic (Figure 4.64). Some microplastics, called microbeads, are made intentionally and are used in many health and beauty products.

**Figure 4.64:** Small pieces of microplastic find their way into the oceans, and may then be washed up on a beach or affect marine wildlife.

## The impact of plastic pollution on marine ecosystems

### Visual pollution

Many people do not like the sight of plastic littering the natural environment – it is a form of **visual pollution** (Figure 4.65). This is a huge problem – for example, it is estimated that the equivalent of 536 plastic bottles are discarded into the Mediterranean Sea every second! The visual consequences of this can be seen on many beaches around the world. Exposure to visual pollution like this can cause anxiety and other mental-health issues.

Figure 4.65: Visual pollution by plastics is often most evident at the edge of bodies of water, such as beaches and riverbanks. Most of the trash pictured on the beach here is plastic.

### Effects on wildlife

Animals can suffer in many ways – for example, by eating plastics or becoming entangled in them. Experts claim that around 56% of all marine mammals are known to have ingested plastic, including whales, dolphins and many species of seals. The most obvious problem this causes is that, once in the animal's stomach, the plastic cannot be broken down by digestion. The stomach is thus permanently full or partially full of plastic, so the animal cannot eat its normal food. In addition, the plastics they have ingested can cause physical damage to the intestines. Similar problems face seabirds, turtles (Figure 4.66) and a range of other marine creatures.

Figure 4.66: Sea turtles often mistake plastic bags for their jellyfish prey and try to eat them.

> **KEY WORD**
>
> **visual pollution:** reduction in the aesthetic value of an area, disrupting ecological systems as a result

Plastic can also harm marine creatures when they get tangled up or otherwise trapped in it. The most severe form of entanglement of marine creatures is when they become trapped inside bags and bottles that have found their way into the ocean (Figure 4.67). If it cannot get out, the animal will die.

Figure 4.67: A fish completely enclosed inside a plastic bag – its chances of survival are slim.

### Bioaccumulation and biomagnification

If marine creatures consume microplastics, the plastic can build up in their bodies and affect not only the animals themselves but also others further up the food chain. Microplastics can both bioaccumulate and biomagnify within marine ecosystems. Observations in the wild and in laboratory experiments have shown that many species, from seaweeds to predators, accumulate microplastics.

Evidence for biomagnification is less solid, but studies have shown that it can occur. In one experiment, it was proven that microplastics in mussels were transferred to crabs when they ate the mussels. Plastics are chemicals, and they can often interact with, and bind to, toxic chemicals in the environment. So, although the plastic may not be subject to biomagnification, toxic chemicals to which it is bound may be.

The extent of the pollution of the oceans by plastic has recently been monitored, and it has been found that there are huge collections of marine debris trapped by ocean currents. The biggest of these is termed the Great Pacific Garbage Patch – a huge mass of plastic pollution in the Pacific Ocean, more than three times the size of France and which comprises an estimated 1.8 trillion plastic pieces.

## Strategies for managing plastic pollution

The management of plastic pollution falls into a number of categories:

- using plastic substitutes
- reducing the use of plastics
- safe, environmentally friendly disposal of plastics
- recycling
- reinforcing all these measures by legislation and enforcement.

**Alternative packaging**

A wide range of alternative materials are in use as packaging and many show advantages over non-biodegradable plastics. These include wool, corrugated cardboard, fungal mycelia, seaweed, palm leaves and milk plastic. Different materials are suitable for different roles, which makes encouraging or enforcing their use somewhat more difficult.

**Avoiding single-use plastics**

Another way of addressing the issue is to reduce how much plastic we use, especially when we only use it once before disposing of it. It is estimated that 1 million plastic bottles are bought every minute around the world. Around 500 billion single-use plastic bags are used every year globally. Avoiding this would obviously dramatically reduce the amount of plastic waste. Many initiatives have been developed to encourage people to re-use plastics.

Experts hope that the use of non-biodegradable plastic will reduce as more biodegradable plastic becomes readily available. This, along with initiatives to collect the plastics that already pollute our environment and action to reduce the disposal of plastic into the environment, may solve the many problems plastic is currently causing our planet.

**Safe disposal**

Generally, disposing of plastic into landfills has a huge number of drawbacks. Such sites take up a lot of space and, of course, the plastic is wasted. Disposal into recycling containers should, in theory, be a safe way of getting rid of such materials. However, it is not always clear what happens to materials disposed of in this way, but ideally either the fabric from which the product has been made is re-used, or the product itself is re-used.

Burning plastic is an alternative disposal method and has the advantage of producing energy that can be used to generate power. The downside is that toxic chemicals are released into the environment when plastics are burnt.

### Recycling plastic

One obvious route to resolving the problem of plastic pollution is to deal with the waste properly. If plastic is biodegradable, it needs to be placed in the right environment to biodegrade efficiently. If it is non-biodegradable, it should be processed in some way to make it less harmful to the environment. Recycling of non-biodegradable plastics is beginning to happen, and many schemes exist to collect plastics (Figure 4.68) and make something useful out of them, including bags, furniture, outdoor fencing and even buildings.

However, there are some issues with recycling plastics. There are many different types of plastic, and each has different properties. Not every plastic is covered by current recycling initiatives. Many products carry information on their label about if and how they can be recycled.

Figure 4.68: Recycling initiatives collect materials from people's homes or provide bins to place items in for recycling.

> **SUSTAINABILITY TIP**
>
> Addressing the problem of plastic pollution is something we can all do in small ways in our everyday lives. For example, when it is safe to do so, use a refillable water bottle rather than buying water in single-use bottles, or find alternatives, such as drinking coconut water straight from the fruit. Look at the labels and buy products that say they are made from recycled plastic if you can.

# 4 Water

**Legislation and enforcement**

All over the world, laws are being passed to reduce single-use plastics. In 2018, the UK banned the use of plastic straws; in 2021, the European Union banned the use of plastic cutlery; and the UAE will be bringing in laws to regulate the use of single-use plastics from 2026. On a global scale, the UN Environment Agency has made a resolution to end plastic pollution, and a treaty has been agreed to by 175 nations.

# Questions

**4.18** Copy and complete the following paragraph about plastics:

Conventional plastics are made from _____ and mostly cannot be _____ by living organisms. Recently, plastics have been made from materials such as corn starch and are termed _____. These newer plastics may or may not biodegrade. Conventional plastics can break down into smaller pieces over time and are termed _____ when they are smaller than _____ in length.

**4.19 a** Even though a particular bioplastic does not biodegrade, why does it have an advantage over a conventional plastic?

**b** Other than the inability to biodegrade, suggest one other disadvantage of a bioplastic.

**4.20** Suggest how plastic pollution might affect:

a  a dolphin

b  tourism

c  a food chain

---

### EXTENDED CASE STUDY

#### The cholera outbreak in Haiti

**Phase 1, October 2010–2015**

On 12 January 2010, at 16:53 local time, Haiti was hit by a devastating earthquake of magnitude 7.0. The epicentre was 25 km west of the capital, Port-au-Prince. The number killed is estimated to have been between 100 000 and 160 000 (government figures state even more, but there are concerns that these figures are inflated).

At the time of the earthquake, the sanitation in Haiti was very poor. Only 71% of the population had access to improved water and 24% to improved sanitation. Despite this, there had not been a case of cholera in Haiti for nearly a century before the earthquake. Within 10 months of the disaster, however, a cholera outbreak had begun, and it spread around the country in just four weeks. By August 2015, more than 700 000 cases and about 9000 deaths had been reported.

Many nations provided aid to Haiti at the time of the earthquake, including a group of UN aid workers flown in from Nepal. Their military base in Haiti was on a tributary of the Artibonite River (Figure 4.69). Unfortunately, sewage had leaked from the military base into the river – this was the source of the cholera outbreak. Most of the people affected in the original outbreak had drunk from the river. The bacterial strain responsible for the outbreak was identified as one closely related to a Nepalese strain.

Several strategies were used to try to control the cholera. These included:

- installing latrines
- thoroughly cooking food
- providing education about hand washing.

By 2014, the number of cases had been significantly reduced, to only about 10% of the peak in 2011. However, every rainy season leads to an increase in the number of cases. Disappointingly, the number of cases also rose dramatically in the last few months of 2014 (Figure 4.70). This is thought to have been caused by:

- heavy, late rainfall
- continued inadequate sanitation
- an assumption that the disease was now under control.

# CAMBRIDGE IGCSE™ AND O LEVEL ENVIRONMENTAL MANAGEMENT: COURSEBOOK

**CONTINUED**

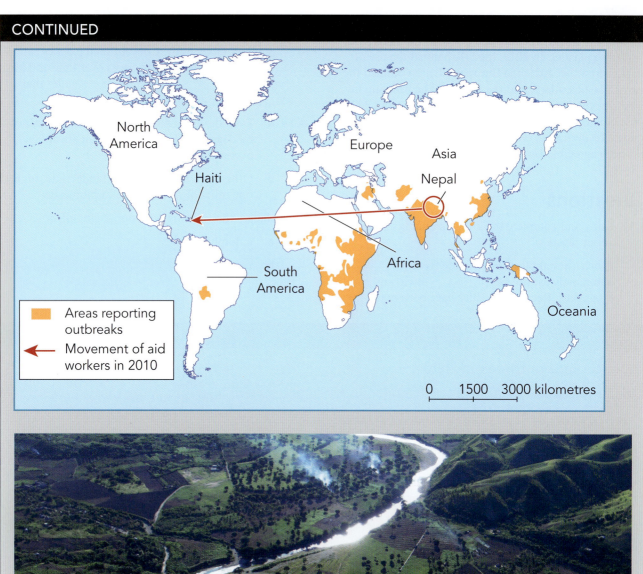

Figure 4.69: A world map showing where cholera has occurred in the recent past. Also shown is where some aid workers travelled from to help in the cholera outbreak of 2010 in Haiti. The picture shows the Artibonite River, the source of the Haitian outbreak.

## CONTINUED

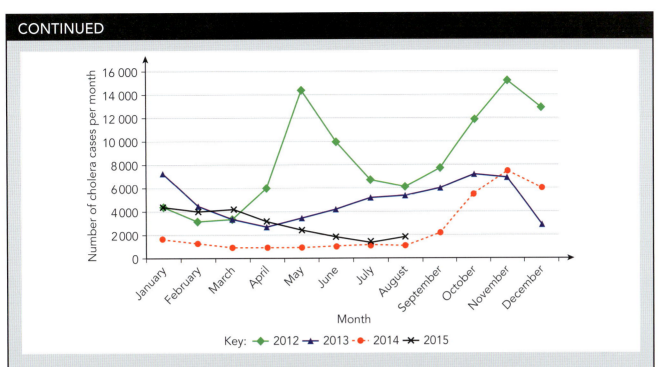

Figure 4.70: New cholera cases in Haiti every month from January 2012 to August 2015.

### Phase 2, October 2019–2022

In October 2022, WHO reported that there had been a resurgence of cholera despite no reported cases for several years. Between 2 October and 6 December 2022, there were 13 672 cases and 283 deaths. WHO cites poor health conditions and limited access to safe drinking water and sanitation facilities as the causes.

### Questions

1. a  It was suggested that some aid workers, carrying the infection, caused the cholera outbreak. Explain why this suggestion has been made.

   b  It was also suggested that the cholera bacteria might have come from a source in South America. Using Figure 4.69, suggest how the cholera bacteria might have reached Haiti from a source in South America.

2. Describe how strategies used to control the outbreak could reduce the numbers of people infected.

3. a  From Figure 4.70, state the month and maximum number of cases in 2012.

   b  From Figure 4.70, state the month and maximum number of cases in 2014.

4. Calculate the percentage reduction in cholera cases from the peak in 2012 to the lowest number in 2014.

5. Describe the pattern of cholera cases recorded in 2015.

6. In 2012, rainfall peaked in May and in November. How does this explain the pattern of cholera cases in that year?

7. To what extent do you agree with the statement that 'Haiti has managed to control the cholera outbreak that began in 2010'?

### Project

Incidences of cholera in a country are related to its level of sanitation. Malaria is not a consequence of poor sanitation, but it is related to the frequency of mosquitos that carry the malarial parasite. In groups, carry out some research into the countries

> **CONTINUED**
>
> that have a high incidence of malaria and those that have a high incidence of cholera. Identify these countries on a world map in two different colours.
>
> The level of wealth of a country impacts its ability to provide good sanitation and potable water to its population. It also depends on the level of health care and the provision of treatment for diseases, including malaria and cholera. In your groups, research the wealth of different nations and their levels of sanitation. See if either is related to the incidence of cholera and/or malaria.
>
> Produce a leaflet/poster/presentation on the state of countries in terms of the health of their populations.
>
> **Further resources**
>
> *Figures on Cholera and Malaria*, The European Centre for Disease Prevention and Control
>
> *Various reports on diseases and health conditions around the world*, World Health Organisation
>
> Country Ranking of Sanitation Services, Mundi Index

## SUMMARY

| |
|---|
| Water exists on Earth in the atmosphere, on the surface, below ground and in the oceans. |
| Water cycles through transpiration, evaporation, condensation, precipitation, interception, surface run-off, infiltration, through-flow and groundwater flow. |
| There are five main oceans: Atlantic, Pacific, Indian, Arctic and Southern. |
| Only 3% of Earth's water is fresh (non-salty). Fresh water can be obtained from rain, snow, surface waters (such as rivers, reservoirs and lakes) and from groundwater (such as aquifers). |
| Water treatment involves screening, sedimentation, filtration and chlorination. |
| Ocean water can be made potable (drinkable) through the process of desalination to remove the salt. Desalination can be carried out by distillation or reverse osmosis. |
| The availability of potable water varies around the world. A country can suffer water scarcity either physically or economically. Urban and rural regions face different challenges in supplying potable water. |
| Dams can be built to satisfy a variety of needs, including flood control, hydro-electric power, irrigation, storage, transport, recreation, tourism and fish farming. |
| Water pollution may come from domestic waste, sewage, plastics, industry and farming. |
| Pollution can cause an increase in infectious diseases, an accumulation of toxic substances, bioaccumulation and biomagnification. |
| The burning of fossil fuels can release oxides of nitrogen and sulfur, which cause acid rain. This affects organisms in lakes and rivers; nutrients that enter the water can lead to a growth of algae, which when they die cause a lack of oxygen and the death of organisms – eutrophication. |
| Better sanitation and sewage treatment, along with greater control and legislation, can improve water quality. |
| Mosquitos are vectors of the malarial parasite; the disease is transmitted via an infected female mosquito biting a non-infected person. |
| Malaria can be controlled by preventing mosquitos breeding or by stopping them from biting humans. |

## CONTINUED

| |
|---|
| Good sanitation, sewage treatment, good hygiene and vaccination can all prevent the transmission of cholera. |
| Exploitation of marine species is caused by overfishing and overharvesting, which impact both the target species and bycatch ones, as well as marine food chains. |
| Marine aquaculture has been carried out on many species, including fish, crustaceans and seaweeds. |
| It can increase food supplies and reduce the exploitation of natural stocks, but it has limitations including the risk of disease and escaped creatures affecting local food webs. |
| Strategies to manage the harvesting of marine species include: the control of boat, net and mesh sizes; sustainable methods; limiting harvesting periods and areas; and international agreements. |
| Oil pollution can come from extraction processes, pipelines, shipping accidents, cleaning ships' tanks at sea and from refineries. It may affect a range of organisms, coral reefs and beaches. |
| Strategies to reduce oil spillages include MARPOL, the use of double-hulled tankers, carrying out regular risk assessments and maintenance. |
| Oil spills can be dealt with using detergents, sorbents, booms and skimmers; oil can also be burnt off in a controlled way. |
| Plastics can be non-biodegradable and made from fossil fuels; some may biodegrade in the right conditions, but the speed of biodegrading depends on several factors. |
| Plastics that are less than 5 mm are defined as microplastics; these come from the breakdown of larger plastics but are also used in some commercial products. |
| Plastic pollution can be visual, but it can also physically harm wildlife through entanglement, being consumed, and by bioaccumulation and biomagnification. |
| Many strategies are being used to reduce plastic pollution, including: using alternatives to plastic, avoiding single-use plastic, safe disposal and recycling, and legislation that is being developed to implement these approaches. |

## SELF-EVALUATION CHECKLIST

After studying this chapter, complete this table.

| I can: | Needs more work | Almost there | Ready to move on |
|---|---|---|---|
| describe the water cycle | | | |
| describe how people can obtain safe, fresh water, and explain what they use the fresh water for | | | |
| name the major oceans | | | |
| discuss the availability of safe drinking water across the world | | | |
| describe the process of desalination, and discuss its benefits and limitations | | | |
| understand the uses, benefits and limitations of dam projects | | | |

## CONTINUED

| I can: | Needs more work | Almost there | Ready to move on |
|---|---|---|---|
| summarise the different causes of water pollution | | | |
| explain the effects of water pollution on human populations and the environment, including bioaccumulation and biomagnification of toxic substances, acid rain, and eutrophication | | | |
| comment on a variety of methods for improving access to good-quality and reliable quantities of water | | | |
| explain the methods used to control and eradicate malaria and cholera | | | |
| describe the impacts of overfishing and overharvesting of marine organisms | | | |
| discuss the benefits and limitations of marine aquaculture | | | |
| describe the strategies to reduce exploitation of marine organisms | | | |
| describe the causes of oil pollution and its impacts | | | |
| discuss the strategies to reduce oil pollution | | | |
| describe the different types of plastics and their impact on water systems | | | |
| explain strategies to reduce plastic pollution. | | | |

# PRACTICE QUESTIONS

1. State **four** purposes of a multipurpose dam project. [4]

2. Sewage treatment is one strategy for improving water quality.

   a. Name and explain **one** other way of improving water quality. [2]

   b. Sewage treatment has two phases: the first is where large particles are removed and the second phase is where bacteria is removed. Explain the methods used to carry out these two phases. [3]

3. Eutrophication is the addition of nutrients to water in lakes and rivers by leaching and nutrient enrichment from inorganic and organic ions.

   Describe the process of eutrophication, and explain why it causes the reduction in oxygen levels in the water of a lake. [4]

4. **Figure 4.71** shows several sources of water pollution.

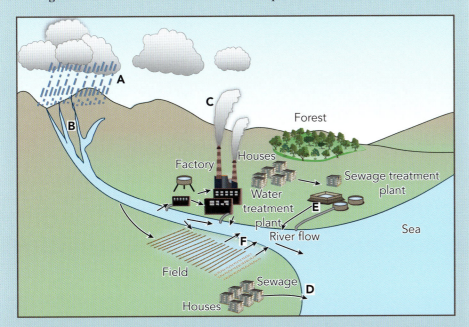

Figure 4.71: Sources of water pollution.

   Use **Figure 4.71** and your own knowledge to answer the following questions.

   a. State the name of the main gas produced by the factory that may lead to death of animals in the river. [1]

   b. Describe how the effluent at D differs from that at E. [3]

   c. Explain how the sewage treatment plant results in this difference. [5]

   d. Discuss the effects that the run-off from the field may have on the ecosystem of the river estuary. [4]

> CAMBRIDGE IGCSE™ AND O LEVEL ENVIRONMENTAL MANAGEMENT: COURSEBOOK

## CONTINUED

5   **Figure 4.72** shows the process of reverse osmosis used in the desalination of sea water.

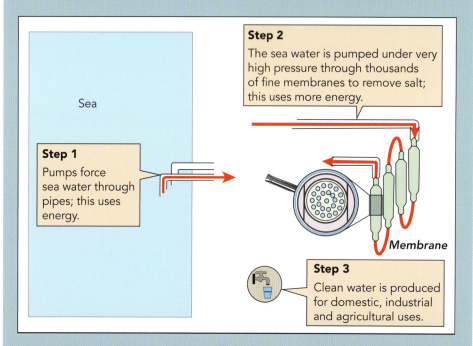

Figure 4.72: A reverse osmosis plant.

   a   With reference to **Figure 4.72** and your own knowledge, describe the process of reverse osmosis. [4]

   b   Desalination has both positive and negative impacts.

   i   Describe **one** positive impact of desalination. [2]

   ii   Describe **one** negative impact of desalination. [2]

6   Malaria and cholera are both diseases related to water that can spread widely after natural disasters such as floods.

   Compare how each of these diseases can spread after a flood. [6]

## CONTINUED

**7** Table 4.6 shows fish catches from 1997 to 2005.

| Year | Catch / thousands of tonnes |
|---|---|
| 1997 | 68.0 |
| 1999 | 91.5 |
| 2001 | 88.0 |
| 2003 | 104.0 |
| 2005 | 131.0 |

**Table 4.6:** Fish catches from 1997 to 2005. Data adapted from: *A Bioeconomic Analysis of Maldivian Skipjack Tuna Fishery* by Solah Mohamed.

a Plot a line graph of the data in **Table 4.7**. [4]

b With reference to the graph you have plotted, state the estimated catch in the year 2000. [2]

c Calculate the percentage increase in the catch between 1997 and 2005. [2]

d Suggest reasons for the pattern shown by your graph. [3]

**8** The following information was presented in the case for farming fish and other animals for meat.

Feed conversion ratio is the calculation of the amount of food given that is converted to animal weight gain. It shows how effective an animal is at turning food into body weight.

Feed conversion ratio can be calculated to show the efficiency level of farmed food as follows:

The weight of food intake divided by the weight gained by the animal.

0.54 kg of food is needed to produce 0.45 kg of salmon. The amounts of feed needed to produce 0.45 kg of three other types of meat are as follows:

meat **A** requires 3.93 kg of food

meat **B** requires 2.66 kg of food

meat **C** requires 0.86 kg of food.

a **Show** this information in the table below. **B** has been completed for you. [6]

| Food type | Feed conversion ratio |
|---|---|
| Salmon | |
| A | |
| B | 5.9 |
| C | |

CONTINUED

    b  Determine how far this information supports the marine aquaculture of fish? [3]

    c  Give **three** other reasons for developing marine fish farming, apart from the possible increased food conversion efficiency. [3]

9  **Figure 4.73** shows the occurrence of microplastics in commercial fish caught in a fresh water lake. **Figure 4.74** shows the occurrence of microplastics in specific fish species caught in the lake.

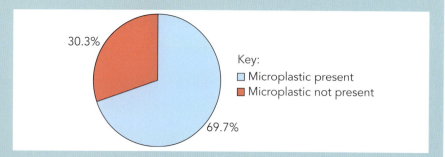

**Figure 4.73:** The occurrence of microplastics in commercial fish caught in a fresh water lake.

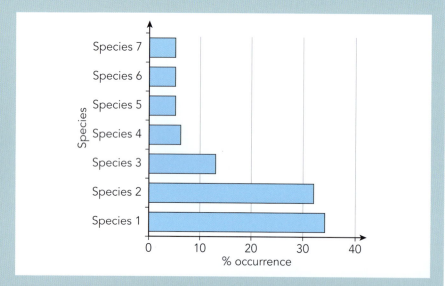

**Figure 4.74:** The occurrence of microplastics in specific fish species caught in the lake.

    a  With reference to **Figures 4.73** and **4.74**, describe the occurrence of microplastics in the commercial fish found in this fresh water lake. [3]

    b  Explain how the microplastics found their way into the bodies of the fish. [3]

    c  Describe **one** method for sustainably managing plastics to reduce the risk of the contamination of ecosystems with microplastics. [2]

## CONTINUED

10 **Figure 4.75** shows the distribution of an oil spill caused by damage to the *Exxon Valdez* in 1989.

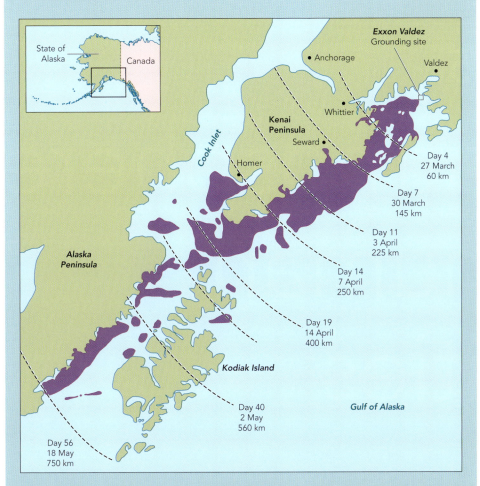

**Figure 4.75:** Distribution of an oil spill damage caused by damage to the *Exxon Valdez* in 1989.

a Describe the distribution of the oil spill caused by the *Exxon Valdez* accident. [2]

b State **two** strategies that have been introduced by **MARPOL** that would have helped to prevent this spill from occurring. [2]

c Give **three** different techniques that can be used to control or clean up oil spills like this one. [3]

# Chapter 5
# The atmosphere and human activities

## LEARNING INTENTIONS

In this chapter you will:

- discover the composition and structure of the atmosphere
- understand how climate and weather are related
- investigate how the natural greenhouse effect works
- learn what greenhouses gases are and give some examples
- explore why there are increased concentrations of greenhouse gases in the atmosphere and what impact this is having
- discover the impacts of climate change
- examine strategies to reduce carbon footprints and manage the impacts of climate change
- consider ways in which we can adapt to climate change, and the advantages and disadvantages of such strategies

# 5 The atmosphere and human activities

## CONTINUED

- learn how acid rain forms
- investigate the impacts of acid rain and strategies to manage its impacts
- explore the causes of ozone depletion in the ozone layer
- consider the impacts of ozone depletion and strategies to manage these impacts.

## BEFORE YOU START

In groups of three or four, make some brief notes on what you know about Earth's atmosphere.

Look at the statements below. Which are true and which are false?

- The composition of the atmosphere has remained the same since Earth was formed.
- The atmosphere is composed of four layers.
- The temperature of the atmosphere decreases with height.
- The pressure of the atmosphere decreases with height.
- Carbon dioxide, methane and water vapour are all greenhouse gases.
- Transport accounts for 15% of global greenhouse emissions.
- Ozone is found throughout the atmosphere.
- Human activity is the main cause of the enhanced greenhouse effect.

Why do you think Earth's atmosphere is essential for life on our planet?

Share your ideas as a class.

## ENVIRONMENTAL MANAGEMENT IN CONTEXT

### The man who survived a supersonic freefall

**Earth's atmosphere** extends 1000 km upwards from Earth's surface, and the Karman line occurs at an altitude of 100 km above sea level. This line represents the boundary between Earth's atmosphere and what is referred to as 'outer space'. On 24 October 2014, a former Google Executive, Alan Eustace (Figure 5.1), took 1 hour and 45 minutes to rise up through the atmosphere with a helium-filled balloon, to a height of 41.4 km. He then jumped from the balloon and fell at speeds of up to 1287 km / hour. Fifteen minutes later, he was back on Earth. Doing this, Eustace broke the world record for the highest freefall parachute jump by just over 2 km, which had been set two years before by Felix Baumgartner.

Eustace faced many dangers on his ascent and descent, and wore a specially designed pressurised spacesuit with a built-in life support system. Pressure decreases with height, so if his suit had failed above 19.2 km (the Armstrong limit), fluids in his exposed body would have boiled. Oxygen levels also fall as pressure decreases, and so he faced the risk of hypoxia (lack of oxygen), as well as freezing to death.

Although Eustace did not jump from the edge of space, he did jump from above the ozone layer and above the height that civilian aircraft fly at. At 41.4 km up, he had 99% of Earth's atmosphere below him, and he fell through two of the four layers of the atmosphere: the stratosphere and the troposphere.

### KEY WORD

**Earth's atmosphere:** a layer of air and water vapour approximately 480 km thick that surrounds Earth

> CAMBRIDGE IGCSE™ AND O LEVEL ENVIRONMENTAL MANAGEMENT: COURSEBOOK

## CONTINUED

**Figure 5.1:** Alan Eustace, who parachuted back to Earth from the stratosphere.

**Discussion questions**

1 What information would you use to determine where the layers of the atmosphere change?

2 What do you think makes jumping from space different to jumping from an aircraft?

## 5.1 The atmosphere

The atmosphere is a layer of gases held to Earth by gravitational force. Gravity and compression mean that 50% of the atmosphere lies within 5.6 km of Earth's surface.

## The structure and composition of the atmosphere

Scientists believe that when Earth formed, it had no atmosphere, but as the planet cooled, gases were released and an atmosphere began to form.

### Components of the atmosphere

Today's atmosphere is composed of nitrogen (mostly the product of volcanic eruptions), oxygen, argon (an inert or **noble gas**), carbon dioxide (cycled through photosynthesis, respiration and the burning of fossil fuels) and ozone. Carbon dioxide and ozone are referred to as 'variable gases' because their quantity can change as a result of processes such as evaporation and transpiration and, in the case of ozone, because of varying rates of formation, pollution and seasonal change. There are also tiny traces of other gases, such as krypton.

Besides these gases, the atmosphere contains **aerosols**, or solid particles (minute particles of dust such as salt, fine sand and volcanic ash), and water vapour (Figure 5.2). Levels of water vapour in the atmosphere vary depending on temperature and pressure, from between 4% above tropical rainforests to 0.2% above the Arctic and Antarctic. **Clean, dry air** is air from which water vapour has been removed.

Table 5.1 shows the composition of the atmosphere.

**Figure 5.2:** The atmosphere contains gases as well as aerosols and water vapour.

### KEY WORDS

**noble gas:** a gas that rarely reacts with other elements because it is stable, previously referred to as inert gas

**aerosols:** sprays containing fine particles and/or droplets that become suspended in the atmosphere

**clean, dry air:** air that contains no water vapour, only gases

198

# 5 The atmosphere and human activities

| Component | % in atmosphere | Importance to life on Earth |
|---|---|---|
| Permanent gases: | | |
| Nitrogen ($N_2$) | 78 | Needed for the growth of plants. |
| Oxygen ($O_2$) | 21 | Produced by photosynthesis and used in respiration. |
| Variable gases: | | |
| Water vapour ($H_2O$) | 0.2–4.0 | Source for all types of precipitation. |
| Carbon dioxide ($CO_2$) | 0.04 | Provides most of the natural greenhouse gases. Vital to the existence of life. Used by plants in photosynthesis and produced by respiration. As plants are primary producers, they support other life. |
| Ozone ($O_3$) | 0.00006 | Absorbs **ultraviolet radiation**. |
| Inert gases: | | Can create an inert atmosphere that protects materials from reacting with oxygen or other gases. |
| Argon (Ar) | 0.90 | |
| Helium (He), neon (Ne), krypton (Kr) | Trace | |
| Pollutants: | | |
| Sulfur dioxide ($SO_2$), nitrogen dioxide ($NO_2$), methane ($CH_4$) | Trace | Can lead to acid rain and the enhanced greenhouse effect. |

**Table 5.1:** The composition of the atmosphere.

The natural balance of gases in the atmosphere is maintained by various cycles, including the nitrogen cycle and carbon cycle. However, human activities can alter the composition in many ways. Deforestation (Figure 5.3) and the burning of fossil fuels add carbon dioxide. Growing rice and keeping some types of livestock increase methane levels. Some gases are reduced by human activity, such as **afforestation** or releasing ozone-destroying **chlorofluorocarbons (CFCs)**.

> **KEY WORDS**
>
> **ultraviolet radiation:** harmful rays from the sun, which are classified into three forms: UV-A, UV-B and UV-C; UV-A and UV-B reach Earth, but UV-C is absorbed by the atmosphere
>
> **afforestation:** planting trees on land that has never been forested
>
> **chlorofluorocarbons (CFCs):** human-made chemicals used in older aerosol sprays, refrigerator / air-conditioner coolants, cleaning solvents and insulating plastic foam manufacturing

**Figure 5.3:** When large areas of forest are cut down, the carbon that the trees contain is released into the atmosphere.

## ACTIVITY 5.1

Table 5.2 shows a detailed breakdown of gases in the atmosphere.

| Gas | Percentage |
|---|---|
| Nitrogen | 78.09 |
| Oxygen | 20.95 |
| Argon | 0.90 |
| Carbon dioxide | 0.04 |
| Other gases | 0.02 |

**Table 5.2:** Percentage of different gases in the atmosphere, to two decimal places.

Create a pie chart to show the composition of the atmosphere.

First, draw a circle using a compass and a pencil. There are 360° in a circle. To construct the pie chart, split up the 360° between the different groups. How many degrees each group gets depends on the size of the group: 3.6° = 1%.

Check that the total number of degrees for all groups adds up to 360° before drawing the segments. Mark the segments on the circle using a protractor (Figure 5.4). The largest segment should be drawn first, by drawing a (vertical) radius from the centre straight up to the top of the circle (at '12 o' clock').

Once you have drawn all the segments, shade or colour them and create a key with suitable labels.

Give your pie chart a suitable title.

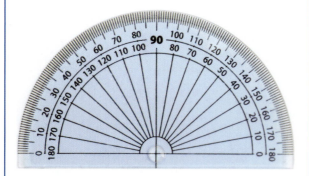

**Figure 5.4:** A protractor.

## MATHS TIP

Remember – pie charts are used when you want to compare a part to the whole. They do not show change over time.

## SELF ASSESSMENT

When you have completed Activity 5.1, look carefully at your completed pie chart and review your own work. Consider the following points:

- Is the pie chart completed in a clear way?
- Are the segments drawn at the correct angle?
- Does the largest segment start at 12 o'clock?
- Have you included a title and a key for the pie chart?

Which features of drawing a pie chart do you need to improve on next time you are asked to do this type of task?

## Structure of the atmosphere

When air pressure is measured at Earth's surface, how much air is above us is actually being measured. When pressure falls, there is less air above; when pressure rises, there is more air above. Atmospheric pressure decreases with height in the atmosphere, but temperature changes are more complicated. Based on temperatures changes, the atmosphere can be divided into four layers, as shown in Figure 5.5.

**The troposphere**

Temperature decreases with height (averaging 6.4 °C / km), because the warming effect of Earth's surface through **conduction** and **convection** gets less as altitude increases. The strength of Earth's gravitational pull declines with altitude, and pressure declines too. The relationship

## KEY WORDS

**conduction:** the process by which heat or electricity goes through a substance

**convection:** the flow of heat through a gas or a liquid

5 The atmosphere and human activities

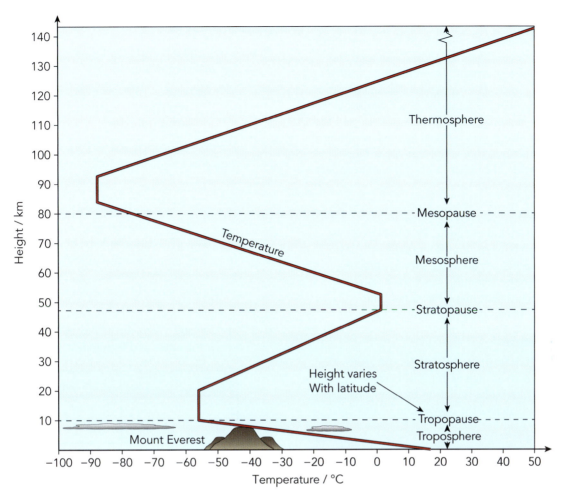

Figure 5.5: The structure of the atmosphere.

between temperature and pressure is important in the troposphere (Figure 5.6). When air moves up in the lowest layer of the atmosphere, the pressure falls (because there is less remaining atmosphere above) and its temperature falls as well. On average, the temperature of the troposphere falls about 6 °C for each 1000 metres up. In contrast, wind speeds increase with height. The top of this layer is marked by the **tropopause**, where temperatures remain fairly constant. This boundary occurs at a height of about 8 km at the poles and 17 km in the tropics. It marks the upper limit to Earth's weather and climate.

> **KEY WORD**
>
> **tropopause:** the upper limit of the troposphere

Figure 5.6: Most clouds form and most weather occurs in the troposphere – the lowest level of the atmosphere.

201

### The stratosphere

The stratosphere extends to nearly 50 km above Earth's surface. Pressure continues to fall, but temperatures increase steadily with height. This situation is called a **temperature inversion**. It is caused by the concentration of ozone, in the ozone layer in the lower stratosphere, which absorbs incoming ultraviolet radiation from the sun. This layer also acts as a shield against incoming meteorites, which burn out when they enter Earth's gravitational field. The upper limit of the stratosphere is marked by the **stratopause**.

### The mesosphere

This layer is 50–80 km in height. Pressure continues to decrease, and temperatures fall rapidly to below −80 °C because there is no water vapour, dust or ozone to absorb the incoming short-wave radiation. Winds can reach speeds up to 3000 km / hour. The **mesopause** marks the upper limit of this layer.

### The thermosphere

This layer is 80–1000 km in height. Temperatures here rise rapidly to as high as 1500 °C because of the absorption of ultraviolet radiation by atomic oxygen. The **thermopause** marks the upper limit of this layer.

---

**KEY WORDS**

**temperature inversion:** when temperatures increase with altitude

**stratopause:** the upper limit of the stratosphere; temperatures remain constant in this boundary layer

**mesopause:** the upper limit of the mesosphere; temperatures remain constant in this boundary layer

**thermopause:** the upper limit of the thermosphere; temperatures remain constant in this boundary layer

---

**PROBLEM SOLVING TIP**

To help you to remember the layers of the atmosphere, devise a memory aid. For example:

**T**he = **t**hermosphere (highest layer)

**M**oon = **m**esosphere

**S**un = **s**tratosphere

**T**ogether = **t**roposphere (lowest layer)

---

## Questions

**5.1** Copy and complete the following paragraph using the words shown in the list:

> ozone    78    oxygen    gases
> nitrogen    argon    gravity
> carbon dioxide    stratosphere

Earth's atmosphere is a mixture of _____, with some liquids and solids, held to Earth by _____. _____ is the most abundant gas (_____%). This is followed by _____. A gas that makes up around 0.90% is _____. Another gas, _____, makes up 0.04% of the atmosphere. Plants make food from this gas via photosynthesis. _____ is a gas found in the lower _____ that absorbs potentially harmful ultraviolet radiation.

**5.2** Table 5.3 shows the composition of the atmosphere. Copy the table and fill in the missing gases, formulae and abundance.

| Gas | Formula | Abundance |
|---|---|---|
|  | $N_2$ | 78.09% |
| Oxygen |  |  |
| Argon |  |  |
|  | $H_2O$ |  |
| Carbon dioxide | $CO_2$ |  |
|  | $CH_4$ | Trace |
| Ozone |  | Trace |

**Table 5.3:** The composition of the atmosphere.

**5.3** Why is carbon dioxide an important gas for life on Earth?

**5.4** Look at Figure 5.7. It has axes of temperature against altitude and the names of the four layers in the atmosphere.

  a  Copy the graph and draw a line to represent the changes in temperature with increasing altitude in the atmosphere.

  b  On the graph, mark with an X the layer in which weather and climate occur, and a Y where ozone is concentrated.

5   The atmosphere and human activities

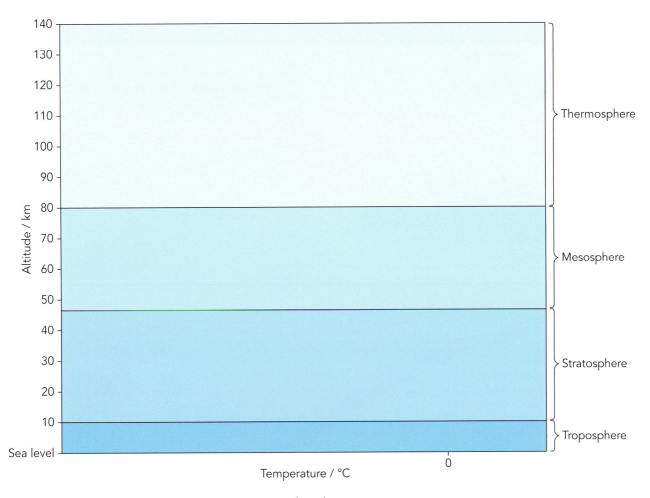

Figure 5.7: A graph showing temperature against altitude.

### FIELDWORK ACTIVITY 5.1

**Investigate the relationship between pressure and temperature**

#### You will need

- a glass
- a small candle that will fit inside the glass
- food colouring
- water
- a saucer

#### Safety

Wear eye protection throughout this experiment and take care when using matches to avoid burns. Follow all safety instructions from your teacher.

#### Before you start

Make sure you have all the equipment ready before you start the experiment.

#### Method

- Put a small amount of water on a saucer and mix in a few drops of food colouring.
- Place a candle in the middle of the saucer and light it with a match.
- Slowly place the glass on top of the candle until it is standing in the water and touching the bottom of the saucer (Figure 5.8).
- Note down what happens next. You might have to wait until the candle goes out.

203

CAMBRIDGE IGCSE™ AND O LEVEL ENVIRONMENTAL MANAGEMENT: COURSEBOOK

### CONTINUED

**Questions**

1 What happened to the water in the saucer when the candle went out?

2 Why do you think this happened?

3 How do you think this relates to what you have learnt about the structure of the atmosphere?

**Figure 5.8:** Use a candle, coloured water and a glass to investigate the relationship between pressure and temperature.

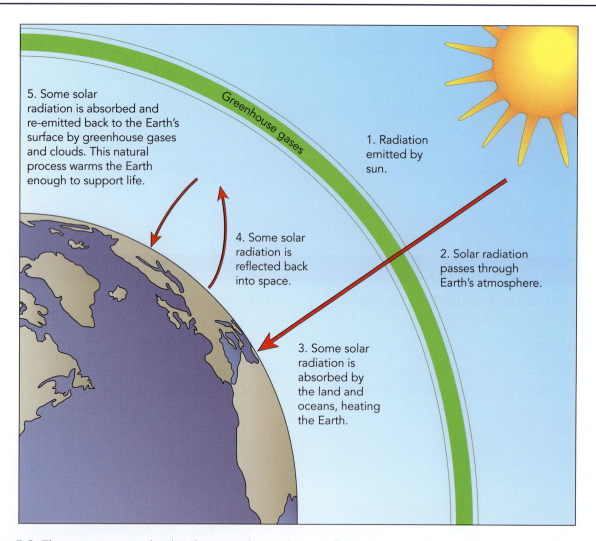

**Figure 5.9:** The processes involved in the natural greenhouse effect.

> **REFLECTION**
>
> Did you find the practical investigation a useful way to understand the relationship between pressure and temperature? Why, or why not? Produce a list of problems that you might have encountered and try to suggest possible improvements for your investigation.

## The natural greenhouse effect

The natural greenhouse effect is the process that helps keep Earth's surface and atmosphere warm (Figure 5.9).

Earth receives incoming **solar radiation** (short-wave radiation) from the sun. About half of this thermal energy is absorbed by Earth's surface, heating the planet. Around 20% is absorbed by the atmosphere, and 30% is reflected back into space by clouds and Earth's surface. As the surface warms, outgoing **solar radiation** (long-wave radiation) is emitted back into the atmosphere.

Greenhouse gases absorb some of this radiation and re-emit it back to Earth's surface. These greenhouses gases make up a small proportion of the atmosphere, but they act like a blanket, trapping the radiation. The greater the concentration of greenhouse gases, the more effectively they return radiation back to Earth's surface. This process maintains Earth's temperature at around 34 °C warmer than it would otherwise be, allowing life to exist.

This atmospheric phenomenon is called the greenhouse effect, because the reflection and absorption of heat warming the atmosphere acts like a greenhouse.

> **KEY WORD**
>
> **solar radiation:** radiation from the sun; this may be short-wave (incoming) radiation or long-wave (outgoing) radiation; as Earth produces very little visible light or ultraviolet radiation, all radiation from the Earth is infrared

## 5.2 Climate change

'Climate' refers to the weather conditions in a location based on the weather over many years. Climate change is therefore any change to those typical conditions.

### Greenhouse gases

As you have seen, greenhouse gases are gases in the atmosphere that absorb solar radiation and emit the energy as thermal (heat) energy. Besides water vapour ($H_2O$), the main greenhouse gases are carbon dioxide, methane and nitrous oxides. Chlorofluorocarbons (CFCs – gases containing fluorine, chlorine and carbon) are also greenhouse gases, but they are artificial. Ozone is a greenhouse gas. These gases stay in the atmosphere for differing amounts of time, as shown in Table 5.4. Unlike other greenhouse gases, water vapour stays in the atmosphere for just a few days.

| Greenhouse gas | % contribution to the greenhouse effect | Number of years gas stays in the atmosphere |
|---|---|---|
| Carbon dioxide | 65 | 200 |
| Methane | 17 | 12 |
| CFCs | 12 | 1000 |
| Nitrous oxides | 6 | 114 |

**Table 5.4:** Some greenhouse gases and the length of time they stay in the atmosphere.

# The causes and effects of increased greenhouse gases in the atmosphere

## Human activities

The increasing global human population, rising living standards and advances in technology have all led to a huge demand in energy, especially from the combustion of fossil fuels. This, combined with industrialisation, has resulted in more carbon dioxide being released (Figure 5.10). Scientists estimate that the concentration of carbon dioxide in the atmosphere before the Industrial Revolution in the late 18th century had a value of approximately 280 parts per million (ppm). Measurements in 2023 put the concentration at over 424 ppm – the highest ever recorded.

Figure 5.10: Increased industrialisation has contributed to the rise in carbon dioxide being released into the atmosphere.

> **KEY WORD**
>
> **enhanced greenhouse effect:** when human activities increase the warming effect of the natural greenhouse effect

The causes of the increase in emissions of greenhouses gases from human activity are outlined in Table 5.5.

| Greenhouse gas | Human activities that increase abundance of gas |
|---|---|
| Carbon dioxide | Combustion of fossil fuels for energy and transport |
| | Deforestation, which reduces the number of plants available to take carbon dioxide out of the atmosphere through photosynthesis |
| | Cement production, as calcium carbonate in the form of limestone is heated to produce calcium oxide (lime) and releases carbon dioxide |
| | Increasing human population and its associated energy usage |
| Methane | Agriculture – increased livestock farming; some livestock release large amounts of methane through their digestion |
| | Manure decomposition and rice production both release methane |
| | Wetland drainage for urban development and food production |
| CFCs | Aerosol sprays, fire extinguishers, refrigeration, air conditioning |
| Nitrogen oxides | Vehicle exhausts, chemical fertilisers |

Table 5.5: Sources of some of the main greenhouse gases emitted by human activity.

## The enhanced greenhouse effect

All these human activities add greenhouse gases to the atmosphere, which results in a phenomenon known as the **enhanced greenhouse effect**. The increased concentrations of greenhouse gases result in more heat being retained in the atmosphere and an increase in Earth's temperature. This is leading to global warming, which is causing climate change. Carbon dioxide is the single-largest contributor to the enhanced greenhouse effect.

## 5 The atmosphere and human activities

### ACTIVITY 5.2

Table 5.6 shows the changes in mean annual atmospheric carbon dioxide measured in parts per million/ppm above the Mauna Loa volcano in Hawaii.

| Year | Mean annual atmospheric $CO_2$ / ppm |
|---|---|
| 1960 | 315.97 |
| 1965 | 320.04 |
| 1970 | 325.68 |
| 1975 | 331.08 |
| 1980 | 338.68 |
| 1985 | 346.04 |
| 1990 | 354.35 |
| 1995 | 360.80 |
| 2000 | 369.52 |
| 2005 | 379.80 |
| 2010 | 389.85 |
| 2015 | 400.83 |
| 2020 | 414.21 |

**Table 5.6:** Changes in mean annual carbon dioxide levels above Mauna Loa in Hawaii.

a  Plot a line graph to show the trend of the data. Put the concentration on the y-axis and year on the x-axis. Make sure the axes are drawn with a ruler and correctly labelled. Use a sensible linear scale so that the plots cover at least half of the graph paper or grid. Carefully plot the data correctly and join up the plots with a ruler.

b  Calculate the mean annual atmospheric $CO_2$ between 1960 and 2020. Plot it as a line on the graph.

c  Describe and explain the evidence for climate change as shown by your graph.

### MATHS TIP

Line graphs are used to show changes over time. It is important that when you draw a line graph, the axis intervals are evenly spaced. Starting the y-axis above 0 can make small changes look extreme.

### PEER ASSESSMENT

Swap graphs with another student. Mark their graph out of 5 for the following points:

- axes drawn with a pencil and a ruler, and labelled correctly (1 mark for each axis)
- sensible linear scale and the plots covering over half the sheet of graph paper
- correct plotting of the data and joined up with a ruler
- a title that describes what the graph shows.

### REFLECTION

Look back at your graph. Did you get the full 5 marks? If not, do you understand what is not correct on your graph? What do you need to work on to improve your skills at plotting graphs? Make some notes and then revise your own graph in light of the feedback.

## Questions

**5.5** Copy and complete the following passage using words from the list. A word may be used more than once.

**greenhouse gases    space    temperature**
**atmosphere    sun    radiation    solar**

Global warming is the increase in _____ of Earth's atmosphere. Earth is naturally warmed by _____ radiation from the _____, which passes through the _____ and is reflected back out to _____. _____ make the atmosphere more effective at trapping _____ radiation. The natural greenhouse effect lets some of the _____ back out of the atmosphere, keeping Earth at the right temperature for plants, animals and humans to survive.

5.6 Describe the natural greenhouse effect.

5.7 Name two greenhouse gases and state a source for each one.

5.8 Explain how deforestation can contribute to the enhanced greenhouse effect.

5.9 Which of the following is not a consequence of the enhanced greenhouse effect?

   sea-level rise
   habitat loss for some animals
   an increase in the use of fossil fuels
   ocean acidification

5.10 Using Table 5.4, explain why we should be more worried about CFC concentrations in the atmosphere than methane.

5.11 Study Table 5.7. Calculate the percentage contribution of carbon dioxide to the enhanced greenhouse effect.

| Gas | % contribution to the enhanced greenhouse effect |
|---|---|
| Carbon dioxide |  |
| Methane | 18 |
| Other gases | 6 |

**Table 5.7:** The contribution of different gases to the enhanced greenhouse effect.

5.12 Study the graph in Figure 5.11, which shows global average temperatures in the atmosphere from 1860 to 2020.

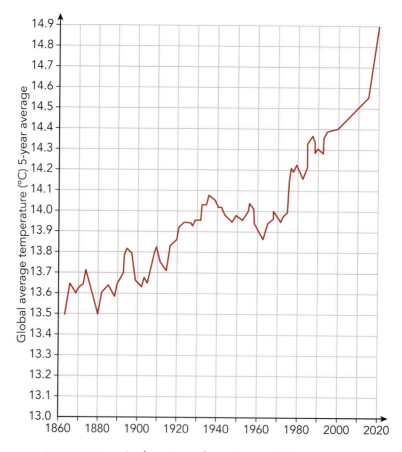

**Figure 5.11:** Global average temperatures in the atmosphere, 1860–2020.

# 5 The atmosphere and human activities

a   State the global average temperature in 1880, 1950 and 2020.

b   What do you think the relationship is between global average temperature and atmospheric carbon dioxide concentration after 1860? Why do you think this is?

## ACTIVITY 5.3

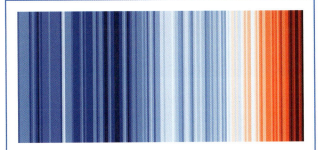

**Figure 5.12:** A warming stripe graph for the world, 1850–2022.

Warming stripe graphs were created by climate scientist Edward Hawkins in 2016. His aim was to show temperature change over time in a way that was simple and easy to understand. Each stripe represents the temperature of a single year, and together the stripes paint a picture of the changing climate.

a   As a class, discuss the trend shown by the graph of global warming stripes (Figure 5.12). Can you see any anomalies – things that are different from the expected pattern or trend? If so, can you explain why they have occurred?

b   In pairs, download from the internet the warming stripe graph for your own country and compare it with the global warming stripe graph. Look for differences and similarities.

c   Extend your research by selecting a country from a continent other than your own. Share your research with the class.

### KEY WORD

**coral bleaching:** the whitening of coral as oceans warm up, disturbing the relationship between coral polyps and algae, causing the coral to eject the algae

## The impacts of climate change

Some scientists believe that we are already experiencing the impact of climate change on our planet because there is a strong correlation between rising average global temperatures and the concentration of carbon dioxide in the atmosphere.

Climate change could have significant impacts on the environment. These include:

- an increase in the temperature of Earth's surface
- an increase in the temperature of the surface of the oceans
- rising sea levels caused by ice sheets, glaciers and permafrost melting and flowing into the oceans; sea levels will also rise as sea water becomes warmer and expands
- ocean acidification – as oceans become more acidic due to increased concentrations of carbon dioxide in the atmosphere, organisms like corals are less able to accumulate calcium carbonate and build a skeleton; **coral bleaching** may occur (Figure 5.13)
- habitat loss as sea-levels rise lead to the loss of low-lying coastal land, and increased erosion and saltwater intrusion
- habitat loss due to extreme events, such as flooding, drought, desertification, storms and wildfires
- disruption to food chains as ecosystems change and plant and animal species move to new areas to find the conditions they need
- increased outbreaks of pests and invasive species
- loss of biodiversity and perhaps even extinction if species cannot adapt to the changed conditions.

**Figure 5.13:** Coral bleaching is a consequence of warming of the oceans because of climate change.

209

Climate change will also affect the human population. Although these impacts are likely to be negative for most people, some people may benefit from them (Figure 5.14). Potential impacts on people include:

- loss of land for settlements and agriculture due to extreme weather events, such as flooding, drought, desertification, storms and wildfires
- increased forced migration as people lose their homes and livelihoods due to rising sea levels
- changes to crop yields: warmer weather may mean that farmers can grow different crops and have longer growing seasons, increasing crop yields, but increased droughts could lead to a decline in crop yields
- if crop yields decline, it could lead to food shortages or famines
- the spread of diseases, such as malaria, due to warmer temperatures

- a negative impact on certain economic activities, such as the skiing industry.

**Figure 5.14:** Climate change could bring benefits to some people. For example, it could cause the Northwest Passage in the Arctic to become ice-free and open up trade routes for shipping all year round.

## CASE STUDY

### Melting ice sheets in Antarctica

**Figure 5.15:** Emperor penguins in Antarctica.

Are we seeing the impact of climate change in Antarctica? Antarctica holds 90% of the world's ice and 70% of the world's fresh water. The sea ice melts and freezes on a seasonal cycle, from a winter maximum to a summer minimum. In 2022 and 2023, however, average monthly temperatures broke records for their warmth, and the sea-ice extent reached record lows. In 2023, the sea ice was 1.42 million km² a smaller than in 2022, when it covered 14.90 million km². This was the lowest extent observed for a southern hemisphere winter since continuous satellite records began in 1978.

The extent of sea ice was low around nearly the whole continent. Some scientists have suggested that warmer ocean temperatures, due to climate change, are a possible cause of the decline.

This loss of sea ice is already having an impact. Less ice cover means an increase in the absorption of solar radiation, as ice has a very high **albedo**. The ground is warmed and air temperatures start to rise, causing even more sea ice to melt. Emperor penguins (Figure 5.15) are an important food source for orca and leopard seals, but scientists discovered that emperor penguin colonies experienced breeding failure where there was total sea-ice loss on a scale that had not been observed before. The penguin chicks were unable to develop the waterproof feathers they needed to survive as the sea ice broke up underneath them. Thousands of chicks drowned or froze to death.

### Questions

1 Using the statistics in the information above, calculate the sea-ice extent for Antarctica in 2023.

2 Give three impacts of the melting ice sheets on Antarctica.

210

## CONTINUED

3  Sea-level rise is one potential impact of melting ice sheets. Look at Figure 5.16, then answer the questions.

   a  What is the projected rise in sea level by 2100 at current levels?

   b  What is the possible increase, by 2100, from Antarctic ice melt?

4  What other impacts might be seen around the world if ice sheets in Antarctica continue to melt?

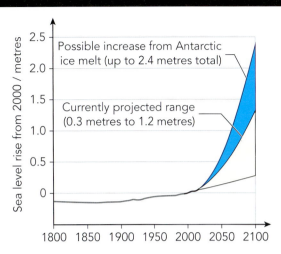

Figure 5.16: Global sea-level rise, 1800–2100 (projected).

### KEY WORD

**albedo:** the proportion of sunlight reflected from the Earth's surface

### ACTIVITY 5.4

In small groups, research the impact of the projected rise in global annual temperatures on the Arctic region. How do the impacts compare with those that may potentially occur in the Antarctic? Remember that not all the impacts may be negative.

Present your findings as a five-minute presentation that you will share with the class.

### REFLECTION

What were the most interesting discoveries you made while listening to the class presentations? Could you do further research on these topics to extend your knowledge and understanding? What learning strategies could you use to help you understand this topic even better?

## Managing the impacts of climate change

To manage the effects of climate change, we need to reduce our **carbon footprint**, cutting down on the amount of greenhouse gases being released into the atmosphere. There are several strategies for this, which can be broadly split into two categories: **mitigation strategies** and **adaptation strategies**. These may be carried out at the international, national and individual levels, and may be short term, or focused on longer-term solutions.

### KEY WORDS

**carbon footprint:** a measure of the impact human activities have on the environment

**mitigation strategies:** local or global strategies that deal with the cause of the problem, reducing or preventing the greenhouse gases that cause climate change, and protecting carbon sinks, such as forests and oceans

**adaptation strategies:** strategies that respond to the impacts of climate change and try to make populations less vulnerable; these tend to be on a local or national scale rather than global scale

## Mitigation strategies

Table 5.8 outlines some of the mitigation strategies that can help to reduce our carbon footprint and as a result limit the impacts of climate change.

> **KEY WORDS**
>
> **climate model:** a computer simulation of the Earth's climate system
>
> **carbon sequestration:** the long-term storage of carbon dioxide and other forms of carbon
>
> **carbon tax:** a tax placed on fossil fuels

| Strategy | Benefits and limitations |
| --- | --- |
| International agreements and policies (for example, the 2015 Paris Climate Conference, at which 195 countries agreed to limit the rise in global temperature to 2 °C) | The serious nature of the problems that climate change creates, and the fact that they affect the whole planet, means that international cooperation is needed to combat them. However, some countries want to develop their industries and do not want to reduce emissions. Countries may not have the money to implement costly strategies to reduce emissions or to use more renewable energy sources instead of burning fossil fuels. |
| Research and **climate modelling** | Climate modelling helps to predict global average temperature changes in the future and can recreate past climates. It allows researchers to test their ideas and scenarios, and see the effects on the climate. However, not all climate models are reliable, and extreme weather events are difficult to predict. |
| Decreased use of fossil fuels and increased use of renewable and nuclear energy | Reducing the use of fossil fuels and using renewable and nuclear energy instead will reduce greenhouse gases and slow the rate of change of global average temperatures. However, some countries will continue to use fossil fuels because they already have the resources and reserves, so extracting and producing the fuel is low cost. Some countries lack the investment and infrastructure for renewable energy and nuclear energy. Producing nuclear energy is very expensive and produces radioactive waste. |
| **Carbon sequestration:** carbon capture and storage (CCS), in which waste carbon dioxide from power stations is captured and transported via pipelines to underground storage sites (Figure 5.17) | This could remove 20% of total carbon dioxide emissions from industrial and energy production sites. However, fitting power stations with the necessary technology is very expensive. Not all countries will have sufficient carbon dioxide storage capacity. Leakage from a site is a possibility; this could contaminate groundwater and put the health of local people and animals at risk. Small earthquakes triggered by the injection of carbon dioxide underground have been reported. |
| Transport policies (for example, a comprehensive public transport system, use of electric or hybrid cars, biofuels, increasing road tax, car-sharing schemes) | In 2023, the global transport sector accounted for 15% of global greenhouse gases, so transport emissions of carbon dioxide need to be reduced as quickly as possible. However, finding new solutions to decarbonise the aviation and shipping industries has not been easy, and changing people's habits to use more public transport takes time. People may not be in favour of the changes, such as increased use of electric cars and road taxes. The changes involved can be more expensive. |
| Taxation: putting a **carbon tax** on carbon-emitting goods | This may reduce remand. However, governments are reluctant to impose this tax, as it can impact on the poorer people in society more than the wealthy. Imposing new taxes can be politically difficult, as businesses could be affected, and it only targets carbon dioxide, not other emissions such as methane. |

| Strategy | Benefits and limitations |
|---|---|
| Energy conservation, including education campaigns and advertising to encourage people to be more energy efficient | Campaigns make people aware of the consequences of their actions on global warming. However, individuals may not feel they can make a difference and are not prepared to make changes. Some of the suggested changes may cost more money to individuals. |
| Use of **artificial intelligence (AI)** to predict future impacts of climate change and mitigate against them | AI can measure changes in icebergs 10 000 times faster than humans can, as well as measuring rates of deforestation and how much carbon is stored in forests. AI uses technology to predict weather patterns and can help communities adapt to climate change, such as by improving access to renewable energy, putting in place waste management systems and encouraging reforestation. AI is being used to help industries decarbonise their operations and to track, trace and reduce their emissions. However, AI has its own carbon footprint, and there is the possible environmental impact of the materials used to manufacture the technology. |
| **Reforestation**, afforestation and **agroforestry** (trees act as **carbon sinks**) | The benefit of planting trees is that they remove carbon dioxide from the atmosphere, and it is a countermeasure against the impacts of deforestation. Trees slow down the rate of climate change. Research has shown that 1 trillion new planted trees could absorb one third of human-caused carbon dioxide emissions. However, a global effort is needed to plant enough trees to make a sizeable impact on global warming. |
| A reduction in the number of children per woman | A reduction in the number of people on Earth would reduce the carbon footprint, but a fall in birth rate can be very hard to achieve. |
| Changes in agricultural practices, such as a reduction in livestock farming and replacing chemical fertilisers with organic fertilisers | Reducing livestock farming limits methane emissions. Nitrogen-based fertilisers are a major source of greenhouse gases; research has shown that they emit more carbon than global aviation and shipping combined, so the use of chemical fertilisers needs to be reduced. Other methods, such as reduced ploughing and planting cover crops, can reduce the amount of carbon dioxide lost from the soil and also improve soil quality. However, some of these changes can lead to a reduction in production and be more expensive to implement, so without financial incentives, farmers are less likely to use such strategies. |
| Making more sustainable lifestyle choices, such as switching from a meat-based diet to a plant-based diet, and buying only seasonal and locally produced food | Research has shown that sustainable lifestyle choices can reduce greenhouse gas emissions by 70% by 2050. In general, people do not often think about how they impact on the planet and will only act if the changes are easy, accessible and affordable. |

**Table 5.8:** Strategies to mitigate the impacts of climate change.

> **KEY WORDS**
>
> **artificial intelligence (AI):** the use of computers and machines that have human-like abilities to solve problems and learn from data supplied to them
>
> **reforestation:** planting trees on land that has recently had tree cover
>
> **agroforestry:** growing trees or shrubs around or among crops
>
> **carbon sink:** a vegetated area where the intake of carbon dioxide from the atmosphere by photosynthesis exceeds its output from respiration, so the net flow of carbon is from the atmosphere into plants

Figure 5.17: Capturing carbon from power plants and piping it into underground storage is one way in which countries and governments are mitigating the potential impacts of climate change.

## Adaptation strategies

Climate change adaptation involves changing our behaviour, practices and infrastructure in ways that allow us to cope with the impacts of climate change. Table 5.9 outlines some of the adaptation strategies that governments and individuals are adopting.

> **SUSTAINABILITY TIP**
>
> Remember that we can all play a role in helping to mitigate and adapt to the effects of climate change. Look around your school or home. If you were redesigning it to better cope with the impacts of climate change, what would you do? Think about building materials, insulation, heating and cooling systems, etc.

| Strategy | Benefits and limitations |
| --- | --- |
| Changes in agricultural practices (growing drought-resistant crops or ones that are resistant to warmer and wetter conditions, more efficient irrigation methods, techniques to conserve soil moisture) | Adaptations will reduce the impacts of crop failure or livestock deaths, which may lead to food insecurity and possible famine. Adaptation can also reduce the possible negative economic impact. Changes require investment, but this does not have to be expensive – for example, providing livestock with shelter from heat. However, limitations to changes are a lack of money and a lack of access to water. Farmers in some LICs will need outside help, especially with costs. |
| Improved flood defences to reduce risks from extreme weather events (flood shelters, houses on stilts, sea walls, storm-surge barriers – see Figure 5.18) | Reducing the impact of flooding from more extreme weather and rising sea levels will also reduce coastal erosion. People will not have to relocate, farmland will not be destroyed, livelihoods can be maintained and economic losses reduced. Coastal habitats will not be destroyed. Wetland vegetation can grow under houses on stilts. However, some of the strategies may be expensive to build and maintain, and coastal habitats may be disturbed. |
| Land-use zoning to ensure that people do not build too close to at-risk coasts or on floodplains | By introducing legislation to reduce building near coasts, there is less chance that homes and industry will be flooded. Important buildings, such as hospitals and schools, should be built away from zones at risk so that they can continue to function. However, it is not always possible to control urban growth, and some people are prepared to live with the risk. |
| New building designs, materials and regulations (improving heat insulation, installing cooling systems and reflective roofing, and carbon sequestration) | By 2050, 1.6 billion people will be living in more than 970 cities regularly exposed to high temperatures, which puts people's lives at risk. Planting urban forests cools the surrounding environment and offers a habitat for wildlife. Traditional designs can be incorporated, such as in Laos where new houses are built with large openings to improve ventilation (Figure 5.19). However, in LICs, settlements are largely self-built and people do not have access to new building materials. New designs may make the houses more expensive to build. |

Table 5.9: Strategies to help people adapt to the impacts of climate change.

# 5 The atmosphere and human activities

**Figure 5.18:** Storm-surge barriers, or flood barriers, allow water to flow through them in normal conditions, but they have special gates that can be closed to block water and prevent flooding during storms or high tides.

**Figure 5.19:** Traditional building designs can be incorporated into new houses. In Laos, large openings improve ventilation.

## Questions

**5.13** Describe two economic impacts of climate change on people.

**5.14** Explain why it may be difficult for countries to reach international agreements on mitigating the impacts of climate change.

**5.15** State two ways in which individuals can take steps to mitigate or adapt to the impacts of climate change on a personal level.

## 5.3 Acid rain

Acid rain is precipitation or atmospheric deposits with a pH value below 5. It is one of the consequences of burning fossil fuels.

### How acid rain forms

Volcanic eruptions emit sulfur dioxide in volcanic gases, but most of the acidity results from burning fossil fuels in factories and power stations, which contain sulfur compounds and release sulfur dioxide ($SO_2$) and nitrogen oxides into the atmosphere. Vehicle emissions add further nitrogen oxides when nitrogen from the atmosphere reacts with oxygen in the high temperature of vehicle engines. This is known as 'dry deposition'. If sulfur dioxide and oxides of nitrogen react with water vapour and oxygen in the atmosphere, weak solutions of nitric and sulfuric acids (sulfurous acid) are created to form acid rain. The equation for this process is:

$$\text{sulfur dioxide} + \text{water} + \text{oxygen} \rightarrow \text{sulfuric acid}$$

Acid rain can be moved by winds for hundreds of kilometres before it falls to Earth, so it can occur at some distance from the source. This is known as 'wet deposition'.

### The impacts of acid rain

The pollutants in acid rain are sulfur dioxide and nitrogen oxides. These can impact both property and the environment. Potential impacts include:

- the acidification of water bodies, such as rivers and lakes, as they become affected by acid deposition
- the poisoning of aquatic and animal life in lakes as acidity levels increase, which can lead to reduced fish populations and impact aquatic food webs (Figure 5.20)
- the acidification of soil as nutrients, such as calcium, are leached out of it
- damage to crops, which can result in a decline in crop yields

- damage to trees and other vegetation, including **defoliation**, as roots are affected by the acidification of groundwater and the ability to photosynthesise decreases
- chemical weathering of limestone and marble buildings and statues (Figure 5.21).

**Figure 5.20:** Acid rain can impact rivers and lakes.

**Figure 5.21:** A limestone carving weathered by acid rain.

> **KEY WORD**
>
> **defoliation:** the process of leaves falling off a plant

## Managing the impacts of acid rain

Governments may implement a variety of strategies to manage the impacts of acid rain.

Reducing sulfur dioxide emissions will reduce the amount of acid rain being created. Flue-gas desulfurisation systems or scrubbers remove sulfur dioxide from the emissions of fossil-fuel power stations and other industries. Scrubbers clean the polluted gas by spraying calcium carbonate or calcium oxide into a large chamber where the calcium reacts with the sulfur dioxide in the flue gas. It is a very efficient method and can remove up to 95% of sulfur dioxide emissions. However, the process uses a lot of energy, because of the high temperatures needed for the process to work. Sometimes, water is used in the scrubbing process. Water will need to be treated afterwards, and this can lead to water pollution if there are any leaks.

**Catalytic converters** use a catalyst to speed up a chemical reaction. This reduces levels of harmful gases, such as oxides of nitrogen from vehicles (Figure 5.22). Catalytic converters have reduced harmful emissions, and this has improved air quality. However, they are expensive to replace and can increase fuel consumption, as extra fuel is needed to keep the converter hot enough to work.

Transport policies can be used to manage the impacts of acid rain by reducing the use of fossil fuels. Governments can encourage the use of public transport by offering greater subsidies, and also walking, cycling and sharing cars can help. Greater use of electric vehicles can help reduce emissions.

> **KEY WORD**
>
> **catalytic converter:** a device fitted to cars to convert polluting exhaust gases into less harmful emissions

**Figure 5.22:** Fitting catalytic converters to vehicles can reduce levels of oxides of nitrogen, which contribute to the formation of acid rain.

## FIELDWORK ACTIVITY 5.2

### Testing the effect of different levels of acidity on the germination of seeds

#### You will need

- filter paper
- five Petri dishes
- a measuring cylinder
- distilled water
- a beaker
- 100 seeds (e.g. mung beans or cress, but make sure the seeds are of the same species and the same age)
- a pen
- 0.5 mol dm$^{-3}$ sulfuric acid
- a syringe

#### Safety

Wear eye protection and take care when handling chemicals. If possible, wear protective gloves. Wash your hands after handling chemicals and never ingest them.

#### Before you start

In this activity, you are going to investigate how differing levels of acidity affect the germination of seeds. Before you start, predict what results you might expect to find based on what you have learnt so far about acid rain. At the end of the experiment, go back to your prediction and see if it was correct or not.

#### Method

- Work in pairs. Place some filter paper in a Petri dish. Using a measuring cylinder, pour 20 cm$^3$ of distilled water into a beaker.
- Carefully pour the 20 cm$^3$ of distilled water into the Petri dish. Spread 20 seeds over the filter paper. Replace the Petri dish lid and label it 'distilled water'. This is your control.
- Prepare the second Petri dish with filter paper and pour 19 cm$^3$ of distilled water into a beaker. Add 1 cm$^3$ of 0.5 mol dm$^{-3}$ sulfuric acid to the water (see Table 5.10, second row) using a syringe. Stir well. Pour this into the second Petri dish, spread 20 seeds over the filter paper and label it '5% acid rain'.

| Amount of distilled water / cm$^3$ | Amount of sulfuric acid / cm$^3$ | Total volume / cm$^3$ |
|---|---|---|
| 20 | 0 | 20 |
| 19 | 1 | 20 |
| 18 | 2 | 20 |
| 17 | 3 | 20 |
| 16 | 4 | 20 |

**Table 5.10:** Dilution table.

- Repeat the procedure with three more Petri dishes. Work down Table 5.10 for the correct concentration of distilled water and sulfuric acid. Label the Petri dishes '10% acid rain', '15% acid rain' and '20% acid rain' accordingly.
- Place the Petri dishes in a warm, dark place for seven days. Temperature, water and light must be kept the same for all five Petri dishes.
- Draw up a suitable table to record your results. Count the number of germinated seeds in each Petri dish and record the results as a percentage.

#### Questions

1. What was the purpose of the control dish in this investigation?
2. List two factors that should have been kept the same in this experiment.
3. Apart from the number of germinated seeds, what else could be recorded in this experiment?

---

### REFLECTION

Was your prediction at the start of the experiment correct? If not, do you understand why not? How could you improve this experiment if you were asked to repeat it?
Discuss your ideas with a partner.

## 5.4 Ozone depletion

### Causes of ozone depletion

The ozone layer prevents the majority of the sun's harmful ultraviolet radiation from reaching Earth. The ozone layer has been consistently depleted in recent decades. This is due to chlorofluorocarbons (CFCs) in aerosols (fine, solid particles in air) and refrigerants (a fluid used in cooling systems) being released into the atmosphere. CFCs are produced by plastic manufacturing, air-cooling systems, smoke, irrigation mist, and more.

### Impacts of ozone depletion

Ozone depletion (Figure 5.24) affects humans and the environment in several different ways.

Without sufficient ozone, higher levels of ultraviolet radiation reach Earth. This can have a dramatic effect on human health and wellbeing. The radiation can disrupt DNA and cause sunburn. This results in increased rates of skin cancer. It can also damage the retina in the eye and cause cataracts (a disease of the eye that clouds the eye's lens).

The radiation may also inhibit the reproductive cycle of phytoplankton, which make up the lowest layer of many food webs. Inevitably, this has implications for all creatures further up the food chain and so may affect the populations of other animals. Changes in the biochemical composition of some plants makes their leaves less attractive as a food source, which also affects the balance in ecosystems. Damage to vegetation may cause a reduction in crop yields.

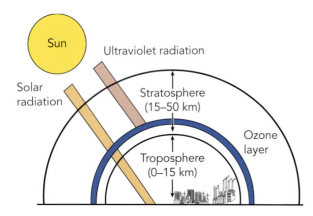

**Figure 5.23:** The ozone layer is found in the lower stratosphere.

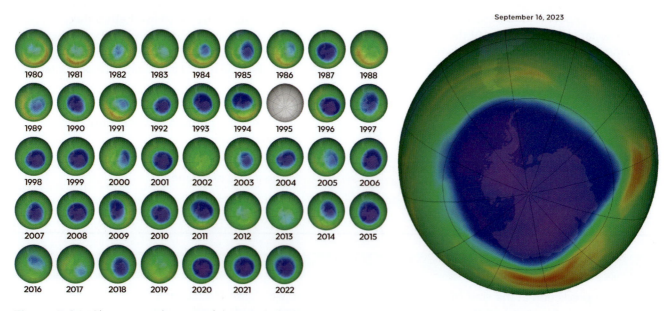

**Figure 5.24:** Changes in the size of the ozone hole, 1980–2023. The ozone depletion is shown by the darker purple and blue towards the centre of the image.

# Strategies to manage the impacts of ozone depletion

The efforts to recover the ozone layer are an example of how international cooperation can have a positive impact. The 1987 Montreal Protocol was signed by 43 countries, which agreed to phase out ozone-depleting substances by 1989. By 2000, a further 131 countries had signed up. By 2021, the use of ozone-depleting substances had fallen by 99.7% compared to 1986. So, to combat ozone depletion, there has been a global reduction in the use of CFCs.

Alternative processes have been introduced, such as pump-action sprays (Figure 5.25), or alternative materials are being used, such as alcohols and hydrochlorofluorocarbons (HCFCs). These alternatives are more expensive and less efficient than using CFCs, but the main problem is that HCFCs are potent greenhouse gases and remain in the atmosphere for a long time. Scientists claim that phasing them out could reduce global warming by 0.5 °C by 2100. By 2030, developed countries are expected to eliminate their use, but developing countries have a later deadline. Further alternatives to using CFCs as a coolant include ammonia and water, and modern air-conditioning units use less coolants now than in the past.

Safe disposal of items containing CFCs, such as old refrigerators, has been encouraged, as leakages happen when fridges and air-conditioning units are disposed of improperly. CFCs can be disposed of safely in special disposal facilities that break CFCs down into non-harmful molecules. However, in some developing countries, disposal facilities are not available, as the countries are unable to afford them.

## Questions

**5.16** Match the pollutant gas to the source.

| Gas | Source of pollutant |
|---|---|
| Methane | Burning fossil fuels |
| CFCs | Keeping cattle |
| Sulfur dioxide | Using aerosols |

**5.17** Copy and complete the following table to show the differences between ozone depletion and the enhanced greenhouse effect.

|  | Enhanced greenhouse effect | Ozone depletion |
|---|---|---|
| Atmospheric layer that absorbs the radiation |  |  |
| Direction of travel of radiation when absorbed |  |  |
| Pollutant gas |  |  |
| Action of pollutant gas |  |  |
| International agreement to combat problem |  |  |

**5.18** Why should people be concerned about a hole forming in the ozone layer?

Figure 5.25: The use of pump-action sprays has helped reduce the use of CFCs.

Figure 5.26: Old refrigerators contain CFCs

> CAMBRIDGE IGCSE™ AND O LEVEL ENVIRONMENTAL MANAGEMENT: COURSEBOOK

## EXTENDED CASE STUDY

### The Maldives' fight for survival

**Figure 5.27:** The Maldives attract thousands of tourists every year – in 2021, tourism accounted for 21.4% of GDP.

The Maldives are on the front line of climate change and are fighting for survival. The country comprises more than 1190 low-lying islands that are less than 1 metre above sea level, arranged around 26 coral atolls in the Indian Ocean. The Maldives are well known for their beautiful beaches and tropical seas, which attract thousands of tourists each year. But the Maldives are also famous for another reason: the possibility that they may be one of the first countries in the world to disappear beneath the ocean because of climate change. NASA predicts that with current rates of global warming, many of the islands could become uninhabitable by 2050.

The Maldives face three potential problems caused by climate change. The first is rising sea levels, due to the melting of ice sheets as water that was previously stored in a frozen state enters into oceans. Sea water also expands as it gets warmer. Not only does a rising sea level threaten to submerge some of the islands, but it is also causing coastal erosion. Of the 186 inhabited islands, 90% have reported severe erosion and resulting land loss. Rising sea levels can also lead to saltwater intrusion, which contaminates groundwater. It has been estimated that 97% of the population now have limited fresh water and rely on rainwater collection.

The second threat to the Maldives as a result of climate change is that seasonal weather patterns are becoming disrupted, making tropical cyclones more frequent and intense. The resulting storm surges increase the rate of coastal erosion and cause salinisation of soil, which makes it harder to grow food.

The third problem is that rising sea levels and temperatures are killing the coral reefs around the islands. A 2016 'bleaching' event killed 60% of the corals in the area, and it is predicted that if annual average global temperatures rise by 1.5 °C by 2050, 70–90% of all corals around the world will be lost. The reefs are essential to the Maldives' survival. Not only are they an essential part of the tropical marine ecosystem, but also local fishermen depend on them, and fishing and fish-processing is the second-largest industry after tourism. The reefs also act as coastal protection, reducing the energy of incoming waves produced by tropical storms.

The warnings over the impact of climate change on the Maldives have been well documented. In 2015, fearing that the population would become environmental refugees, the government planned to purchase land in Sri Lanka, India or Malaysia, and hence relocate the population.

More recent strategies have focused on protecting the islands, and 50% of the national budget is spent on adaptation strategies:

- Breakwaters (concrete blocks and boulders that extend from the coast or are located offshore, to absorb wave energy) have been put in place off Malé, and a 3-metre-high concrete seawall made of tetrapods (Figure 5.28) surrounds the capital.
- Houses are built on stilts to protect against storm surges and flooding. Floors on new homes have to be at least 1 metre above high tide. Where this is not possible, ceilings must be high enough to accommodate a subsequent 0.6-metre elevation of floor levels as the sea level rises. Important public buildings are constructed at higher elevations than other buildings.

5 The atmosphere and human activities

CONTINUED

- An artificial elevated island called Hulhumale (also referred to as 'City of Hope'; Figure 5.29) was formed from reclaimed land and sand pumped from the sea floor. It is 2 metres above sea level and is now the fourth-largest island in the Maldives.
- There are plans to ultimately house most of the population in high-rise blocks of flats. Close to the island, there are plans to construct 5000 floating homes and a golf course, creating the world's first floating city. Four new islands are planned near the Addu Atoll for new tourist resorts.

Figure 5.29: Hulhumale is a new, artificial island on the Maldives.

Figure 5.28: Tetrapods are concrete structures that interlock and reduce the energy of the waves.

Mitigation strategies that have been used include preserving the seagrass meadows and mangroves, which act as carbon sinks. This is sometimes referred to as 'blue carbon'. There is a ban on coral-reef mining to protect the reefs, and the Maldives government has announced that it plans to achieve net-zero carbon emissions by 2030.

At the COP27 conference in Egypt, the most-polluting industrialised countries agreed to set up a 'loss and damage' fund, recognising that low-lying islands, such as the Maldives, are bearing the brunt of climate change. The potential disappearance of the Maldives may not be inevitable.

Questions

1. Explain why sea level is expected to rise in the Maldives.
2. Why is the Maldives vulnerable to sea-level rise?
3. Create a table with three columns to record the social, economic and environmental impacts of sea-level rise on the Maldives.
4. Why do you think a floating golf course is planned?
5. Complete the following two sentences in as much detail as possible:

    One strategy the government of the Maldives islands is using to reduce the impact of rising sea levels is _____. This strategy will help the problem of sea-level rise because _____.

Project

Other island communities in the world are also vulnerable to rising sea levels. Select an island from the following list, or choose one not on the list but that you are interested in. Write a report discussing the social, economic and environmental impacts of sea-level rise on the island and the strategies for limiting the impacts. Use images to illustrate your points.

Suggested islands: Solomon Islands, Fiji, Kiribati, the Republic of Palau, Cape Verde Islands, Tangier Islands, the Seychelles and the Bahamas.

CAMBRIDGE IGCSE™ AND O LEVEL ENVIRONMENTAL MANAGEMENT: COURSEBOOK

### CONTINUED

**Further resources**

*Which islands will become uninhabitable due to climate change first?*, Live Science

*Kiribati and climate change*, Iberdrola

*Sea Level Rise and Implications for Low-Lying Islands, Coasts and Communities*, IPCC

### ACTIVITY 5.5

Imagine you have been asked by the Maldivian government to help plan the strategies to manage the impacts of climate change. They would like you to explore the extent to which mitigation is the most effective strategy in reducing the impacts of climate change on their islands. Work in pairs.

**Student 1:** You will argue that mitigation is the most effective strategy. You need to give examples and also discuss why adaptation strategies may not be suitable for the Maldives.

**Student 2:** You will argue that adaptation strategies are the most appropriate for the Maldives, giving examples and reasons why.

On your own, prepare a brief presentation, giving your side of the argument, then present it to your partner. Listen carefully to your partner's presentation, make notes and ask questions to clarify any information at the end of the presentation.

After both presentations, work together to produce a brief summary of your points and reach a conclusion in order to produce a plan for the Maldives.

### REFLECTION

Which part of this activity did you find most useful? Was it the researching, compiling the information, presenting or listening? Think how this could help you with revision techniques.

### SUMMARY

| |
|---|
| The atmosphere is composed of four layers: troposphere, stratosphere, mesosphere and thermosphere. |
| Ozone is concentrated in the stratosphere. |
| The composition of air in the troposphere is 78% nitrogen, 21% oxygen, and varying amounts of carbon dioxide, argon and water vapour. |
| A greenhouse gas absorbs radiation and emits the energy as thermal heat. |
| Greenhouse gases include carbon dioxide, water vapour and methane. |
| Greenhouse gases create the natural greenhouse effect by allowing short-wave radiation from the sun to reach Earth's surface but trap and re-emit the long-wave radiation reflected from the Earth. |
| Human activities are enhancing the greenhouse effect and causing climate change by increasing the levels of greenhouse gases. |
| Climate change can have many impacts that affect both people and the environment. |
| The impacts of climate change can be managed by mitigation and adaptation strategies. |
| Acid rain is a result of the release of sulfur dioxide and oxides of nitrogen. |
| Acid rain can have impacts on people and the environment. |

5 The atmosphere and human activities

## CONTINUED

| |
|---|
| Strategies to manage the impact of acid rain focus on tackling the emissions of sulfur dioxide and oxides of nitrogen. |
| The depletion of ozone in the stratosphere is a result of emissions of CFCs. |
| Ozone depletion has led to the ozone hole and has impacts on people and the environment. |
| The Montreal Protocol in 1987 led to a successful international agreement to manage emissions of CFCs. |

## SELF-EVALUATION CHECKLIST

After studying this chapter, complete this table.

| I can: | Needs more work | Almost there | Ready to move on |
|---|---|---|---|
| describe the structure and composition of the atmosphere, including its different layers and the proportions of gases it contains | | | |
| describe the difference between weather and climate in terms of timescale | | | |
| describe how the greenhouse effect raises atmospheric temperatures enough to support life on Earth | | | |
| state what a greenhouse gas is, and name the main greenhouse gases and their sources | | | |
| explain why concentrations of greenhouses gases in the atmosphere are increasing and the impact this is having | | | |
| describe and explain the impacts of climate change | | | |
| discuss strategies used to reduce carbon footprints and the impacts of climate change | | | |
| describe some strategies for climate change adaptation, and discuss their benefits and limitations | | | |
| describe how sulfur dioxide and oxides of nitrogen create acid rain | | | |
| describe and explain the impacts of acid rain | | | |
| discuss the impacts of acid rain and strategies to manage its impacts | | | |
| describe the concentration of ozone in the stratosphere | | | |
| explain the depletion of ozone in the stratosphere | | | |
| discuss the impacts of ozone depletion and the strategies to manage them. | | | |

223

PRACTICE QUESTIONS

1  Excluding water vapour, state **two** gases that account for nearly 99% of Earth's atmosphere. [2]

2  **Figure 5.30** shows the approximate altitude of the layers of Earth's atmosphere.

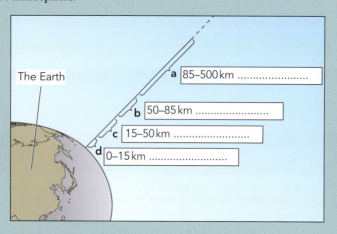

**Figure 5.30:** Altitude of the layers in Earth's atmosphere.

   a  Give the correct label for each layer. [4]
   b  State which layer has the highest concentration of ozone. [1]

3  Explain the role of greenhouse gases in contributing to the natural greenhouse effect. [3]

4  It has been estimated that 924 kg of carbon dioxide are emitted for every 1 tonne of cement produced. Cement is sourced from limestone. **Table 5.11** shows the amount of cement manufactured in India between 2012 and 2022.

| Year | Cement manufactured / million metric tonnes |
|---|---|
| 2012 | 230 |
| 2022 | 379 |

**Table 5.11:** Cement manufactured in India, 2012–22.

   a  Calculate how much more cement is manufactured in 2022 compared to 2012. [1]
   b  Calculate the percentage change in the amount of cement manufactured in India between 2012 and 2022. **Show** your workings and give your answer in tonnes. [1]
   c  Calculate how many tonnes of carbon dioxide are produced from India's cement production in 2022. Show your workings. [1]
   d  Suggest **two** reasons for the increase in cement manufactured in India. [2]

## CONTINUED

5 Global cement manufacture accounted for 8% of the world's carbon dioxide emissions in 2023.

    a Suggest **two** other human activities that have increased carbon-dioxide emissions. [2]

    b Name **three** strategies that can be used to reduce carbon-dioxide emissions. [3]

6  a Acid rain typically has a pH value of less than 5.6.

      State whether a pH of 2.5 is more or less acidic than a pH of 5.6. [1]

   b **Table 5.12** shows two pollutants, their source and effect on the environment. State the missing pollutant. [1]

| Pollutant | Source of pollutant | Effect of pollutant on environment |
|---|---|---|
|  | Combustion of fossil fuels | Acid rain |
| Oxides of nitrogen | Nitrogen from the atmosphere and vehicle engines | Acid rain |

Table 5.12: Sources of pollutants and their effect on the environment.

   c Describe how acid rain forms. [3]

   d Suggest **three** strategies that could be used to manage the impact of acid rain. [3]

7 The ozone layer is part of one of the layers of the atmosphere.

   a State the gas responsible for depleting the ozone layer. [1]

   b State **two** impacts of ozone depletion. Explain these impacts.

    Impact 1..................................................................................

    Explanation............................................................................

    Impact 2..................................................................................

    Explanation............................................................................ [4]

## CONTINUED

8   **Figure 5.31** shows the world's consumption of ozone-depleting substances between 1986 and 2021.

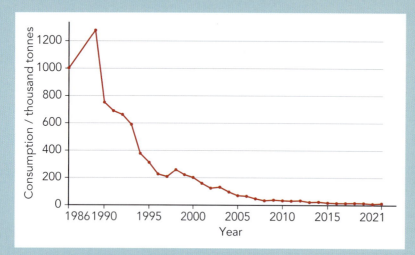

Figure 5.31: World consumption of ozone-depleting substances, 1986–2021.

a   With reference to **Figure 5.31**, describe the trend in the consumption of ozone-depleting substances between 1986 and 2021. [3]

b   The production of ozone-depleting substances was banned by an international agreement in 1987. Explain why an international agreement was needed. [3]

### MATHS TIP

Remember to put the units in your answer if they are not provided for you.

# Chapter 6
# Ecosystems, biodiversity and fieldwork

**LEARNING INTENTIONS**

In this chapter you will:

- explore the different components of an ecosystem
- learn about biotic (living) and abiotic (non-living) factors in ecosystems
- explore some of the relationships between living things within an ecosystem
- examine the processes of pollination and photosynthesis
- learn how energy flows along food chains and webs within an ecosystem
- use pyramids of numbers and pyramids of energy to describe food chains
- understand the process of aerobic respiration
- investigate how carbon cycles within an ecosystem
- explore how forests are lost and the consequences of deforestation
- discover why we need strategies for the sustainable management of forests
- consider a variety of strategies for conserving biodiversity, and their advantages and disadvantages
- learn how to apply the scientific method to data collection
- estimate biodiversity using random and systematic sampling
- discover how to measure populations using a variety of techniques, and consider their pros and cons.

## BEFORE YOU START

List at least three ecosystems you think you could find within 15 km of your school or home. Share your ideas with a partner, noting any similarities and differences between your lists.

Now list some ecosystems on a different continent that you may have read about or seen on television. Again, compare your list with your partner's, noting similarities and differences.

In your pairs, choose one of your local ecosystems and one from a different continent and compare them, considering how they are similar and how they are different.

## ENVIRONMENTAL MANAGEMENT IN CONTEXT

### The sixth extinction?

Life on Earth arose more than 3 billion years ago. The number of species that have gone extinct over that vast period far outnumbers those alive today. So, extinction is normal: species are only expected to exist for a geologically short period of time. Geological evidence suggests that, on average, species of mammals exist for only about 1 million years. The so-called background level of extinction of species is about 10 / year. One of the greatest dilemmas for humans in the early 21st century is the current extinction rate, which stands at 27 000 species / year according to some estimates.

There have been five mass extinctions in the past. The largest of these was the Permian extinction, or Great Dying. This happened 280 million years ago, when 96% of all species alive at that time were lost. All life on Earth now is descended from the 4% of species that survived the Permian extinction. However, although the Permian was the biggest, the Cretaceous–Tertiary extinction of 65 million years ago is the best known. This is when the dinosaurs, which had existed for millions of years, were wiped out.

So, why are we worried if mass extinctions are part of the natural process? The possible sixth extinction event, which we are living through now, is different in several ways. First, the rate of extinction is much faster than during any of the previous five. It is estimated that we could have lost as many as 67% of all species by 2100, compared with the number that existed at the end of the 19th century. That is a huge loss in just 200 years. The other five great extinction events took place over many thousands of years.

In this chapter, you will learn why there are so many species and how they interact with each other and the non-living environment. You will find out about the threats to these species and the places in which they live. Finally, you will study strategies for conserving species and their environment.

Figure 6.1: Life in the sea in the Devonian period, 419–358 million years ago. These organisms are all extinct.

### Discussion questions

1. Is it important to try to slow the rate of extinction we are currently seeing? List some reasons why.

2. Do you think we can stop extinction altogether? Explain your answer.

# 6 Ecosystems, biodiversity and fieldwork

## 6.1 Ecosystems

An ecosystem is defined as all the living things, together with all the non-living things, in an area. These biotic (living) and abiotic (non-living) components interact with each other.

## Components of an ecosystem

All living things in an ecosystem can be described at a number of different levels. They can also be discussed in terms of what they do within the system.

**Populations** are made up of all the individuals of the same **species** in an area. Examples of populations include all the frogs in a pond, all the drongos (a bird) in a forest or all the elephants in a national park.

**Communities** are made up of all the species that are characteristic of a particular ecosystem. Examples include all the different species of animal in the Arctic tundra or all the plants in the Arctic tundra, representing the animal and plant communities respectively.

Living things are found in a **habitat** within an ecosystem. A habitat is the place where the population of an organism lives, finds food and reproduces. Within its habitat, an organism has a particular role in terms of its interactions with other species and its effect on the environment. This is called its **niche**.

The fact that there are so many niches to fill in Earth's ecosystems is the reason why there are so many species. This may seem to be something of a paradox. For example, all plants make food from sunlight. However, plants that can make food in a desert climate are very different from those that do the same thing on the rainforest floor, which are different again from those that do it in the canopy of the same forest. The niche can be summarised in a very simple way – for example, a **predator** is an animal that eats **prey**. However, a much more well-defined niche would be that of the green woodpecker, which eats prey like any other predator but whose prey consists almost entirely of ants (Figure 6.2). An **apex predator** is one at the top of the food chain, with no predators of its own. When the apex predator dies, its body will be decomposed by organisms, such as bacteria, fungi and scavengers.

**Figure 6.2:** A green woodpecker searching for ants. Note its long, sticky tongue, probing into the ground.

### KEY WORDS

**population:** all the organisms of one species living in a defined area

**community:** a group of populations of different species that live together in an area and interact with each other

**species:** a group of organisms that can reproduce with one another and create fertile offspring

**habitat:** the place within an ecosystem where an organism lives

**niche:** the role of a species within its ecosystem

**predator:** the organisms within an ecosystem that prey on other organisms

**prey:** animals that are eaten by other animals

**apex predator:** an animal that kills and eats other animals, but which is not normally killed and eaten by any other animal

## Biotic and abiotic components

Habitats and niches include both **biotic** and **abiotic** factors.

### KEY WORDS

**biotic:** living components of the environment that may affect other living things

**abiotic:** non-living components of the environment that may affect living things

## Biotic factors

Green plants, which make glucose in a process called **photosynthesis**, are known as **producers**. Animals called **herbivores** eat the plants, and animals called **carnivores** eat the herbivores.

Herbivores and carnivores are both consumers – one consuming plants and the other consuming animals. A plant-eating consumer is a **primary consumer** and an animal-eating one is a **secondary consumer**. If an animal eats an animal that itself eats an animal, it is a **tertiary consumer**. If the animal (or other organism, such as fungi) consumes the dead bodies of plants or animals, it is called a decomposer.

> **KEY WORDS**
>
> **photosynthesis:** the process by which plants make (synthesise) glucose using carbon dioxide and water, with sunlight as the source of energy which is captured by chlorophyll in plants
>
> **producer:** an organism within an ecosystem that can carry out photosynthesis
>
> **herbivore:** another name for primary consumer
>
> **carnivore:** another name for secondary and tertiary consumers
>
> **primary consumer:** an organism within an ecosystem that derives its food from producers
>
> **secondary consumer:** an organism within an ecosystem that derives its food from primary consumers
>
> **tertiary consumer:** an organism within an ecosystem that derives its food from secondary consumers

## Abiotic factors

Abiotic factors affect (and are also affected by) living things. The major abiotic factors are described in the following sections.

### Temperature

Temperature is usually expressed as degrees Celsius (°C). Living things have a range of temperatures within which they can survive (Figure 6.3). For example, flatworms are distributed in mountain streams according to how hot or cold the water is. One species lives high up in the mountains where the water is colder, and another lives lower down where the water is warmer.

**Figure 6.3:** There is not much water in the Simpson Desert in Australia, but some things can still live there.

### Water

Water is essential for all life. It is a raw material for photosynthesis and is necessary for chemical reactions. However, living things can survive without water in liquid form. For example, some beetles that live in stored products, like flour, only use the water they make themselves during respiration.

Plants get water from the soil, so the water content of soil is an important factor in determining exactly where a plant species lives. For example, cacti are adapted to survive in soil with very little water (Figure 6.4). The roots of plants that live in soil saturated with water (waterlogged) are adapted to function in low-oxygen conditions (Figure 6.5).

**Figure 6.4:** In this barrel cactus, you can see the shallow roots, which are designed to access rainfall straight away, as well as the long 'tap' roots, adapted to search for water deep underground.

## 6 Ecosystems, biodiversity and fieldwork

Figure 6.5: Plants such as rushes and rice are adapted to grow in very wet conditions, such as waterlogged fields.

## Oxygen

Oxygen makes up about 20% of the gas in air; the rest is mainly nitrogen. However, the absolute quantity of oxygen decreases as altitude increases. At the top of a high mountain, there is much less oxygen than there is at sea level. In water, the amount of oxygen is usually expressed as parts per million (ppm).

Oxygen is not very soluble in water, so all aquatic organisms have special adaptations to ensure they get enough. For example, they might have gills or take in oxygen through their skin. Rushes have a spongy stem that allows oxygen to move down from the air to the roots (Figure 6.6).

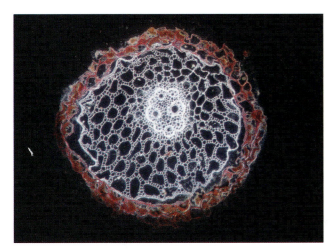

Figure 6.6: A cross-section of a rush stem showing the air spaces to allow oxygen to move down to the waterlogged roots.

## Carbon dioxide

Carbon dioxide is the basis for all the food on Earth – the food that plants make and that everything consumes. Carbon dioxide is constantly cycled, as plants take it in and process it via photosynthesis, combining it with water and making sugar. This sugar (and other food made from it) is used by the plants themselves, animals and other living things, such as microbes, in a process called **respiration**. In this process, the energy in the food is released for use by the organism, and the carbon dioxide re-enters the atmosphere.

## Salinity

Salinity – how salty something is – is measured as parts per million (ppm) or parts per thousand (ppt) of salt, or as a concentration (for example, milligrams / litre).

Salinity mainly affects aquatic animals. All marine species live in water that has 35 ppt of salt, whereas in fresh water there is none. Water with a salinity that is less than 35 ppt but more than zero is referred to as **brackish water**.

In some cases, such as salt marshes, the water in soil is saline. Plants that live in saline water are adapted in various ways – for example, mangroves secrete the excess salt from their leaves (Figure 6.7). Salty soil can arise as a result of poor irrigation practices (see Chapter 3) and this can be a serious problem for farmers trying to grow crops.

Figure 6.7: Mangroves may get rid of salt from the water that is taken up by their roots through the leaves or bark.

### KEY WORDS

**respiration:** the process by which living things release energy from food to carry out the processes of life, such as movement

**brackish water:** water that is salty but not as salty as sea water

231

CAMBRIDGE IGCSE™ AND O LEVEL ENVIRONMENTAL MANAGEMENT: COURSEBOOK

## Light

Light is measured in various ways and expressed as lumens. Light is essential for photosynthesis, so nearly all living things depend on it. With no light, there will be no food. However, some plants are adapted to living in low light levels and can support a community of animals.

## pH

pH is a measure of how acid or alkaline water, or an aqueous solution, is. It is expressed as a number without units on the pH scale (see Chapter 4). The pH of the sea is relatively stable, but the pH can vary a lot in fresh water. For example, decomposing leaves add humic acid to the water, reducing the pH to less than 7. The pH of soil water is a very important factor for plants. Some plants are acid-loving, requiring a soil with an acidic water content. Other plants cannot survive in acidic soils at all.

# Biotic interactions

Living things interact in a variety of ways, including those discussed in the following sections.

## Native and invasive species

**Native species** are those that have lived in an area for a very long time and have adapted to the characteristics of that place. **Invasive species** are ones that have entered the area from outside, often due to human actions.

Invasive species can be extremely damaging to an ecosystem. All species have predators, but there is usually a balance between native predators and prey in an area. However, invasive species may have predatory strategies to which native animals have not adapted. For example, in Australia, invasive cane toads produce toxic secretions that native species are not resistant to. Invasive species may also compete with native species for resources.

Table 6.1 shows some examples of how invasive species have affected native wildlife.

> **KEY WORDS**
>
> **native species:** a species that occurs naturally in an area and which has adapted to conditions in that area
>
> **invasive species:** a species that is not native to an area, and whose presence may cause environmental or ecological harm

| Species | Area to which it was introduced | Area from which it was introduced | Reason for introduction | Problems caused |
|---|---|---|---|---|
| Cane toad | Australia | South and Central America | To control cane beetles, which eat sugar cane | Poisonous to native predators, so native populations declined (e.g. quoll numbers declined by 97%) |
| Kudzu | USA | Japan and China | Sturdy ornamental plant introduced to try to prevent soil erosion | Very fast-growing (30 cm per day); smothers other vegetation, impacting animals that rely on those plants |
| *Prosopis* | Ethiopia | South and Central America | A flowering plant introduced to provide shade, timber, forage, food and medicine | Invades farmlands – about 0.8 million hectares in Ethiopia alone |

Table 6.1: Some examples of invasive species and the problems they cause.

232

6 Ecosystems, biodiversity and fieldwork

ACTIVITY 6.1

Figure 6.8: Cane beetles damage cane crops and are a major pest in Australia.

Read the following facts about cane beetles (Figure 6.8) and cane toads.

Cane beetles (native to Queensland, Australia):

- The adults eat sugar cane plant leaves.
- The larvae (grubs) eat the roots underground where they spend 3–4 months feeding.
- The eggs are laid 20–45 cm deep in the soil.

Cane toads (introduced to Queensland, Australia):

- They have no natural predators in Queensland.
- The females lay more than 30 000 eggs in a year.
- They eat insects, frogs, small reptiles, birds and mammals.
- They are poisonous at all stages in their life cycle.
- They do not dig for food.
- They will breed at any time of year, as long as there is water present.
- They go from egg to adult in one year.
- They cannot climb.

Rank the features of the toads in terms of their importance in ensuring that the toad:

- failed to control cane beetles in Queensland
- has become a major pest in Queensland.

In pairs, compare and explain your rankings. Discuss any differences. Try to agree on a final ranking of the features.

## Competition

Living things need a range of resources from the environment, including other living things and non-living components such as water and oxygen. Many more young of a species are produced than will survive, so there is often competition for the resources. Those individuals that are least well adapted to the current conditions will die earlier or fail to reproduce.

## Predation

An animal that eats another animal is called a predator (Figure 6.9). Examples of familiar predators include lions and tigers. However, there are also many predators in the insect world and in the sea. Beetles eat earthworms and insect larvae, and marine predators range from small fish to the great white shark.

## Pollination

The male gametes (sex cells) of many animals swim through an aqueous (watery) environment to the

Figure 6.9: The harpy eagle – an apex predator in the Amazon. It has been recorded as having up to 116 different prey items, including sloths and monkeys.

female gamete (egg cell). However, flowering plants do not reproduce like this. Male sex cells are found in a structure called a **pollen grain**, which is made in the anther. The pollen grain is either blown about by the wind (as in many grasses and trees) or carried by insects (such as bees and many flies; Figure 6.10), birds and mammals (for example, bats).

With insect-pollinated flowers, the insects are attracted by brightly coloured petals, which are often scented. In addition, the flower provides nectar, which further attracts the insects. Furthermore, the pollen tends to be rather sticky, not particularly light and less abundant than in wind-pollinated flowers.

With wind-pollinated flowers, the anther often hangs outside the flower so that they can be easily blown by the wind, and there is no need for attractive petals, scent or nectar. Pollen in wind-pollinated flowers is light and very abundant; this type of pollen is the main cause of hay fever, which is an allergic reaction to it.

In both cases, the pollen grain lands on the stigma of another flower and sends out a tube. This tube grows down to where the female gamete (egg) is. Here, the egg is fertilised and from this an embryo develops. The embryo is enclosed in a seed, along with a food store. Seeds (sometimes one, sometimes many) are packaged in fruits. The embryo can grow into a new plant, using the food store at the start until it can make its own food through photosynthesis.

**Figure 6.10:** Bees are essential pollinators. They carry pollen from the anther of one flowering plant and deposit it on the stigma of another.

> **KEY WORD**
>
> **pollen grain:** the structure in plants that contains the male sex cell; it is carried to the female organ by pollination

## Questions

**6.1** A species of plant is found growing in a narrow zone at the edge of woodland bordering an open field.

    **a** Suggest two biotic factors that may be involved in restricting it to this zone.

    **b** Suggest two abiotic factors that may be involved in restricting it to this zone.

**6.2** Copy and complete the passage using the following words:

    population   species   community   niche   habitat

    An ecosystem contains a number of _____ of animals and plants, each of which has a _____, lives in a particular _____ and occupies a _____. They all live together in a _____.

> **PROBLEM-SOLVING TIP**
>
> When you are asked to 'suggest' something in a task, you may have been given a scenario that you will not have studied directly, so you will need to apply your existing knowledge to this new situation. In the previous questions, you can apply what you have learnt to suggest appropriate factors for the given scenario.

## Photosynthesis

Plants trap energy in the form of light from the sun in photosynthesis. Photosynthesis is a complicated process, but it can be summarised as if it was a single-step chemical reaction:

$$\text{carbon dioxide} + \text{water} \xrightarrow[\text{chlorophyll}]{\text{light}} \text{glucose} + \text{oxygen}$$

The plant converts glucose into other substances that it needs, such as starch, cellulose and proteins. Energy is released from the rest of the glucose in a process called respiration

Other elements (minerals) from the soil, such as nitrogen, are needed to form other substances, such as proteins. However, in all cases, chemical energy remains stored in the substance.

Plants get the carbon dioxide they need for photosynthesis from the atmosphere through pores in their leaves (stomata; Figure 6.11). The plants get water from the soil through their roots. A green pigment in the leaves called chlorophyll captures light energy from the sun, which is then used to split the water into hydrogen and oxygen. The hydrogen is added to carbon dioxide to make glucose. Any oxygen that is not used in respiration is given off to the atmosphere.

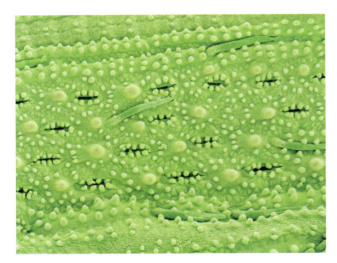

**Figure 6.11:** Plant leaves are covered in tiny holes, called stomatal pores, through which carbon dioxide diffuses.

# Energy flow in ecosystems

The basis of all life on Earth is energy, which comes mainly from the sun as light. Energy enters the living world via photosynthesis and is then passed from plants to animals along food chains within food webs.

## Food chains and food webs

Look back at the previous section on 'Biotic factors'. All these components in an ecosystem – from producers to tertiary consumers – interact with each other. At a basic level, this relationship can be shown in a **food chain**:

producers → herbivores (primary consumers) → 1st carnivores (secondary consumers, predators) → 2nd carnivores (tertiary consumers, also predators)

In reality, the picture is not so simple. In a garden, there might be plants with leaves that, when they fall to the ground, are eaten by earthworms. In turn, the earthworm is eaten by a bird, which could be eaten by a snake.

leaves → earthworm → bird → snake

However, the leaf might also be eaten by a slug or a woodlouse, the worm by a fox or a shrew, and the bird by a fox. You can show all these relationships (and more) in a diagram called a **food web**, which gives a more accurate picture of how biotic components in an ecosystem interact (Figure 6.12).

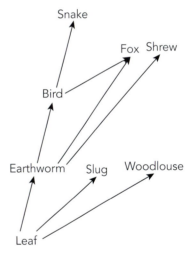

**Figure 6.12:** A food web.

> **KEY WORDS**
>
> **food chain:** a diagram showing the relationship between a single producer and primary, secondary and tertiary consumers
>
> **food web:** a diagram showing the relationship between all (or most) of the producers and primary, secondary and tertiary consumers in an ecosystem

# CAMBRIDGE IGCSE™ AND O LEVEL ENVIRONMENTAL MANAGEMENT: COURSEBOOK

Any change in one part of the food web can cause changes in any other part. So, if the weather is poor and plants do not grow very well, everything will be affected. If snake numbers fall because they are killed by humans, there may be an increase in the number of birds, which might eat more earthworms, causing earthworm numbers to decline.

## Questions

The following questions refer to the drawing of a woodland ecosystem in Figure 6.13.

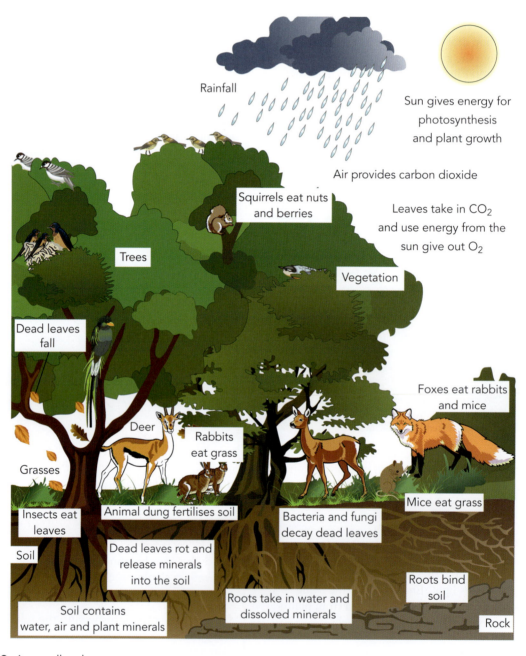

Figure 6.13: A woodland ecosystem.

6 Ecosystems, biodiversity and fieldwork

6.3 Copy and complete the following information:

In the woodland _____ shown, all the energy for life comes from the _____. The energy is in the form of _____ and is trapped by plant leaves in a process called _____. This produces the gas _____ and uses the gas _____ _____. The glucose made in this process is converted into everything that the plant needs. Organisms like plants that make glucose are called _____. Also in the woodland are pictures of some consumers: _____, _____, _____, _____, _____, _____ and _____.

Some of the consumers are predators, such as the _____ and some _____. Animals and plants both use the food they either eat or make to supply energy for their lives. This energy is released in a process called _____. This process also releases the gas taken in by plants.

All the living things in the picture live in a particular habitat. The mice live in the _____, the birds live in _____ and bacteria live in the _____.

6.4 Some abiotic (physical) factors are shown in Figure 6.13. List these factors.

6.5 Copy and complete the following two food chains:

a grass → _____ → foxes

b _____ → insects → _____

6.6 a Using Figure 6.14, copy and complete the food web shown for the whole woodland in Figure 6.13.

b Which animal is not shown on the food web?

c There are five populations of animals in this woodland: deer, rabbits, foxes, squirrels and mice. In addition, there will be many populations of insects and birds of different species. All the animals in the woodland live in a _____.

6.7 a Choose two animal species from the woodland shown and say what you think their niche is.

b Name two animal species that might be in competition with each other in this woodland and suggest what they are competing for.

c Name one predator in the woodland.

d Name one living thing in the woodland that needs to be pollinated and suggest a pollinator, also shown in Figure 6.13.

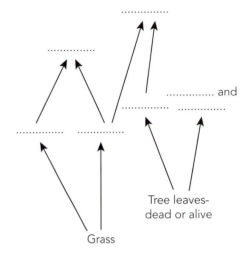

Figure 6.14: A woodland ecosystem food web.

## Pyramids of energy

A plant needs some energy for its own life processes. It gets this not from the light it traps, but from the chemical energy it stores in the form of sugars and other substances it makes. The energy comes from the process of respiration. During respiration, glucose and oxygen are used up, and water and carbon dioxide are produced as waste products. The energy created is used for the processes the plant needs (for example, transporting food and making proteins) and given off to the environment as heat.

Only the energy that is left in the material a plant does not use is available to a consumer. This is about 10% of the energy that the plant fixed from sunlight. This energy flow can be shown in a simple diagram (Figure 6.15a). The same relationship occurs at the next **trophic level** (Figure 6.15b).

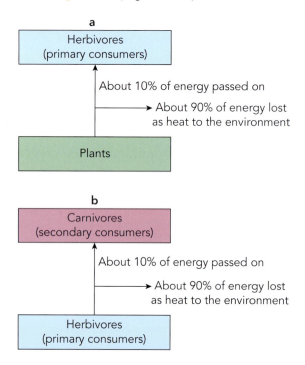

**Figure 6.15: a** Energy flow between the first and second trophic levels. **b** Energy flow between the second and third trophic levels.

Animals in the higher trophic (or feeding) levels need energy – for example, to move, digest food and excrete waste products. This energy is released from their food in respiration, but that process is not 100% efficient, and much of the energy is lost into the environment as heat.

When a consumer eats a plant, it gets two things:

- chemical energy from the starch, simple sugars and other compounds
- various materials, such as nitrogen, that are also present in these substances.

The minerals are not lost because, when consumers die, their bodies break down. The minerals in the dead bodies are released and are once again available to living things. It is important to know this difference: energy flows through ecosystems, but minerals cycle round ecosystems.

Together, the two parts of Figure 6.15 form a **pyramid of energy** (Figure 6.16).

You can see that after two steps, the energy available to a consumer is just 10% of 10% of the energy available from the sun, which is only 1%. After three steps, it is only 0.1%. This is why food chains never have more than four or five links: there is just not enough energy left to support another trophic level. The quantity of energy present in each level, and flowing between them, is measured in kilojoules (kJ).

## Pyramids of numbers

Look back at the food web in Figure 6.12. This offers a more detailed picture of a simple food chain, but even the food web is not likely to be the whole story. What eats the woodlice, slugs and shrews? What else do snakes, foxes, birds and earthworms eat? Real food webs are very complicated.

A way of simplifying this information is to think of the numbers of producers and consumers found in the ecosystem. For example, in a lake, millions of tiny plants are being fed on by thousands of tiny animals. In turn, these are eaten by hundreds of small fish, which in turn are eaten by dozens of larger fish. Standing by the side of the lake might be a few herons and egrets, eating the big fish.

This information can be represented in a diagram called a **pyramid of numbers** (Figure 6.17). Here too, the pyramid shape reflects the loss of energy at each trophic level. It is this energy loss at each level (about 90%) that underlies the reduction in numbers in the pyramid of numbers.

> **KEY WORDS**
>
> **trophic level:** a feeding level within a food chain or web
>
> **pyramid of energy:** a diagram that represents the energy found at different trophic levels of an ecosystem
>
> **pyramid of numbers:** a diagram that represents the numbers of organisms at each feeding (trophic) level in an ecosystem by a horizontal bar whose length is proportional to the numbers at that level

6 Ecosystems, biodiversity and fieldwork

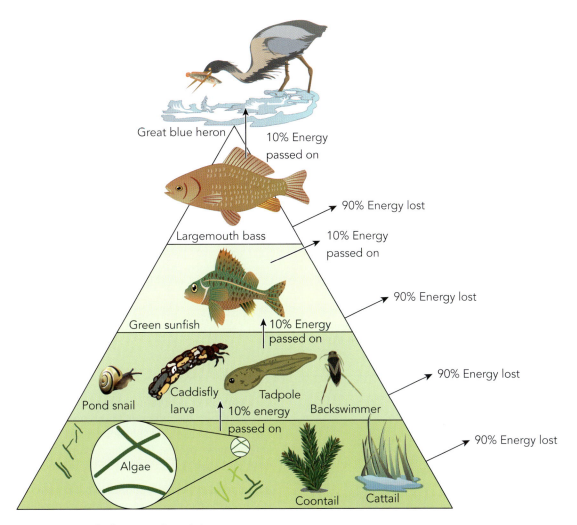

Figure 6.16: A pyramid of energy for a lake.

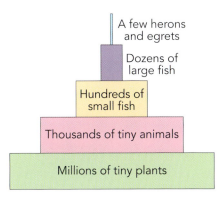

Figure 6.17: A pyramid of numbers for a lake ecosystem.

### SUSTAINABILITY TIP

Due to the small quantity of energy reaching animals in a food chain, it is energy inefficient to eat them. Consider swapping animal-based food with plant-based food for part of your diet.

> **WORKED EXAMPLE**
>
> ### Percentages
>
> If 720 kJ entered a trophic level and 62.8 kJ of this was lost as heat, what percentage of the energy was lost as heat?
>
> **Step 1** Divide the energy lost as heat by the total amount of energy entering the trophic level:
>
> 62.8 ÷ 720 = 0.087
>
> **Step 2** Multiply your answer by 100 to make it into a percentage.
>
> 0.087 × 100 = 8.7%.
>
> ### Now you try
>
> If 1740 kJ of energy entered a trophic level and 156 kJ was lost as heat, what percentage of the energy was lost as heat?

## Aerobic respiration

Respiration occurs in all living things, including microorganisms that break down dead organisms. The overall equation for respiration is:

glucose + oxygen → carbon dioxide + water

Energy is released during aerobic respiration. It should not be shown in the word equation.

When microorganisms break down dead organisms, the process is called decay or decomposition. Carbon dioxide is also returned to the atmosphere by burning (combustion). This is important in relation to the removal of forest, when much of the forest material that is cut down is burnt.

> **ACTIVITY 6.2**
>
> In pairs, carry out some further research on the processes of photosynthesis and respiration. Create a short presentation to compare the two processes. Join up in groups of four to deliver your presentation to another pair.

> **PEER ASSESSMENT**
>
> In your groups of two pairs, give each other feedback on your presentations from Activity 6.2. Name two things that the other pair did well in their presentation and suggest one thing that could have been improved.

## The carbon cycle

As a consumer is obtaining energy from the level below, it is acquiring the minerals that it needs. These include carbon, oxygen, sulfur, phosphorus and nitrogen, among many others. The minerals are stored in different ways and then transferred by various processes.

All mineral cycles have the same basic pattern. In the carbon cycle, the stores are carbon dioxide in the atmosphere, carbon in fossil fuels (coal, petroleum and natural gas) and various carbon compounds in organic matter (in living and dead animals and plants). The transfers take place by photosynthesis, respiration, feeding, decomposition, formation of fossil fuels and combustion (Figure 6.18).

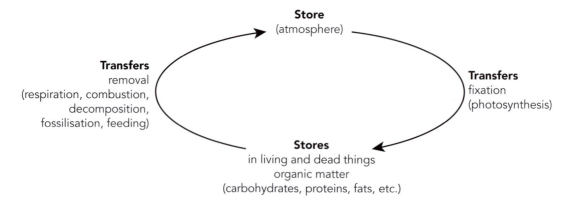

**Figure 6.18:** General diagram of mineral cycles. Situation for the carbon cycle shown in brackets.

6 Ecosystems, biodiversity and fieldwork

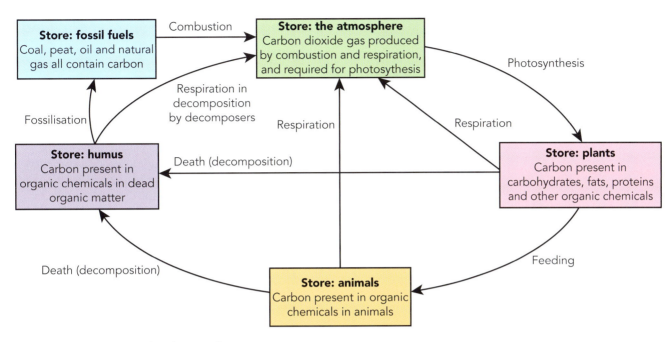

Figure 6.19: A detailed carbon cycle.

In simple terms:
- The store is carbon dioxide in the atmosphere.
- Fixation takes place by photosynthesis.
- Carbon is found within living things in carbohydrates, proteins, fats and other chemicals.
- Carbon is removed from living things by respiration, which returns the carbon dioxide to the atmosphere.

Figure 6.19 shows the carbon cycle in more detail.

## Questions

6.8 In a study of the organisms in a food web, it was found that 3000 kJ of energy were present in the herbivores, 450 kJ in the carnivores and 40 000 kJ in the plants.
   a Sketch a pyramid of energy for this food web.
   b Calculate the percentage efficiency of energy transfer from:
      i  plants to herbivores
      ii herbivores to carnivores.
   Show your working for both parts of the question.

6.9 State the location of a store of carbon in the carbon cycle.

6.10 State examples of substances in living things that contain carbon.

6.11 Compare and contrast respiration and decomposition.

### REFLECTION

How confident do you feel in your understanding of cycles in general and the carbon cycle in particular? What could you do to increase your level of confidence? Did Activity 6.2 and Figures 6.18 and 6.19 help? If so, can you explain why?

## 6.2 Forest ecosystems

Forests cover about 40 million km² of the Earth's land area – about 30%. They are important due to their influence on climate, rainfall patterns, and the provision of timber and other raw materials. It is estimated that 1.6 billion people depend on forests for their livelihood. It gives them food, fuel and shelter.

# Causes of deforestation

Deforestation is a major cause of habitat loss, but how extensive is deforestation and what causes it? In Africa, South America (especially Brazil) and Indonesia, significant forest losses occur. In 2022, 4.1 million hectares of forest were lost. Nearly 1.8 million hectares (43%) of this loss occurred in Brazil. The Democratic Republic of the Congo came next with 0.5 million hectares (12.5%) lost, closely followed by Bolivia with 9.4% and Indonesia with 5.6%. From a total tree cover of 2572 million hectares in the top countries for deforestation, 320 million hectares were lost in the first 22 years of the 21st century (12%). It is worth noting, however, that not all forest is permanent, and there have been gains too – about 130 million hectares during the same period.

## Logging and timber extraction

The most obvious cause of deforestation is the need for the wood itself. Wood has been used by humans for thousands of years. It can be used for building and furniture-making, but also for paper-making. It is also a source of energy when burnt. The word 'timber' can refer to wood or to the products made from wood in the form of boards and planks. Logging, in its broadest sense, is the process by which wood is extracted from a forest and made into timber (Figure 6.20). This timber is needed for products ranging from luxury furniture to paper, which are all in high demand.

**Figure 6.20:** Logging is the cutting down of trees to sell as timber in industries such as construction and paper-making.

## Farming, roads, settlements and mining

Deforestation also takes place to clear land for farming, roads and settlements. In tropical forests, the logging itself is not necessarily very damaging. Only some species are suitable for creating timber, so logging tends to be selective, and such a process can be beneficial to the forest. However, logging and timber extraction often involve opening up the forest. Creating roads for the vehicles associated with the logging process is probably the single most damaging aspect of the process. Logging itself may lead to only 10% of the deforestation in an area. It is the agriculture and settlement that follow, encouraged by the logging roads, that cause the greatest loss of trees. As people establish themselves in an area, other activities follow. If profitable deposits of rocks and minerals are found, extraction may occur, which can lead to further deforestation.

Figure 6.21 shows that agriculture in all its forms (subsistence and commercial, together with pasture for animals) is the cause of about 80% of all deforestation, while mining and the construction of settlements, hydro-electric power stations (HEPs) and roads cause only a small faction (as part of 'other'). So, roads lead directly to only a small amount of deforestation, but they are instrumental in opening up the forest to other activities.

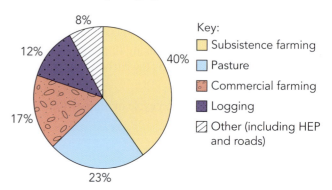

**Figure 6.21:** The causes of deforestation as percentages of the total figure.

## Hydro-electric power stations

The creation of hydro-electric power stations can result in large areas, often forest, being flooded. For example, the creation of the Balbina Dam in Brazil caused the loss of over 2500 km² of tropical rainforest.

## Climate change

Deforestation is playing a big part in global warming and, therefore, climate change. However, climate change may also be causing deforestation, as it increases the frequency and severity of wildfires. Increased incidences of storms and other extreme weather events, more frequent outbreaks of insects, and the presence of invasive species in an area can all be caused by climate change and play a part in deforestation.

# Impacts of deforestation

## Habitat loss

As you have seen, biodiversity is lost when habitats are lost. Tropical forests, in particular, are centres of great biodiversity, so the loss of habitats in these forests is particularly serious. The trees in large forests are not only home to many rare species but also a massive **carbon store**.

> **KEY WORD**
>
> **carbon store:** a mature vegetated area where the intake of carbon dioxide from the atmosphere by photosynthesis equals its output from respiration, so the mature plants store carbon

## Soil erosion and desertification

The forest reduces the impact of heavy rainfall on the ground, which limits soil erosion. When forests are lost, therefore, soil erosion often occurs. In addition, tree roots hold the soil in place, and the layer of fallen leaves and branches on the forest floor protects the soil. After deforestation, an area that once supported luxuriant growth may slowly become a desert, as a result of desertification (see Chapter 4).

## Silting and flooding

Silting occurs when rivers and lakes become filled with sediment, usually from eroded soil, as material washed off the land ends up in water bodies. Water quality may be reduced, and the river or lake may start to fill up, which can eventually lead to flooding (Figure 6.22). Floods also become more frequent as the removal of trees reduces the water-holding capacity of the soil.

## Global warming

Almost all scientists agree that the levels of greenhouse gases in the atmosphere are rising – especially carbon dioxide levels – and this is causing global warming. The main cause of the rise in carbon dioxide is the burning of fossil fuels (see Chapter 5), which accounts for about 87% of all human carbon dioxide emissions. Following that come changes in land use – most importantly, deforestation – at about 9% and then other industries at about 4%.

**Figure 6.22:** Flooding is just one impact of deforestation, as soil erosion causes a build-up of sediment in rivers, like this one in Colombia.

Trees remove carbon dioxide from the atmosphere during photosynthesis. As deforestation reduces the number of trees, it also reduces how much carbon dioxide forests can remove. However, trees also give out carbon dioxide through respiration. If the rates of photosynthesis and respiration are the same, then the removal of trees will have no effect on atmospheric carbon dioxide levels. Nonetheless, the permanent removal of trees leads to large quantities of carbon dioxide being released when they are burnt or when they decompose. In addition, the machinery used for logging and timber extraction burns fossil fuels, releasing more carbon dioxide.

## Changes to rainfall patterns

Deforestation can lead to a significant reduction in rainfall in the deforested areas. A 2023 study showed a reduction of 0.25% in rainfall for every 1% of forest lost. This can have a knock-on effect, as less rain may mean more forest fires, poorer tree growth and thus more deforestation. This leads to a vicious cycle in the process of deforestation and its impacts.

## Loss of biodiversity and genetic depletion

Because forests, and rainforests in particular, are such important centres of biodiversity and genetic diversity, their loss causes particularly dramatic examples of habitat, biodiversity and genetic loss (see 'Forests as a genetic resource' section). The situation is even more worrying when you consider that we may be unaware of the identity of the majority of species that live in these forests.

## Questions

**6.12** A large area of mature rainforest has been cleared to plant fast-growing oil palm trees. Suggest how this might affect:

    **a** the level of carbon dioxide in the atmosphere

    **b** biodiversity in the area.

**6.13** Table 6.2 shows the results of a study of the reasons for deforestation in the Amazon.

| Reason | Percentage |
|---|---|
| Cattle grazing | 60 |
| Subsistence farming | 30 |
| Commercial agriculture | 2 |
| Logging | 4 |
| Other | 4 |

**Table 6.2:** Reasons for deforestation in the Amazon, 2006.

    **a** Copy and complete the blank pie chart using data from Table 6.2.

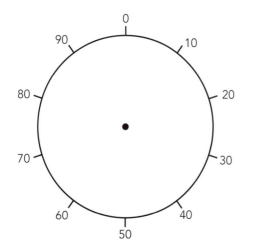

    **b** In 2006, 14 285 km² of the Amazon forest were lost. Calculate how much of this was lost due to subsistence farming. Show your working.

## The need for sustainable management of forests

Ecosystems, such as forests, can be managed in all kinds of ways, but ideally that management would be done sustainably. Sustainable management takes into account the needs of all parties – that is, the environment itself, the wildlife that lives there and the humans who want to use it. The challenge of sustainability is to meet all these needs in both the present and the future.

### Climate regulation: carbon sinks and carbon stores

When a forest is growing, it takes in more carbon dioxide in photosynthesis than it gives out in respiration, because most of the trees in it are relatively young. This makes it a carbon sink. A mature forest, in which most of the trees are old and not growing actively, takes in and gives out the same quantity of carbon dioxide (Figure 6.23). This makes is a carbon store.

### The water cycle and flood control

Forests add water to the atmosphere in the process of transpiration (see Chapter 4). This leads to the formation of clouds. Eventually, the clouds release the water as precipitation. When forests are cut down, this process is reduced, which can lead to local droughts in the area of deforestation. Forests generate moisture in the atmosphere, which can also affect rainfall around the world. For example, deforestation in the Amazon is now thought to influence rainfall from Mexico to the US state of Texas. The level of precipitation in the American Midwest seems to depend on the state of the rainforest in Central America, and that of China and the Balkans is influenced by deforestation in Asia.

As you have seen, the loss of forests can lead to silting, which in turn can lead to floods as rivers and lakes lose their capacity to hold water. Direct run-off of water from bare soil when trees are removed can also lead to floods. In both cases, afforestation – the planting of trees – can help reverse the damage.

# 6 Ecosystems, biodiversity and fieldwork

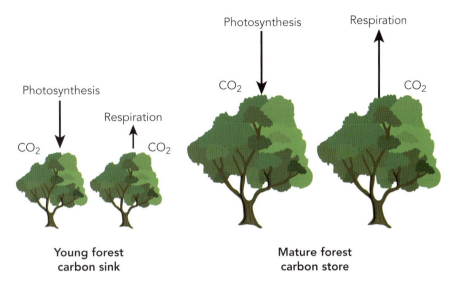

**Figure 6.23:** Movements of carbon dioxide into (in photosynthesis) and out of (in respiration) trees in young and mature forests.

## Prevention of soil erosion

Forests help to prevent soil erosion in a number of ways:

- By intercepting rain, the forest reduces heavy rainfall on the forest floor.
- Debris, such as leaves, on the forest floor slows run-off.
- The roots of trees hold the soil in place.
- Trees reduce wind speed over the soil, especially at the coast where they reduce erosion by absorbing energy from storms.

Figure 6.24 illustrates what happens when trees are removed.

## Forests as a genetic resource

As recently as 10 000 years ago, people were still gathering plants and hunting animals for food. Then, at around that time, some human populations learnt to plant seeds. At first, the plants grown from these seeds would have given an unpredictable, but often small, yield. Unintentionally, the plants that gave a good yield were selected for the next generation. This was an early form of **selective breeding**. This marked the start of the agricultural revolution and since then, people have intentionally selected the crops most likely to give high yields.

The process has been hugely beneficial in providing food for the growing human population. However, experts are concerned that modern types of crop plants may not be able to adapt to changes in the future, such as those caused by climate change. Efforts have been made to retain populations of ancient types of important crop plants. However, no matter how successful these projects are, it is important to retain biodiversity in the wild, including that of forests. The characteristics of wild varieties of modern crop plants may prove useful in the future.

The species and genetic diversity that exist in the wild may have many uses that we have not yet discovered. A large proportion of medicines that we use have come from wild plants and animals. It is possible that other useful products may exist in the forest ecosystem. Deforestation, leading to the loss of biodiversity, could mean that valuable products are never discovered. This loss of species containing potentially useful genes is known as 'genetic depletion'. Habitat destruction reduces genetic diversity and may even lead to species becoming extinct, when the genetic loss becomes irretrievable (Figure 6.25).

### KEY WORD

**selective breeding:** the process of choosing only plants and animals with desirable characteristics to reproduce

245

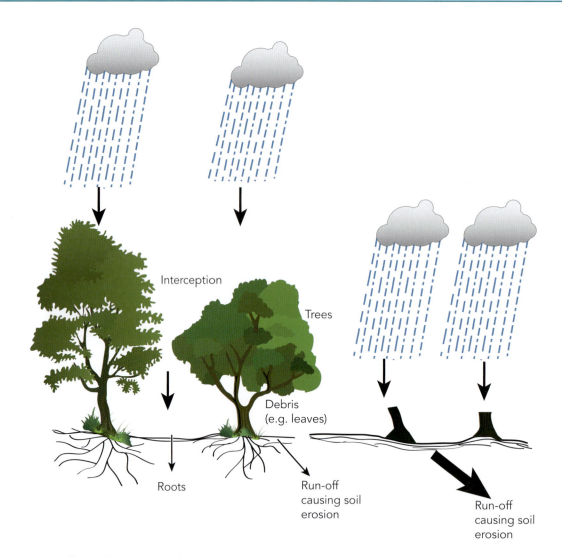

Figure 6.24: The effect of tree removal on soil erosion.

Figure 6.25: Jaguars have no sub-species, so it is important that their populations remain connected to maintain genetic diversity. Deforestation separates jaguars into smaller breeding groups, which makes them vulnerable.

## Forests for medicine, food and raw materials

Trees and the plants that grow under and on them have always been used by those who live in or near forests, for a wide range of purposes. For example, the kapok tree has a wide range of uses to West African people (Figure 6.26). The fruits are used for medicines, pillow-making and blocking holes in canoes. The oil from the seed is used to treat rheumatism, to make soap and as a fire-lighter. The leaves are eaten in soups and fed to goats. The ash is used to spread around crops as a mulch. The bark is used as a cleansing mouthwash and the roots as a treatment for leprosy. Bees use the tree for food and thus provide honey, and an edible mushroom grows around its base. If one tree can supply medicine, food and raw materials in this way, it is clear that a forest is a treasure chest full of useful products.

**Figure 6.26:** The bark, berries, roots, leaves and other parts of the kapok tree are used for a wide range of purposes, from medicine to boat-building.

## Ecotourism, recreation and education

**Ecotourism** is responsible travel to a natural area that promotes conservation of the environment. Ecotourism is both a reason to manage forests sustainably and a method by which this can be achieved. Ecotourism takes many forms: it could mean visiting simply to appreciate the natural beauty of an area, or participating in activities to help conserve that area. Ecotourism may even involve exploiting a location in a sustainable way. Like all human activities, ecotourism may be mainly economic in focus, with success measured by income. On the other hand, it may be focused on sustainability, with success measured by a limit on numbers of visitors.

Ecotourism brings with it opportunities for recreation, with activities such as birdwatching, botanising, hiking, orienteering, cycling and many others. All this provides a good opportunity to educate visitors on the importance of sustainability in forest management. There are many schemes around the world designed to educate children and adults about the benefits of experiencing the natural world in a sustainable way.

> **KEY WORD**
>
> **ecotourism:** tourism in which the participants travel to see the natural world, ideally in a sustainable way

# 6.3 Managing biodiversity

There is a very strong case for the **conservation** of natural ecosystems and their associated biodiversity. In addition, conservation can include the protection, preservation, management and restoration of wildlife and habitats.

> **KEY WORD**
>
> **conservation:** the protection and management of natural areas

## Conservation strategies for natural ecosystems

A wide range of strategies are applied to conservation.

### Sustainable harvesting and sustainable forestry

Any action described as sustainable must meet the needs of the present without denying the needs of future generations. This means that we need to find ways of taking the wild animals and plants that are required now, but still leave enough for people in the future. Perhaps the best-known examples of harvesting wild animals and plants are fisheries, forestry and medicinal plants. Some of the successes and failures of harvesting wild fish are covered in Chapter 4.

Many plants have medicinal properties because of the various substances they produce. Wild plants are often better than cultivated varieties, which may only produce small quantities of the useful chemicals and sometimes none at all. There have been many attempts to control the harvesting of wild medicinal plants. These are usually guided by a management plan, which assesses the abundance of the plant, then investigates its growth rate, reproductive biology and what impact harvesting would have. This should reveal the yield that can be sustained by the wild population. Finally, a management plan will include details of how the harvesting should be monitored.

One example of sustainable forestry is the practice of selective logging. This involves removing only the mature trees of the species of value. Other species, and immature trees of the valued species, are left, allowing the forest to repair itself. Non-valued trees still provide habitat for many species, and the immature valued trees can be used years later.

## National parks and reserves

In response to the need to protect the wildlife of an area, a government may designate it as a specially protected region, covered by certain laws. National parks and wildlife and ecological reserves differ mainly in size.

The world's first national park, Yellowstone National Park in the USA, was established in 1872. It has an area of 8983 km², which protects nearly 2000 species of plants and nearly 60 large mammals, including the grey wolf (Figure 6.27), lynx and bison. There are now 59 national parks in the USA, with a total area of 210 000 km² (2.18% of the country's total area). Canada, itself a very large country, has the largest area of land protected by national parks, at 377 000 km², representing 3.78% of the country's land. In contrast, the Central American countries of Costa Rica and Belize have 25% and 38%, respectively, of their land area protected by national parks. The largest national park in the world is the Northeast Greenland National Park, covering 972 001 km². Worldwide, there are about 113 000 national parks, which cover about 6% of Earth's land surface, or about 149 million km².

**Figure 6.27:** Grey wolves were reintroduced to Yellowstone National Park in 1995, where they are now an important part of the ecosystem.

Governments have been slower to protect marine ecosystems, but they are making a start. The largest marine park in the world protects the Chagos Islands and their surrounding waters in the Indian Ocean. This park has a total area of 544 000 km². The Great Barrier Reef Marine Park off the east coast of Australia protects an area of 345 000 km².

National parks have detailed management strategies that vary according to the nature of the park. Governments implement laws that ban or limit activities, such as hunting and logging. Even the collection of wildflowers may be restricted or banned. However, it is sometimes difficult to stop these activities, and enforcement can require a combination of regular inspection and the threat of large fines or imprisonment for breaking the law.

Although national parks are not established to be tourist destinations, extensive facilities for tourists are usually provided, including systems of roads, car parks and nature trails. Visitors may be charged an entry fee, and there are strict rules governing how tourists must behave in the park.

People living in wildlife and ecological reserves may feel they are in competition with the natural world around them. An example of this arose in Australia, when attempts were made to set up ecological reserves on several rivers. Some people felt that these reserves were necessary and that the water was there for the creatures that live in it, but others believed that the money being spent protecting fish and other wildlife would be better used tackling issues that affected local people. The ultimate goal of a successful ecological or wildlife reserve is to balance the needs of people and wildlife. This can only be achieved with a strategy that protects the wildlife and is part of a system that people want and need.

## Wildlife corridors

Wildlife corridors are areas of land that link large reserves or other wildlife areas. When natural habitats are fragmented, the remaining areas may be acquired and set up as reserves. However, many species are unable to maintain a viable population in smaller areas. For example, some species are so dependent on trees that they never come down to the ground, so even if another forested area is only metres away, individuals within the two areas may not be able to mate or interact in other ways. A corridor of trees between the two areas can provide a solution to this problem (Figure 6.28).

## Seed banks

When habitats become severely threatened or even destroyed, the last resort for conserving the species within them may be to put them into zoos (in the case of animals) or seed banks (in the case of plants).

Wild plant populations can be destroyed by habitat destruction caused by factors such as floods, fire, climate change and over-harvesting. Wild plants may carry genes that could be used in crop plants to confer resistance to pests and diseases. If it is not possible to

# 6 Ecosystems, biodiversity and fieldwork

Figure 6.28: Wildlife corridors can take the form of special crossings built to connect parts of a habitat that have been separated by roads.

Figure 6.30: Outside of the Global Seed Vault on the island of Svalbard, Norway. The site is dug into a mountain on land inside the Arctic Circle at 78 °N.

protect the area where the plants live, the species can be preserved as seeds in seed banks.

Seeds, rather than living plants, are stored because they need less space, so more species can be stored. Also, most plants produce large numbers of seeds, so collecting small samples of seeds is unlikely to damage the wild population. Finally, seeds are easier to store than whole plants because they are dormant and need minimal care. Figure 6.29 shows the process of seed storage, and Figure 6.30 shows the Global Seed Bank on the island of Svalbard, at about 78 °N.

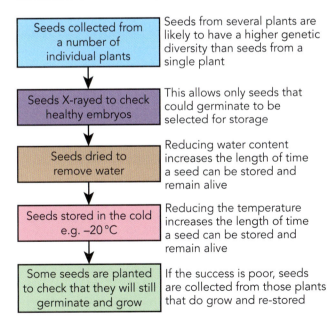

Figure 6.29: The stages in the storage of seeds in a seed bank.

## Zoos and captive breeding

Zoos have three main roles in conservation. Firstly, they provide important education about the illegal trade in animals and their products, and the need to maintain biodiversity. Secondly, zoos are involved in scientific research on the control of diseases, animal behaviour and techniques to improve breeding success. Thirdly, zoos have a very important role in captive-breeding programmes to increase species numbers, thereby reducing the risk of extinction (Figure 6.31). Animals bred in captivity are released into the wild when habitats have been restored.

These programmes try to maintain the genetic diversity of a species, which is reduced by inbreeding and could result in reduced adaptability if the species is placed back into the wild. However, zoos often have only a small number of individuals of a particular species, so they take a variety of approaches to avoid these issues:

- Organisms are not allowed to breed repeatedly with the same partner.
- A variety of partners for an organism can be achieved by in-vitro fertilisation and swapping individuals between zoos.
- All zoos use a database called a studbook to record the breeding history of individuals in captivity.

249

**Figure 6.31:** In 2023, two Sumatran rhinos were born as part of a captive-breeding programme at a sanctuary in Indonesia, in a small but significant step for the conservation of this critically endangered species.

## Ecotourism

Tourism can be an important source of income for a country or a region, but it can also be very damaging. Habitats are sometimes destroyed to provide accommodation, such as hotels, for tourists. The often huge but temporary increase in the population of an area leads to increased pollution and other problems. Sustainable tourism is tourism that is managed in a way that prevents damage to habitats and provides what people want. Ecotourism is a form of sustainable tourism that is guided by environmental principles. Measures are taken to safeguard the wildlife of the area, and the natural resources are used in a sustainable way. The key to successful sustainable ecotourism is realising that the growth of the tourist industry depends on maintaining the environment.

## International cooperation against the animal trade and the regulation of trade in vulnerable and endangered species

The Convention on International Trade in Endangered Species of Wild Fauna and Flora (CITES) is an international agreement between governments. It is designed to ensure that international trade in plants and animals does not threaten the survival of any of these species.

The need for such an organisation was proposed in 1963, and it finally came into being in 1973. To date, it has been signed by 183 countries. It currently offers protection – at different levels – to over 36 000 species of animals and plants. Species threatened with extinction in the very near future represent 3% of this total. International trade in these species is prohibited. A further 97% of the total are not threatened with immediate extinction, but may become threatened if trade is not regulated. In these cases, trade is allowed but is carefully monitored. A third category, representing just 1%, requires cooperation between two different parties before trade can happen.

The bulk of CITES' work is in the regulation of trade in animals (78% of the 10 million transactions over the last decade). However, despite this, $360 billion worth of organisms are traded each year, and only a minority of countries (14 out of 183) have an up-to-date electronic system in place to streamline the regulation. There is still much work to be done.

### ACTIVITY 6.3

One very popular form of ecotourism is whale watching. People travel to areas where whales can be found, stay in local accommodation and then go out in boats on day trips to see the whales.

One definition of ecotourism is that it involves travelling to natural areas that conserve the environment, and improves the welfare of the local people.

In small groups, discuss the ways in which whale watching as described meets this description, and ways in which it does not. If possible, find out more about whale watching to support your arguments. Use the internet and any other resources available.

At the end of your discussion, try to reach a consensus on whether, overall, whale watching is a sustainable form of ecotourism. Present your arguments to another group or the class. Did any groups reach a different decision to yours?

# 6 Ecosystems, biodiversity and fieldwork

## CASE STUDY

### The scarlet macaw in Costa Rica

Of 146 species of New World parrots, over 40 are threatened. The scarlet macaw is one of these (Figure 6.32). In Costa Rica, by the late 20th century, they occurred in only two areas: the Osa Peninsula and the Central Pacific Conservation Area (CPCA). Populations in a 560 km$^2$ area of the CPCA were monitored from 1990 until 2003 and managed from 1995 until 2003.

Figure 6.32: A pair of scarlet macaws in flight.

The birds are most visible during their daily flights between nocturnal roosting areas and feeding sites. For this reason, counts of the birds were made during their daily flights, from May 1990 until October 1994. The results of this monitoring are shown in Figure 6.33.

The study at this stage confirmed a decline in numbers, and so a macaw conservation strategy was developed at a workshop in 1994. The strategy focused on minimising chick poaching, the enhancement of habitats and community education. Subsequently, nest boxes were constructed and natural nests were protected. This was done under the auspices of the association for parrot protection, LAPPA. This organisation worked with ranchers, park workers, scientists, the local community and ecotourism organisers. The strategy also included raiding poachers' homes, confiscating poached chicks and tree-climbing equipment, arresting poachers, and writing newspaper articles that criticised named poachers. The effect of this strategy on macaw numbers is shown in Figure 6.34.

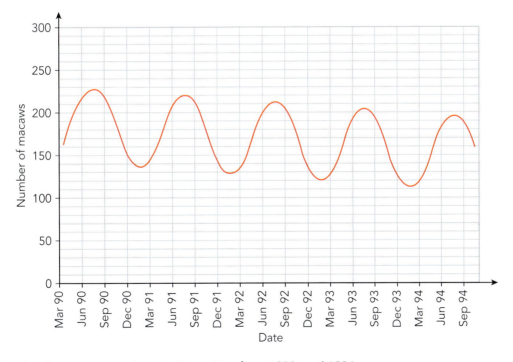

Figure 6.33: Scarlet macaw numbers in Costa Rica from 1990 until 1994.

> **CONTINUED**
>
>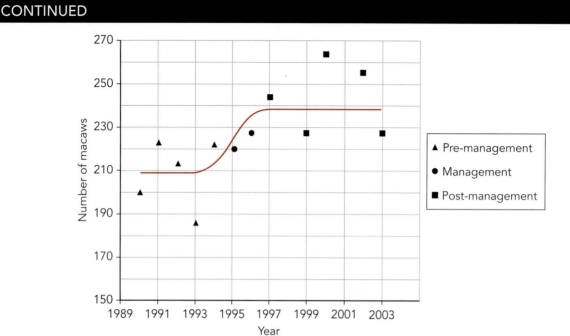
>
> **Figure 6.34:** Scarlet macaw numbers between 1989 and 2003. The population was subject to management between 1995 and 1997.
>
> The Central Pacific scarlet macaw population is important for ecotourism. In 1994, more than 40 000 tourists spent $6 million during visits to the area. It was reported that most of the tourists came to see the scarlet macaw. It was also reported that less than 10% of the money generated by tourism went to the local community. More recently, it has been reported that tourism in the Central Pacific region employs more adult Costa Ricans than any other industry. The hope is that chick poaching will stop when communities see that the income from conserving macaws is greater than from poaching them.
>
> **Questions**
>
> 1. Using Figure 6.33, calculate the average yearly rate of loss of birds from 1990 to 1994.
>
> 2. Using data from Figures 6.33 and 6.34, suggest how successful the experimental conservation strategy, started in 1994, has been.
>
> 3. Explain why scarlet macaws are said to be worth more alive in the wild than either dead or caged as a pet.

### CRITICAL THINKING TIP

The data in the case study is 30 years old. Does this matter? When considering data, ask yourself about the quality of the data. For example, who gathered the information and compiled the data? What was their motive for doing so?

## Classifying organisms in terms of their threat level

There are two systems in place to classify how threatened a species is: one is operated by CITES and the other by the International Union for the Conservation of Nature (IUCN). The IUCN's system is better known, because the organisation manages the 'Red List of Threatened Species' and categorises species in terms of their threat level. The IUCN list features 10 categories, but three of them – 'no data', 'not evaluated' and 'conservation dependent' – are usually omitted from the standard lists (Table 6.3).

# 6 Ecosystems, biodiversity and fieldwork

| EX Extinct |
| --- |
| EW Extinct in the wild |
| CR Critically endangered |
| EN Endangered |
| VU Vulnerable |
| NT Near threatened |
| LC Least concern |

**Table 6.3:** The IUCN list of organism classification in relation to the threat level; 'critically endangered', 'endangered' and 'vulnerable' are also grouped under a general category of 'threatened'.

**Figure 6.35:** Extinct: A Tasmanian tiger, or thylacine, in captivity around 1930. The species is believed to have become extinct in the early 20th century.

**Figure 6.36:** Extinct in the wild: The Guam kingfisher went extinct in the wild due to the introduction of brown tree snakes to the island of Guam during the Second World War. There are about 200 birds in captive-breeding facilities in the USA and on Guam.

**Figure 6.37:** Critically endangered: *Mezoneuron kauaiense* in Hawaii.

**Figure 6.38:** Endangered: The Yangtze finless porpoise.

253

Figure 6.39: Vulnerable: A Snares crested penguin on Enderby Island, New Zealand.

Figure 6.40: Near threatened: White rhinos are the least threatened of the five rhino species, but they are still classified as 'near threatened'.

Figure 6.41: Least concern: A male narwhal shows his tusk in a mating ritual.

# The benefits and limitations of conservation strategies for natural ecosystems

The strategies explored previously all have both positive and negative aspects, or benefits and limitations. Table 6.4 summarises the main ones.

| Strategy | Benefits | Limitations |
|---|---|---|
| Sustainable harvesting of wild plant and animal species | Already being used<br><br>Reduces the environmental footprint of farming<br><br>Can be done stage by stage rather than all at once; not just for large-scale farms<br><br>Reduces use of chemicals, such as pesticides and herbicides<br><br>Hands back control to farmers | Unlikely to offer some of the benefits of conventional farming<br><br>There is debate about some of the claims as to what sustainable farming achieves<br><br>Financial risk for farmers<br><br>Difficult to get farmers to introduce it when the benefits are not clear<br><br>May require costly education of farmers<br><br>Sustainable farming is only being used in certain areas and may not be suited to others for geographical and meteorological reasons<br><br>Certain foods and products, although relatively unsustainable to farm, may be required for the health or religious beliefs of some people |

| Strategy | Benefits | Limitations |
|---|---|---|
| Sustainable forestry | Preserves trees and forests and the benefits that they give<br>Avoids the displacement of local people<br>Can support other economic activity, such as tourism | Priorities are not always clear, with some people prioritising economic gains and others environmental protection<br>Rather than forestry, individuals and governments might wish to convert the land to other uses |
| National parks and reserves | Provide services in the preservation of biodiversity, together with recreational and educational activities<br>Economic benefits due to the attraction of tourists<br>May provide climate-regulation services, particularly if forested<br>Provide benefits for health and wellbeing | Overcrowding is often a problem in national parks and reserves<br>National parks, particularly due to their large size, may have a negative effect on local communities, leading to feelings of exclusion<br>It is often a major economic challenge to maintain the infrastructure |
| Wildlife corridors | There is much evidence that they work<br>They facilitate general day-to-day movement as well as migration<br>Improve gene flow between small populations<br>Avert conflicts between humans and animals | May encourage the spread of unwanted and invasive species<br>May lead to increased fire risk<br>May create a bottleneck, leading to increased predation |
| Seed banks | Replenish seeds lost due to disasters<br>Should preserve enough genetic variety to allow the development of new strains | Cannot be used for the conservation of all plants |
| Zoos and captive breeding | Excellent for education<br>Allow research<br>Can save species from extinction | Harm animals both psychologically and physically |
| Ecotourism | Good for health and wellbeing<br>Helps in understanding other cultures<br>Relatively inexpensive<br>Can provide employment for local people | There are safety issues<br>The discomfort may be a limitation for some people |
| International cooperation against the animal trade and regulation of trade in vulnerable and endangered species | Exerts control over a multi-billion-dollar industry<br>Can help in limiting the spread of diseases | Relatively susceptible to corruption; permits can easily be bought for the right sum of money<br>May be influenced by politics |
| Classifying organisms in terms of their threat level | Allows efforts and funding to be targeted to the most vulnerable habitats and species | There is not enough data to classify some species |

**Table 6.4:** The benefits and limitations of strategies for conserving the biodiversity and genetic resources of natural ecosystems.

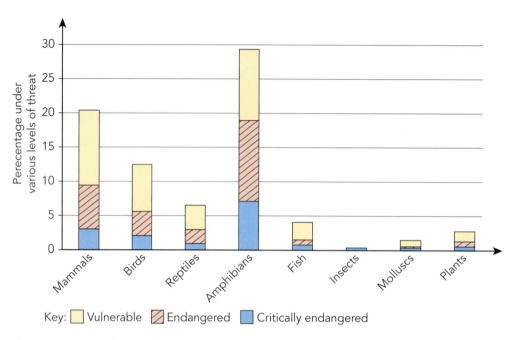

Figure 6.42: The percentage of major groups of living things under threat.

## Questions

6.14 Suggest why plants are often conserved by creating a seed bank, whereas animal conservation is often carried out in a zoo.

6.15 Suggest how reserves and wildlife corridors might be used together to conserve biodiversity and genetic resources over a large area.

6.16 Most groups of living things have some species that are under threat of decline or even extinction. A study found the data shown in Figure 6.42 for some major groups:

   a  Discuss the extent to which these data support the view that all wildlife is under increasing threat.

   b  State the percentages of mammals, birds and amphibians that are endangered.

# 6.4 Fieldwork investigations

Throughout your studies of environmental management, you will need to demonstrate your skills in carrying out investigations and making judgements. Many of the features of fieldwork investigations are covered in Chapter 1. Here, we are going to look at some of these techniques in more detail and consider how they can be applied to measuring populations of species.

## The scientific method

Since the 17th century, it has been common to try to answer questions about the way the world works using the scientific method. Figure 6.43 summarises the steps involved in this.

# 6 Ecosystems, biodiversity and fieldwork

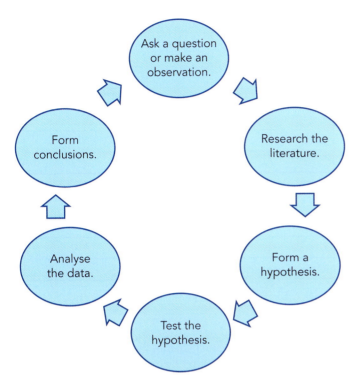

**Figure 6.43:** A simple representation of the steps in the scientific method.

A scientific investigation may be observational or experimental. For example, imagine you want to look at the effect of the level of nitrate in the soil on plant growth. You could do this by measuring nitrate levels in soils and measuring the growth of the plants in those soils. This is an observational fieldwork approach. However, you could also conduct an experiment in which you deliberately create different nitrate levels in a range of soils, then grow plants in them. This would be a laboratory-based experimental approach.

In general, an experimental approach is likely to provide more valid data. In an observational study, such as the previous example, other factors might affect plant growth, such as soil pH, soil water content and soil temperature. That means it would not be clear which of these – or indeed any other factors – was affecting the growth. In the experimental approach, the artificially created soils could be made to have the same pH, the same water content and be kept at the same temperature. In this way, any effect of the different soils is more likely to be due to the nitrate level than anything else. In some situations, however, it is not possible to set up an experiment, and so an observational study is needed.

## Applying the scientific method to collecting reliable data

### Suggest aims and hypotheses

Planning an investigation involves formulating an aim (or guiding question) or a hypothesis. A hypothesis is usually based on prior knowledge or observations. In the previous example, the hypothesis could be: 'Increasing nitrate levels in the soil leads to an increase in plant growth'. A hypothesis can be accepted or rejected by testing. This is achieved through data collection and analysis. A good hypothesis should:

- be a statement, not a question
- be a prediction with cause and effect
- state the independent and dependent variables being tested
- be short in length.

As part of your plan, you should also identify the way you intend to collect and record your data. This involves choosing a sampling strategy and technique. You can find out more about these in the following sections and in Chapter 1.

An investigation may also require a **control**. The group that receives the treatment is the experimental group, the group that does not is the control group.

For example, in the investigation to look at the effect of nitrate on plant growth, you would need to grow some plants in a soil that is not enriched with nitrate – this would be the control.

> **KEY WORD**
>
> **control:** in an investigation, an object or system that is not changed, so it can be compared with similar objects or systems that are intentionally changed

### Understanding variables

The hypothesis is basically a testable prediction that proposes a relationship between two variables. A variable is something that can be measured, and which may change over space or time in an investigation.

An independent variable is not changed by other variables. It either has different values in a natural setting or is made to have different values by the person carrying out the experiment. In the investigation testing the effect of nitrate levels on plant growth, the independent variable is the level of nitrate in the soil. These levels will vary in different natural settings, or they can be manipulated in the course of an investigation.

A dependent variable is usually the variable that is being measured. In our example, the dependent variable is plant growth, which might be measured by plant height or plant mass.

There will also be other variables in an investigation – for example, pH, water content and temperature. In a fieldwork investigation, you would need to take these variables into account by measuring them at various sites. They are measured variables. In some investigations, you may be able to keep the variables constant at predetermined values. In this case, they are referred to as **control variables.**

> **KEY WORD**
>
> **control variable:** in an experiment, a factor that is kept constant

> **SCIENCE TIP**
>
> One way to remember how to write a hypothesis is that the dependent variable will depend on the independent variable.

> **SCIENCE TIP**
>
> The previous information should help you to not confuse control variables and a control. Make sure that you know the difference between the two.

## Repeats and replicates

Repeats and replicates are another common feature of scientific experiments or observations. They are carried out to check the level of variability in measurements taken during an investigation. Repetition is when the same scientist conducts the same experiment multiple times. Replication is when other scientists conduct the experiment using the same procedure. In environmental management, you are most likely to encounter repetition rather than replication.

Table 6.5 shows the measured heights of some plants in two fields, A and B.

| Plant number | Height (cm) Field A | Height (cm) Field B |
|---|---|---|
| 1 | 11 | 11 |
| 2 | 23 | 9 |
| 3 | 17 | 7 |
| 4 | 14 | 12 |
| 5 | 25 | 8 |
| 6 | 19 | 7 |
| 7 | 10 | 9 |
| Mean (average) | 17 | 9 |

**Table 6.5:** The measured heights of plants in two fields.

If only one plant had been measured in each field (plant 1), you might conclude that the plants are the same height in these two fields. But by measuring seven plants – repeat measurements – you can see that, on average, the plants in field A are taller than those in field B.

## Identifying and processing anomalies

In another example, the averages are the same but they come from very different sets of results (Table 6.6).

| Plant number | Height (cm) Field A | Height (cm) Field B |
|---|---|---|
| 1 | 3 | 1 |
| 2 | 4 | 1 |
| 3 | 5 | 10 |
| Mean (average) | 4 | 4 |

**Table 6.6:** The measured heights of plants in two fields.

This second set of results illustrates another use of replication – to identify anomalies (see Figure 6.44). From the measurements of two plants in field B, it might look as if they are quite short. However, a third plant was much taller. You might decide that this plant height result is anomalous – an outlier – and decide to ignore it in your further analysis. Alternatively, you might feel it is necessary to explain the anomaly. For example, further inspection of field B might show that the 10 cm plant is growing near some manure, which would explain its unusual height.

# 6 Ecosystems, biodiversity and fieldwork

**Figure 6.44:** Watch out for anomalies in the measurements you take in the field.

## Record and analyse data and draw conclusions

Once you have designed your investigation, it is time to carry it out. In doing so, you will gather data that must be recorded. It is important to decide how you will record your data – in a table, for example – before you start collecting it. You can find detailed information on the best ways to record and analyse data, and how to draw conclusions from your investigations, in Chapter 1.

# Sampling strategies

Before biodiversity can be properly managed, it needs to be measured. One of the things this involves is estimating the population size of species. The populations of individual organisms and numbers of different species can be huge, so it would be impossible to count all of them. Instead, scientists use samples, in which they count a subset of the whole. There are two main strategies for sampling: random sampling and systematic sampling.

## Random sampling

**Random sampling** is when samples are selected in such a way that every possible place from where data may be gathered has an equal probability of being chosen to every other place. For example, if you wanted to find out people's thoughts on an issue and you wanted a random sample, you might ask people in the order dictated by a set of random number tables or a random number generator on a calculator. So, if you had up to 100 people to whom you could address your questionnaire, you might ask people in this order:

10 24 85 79 98 78 33 40 50 3 18 97 23 53 60 71 31 44 86 90

This would give you a sample of 20 out of the 100.

On another occasion, you might sample the following:

61 88 10 49 56 8 45 1 100 82 68 3 65 54 37 51 89 50 30 57

Both sets of numbers were generated randomly. Or you could just wander around until you had asked 20 people your questions!

## Systematic sampling

**Systematic sampling** is when samples are selected in a predetermined way. In the previous example, out of 100 people to whom you want to present a questionnaire, you might ask every fifth person that you come across or that enters the room through a particular door. You might ask older people, and 20 of them if that was appropriate, or all the females in a group of men and women. All of these would be systematic samples.

> **KEY WORDS**
>
> **random sampling:** a sampling method in which an area is divided into a grid or given coordinates from a map and the sampling device is placed using random number tables or a random number generator to locate sampling points within this area. For a questionnaire, people may be selected by random selection from a phone book.
>
> **systematic sampling:** a sampling method in which the sampling device is placed along a line or some other predetermined pattern; the most common pattern is the line of a transect; questionnaires can also be applied systematically. The predetermined pattern maybe every nth metre or every nth person.

# Sampling techniques

There are two main groups of methods for sampling and measuring biodiversity. One group uses techniques for sampling organisms that do not move about (sedentary organisms), such as plants and animals like barnacles and limpets. The second group uses techniques for sampling non-sedentary organisms, which usually involve some sort of trap to catch the organisms. You were introduced to some of these techniques and the apparatus in Chapter 1. Here, you will see how they could be used to measure species.

259

## Quadrats and transects

For sedentary organisms, sampling can be done with a **quadrat**. The plants enclosed within the quadrat can then be counted. In some cases, counting individual plants is still not possible, so you will need to make an estimate. The most common of way of estimating plant numbers is to use an estimate of cover.

One way to use a gridded quadrat is to count the number of squares that the plant appears in and take the total to be the percentage cover. In the example in Figure 6.46, this would give 11% for B and 14% for A. You can then say that the percentage cover of C is 100 − (11 + 14) = 75%.

Another method is to count each square in which the plant occupies more than half of the area. This gives 7% for B and 9% for A, so C is 87%. These numbers do not add up to 100 because of the rounding effect.

When sampling biodiversity, it is important to consider where you place a quadrat. If you want to compare two areas, you should use a random sampling strategy by placing the quadrat randomly in each (Figure 6.46b). If your aim is to see how the species change along a gradient in the environment, you should use systematic sampling, placing the quadrat along a line called a **transect** (Figure 6.46a). An example of an environmental gradient is the change in light intensity from the shade of a woodland into an open field.

In systematic sampling, the quadrat can be placed along the transect line at either regular or irregular intervals. Figure 6.46a shows quadrats placed at regular intervals.

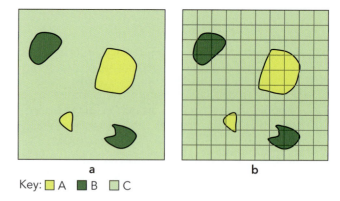

Key: ☐ A ■ B ☐ C

**Figure 6.45:** An area of grassland (C) with patches of other plants (A and B). It is difficult to estimate percentage cover, but if a gridded quadrat, as shown on the right, is placed over the area, it is easier to make this estimation.

In random sampling, it is best to lay out a grid in each of the areas to be sampled. The position of the quadrats is then determined using random coordinates from a set of random number tables or a random number generator. For example, the coordinate generated might be 4, 2. The quadrat would then be placed 4 units (say, metres) along one axis (say, $x$) and 2 along the other, $y$. This is shown in Figure 6.47.

### KEY WORDS

**quadrat:** a frame of known area used to sample organisms that do not move, such as plants

**transect:** a sampling method in which sampling devices are laid out along a line already placed across an area

6 Ecosystems, biodiversity and fieldwork

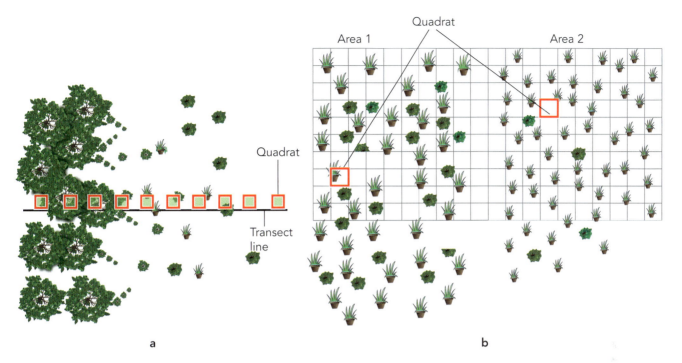

a     b

**Figure 6.46:** Systematic sampling using quadrats along a transect is appropriate in the situation shown in **a**. Random sampling – placing quadrats using random number tables in a pre-marked grid – is appropriate in the situation shown in **b** in which area 1 is being compared to area 2.

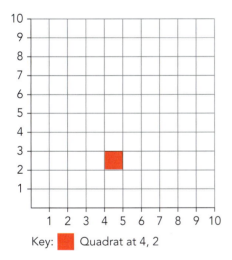

Key: ■ Quadrat at 4, 2

**Figure 6.47:** A grid showing the position of quadrat at coordinates 4, 2.

### FIELDWORK TIP

Never throw quadrats in the hope that they will land in places that will give you a random sample. Scientifically, this technique has been shown to oversample the centre of an area. There is also a risk that the quadrat may hit someone and cause injury.

261

# WORKED EXAMPLE

## Converting data

Often when estimates of numbers are made using quadrats, researchers will then try to work out the total number in an area.

A study obtained the following results for the number of dandelions (a weed) in a pasture in ten randomly placed 1-metre square quadrats. The pasture was 100 metres square.

| Quadrat number | Tally of number of dandelions |
|---|---|
| 1 | 𝍤𝍤 |
| 2 | 𝍤 II |
| 3 | III |
| 4 | 𝍤 |
| 5 | IIII |
| 6 | 𝍤 𝍤 𝍤 |
| 7 | 𝍤 𝍤 |
| 8 | III |
| 9 | 𝍤 |
| 10 | II |

Table 6.7: Tallies of the number of dandelions in the pasture per quadrat.

Estimate the number of dandelions in the entire pasture using Table 6.7.

**Step 1** Convert the tallies into real numbers.

𝍤 = 5

The table then becomes:

| Quadrat number | Tally of number of dandelions | Number of dandelions |
|---|---|---|
| 1 | 𝍤 𝍤 | 10 |
| 2 | 𝍤 II | 7 |
| 3 | III | 3 |
| 4 | 𝍤 | 5 |
| 5 | IIII | 4 |
| 6 | 𝍤 𝍤 𝍤 | 15 |
| 7 | 𝍤 𝍤 | 10 |
| 8 | III | 3 |
| 9 | 𝍤 | 5 |
| 10 | II | 2 |

Table 6.8: Number of dandelions in the pasture per quadrat.

**Step 2** Calculate the total number of dandelions in the ten quadrats (64) using Table 6.8.

**Step 3** Calculate the mean average number of dandelions per quadrat (64 ÷ 10 = 6.4).

**Step 4** Calculate the total area of the pasture in metres$^2$. It is 100 metres × 100 metres, which is 10 000 metres$^2$.

**Step 5** Multiply the average number of dandelions in a quadrat (6.4) by the area of the pasture in metres$^2$ (10 000) = 6.4 × 10 000 = 64 000 dandelions.

## Now you try

Figure 6.48 shows two fields being compared for the number of daisies in them. Each square is 1 metre$^2$. Each dot is 1 daisy.

Estimate the number of daisies in field A and in field B.

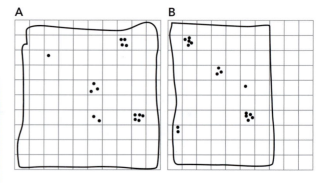

Figure 6.48: Two fields being compared for the number of daisies.

6 Ecosystems, biodiversity and fieldwork

> **SELF-ASSESSMENT**
>
> On a scale of 1–5, where 5 is very confident and 1 is not at all confident, how confident do you feel about working with counts from investigations using quadrats in sites of a known area? If you graded yourself at confidence levels 1, 2 or 3, look back through the information on using quadrats and the Worked example 'converting data' – note down the area for which you need more support or practice.

## Pitfall traps

For organisms that move, a variety of trapping methods can be used to estimate biodiversity as well as population size.

A pitfall trap (Figure 6.49) is a common device used for small animals moving about on the ground. A pitfall trap consists of a jar sunk up to its rim in the soil. The top may or may not be covered (depending on whether it is likely to rain), and the trap should be inspected and emptied regularly.

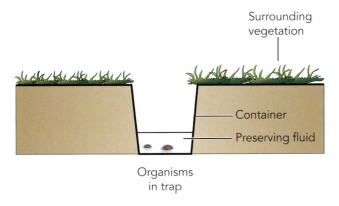

Figure 6.49: A pitfall trap without a cover.

Traps can be placed systematically (for example, along a transect) or randomly (for example, in places selected on a grid with random numbers). So, a transect line or random set of samples – as set out for plants – can also be used to sample this type of animal. However, pitfall traps measure the level of activity of the animals as well as their numbers. So, for example, if a population of 100 beetles was running about in an area where pitfall traps had been placed, it might be that, after a day, 17 beetles in total were caught. On another occasion, in the same area with the same number of pitfall traps but on a warmer day, the 100 beetles were running about more quickly and, therefore, more likely to be trapped and so you caught, say, 31. The population is still, of course, 100 in the area, so the level of activity has affected the catch.

## Sweep nets and pooters

Other techniques for sampling small animals, such as insects in short vegetation or on trees, involve catching them in a net of some kind, often a **sweep net** (Figure 6.50). The animals or insects can then be transported back to a laboratory for careful identification. A **pooter** is a simple piece of equipment for getting the animals out of the net and into a specimen container (Figure 6.51).

Figure 6.50: A sweep net.

> **KEY WORDS**
>
> **sweep net:** a bag-shaped net with a handle, used for catching insects
>
> **pooter:** a device for retrieving small animals from devices, such as nets and pitfall traps

263

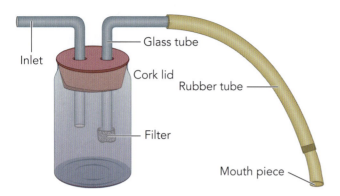

**Figure 6.51:** A pooter.

## Aerial photography and drones

For larger animals, such as small mammals like mice and voles, other kinds of traps can be used. For very large animals, such as zebras and wildebeest, counting is used, often taking advantage of technology, such as aerial photography from an aeroplane or a drone (Figure 6.52).

**Figure 6.52:** Aerial photography showing a group of walruses.

## Automated sampling

Automated sampling is a new technique. It can be applied in many different ways, but a common one is the trail camera or camera trap (Figure 6.53). These battery-operated devices can be left outside unattended for many weeks and set up to record every so often, or when there is movement detected. Recently, one of 80 trail cameras that had been set up in the jungles of northern New Guinea captured images of an animal that had not been seen since 1961 – the Attenborough's long-beaked echidna.

The benefit of such equipment is that it can record a lot of data with very little labour involved. However, the problem is that after recording, finding relevant and interesting data is often very labour intensive.

**Figure 6.53:** Trail cameras can be positioned in or on trees, or hidden in appropriate places at ground level.

## When to use random or systematic sampling

When designing an ecological investigation, scientists have to decide whether the quadrats, traps or sweep nets should be positioned or used in a systematic or random fashion. As a general rule, if the investigation is looking at how distribution changes over an environmental gradient, systematic sampling is best. For example, if you wanted to look at the effect of a road on vegetation, you would use this method (Figure 6.54).

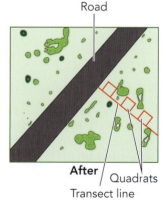

**Figure 6.54:** To investigate the effect that building a road has had on the plants growing on either side, a transect with quadrats laid at regular intervals along it can be used to sample the plants.

If your investigation requires you to compare areas, then random sampling using a grid is the most suitable method. For example, to compare the insect populations between an area grazed by animals and an area that is not grazed, pitfall traps could be set out randomly in both areas using a grid and random number tables.

## Questions

**6.17** Match the following studies (**a** to **d**) with the potential sampling methods (**i** to **iv**) – the first one has been done for you:

a   The distribution of ground-living beetles along the side of a road heading from the countryside into a town. (**iii**)

b   The distribution of plants on either side of a heavily used footpath across a field.

c   A comparison of the numbers of scale insects (an insect that sucks sap from plants and stays in one place all its life) in a field grazed by sheep with the numbers in a field where sheep do not graze.

d   A comparison of the numbers of grasshoppers in a field that is mown with the numbers in a field that is not mown.

   i   Pooters used to collect insects from quadrats in two different fields, placed using coordinates generated by the throw of dice.

   ii  Quadrats placed in two different fields using coordinates generated by the throw of dice.

   iii Pitfall traps placed in a line a fixed distance apart.

   iv  Quadrats placed 10 metres apart in a line.

# Benefits and limitations of sampling techniques for measuring species populations

All the sampling techniques described previously have advantages and disadvantages. These are outlined in Table 6.9.

| Method | Advantages | Disadvantages |
| --- | --- | --- |
| Quadrats | • Quick<br>• Inexpensive<br>• Portable | • Not always very accurate<br>• Unless many quadrats are placed, the sample can be unintentionally biased |
| Transects | • Quick<br>• Inexpensive<br>• Portable | • Often used in inappropriate situations, so care must be taken when deciding whether or not to use a transect |
| Pitfall traps | • Inexpensive<br>• Easy to set up and use | • Often kill the organisms captured<br>• May over-sample or under-sample<br>• Count may not reflect actual numbers, as numbers caught may also depend on activity |
| Sweep nets | • Inexpensive<br>• Easy to use | • Count may depend on many things, such as time of day, weather, etc.<br>• Can damage vegetation<br>• Only useful in quite tall vegetation |
| Aerial photography | • Can cover large areas quickly<br>• Counts can be very accurate as can be studied at length | • Expensive<br>• Not suitable for use in forested areas |

| Method | Advantages | Disadvantages |
|---|---|---|
| Drones | - Inexpensive<br>- Easy to operate<br>- Counts can be very accurate as can be studied at length | - Not suitable for use in forested areas<br>- Many restrictions on use are coming into force |
| Automated sampling | - Labour non-intensive once set up<br>- Can generate large amount of data | - The amount of data generated can itself become a problem; analysing it can take many hours, looking through all the photographs, many of which may be of no interest |

Table 6.9: The benefits and limitations of sampling techniques for measuring the populations of species.

### FIELDWORK ACTIVITY 6.1

#### Studying the distribution and abundance of plants

You can practise these skills either in the laboratory or in the field. Work in pairs or small groups.

#### Field study

**You will need**

- a quadrat
- a long tape measure (30 metres)
- a method for generating random numbers (e.g. a mobile phone app)
- a simple field guide to whatever it is you are going to investigate (e.g. wildflower plants).

If you do not have a quadrat, you can make one from two rulers (Figure 6.55).

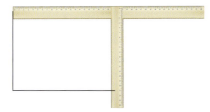

Figure 6.55: Two metre rulers used to make a 50 cm quadrat.

**Safety**

If you are carrying out your investigation in the field, dress appropriately for the weather. Be aware of traffic or any other hazards in the area where you are working, such as cliffs or bodies of water. Make sure you are supervised by an adult and have a charged mobile phone so you can keep in contact with others.

**Before you start**

You will first need to decide on a question you are going to try to answer with your study. For example:

- Are nettles (or any other plant) found more commonly in bright light or dull light?
- Does mowing affect the number of clover plants in an area?
- How does trampling on a path affect plants?
- How do seaweeds change from the high-tide mark to the low-tide mark on a rocky shore?

Next, decide whether you are going to use a random or systematic sampling method. For example, if you are looking at the distribution of a plant along a gradient of light intensity, you will need to use a systematic method. If you are comparing two different areas, such as mown/grazed and not mown/grazed, it will be random.

Draw the table in which you will record your results.

**Method**

Systematic: Lay out your tape measure along the line where you think there might be a gradient.

Random: Set up a grid in each of the areas to be compared (say, 10 x 10 metres, but it must be appropriate to the size of the areas you are comparing).

# 6 Ecosystems, biodiversity and fieldwork

## CONTINUED

Place your first quadrat. If using systematic sampling, place it at the first station on your tape (see Figure 6.46a).

If using random sampling, generate a pair of random coordinates and then find that spot on your grid (see Figure 6.47).

Make an assessment of abundance inside the quadrat. This could be a count of numbers or an estimate of percentage cover.

Record the results for your first quadrat in the table.

Move on to the second quadrat. This will be your next station on the transect line if using systematic sampling, or a second set of random coordinates if using random sampling.

Continue until you have done enough samples. If you are working along a transect line, you should have decided on how many quadrats to do before you start, taking into account the length of the line. If you have laid out a 100-metre line, ten quadrats (one every 10 metres) is about right. For random sampling, do up to ten in each area.

Record all your results in your table.

Transfer the results into a suitable diagram if appropriate.

### Laboratory study

If you cannot carry out this activity in the field, you can do it inside.

Figure 6.56 shows an example area with plants and a grid.

### You will need

- a copy of the top half of Figure 6.56, which you can then print out (you could have one or more copies of the area to use, or stick several together to create a larger area)
- quadrats to sample the artificial plant population
- a copy of the grid traced onto tracing paper.

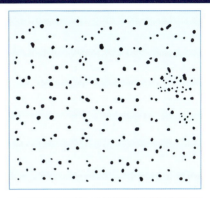

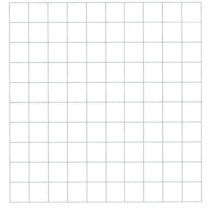

**Figure 6.56:** Plant population and grid to lay over it.

### Method

Place the quadrat over the artificial plant population and count the number of plants within the quadrat.

Record your results in a table.

You could use the example area to create two areas and imitate a comparison via random sampling.

### Questions

1. Some students decided to sample the distribution of litter on a beach to see where it was most commonly found: near the low-tide level or further inland. Explain whether they should use random or systematic sampling.

2. Another group were sampling litter on two fields: one near a school and the other near a golf course. Explain whether they should use random or systematic sampling.

# ACTIVITY 6.4

Look back through this chapter at all the Key words that have been defined. Collect these in your notebook and then use them to write a crossword to give to a partner to check their understanding. Figure 6.57 shows an example, but you should start from scratch with your own crossword.

When you have created your crossword, swap it with a partner and time yourselves to see who can complete the crossword first.

**Across**

2   The place within an ecosystem where an organism lives
4   All the living things (biotic components) together with all the non-living things (abiotic components) in an area
5   Living components of the environment that may affect other living things

**Down**

1   All the organisms of one species living in a defined area
3   A group of populations of different species that live together in an area and interact with each other

Figure 6.57: An example of a crossword.

# REFLECTION

The point of making the crossword was to help you remember the definitions of what are likely to be a lot of new words. Was this helpful? Would you have preferred to have had a crossword that was already created and you just had to fill it in with all the words you need to know? If so, why? Did it help to compete with a partner? If so, why do you think that was? What other ways can you think of to help you remember these definitions?

## 6 Ecosystems, biodiversity and fieldwork

## CASE STUDY

### Mayan Biosphere Reserve, Guatemala

The Mayan Biosphere Reserve in northern Guatemala contains part of one of the largest areas of tropical forest in Central America. It has core areas, which include national parks and wildlife reserves (Figure 6.58). The reserve contains lowland forest, savannah, pine forest, lakes, lagoons, rivers, wetlands and some mangrove forests. The core areas are the only parts of the reserve where laws govern the conduct of people.

The transition zone consists of mainly tropical forest dedicated to the harvesting of date palms, chicle gum, allspice and timber. These activities are encouraged as a way of giving the locals a livelihood that does not involve 'slash and burn'. With slash and burn, vegetation is cut down and burnt, and then crops can be grown on the land for a few years afterwards (see the Extended case study at the end of this chapter).

The buffer zone in the south is an agricultural landscape with some forest. The population of this area has grown during the last 30 years, mostly in regions south of the reserve. Archaeological sites in the reserve include Tikal, a Mayan city which gets as many as 180 000 visitors / year.

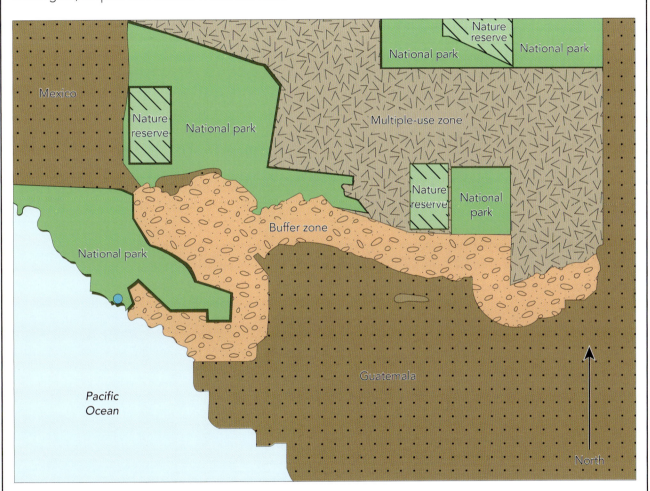

Figure 6.58: Map of the Mayan Biosphere Reserve in northern Guatemala.

## CONTINUED

In 2008, President Alvaro Colom of Guatemala announced the Cuatro Balam initiative to increase tourism in the reserve, focusing on the archaeological sites. The plan is designed to help the conservation of biodiversity and archaeology, at the same time as encouraging economic development in the region. One aim is to attract 12 million visitors to the region. Key features of the plan include a small train that will carry tourists to and from the archaeological sites, and a new university that will promote the study of the region's biodiversity and genetic material, as well as Mayan studies. Colom said that some of the planned objectives could be achieved within just two years, while others would take up to 15 years to realise. He also said that to achieve any of this, the region would have to be protected from invasive farmers, ranchers and drug traffickers, who are concentrated in the western part of the reserve.

Research carried out in the Mayan reserve relates to:

- population studies of the Mexican crocodile
- the ecology of various bird species
- the biology and conservation of parrots
- measuring the abundance of fauna
- fishery pressures in the San Pedro River
- management of natural resources
- the impacts of tourism
- the impacts of subsistence hunting on populations of jaguars and pumas
- the biodiversity and potential uses of vascular plants in the rainforest
- development of communities near Flores, through the hunting and conservation of the ocellated turkey (*Pavo ocelado*)
- the harvesting of traditional non-timber forest products, such as chicle and xate.

### Questions

1 Suggest the possible benefits of the Cuatro Balam plan to:

    a local people

    b the world in general.

2 Suggest how 'hunting and conservation' of the turkey *Pavo ocelado* can both be achieved in the same area.

3 Explain how the biodiversity of plants in the rainforest can be studied.

## EXTENDED CASE STUDY

### Deforestation in Madagascar

Madagascar is a large island off the east coast of southern Africa. It became isolated from all other land masses about 90 million years ago. During most of the time between then and the present day, the animals and plants have been left alone. This means that over 90% of the organisms living on the island live only there and nowhere else on Earth: they are endemic to Madagascar. About 2500 years ago, humans arrived on the island. Since then, over 90% of the once-lush forest has been lost (Figure 6.59).

Much of this deforestation has occurred quite recently, and is largely due to slash and burn, which is called *tavy* in Madagascar. This is a valued agricultural technique and is also of cultural significance. Parcels of land pass from the family that first cleared them to the descendants of those people. The areas are carefully selected by taking account of the species already there and the colour of their leaves, which are both indicators of how fertile the soil is. A hectare (0.01 km$^2$) or so of forest is cut down and then burnt. No trees are left. Burning turns the cleared vegetation into ash, which is rich in minerals. It also destroys potential pests and weeds. The resulting area is planted, usually with rice. The cleared land can usually support a rice crop for only two years, giving a yield of about 900 kg / hectare / year. It is

# 6 Ecosystems, biodiversity and fieldwork

**CONTINUED**

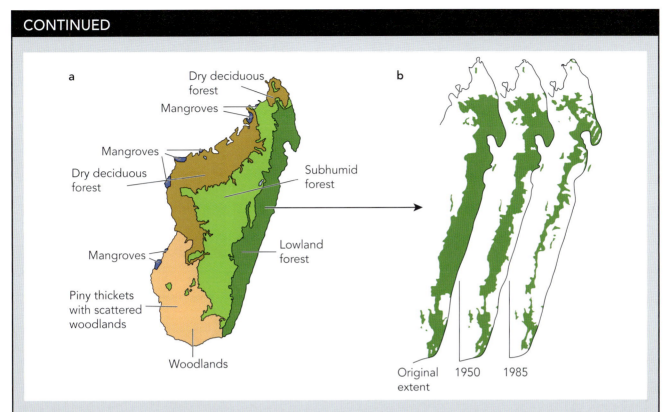

Figure 6.59: **a** The main vegetation zones of Madagascar. **b** Loss of eastern humid forests since human colonisation 2500 years ago.

then left to recover, usually for four years. The vegetation that has grown in those four years is cut and burnt again, and rice is cultivated for two more years. This sequence can be repeated once more, but after that the area is useless for further cultivation.

There is also quite a big world market for timber from Madagascar. The eastern part of the island has a band of tropical rainforest, and it is from here that most of the valuable trees are taken. The most important of these are ebony and rosewood, which can be worth $1000–2000 / tonne.

Many of the profoundly poor people of the country can earn a little money from the sale of charcoal. This is made from many types of wood, leading to further deforestation. In this case, it is the spiny forests of the south-west that are very badly affected.

*Tavy* is a very controversial practice both inside Madagascar and internationally. Primary rainforest, much valued for reasons already discussed, is turned into secondary growth and, ultimately, grassland. Deforestation leads to desertification, extensive soil erosion and nutrient loss. Minerals are lost because of leaching and are taken out in harvested crops, together with some (mainly carbon and nitrogen) that is burnt off.

In the short term, levels of soil minerals increase, but they soon decline again. Over the long term, nutrient loss is ongoing. One study has shown that nutrient levels in the soil had increased by about 25% two years after *tavy* and were back to the starting point within six years. The same study showed that after 160 years of *tavy* cycles, nutrient levels had fallen by 25% from the beginning of the cycle and that the trend was consistently downward.

The soils of Madagascar, like those in most tropical regions, are laterites (Figure 6.60 a, b). These soils are rich in iron compounds and deep red in colour. From space, astronauts have seen red-stained water in many river estuaries, prompting them to describe the island as 'bleeding to death' (Figure 6.60 c).

271

**CONTINUED**

Figure 6.60: **a** Laterite soils in Madagascar, showing the plant cover almost completely removed. **b** Severe erosion of the land in Madagascar. **c** The estuary of the River Betsiboka showing silt from the lands in the interior being washed out to sea.

Along with the forests and their soils, many of the large animals that once lived in Madagascar have been lost. The biggest of these includes the giant elephant birds, of which there used to be eight species. The list also includes two species of hippopotamus, a large species of fossa and over 12 species of lemurs.

Lemurs are a group of primates that are endemic to Madagascar. There are currently thought to be about 100 species left, but eight are critically endangered, 18 are endangered, 15 are vulnerable and 4 are near threatened. Of the remaining 55, 8 are of least concern, but for the rest there is simply not enough information to decide their status.

### Questions

1. Explain what is likely to happen to lead to the recovery of a plot that has undergone *tavy*.

2. If the level of nitrate in a soil before *tavy* was 5 g / kg, use the information in the case study to calculate what it would be:
   
   a. Two years after *tavy*
   
   b. 160 years after *tavy*.

3. Explain the causes and consequences of the observation by astronauts that Madagascar is 'bleeding to death'.

4. Calculate the total yield from a hectare of land cleared by *tavy* after 18 years of this process.

5. Suggest two reasons why it might be difficult for the Madagascar government to control deforestation.

6. Suggest why the loss of animal species may be an issue for the people of Madagascar.

### Project

*Tavy* is the word for slash and burn agriculture in Malagasy, the language spoken in Madagascar. In groups, carry out some research on the practice of slash and burn agriculture around the world. You could look at it under a number of headings, including, but not limited to, the following:

- names for slash and burn in other languages
- reasons for slash and burn being used
- benefits of slash and burn
- problems caused by slash and burn
- alternatives to slash and burn
- incidences of slash and burn by country or region (there would be an opportunity to include visuals here, such as pie charts and/or bar graphs).

Use your research to produce a poster, PowerPoint presentation or other visual with the title 'Slash and burn agriculture throughout the world'.

# 6 Ecosystems, biodiversity and fieldwork

## CONTINUED

**Further resources**

*What is Slash and Burn Farming?*, Rainforest Saver

*Slash-and-Burn Agriculture: Can It Be Sustainable Again?* Treehugger

## SUMMARY

| |
|---|
| A range of physical, non-living (abiotic) factors interact with living things (biotic). These include temperature, water availability, pH and humidity. |
| Living things interact with each other, mainly by eating or by being eaten. |
| The links between the eaters and the eaten is called a food chain or food web. |
| Food chains allow energy to flow from one organism (the eaten) to others (the eaters). |
| The flow of energy can be depicted in a pyramid of energy. |
| All food on Earth is made in synthetic processes in plants and some bacteria. In plants, this is called photosynthesis. |
| As well as energy, nutrients are passed along food chains and webs. |
| Unlike energy, which is lost as heat along the way, nutrients (such as carbon) can be recycled, in nutrient cycles. |
| Human action is causing the loss of habitats around the world. A major habitat that is being lost in this way is forests. |
| Forests are lost through logging, various farming activities, the construction of roads and settlements, mining and quarrying, hydro-electric power station construction, and climate change. |
| Loss of habitat leads to loss of species and, therefore, diversity. We also lose the environmental services that habitats provide, so these losses need to be managed. |
| Trees act as carbon sinks and stores, and have important roles in the cycling of water and flood control. In addition, they prevent soil erosion, and forests are a vast resource for raw materials, medicines and food. |
| In order to manage habitats, we need as much information about them as possible. Sampling allows us to estimate the diversity of life within them – the biodiversity. |
| Once we have surveyed a habitat or ecosystem, we can then use a variety of strategies to help in its conservation, all of which have benefits and limitations. |
| Conservation strategies include: setting up protected areas, local reserves and national parks; the creation of seed banks and breeding programmes in zoos; and international efforts to control trade in endangered species. |

## SELF-EVALUATION CHECKLIST

After studying this chapter, complete this table.

| I can: | Needs more work | Almost there | Ready to move on |
|---|---|---|---|
| describe the different components of an ecosystem | | | |
| identify the biotic (living) and abiotic (non-living) factors in ecosystems | | | |
| discuss the relationships between living things within an ecosystem | | | |
| describe the processes of pollination and photosynthesis | | | |
| explain how energy flows along food chains and webs within an ecosystem | | | |
| use pyramids of numbers and pyramids of energy to describe food chains | | | |
| understand the process of aerobic respiration | | | |
| describe how carbon cycles within an ecosystem | | | |
| explain how forests are lost and the consequences of deforestation | | | |
| state why we need strategies for the sustainable management of forests | | | |
| discuss a variety of strategies for conserving biodiversity, and their advantages and disadvantages | | | |
| apply the scientific method to data collection | | | |
| estimate biodiversity using random and systematic sampling | | | |
| measure populations using a variety of techniques, and consider their pros and cons. | | | |

# 6 Ecosystems, biodiversity and fieldwork

## PRACTICE QUESTIONS

1   **Figure 6.61** shows terms relating to ecosystems and their descriptions.

   Draw **one** line from each term to its correct description. [3]

| Term | Description |
| --- | --- |
| carnivore | an animal that eats plants, changing the energy from the sun stored in plants into meat that can be eaten by other animals |
| predator | an organism that can carry out photosynthesis |
|  | an organism that derives it food from secondary consumers |
| primary consumer | an organism that preys on other organisms |
| producer | an animal that eats meat |

**Figure 6.61:** Terms relating to ecosystems.

2   Ecosystems contain both biotic and abiotic factors.
   a   i   Define biotic. [1]
       ii  Define abiotic. [1]
   b   i   Name **two** biotic factors of a desert ecosystem. [1]
       ii  Name **two** abiotic factors of a desert ecosystem. [1]

3   Photosynthesis is the process by which plants trap energy in the form of light from the sun.
   a   Give the word equation for photosynthesis. [2]
   b   Explain how plants use glucose. [1]
   c   State the role of chlorophyll in the process of photosynthesis. [2]

4   Between 2001 and 2023, the world lost 488 million hectares of tree cover. This is significant because trees play an important part in regulating the climate.
   a   Explain the difference between a carbon sink and a carbon store. [2]
   b   Agriculture is responsible for around 80% of all deforestation.
       Describe how agriculture contributes to deforestation. [3]
   c   i   Suggest **two** impacts of deforestation. [2]
       ii  Suggest **one** example of a sustainable forestry practice and explain how it works. [2]

CONTINUED

5   **Figure 6.62** shows changes in an area of wetland in the US state of Minnesota over the past 150 years.

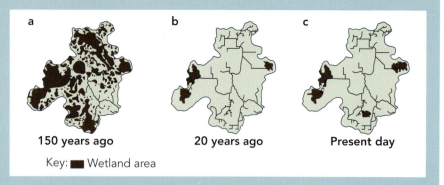

**Figure 6.62:** Changes in an area of wetland in the US state of Minnesota.

   a   Describe the changes that have occurred between these three periods. [3]

   b   i   Give **one** strategy that could be used to conserve the remaining wetlands. [1]

       ii  Give **one** strategy that could be used to extend wetland cover in this state. [1]

6   Two species of flatworm, **A** and **B**, were studied. They were found living in streams both alone and together. When alone they were found in the temperature ranges as follows:

   A = 8.5–19 °C and B = 8.5–23 °C.

   At temperatures above 23 °C, neither was found.

   In streams where both flatworms occurred, **A** was not found at all in temperatures above 14 °C.

   Suggest two reasons for this, assuming that both species eat the same food. [2]

7   **Figure 6.63** represents the numbers in each of four trophic levels in a woodland ecosystem.

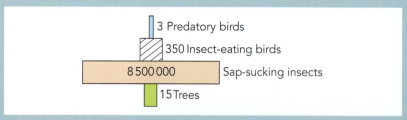

**Figure 6.63:** The numbers in each of four trophic levels in a woodland ecosystem.

## CONTINUED

a State which trophic level the sap-sucking insects belong to. [1]

b Some students told their teacher they were surprised that the diagram did not form a pyramid shape.

With reference to **Figure 6.63**, explain why the tropic levels in this woodland do not form a pyramid shape. [3]

c The information below was collected about the organisms in **Figure 6.63**. Using this information and **Figure 6.63**, sketch an annotated pyramid of energy for this woodland food web. [4]

energy in 15 trees = 75 000 000 kJ

energy in sap-suckers = 680 000 kJ

energy in insect-eating birds = 7 500 kJ

energy in predatory birds = 3000 kJ

8 Avocado-tree farmers reported that their crops were being eaten by a pest. They wanted to find out how well a pesticide worked against the pest. To investigate, a student marked out two sample areas of the same field as shown in **Figure 6.64**.

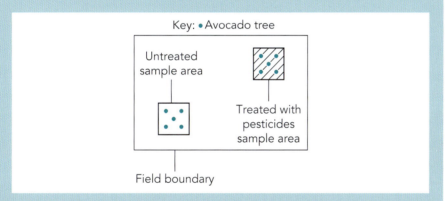

Figure 6.64: The two sample areas in the same field.

a Give **one** reason why the student used two areas in the same field. [1]

b Describe **one** sampling strategy the student could have used to locate the positions of the avocado trees. [1]

c All avocado fruit on the trees selected were picked and removed. The avocado fruit infected with the pest were recorded in a table.

  i Suggest **one** way in which the student could carry out this work safely. [1]

## CONTINUED

ii  Table 6.10 shows the data recorded. Calculate the total number of avocados removed in the sample area treated with pesticides. [2]

|  | Sample area treated with pesticide | | Sample area untreated with pesticide | |
|---|---|---|---|---|
| Avocado tree | Avocados removed | Avocados infested | Avocados removed | Avocadoes infested |
| 1 | 56 | 10 | 60 | 25 |
| 2 | 48 | 8 | 55 | 22 |
| 3 | 51 | 9 | 45 | 18 |
| 4 | 42 | 5 | 50 | 28 |
| 5 | 33 | 6 | 46 | 19 |
| Total |  | 38 | 256 | 112 |

Table 6.10: Results of an investigations into how well a pesticide worked against an avocado pest.

iii  Calculate the percentage infestation for the treated and untreated sections of the field. Give your answers to the nearest whole number. [3]

iv  Determine a suitable conclusion for the investigation. [2]

9  Figure 6.65 shows a transect laid out.

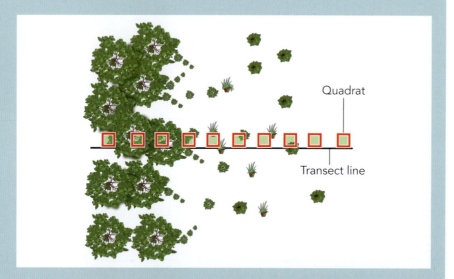

Figure 6.65: A transect laid out for a fieldwork investigation.

a  State the sampling strategy being used in this investigation. [1]

### CONTINUED

**b** Table 6.11 shows the results of data collected from three different transects in this area.

| Transect | Quadrat 1 | Quadrat 2 | Quadrat 3 | Quadrat 4 | Quadrat 5 | Quadrat 6 | Quadrat 7 | Quadrat 8 | Quadrat 9 | Quadrat 10 |
|---|---|---|---|---|---|---|---|---|---|---|
| 1 | 3 | 4 | 3 | 5 | 7 | 9 | 8 | 3 | 1 | 1 |
| 2 | 4 | 3 | 5 | 4 | 8 | 8 | 7 | 2 | 1 | 2 |
| 3 | 2 | 2 | 1 | 2 | 3 | 2 | 4 | 2 | 3 | 1 |

**Table 6.11:** The results of data collected in three different transects.

    **i** Identify the quadrat that had the highest number of species. Give the transect and the quadrat number in your answer. [1]

    **ii** Identify the transect that contains data that does not fit the pattern of the other two transects. [1]

    **iii** Explain why the number of species decreased in the forested portion of the transect. [2]

**c** Identify **two** other sets of data that the investigators could have collected at the same time as collecting information on the number of species. [2]

**d** The investigator used a quadrat that was 0.5 m x 0.5 m to carry out the sampling. Considering the plant species being sampled, identify **one** limitation of this quadrat size. [1]

**10.** A scientist wants to use a random sampling method to estimate the population of yellow daisies in a field.

Describe a random strategy to estimate the population of the daisies. Your answer should include a method to select an area, collect and record your data, and estimate the population of daisies in the field. [5]

# Chapter 7
# Natural hazards

### LEARNING INTENTIONS

In this chapter you will:

- learn about the structure of the Earth
- find out where the seven continents are in the world
- examine the causes and global distribution of earthquakes and volcanoes, and relate them to Earth's structure
- discover the features of earthquakes and volcanic eruptions
- explore the impact that tectonic events have and strategies for managing these impacts
- consider the benefits of living near volcanoes
- investigate the location and conditions needed for tropical cyclones to form
- explore the impacts of tropical cyclones and strategies for managing them at different stages
- investigate what causes flooding
- examine the impacts of flooding and investigate strategies for managing these impacts
- consider the benefits provided by flooding
- investigate a lack of rain and climate change as causes of drought
- explore the impacts of drought and strategies for managing it at different stages.

7  Natural hazards

### BEFORE YOU START

Work in pairs. List as many **natural hazards** as you can think of, then rearrange the list to rank them, first in terms of deaths and then in terms of the impact they might have on the local economy, where 1 causes the most deaths or has the greatest economic impact.

In your pairs, discuss why people live in areas at risk from natural hazards. Give examples where possible. Do you think it is possible to predict **natural disasters**? Why, or why not? Share your ideas with the class.

As a class, decide which of the following numbers matches which statement (**a–f**):

1350   45 000   27   55   46   700

a  the temperature in °C of the ocean surface required for the formation of a tropical cyclone

b  the average speed of a tsunami in kilometres per hour

c  the number of active volcanoes that erupt each year

d  the number of earthquakes that are measured each day

e  the average number of people who died from natural hazards between 2012 and 2022

f  the percentage of land that is desertified in Africa.

### KEY WORDS

**natural hazard:** a physical event that has the potential to cause loss of life or injury, and to damage property and infrastructure; a natural hazard may cause a natural disaster

**natural disaster:** when a natural hazard, such as an earthquake, causes damage and the people affected are unable to cope effectively

### ENVIRONMENTAL MANAGEMENT IN CONTEXT

#### Predicting the impossible?

In Yellowstone National Park in the north-west of the USA, there is a volcano. But this is not just any volcano – it is a **supervolcano**. A supervolcano is when an eruption measures **magnitude** 8 or more on the Volcano Explosivity Index and creates deposits that are greater than 1000 km³. If this volcano were to erupt today, experts suggest that at least 90 000 people would be killed instantly and a 3-metre layer of ash would cover Earth's surface for up to 1000 km away. Global food shortages would also occur as world temperatures dropped.

This volcano has had three super eruptions in the past: 2.1 million years ago, 1.3 million years ago and 640 000 years ago. The time period between these events ranges from 600 000 to 800 000 years, and some experts say that we are long overdue an eruption. The United States Geological Survey (USGS) constantly monitors the supervolcano, but it does not have sufficient data to establish a meaningful recurrence interval, and no one knows when the next eruption will be, simply because it cannot be predicted with any precision.

In 2015, scientists estimated that 800 million people worldwide lived within 100 km of an active volcano. For example, more than 70% of Indonesia's population live within 100 km of one of the country's 130 active volcanoes, which could potentially erupt at any time. That's over 175 million people. Also, 8.6 million Indonesians live within 10 km of an active volcano, which means they are within range of a dangerous pyroclastic flow.

### KEY WORDS

**supervolcano:** a volcano that erupts at least 1000 km³ of material

**magnitude:** a measure of how strong or violent an earthquake is

CAMBRIDGE IGCSE™ AND O LEVEL ENVIRONMENTAL MANAGEMENT: COURSEBOOK

### CONTINUED

As the world's population grows, the exposure of humans to natural disasters caused by natural hazards, like volcanic eruptions, will only increase. Natural hazards have the capacity to kill, injure and disrupt lives. Between 2010 and 2020, natural hazards are believed to have killed over 450 000 people worldwide. Approximately 930 000 people were injured, 12 million were made homeless and the total economic loss was estimated at more than $4 trillion.

The impact of a natural hazard can continue long after the event has passed. We cannot change when, where or how frequently natural hazards occur, but we can try to predict, prepare and manage the causes, so that we can minimise the impacts.

**Discussion questions**

1. What do you think the Volcano Explosivity Index is? What other scales can you think of that are used to measure the strength of natural hazards?
2. Why do you think global temperatures drop after a large volcanic eruption? Can you name any volcanic eruptions besides the one at Yellowstone that have had this impact?
3. Suggest why so many people in Indonesia live close to an active volcano.

**Figure 7.1:** Yellowstone National Park Grand Prismatic Spring.

## 7.1 Earthquakes and volcanoes

### What is a natural hazard?

A natural hazard is a physical event that has the potential to cause loss of life or injury, and to damage property and infrastructure. Natural hazards can be short-term events that last just a few minutes, or long-term events that can happen over several years. They can be classified in a number of different ways, but the most common way is based on the cause of the hazard, including:

- geological hazards – for example, earthquakes and volcanic eruptions; these are sometimes referred to as **tectonic events**
- climatic hazards – for example, tropical cyclones, floods and droughts (Figure 7.2).

The term 'natural hazard' does not refer to just any physical event occurring in the natural world. People and property need to be put at **risk** by the event for it to be a natural hazard. Volcanic explosions may look dramatic, but it is estimated that half of all deaths attributed to eruptions are from just five recorded events. The natural hazard that occurs most frequently is flooding, but between 2010 and 2020, earthquakes have killed more people, as shown in Table 7.1.

### KEY WORDS

**tectonic event:** a hazard caused by tectonic plate movement, such as earthquakes and volcanic eruptions

**risk:** the probability of a natural hazard occurring, and the losses or damage that might result from that natural hazard

282

# 7 Natural hazards

**Figure 7.2:** Between June and September 2023, widespread drought in Indonesia affected nearly 19 million people.

| Natural hazard | Number of deaths from natural hazards, 2010–20 |
|---|---|
| Earthquakes | 268 888 |
| Floods | 56 589 |
| Storms | 29 332 |
| Drought | 20 957 |
| Volcanoes | 1 394 |

**Table 7.1:** The number of deaths from different natural hazards, 2010–20.

> **MATHS TIP**
>
> Remember that percentage values are equivalent to fractions – for example, 25% is a quarter, 50% is half and 75% is three-quarters.

## WORKED EXAMPLE

### Percentages

Working out percentages is an important skill that you will use in many topics on your Environmental Management course.

Study Table 7.1. Calculate the percentage of natural hazards between 2010 and 2020 that were drought events. Give your answer to one decimal place.

**Step 1**   Add up the data values to give a total = 377 160.

**Step 2**   Take the number of drought events and divide it by the total: 20 957 ÷ 377 160 × 100 = 5.6%

### Now you try

Study Table 7.1. Calculate the percentage of natural hazards between 2010 and 2020 that were earthquake events. Give your answer to one decimal place.

## The structure of the Earth

Two of the main natural hazards are earthquakes and volcanic eruptions. To understand the causes and effects of these geological hazards, it is important to understand the structure of the Earth (Figure 7.3).

The inner core of the Earth reaches temperatures of 5000–6000 °C. It is solid because of the intense pressure from overlying rocks. Pressure is 3 million times greater here than at the surface. It is made of iron and nickel. The outer core reaches temperatures of 4000–5000 °C. It is liquid and made of iron and nickel. The mantle accounts for more than 80% of the volume of the Earth. It is made up of mainly silicate minerals. The lower mantle is sometimes called the asthenosphere and has a temperature of 1000–1200 °C. It behaves like a plastic and flows slowly due to convection currents created by heat from the core. The upper part of the mantle is more brittle and joins with the top layer of the Earth (the crust). This is called the lithosphere.

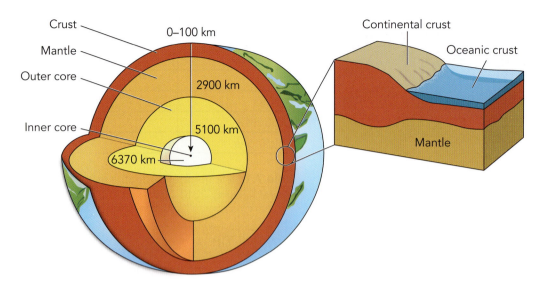

Figure 7.3: The structure of the Earth, showing the two types of crust: oceanic and continental.

| Oceanic crust | Continental crust |
| --- | --- |
| Mainly made of **basalt** | Mainly made of **granite** |
| Thinner (average depth is 6 km) | Thicker (average depth is 35 km but it can be over 100 km under mountain ranges) |
| Denser (heavier: 3 g cm$^{-3}$) | Lighter (2.6 g cm$^{-3}$) |
| Younger | Older |
| It can sink and is continually being renewed and destroyed | It cannot sink and is neither destroyed or renewed |

Table 7.2: The main features of oceanic and continental crusts.

The two types of crust and their different features are summarised in Table 7.2. Remembering the differences between oceanic and continental crust will help you understand the processes related to the theory of **plate tectonics**, which is key to understanding tectonic hazards like earthquakes and volcanic eruptions.

> **KEY WORDS**
>
> **basalt:** a fine-grained extrusive igneous rock formed by the cooling of lava at constructive plate margins
>
> **granite:** a coarse-grained intrusive igneous rock comprising the minerals quartz, feldspar and mica; it is formed at destructive plate margins

> **KEY WORD**
>
> **plate tectonics:** a theory developed in the 1960s that helps explain the formation of some of the important features on Earth's surface and how the continents move

## The continents

The surface of Earth that we see and stand on is split into seven continents: Africa, Antarctica, Asia, Europe, North America, South America and Oceania. These landmasses are separated by five major oceans: the Arctic, the Atlantic, the Indian, the Pacific and the Southern. Figure 7.4 shows the location of these continents and oceans.

## 7 Natural hazards

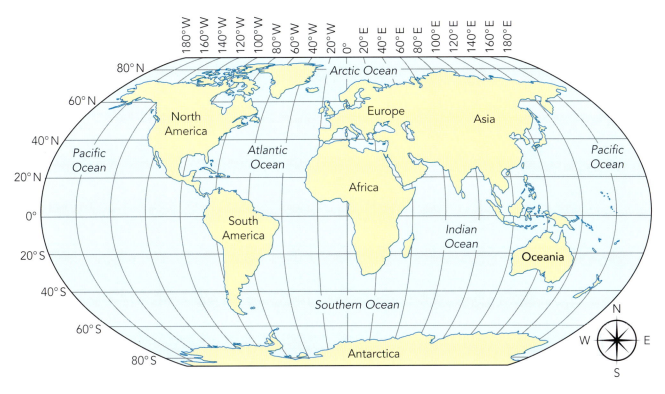

**Figure 7.4:** A world map showing the seven continents and five major oceans, as well as lines of longitude and latitude.

### PROBLEM-SOLVING TIP

When looking at a map or globe, you will see they often include a grid of lines showing latitude and longitude. Lines of latitude are sometimes called parallels because the lines run parallel to the equator. These lines are numbered in degrees, with the equator at 0°, the North Pole at 90° north and the South Pole at 90° south. Other important latitude lines include the Tropic of Capricorn and the Tropic of Cancer. Lines of longitude are called meridians, with the prime meridian at 0°. They run to 180° east and west around the globe. To find a location, first read the latitude coordinate and then the longitude coordinate. For example, in Figure 7.4, the continent found at 20° south and 120° east is Oceania.

### ACTIVITY 7.1

Look at Figure 7.4. In pairs, work out the answers to the following:

a  What continent is 40° north and 120° west?

b  What ocean is found at 40° south and 0°?

c  What continent is found at 40° north and 100° east?

d  What continent is found at 40° north and 20° east?

285

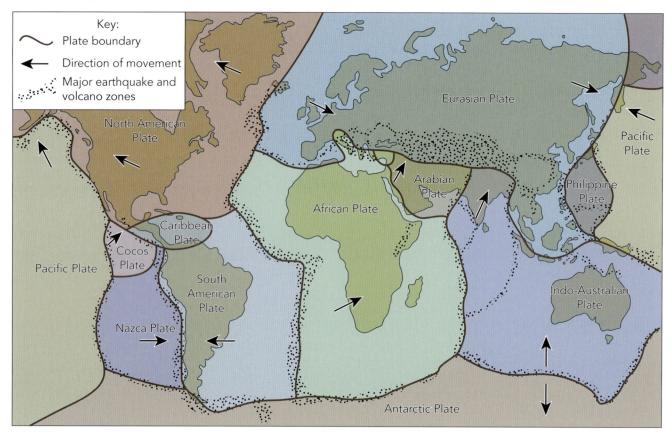

Figure 7.5: The distribution of tectonic plates and zones of tectonic activity.

Beneath the continents and oceans, Earth's surface is not a continuous layer but is fractured. The sections are called tectonic plates, and they are made up of the crust and upper mantle. This is called the **lithosphere**. The surface of Earth is divided into seven major and eight minor plates, which move around on the **asthenosphere** (Figure 7.5).

> **KEY WORDS**
>
> **lithosphere:** the outer and rigid layer of the Earth, comprising the crust and the upper part of the mantle
>
> **asthenosphere:** the layer of Earth below the lithosphere; it is hotter and weaker than the lithosphere and is capable of plastic flow (deformation of material that remains rigid)

> **ACTIVITY 7.2**
>
> In pairs, discuss and then describe in writing an imaginary journey to the centre of Earth. Use diagrams to help with your description. You should try to describe the characteristics of the different layers of Earth – for example, the different physical states of each layer and their composition. Remember, the crust is made up of continental and oceanic crusts.